CQ GUIDE TO

CURRENT AMERICAN GOVERNMENT

Fall 1999

CQ PRESS

A Division of Congressional Quarterly Inc.

D1318715

Congressional Quarterly Inc.

Congressional Quarterly Inc., an editorial research service and publishing company, serves clients in the fields of news, education, business, and government. It combines the specific coverage of Congress, government, and politics contained in the *CQ Weekly* with the more general subject range of an affiliated service, the *CQ Researcher*.

Under the CQ Press imprint, Congressional Quarterly also publishes a variety of books, including college political science textbooks and public affairs paperbacks on developing issues and events, information directories, and reference books on the federal government, national elections, and politics, including the *Guide to the Presidency*, the *Guide to Congress*, the *Guide to the U.S. Supreme Court*, the *Guide to U.S. Elections*, and *Politics in America*. CQ's A-Z Collection is a four-volume reference series providing essential information about American government and the electoral process. The *CQ Almanac*, a compendium of legislation for one session of Congress, is published each year. *Congress and the Nation*, a record of government for a presidential term, is published every four years.

CQ publishes the *Daily Monitor*, a report on the current and future activities of congressional committees. An online information system, cq.com, provides immediate access to CQ's databases of legislative action, votes, schedules, profiles, and analyses.

Copyright © 1999 Congressional Quarterly Inc.
1414 22nd Street, N.W., Washington, D.C. 20037

CQ Books on the Web: http://books.cq.com
CQ Books Customer Service: (800) 638-1710; (202) 822-1475

Printed in the United States of America

ISSN: 0196-612X
ISBN: 1-56802-111-9

Contents

Contents

Introduction

Congressional Quarterly's *Guide to Current American Government* is divided into four sections — foundations of American Government, political participation, government institutions and politics and public policy — that correspond with the framework of standard introductory American government textbooks. Articles have been selected from the *CQ Weekly* to complement existing texts with up-to-date examinations of current issues and controversies.

Foundations of American Government. Fundamental aspects of the U.S. Constitution and the federal government are the focus of this section. The articles include the impeachment of President William Jefferson Clinton by the House of Representatives, the Senate trial that followed and the president's ultimate acquittal. The rules governing the Senate impeachment process are featured, as is the first federal impeachment, which was brought against Senator William Blount in 1798.

Political Participation. This section reviews current issues in electoral politics. Because 1999 is an off-election year, the focus of this chapter is primarily voting blocs and interest groups. One article features the Republicans' difficulty in attracting female voters, long a Democratic stronghold. In interest group politics, the debate over managed health care reform is illustrated by the two opposing sides — the insurance industry and the medical community.

Government Institutions. Aspects of Congress, the presidency, the judiciary and the bureaucracy are discussed in turn. CQ editors look at the aftermath of the impeachment and its impact on Congress, examining how members will fare with the media and what role scandal will play with voters. A feature on House majority whip Tom DeLay, R-Texas, uncovers the force that spearheaded the impeachment effort and drives the House GOP. The section on the presidency is defined by the president as he dealt with impeachment and faced the Senate trial; Clinton's successes in the 105th Congress, accomplished primarily through thwarting the Republican agenda; and Clinton's policy aspirations for the rest of his term as laid out in his State of the Union address. The judiciary article examines the role of the independent counsel law and the debate over its reauthorization. Bureaucracy is examined through the struggle over the census process, with mayors in major cities citing flaws in the current system that are costing their jurisdictions millions of dollars in federal funds.

Politics and Public Policy. This section provides in-depth coverage of major social policy issues, including the effects of welfare overhaul on the states, the status of Medicare reform following the report of the National Bipartisan Commission on the Future of Medicare and proposed legislation that would reshape the banking industry. Also included is a feature on the politics of organ transplant allocation, an issue that seems far removed from Capitol Hill, but a closer look reveals that national lawmakers are carefully considering federal regulation. The final feature in this section details the House vote on gun control measures.

By reprinting articles largely as they appeared originally in the *CQ Weekly*, the *Guide's* editors provide a handy source of information about contemporary political issues. The date of original publication is noted with each article to give readers a time frame for the events that are described. Although new developments have occurred subsequently, updates of articles are provided only when they are essential to an understanding of the basic operations of American government. Page number references to related and background articles in the *CQ Weekly* and the *CQ Almanac* are provided to facilitate additional research on topical events. Both are available at many school and public libraries.

Foundations of American Government

The U.S. Constitution is the basis of the organization of the U.S. government. The constitutional framers divided power among the three branches of government—the legislative, judicial and executive. The framers also put into place a system of checks and balances with the idea of keeping one branch from gaining power at the expense of the others. Of the checks and balances spelled out in the Constitution, one of the most powerful is the use of impeachment.

On December 19, 1998, the U.S. House of Representatives approved two articles of impeachment against President William Jefferson Clinton. It was only the second time in the history of the United States that a president had been impeached. The impeachment had been voted primarily along party lines: a Republican majority voted to impeach a Democratic president.

The articles in this section follow the impeachment process from the House votes through the Senate trial and ultimately, the acquittal of President Clinton. CQ editors delve deeply into one of the most critical constitutional crises of this century, covering both the legal and political aspects.

The first article focuses on the impeachment vote and includes summaries of the four articles of impeachment under consideration, and explanations from members who voted against party lines, both Republicans and Democrats.

Another article defines the rules that guide the Senate procedures during the impeachment trial, with the constitutional provisions applied directly to the circumstances of Clinton's trial. In a brief vignette, the first case of impeachment, against Senator William Blount in 1798, is featured, illustrating the difficulties inherent in such a drastic disciplinary action against a government official.

The final article in this section covers the trial's closing and the Senate's acquittal of the president on both articles of impeachment. Included in this piece are the votes by the senators, along with analyses by several high-profile senators of the legal process that played out during the trial. The political drama that surrounded the trial also is detailed, along with much of the behind-the-scenes maneuvering. Also in this article is the revelation that Independent Counsel Kenneth Starr, whose lengthy and excruciatingly detailed report instigated the impeachment process, would be the subject of a Justice Department investigation. Starr and his staff may have improperly questioned Monica Lewinsky, a former White House intern, in a Virginia hotel room in January 1998 about her affair with the president.

House Accuses Clinton Of Perjury, Obstruction

With a historic impeachment vote only hours away, House members give Robert L. Livingston a standing ovation after he shocked the chamber by announcing his resignation.

The Dec. 19 impeachment of William Jefferson Clinton culminated an era of intensely bitter partisanship in Washington and brought into sharp focus the public interest in the private lives of elected officials.

The votes occurred amid a bizarre juxtaposition of historic events, with the nation watching as television networks pre-empted regular programming.

Republicans pushed forward with impeachment as bombs rained down on Iraq and a few hours after their newly anointed leader, Speaker-in-waiting Robert L. Livingston of Louisiana, dropped a bombshell by announcing he would resign in response to a

sex scandal of his own. A leaderless, lame-duck session of the 105th Congress impeached Clinton despite public opposition and with the concurrence of only a handful of Democrats.

The House approved two articles of impeachment — one on perjury, one on obstruction of justice — related to Clinton's affair with former White House intern Monica Lewinsky and his subsequent attempts to cover it up. It rejected two associated charges. (*Box, p. 5*)

Clinton, who once claimed the mantle of a new generation of leaders, became only the second president to be impeached — and the first who had been elected to the presidency. A student of history, Clinton has indelibly stained his legacy with actions that even his

CQ Weekly Dec. 22, 1998

most fervent supporters condemn. His fate now rests with the Senate.

Republicans crushed attempts to mete out a lesser penalty of censure. They argued that Clinton had lied under oath, and that impeachment was the only constitutional route to demonstrate that no one — not even the president — was above the law. Democrats responded that impeachment was too drastic for misdeeds emanating out of a desire to hide an extramarital affair.

Livingston provided an exclamation point to the arguments about the purity of public officials. After acknowledging his own sexual indiscretions two days earlier, he stunned colleagues by announcing that he would resign from the House rather than become its Speaker in the 106th Congress.

"Who can possibly absorb this?" asked Marge Roukema, R-N.J., who had strongly defended Livingston after he had acknowledged his affairs. "We're tortured — not only hearts, but souls."

Livingston suggested that Clinton take responsibility for his own actions and follow his example. But Clinton stood steadfast against talk of resignation. Two busloads of Democratic members joined him at a South Lawn ceremony shortly after the final vote. Standing with Vice President Al Gore and first lady Hillary Rodham Clinton, he pledged to serve "until the last hour of the last day of my term." (*1998 CQ Weekly, p. 3362*)

Public opinion, a fickle but potent ally in some of Clinton's darkest days, stood with him. An NBC News poll conducted Dec. 19 found that 72 percent of the public approved of his job performance. Only 34 percent said he should resign. Other quick polls showed that his approval ratings ticked upward after the vote.

The case now heads to the Senate and the second presidential impeach-

ment trial in the nation's history. The first such trial, in 1868, ended one vote short of the two-thirds needed to remove Andrew Johnson.

The odds against Clinton's conviction are steep. Republicans seem unlikely to garner the necessary votes of at least 12 Democrats. Still, the outcome is unscripted as the chamber faces a maze of arcane rules and potentially torrid evidence.

The public's wide but shallow support for Clinton, combined with their distaste for a protracted trial steeped in the president's sexual proclivities, could play a role. The quest for a censure resolution could grow, but that would require Congress' diminishing ranks of centrists to reassert themselves.

Another obstacle to finding a middle ground is that conservatives have been loath to consider an alternative punishment short of impeachment. Republican senators likely will feel some of the same pressure from their right flank as their House colleagues did to advance the case against Clinton as far as possible.

The Republican drive to impeach Clinton is viewed by some historians as the latest example of a resurgent Congress eager to dominate the executive branch. Most agree that the threshold for impeachment has been lowered below the abuses of public power that led to the forced resignation of President Richard M. Nixon in 1974.

Fallout could be vast even in the 106th Congress. The fiery speeches on both sides, and the Democrats' characterization of the GOP-led effort as a "coup d'état," hardly portend the level of trust required to deal with such vexing issues as overhauling Social Security and protecting managed care patients.

The poisonous atmosphere prompted leading congressional Republicans to cast aspersions on the timing of

Clinton's bombing of Iraq, which began on the eve of the scheduled impeachment debate and ended shortly after the last votes were cast. (*1998 CQ Weekly, p. 3359*)

The immediate task for Republicans is to find a new successor to outgoing Speaker Newt Gingrich, R-Ga., before the new Congress convenes Jan. 6. With Clinton's impeachment a foregone conclusion, Republicans engaged in a frenzied attempt to designate a new Speaker in the few hours before they left the Capitol — with all signs pointing to an affable, low-key conservative, Dennis Hastert, R-Ill. His selection would ratify the clout of his mentor, Majority Whip Tom DeLay, R-Texas, who rode herd on the GOP impeachment effort.

It was DeLay who, while choked with emotion during the floor debate, praised Livingston and his decision to resign. Livingston, he said, demonstrated that the decision to impeach Clinton was "a debate about relativism versus absolute truth."

That debate is destined to resound in the halls of the Capitol and the rest of the country for a long time. As Richard H. Baker, R-La., asked: "Where in God's name does the line of the private right to know end, and the individual right of personal liberty begin?"

Floor Dynamics

After weeks of buildup and days of frantic scrambling to keep up with events, members of both parties were somber as the day of the vote arrived.

Judiciary Committee Republicans kicked off the debate Dec. 18 with short speeches summarizing the charges against Clinton. "The president was obliged, under his sacred oath, to faithfully execute our nation's laws," said James E. Rogan, R-Calif. "Yet he repeatedly perjured himself and obstructed justice."

All was upstaged by Livingston's shocking announcement from the floor early the next day that he would abandon his quest for Speaker and resign from the House in six months.

It was a moment of high drama. Livingston began by describing the case against Clinton and said the president had the power to heal the wounds he caused: "You, sir, may resign your post."

Democrats erupted at the frontal assault from a GOP leader. "No," they shouted repeatedly. A group, led by Maxine Waters, D-Calif., yelled, "You resign, you resign." Livingston held up his right hand as if to tell them to wait. He then delivered the body blow.

"I can only challenge you in such fashion if I am willing to heed my own words," he said. "I must set the example that I hope President Clinton will follow. I will not stand for Speaker of the House."

After listening to his last words in stunned silence, members of both parties gave Livingston a standing ovation as he left the floor. He strode to the sanctuary of his nearby office, followed by Republicans urging him to reconsider. They were joined by a number of Democrats who admired Livingston's bipartisan impulses as chairman of the Appropriations Committee and had looked forward to his speakership.

Livingston's mind was made up. Within minutes, the next campaign for Speaker was under way in earnest. Members huddled in lobbies and hallways to discuss the turn of events. During the vote on the first article of impeachment, DeLay and Bill Paxon, R-N.Y., were clearly working the floor, steering members to talk to Hastert at the back of the chamber.

Livingston's decision became as much a focus of debate as impeachment itself. Several Democrats, in a curious twist, said that Livingston's resignation was as misguided as the impeachment effort.

"It is a surrender to a developing sexual McCarthyism," said Jerrold Nadler, D-N.Y. "We are losing sight of the distinction between sins, which ought to be between a person and his family and his God, and crimes, which are the concern of the state and of society as a whole."

Judiciary Committee Chairman Henry J. Hyde, R-Ill., responded that the issue was indeed one of crimes — perjury and obstruction of justice, saying Clinton's impeachment grew out of

"equal justice under the law, that's what we're fighting for."

The Democrats' most impassioned plea came from Minority Leader Richard A. Gephardt, D-Mo., who entwined Livingston's decision with Clinton's impeachment and said, "We are now rapidly descending into a politics where life imitates farce.

"Fratricide dominates our public debate and America is held hostage with tactics of smear and fear. Let all of us here today say no to resignation, no to impeachment, no to hatred, no to intolerance of each other, and no to vicious self-righteousness."

He, too, got a standing ovation, as well as bear hugs from fellow Democrats.

Republicans first prevailed on a procedural vote that prevented Democrats from offering a resolution to censure Clinton. That vote was 230-204. Democrats responded by briefly walking out in protest. (*1998 CQ Weekly, p. 3372*)

They returned for the formal voting on H Res 611, which contained four articles of impeachment.

The first article, accusing Clinton of committing perjury in his Aug. 17 grand jury testimony, passed easily, 228-206. Five Democrats and five Republicans crossed party lines. Members had said this was the most likely to be approved because, unlike his deposition in the Paula Corbin Jones sexual harassment case, there was no question that his testimony was material to the investigation by Independent Counsel Kenneth W. Starr. (*1998 CQ Weekly, p. 3372*)

House Managers To Prosecute Case

Henry J. Hyde, R-Ill.
F. James Sensenbrenner Jr., R-Wis.
Bill McCollum, R-Fla.
George W. Gekas, R-Pa.
Charles T. Canady, R-Fla.
Steve Buyer, R-Ind.
Ed Bryant, R-Tenn.
Steve Chabot, R-Ohio
Bob Barr, R-Ga.
Asa Hutchinson, R-Ark.
Christopher B. Cannon, R-Utah
James E. Rogan, R-Calif.
Lindsey Graham, R-S.C.

The second article, charging Clinton with perjury in a deposition in the Jones lawsuit, failed, 205-229. Besides questions of its relevance to the case, the lawsuit was eventually dismissed. (*1998 CQ Weekly, p. 3372*)

The third article, charging Clinton with obstructing justice, passed 221-212. Five Democrats voted for it, while 12 Republicans voted against. This charge was also seen as strong because it included Clinton's attempts to find Lewinsky a job, possibly in return for her silence, and his alleged witness tampering involving his secretary, Betty Currie. (*1998 CQ Weekly, p. 3372*)

A fourth article, charging that Clinton violated his oath of office in providing misleading statements to 81 questions posed by the Judiciary Committee, failed, 148-285. A number of Republicans saw this as a reason to be angry at Clinton, but not to impeach him. (*1998 CQ Weekly, p. 3372*)

After voting on the impeachment articles, the House authorized the appointment of 13 Republican Judiciary Committee members to prosecute the case in the Senate. The contingent walked across the Capitol, where Hyde presented a leather-bound parchment to Secretary of the Senate Gary Sisco. The House will have to reappoint managers in January, but that move is likely to be cast as procedural.

Republicans Unify

The vote to impeach Clinton represented a remarkable turnaround.

It occurred less than seven weeks after Democrats picked up a net of five House seats in the Nov. 3 election. Most observers cited the Republicans' disappointing showing — they had hoped to gain at least 20 seats — and public opposition to impeachment in declaring the effort all but dead.

Earlier in the month, the Judiciary Committee seemed to be lurching out of control with diversions into campaign finance issues and other sexual conduct allegations against Clinton. But by the time the panel voted for four articles of impeachment Dec. 11-12, it had become obvious that the effort was steaming ahead. (*1998 CQ Weekly, p. 3290*)

Perhaps the single biggest factor was the determination of the House Republican leadership to deny a floor vote on a resolution censuring Clinton.

Republican members denied that their arms were twisted.

The Articles of Impeachment Considered by the House

Summaries of the articles of impeachment (H Res 611) against President Clinton as recommended by the House Judiciary Committee, followed by the Dec. 19 votes by the House:

ARTICLE I: Perjury before a federal grand jury on Aug. 17, 1998.

In its report (H Rept 105-830), the committee concluded Clinton lied about "the nature and details of his relationship" with former White House intern Monica Lewinsky; about his testimony in a Jan. 17 deposition in a sexual-harrassment suit filed by former Arkansas state employee Paula Corbin Jones; about statements he allowed his lawyer to make; and about "his corrupt efforts to influence the testimony of witnesses and to impede the discovery of evidence." Though he acknowledged an "improper relationship," Clinton resorted to "legal hairsplitting . . . to bypass the requirement of telling the complete truth."

Adopted: 228-206

ARTICLE II: Perjury in his Jan. 17 deposition in the Jones case.

The committee concluded that Clinton lied to Jones' lawyers about his relationship with Lewinsky, about gifts he had given her, and about efforts to conceal the relationship, including help given to Lewinsky in her pursuit of a job in New York.

Rejected: 205-229

ARTICLE III: Obstruction of justice.

The committee found that Clinton, "using the powers of his high office," engaged in a plan "to delay, impede, cover up and conceal" his involvement with Lewinsky and subsequent lies. The scheme included encouraging Lewinsky to file a false affidavit in the Jones case and making misleading statements to secretary Betty Currie when he knew she was likely to be a witness in the case.

Adopted: 221-212

ARTICLE IV: Abuse of power.

The committee said Clinton continued "a pattern of deceit and obstruction of duly authorized investigations" in his answers to 81 "requests for admission" that were submitted to him by the panel. "Several" of the president's answers "are clearly perjurious, false and misleading," the report says. It also accused Clinton of lying about his infidelities in six public statements, and of lying to Cabinet members and White House aides "knowing that they would repeat his false statements to the American public." His deceptions "caused millions of tax dollars to be spent by not only the Office of the Independent Counsel [Kenneth W. Starr] in its duly authorized investigation, but also by White House lawyers, communications employees and other government employees, who were utilized to help perpetuate the president's lies and defend him."

Rejected: 148-285.

Yet they were subjected to a fusillade of arguments by DeLay that nothing short of impeachment should be considered. Livingston, then in reluctant but firm control of the approaching session, picked up the call Dec. 12.

This decision had a direct impact on a group of 20 to 30 members, most of them moderates from districts that Clinton carried in 1996. Many of them were willing — some anxious to — consider something short of impeachment.

With censure foreclosed as an option, wavering Republicans were forced to confront the fact that if they voted against impeachment, it could appear as though they were defending Clinton. Each announcement in favor of impeachment increased pressure on other Republicans to follow suit or be left outside the GOP mainstream.

Efforts among some GOP moderates to push a censure alternative — backed, in one form or another, by Amo Houghton of New York and

Michael N. Castle of Delaware, as well as by former President Gerald R. Ford and 1996 presidential nominee Bob Dole — fell flat. And some moderates — particularly Christopher Shays of Connecticut and Roukema — said censure was not a good option.

"Historically, moderate Republicans have placed special emphasis on ethics and honor," said John J. Pitney Jr., an associate professor of government at Claremont McKenna College in California. "So this is exactly the kind of issue on which they're likely to oppose Clinton."

House Republicans made a concerted effort to put impeachment in a particular context. Hyde said impeachment simply meant there was sufficient evidence to convene a Senate trial. Bill McCollum, R-Fla., argued that even if the Senate acquitted Clinton, impeachment would serve essentially as a censure.

The impeachment drive may have also picked up steam when Clinton's

two most prominent and unpopular adversaries — Gingrich and Starr — faded from the scene.

Their absence made it harder for Democrats to demonize Republicans. It also put more focus on the actions that got Clinton into trouble.

Clinton's Mistakes

Clinton developed a well-earned reputation during his career for his astute political instincts, tapping into public support and disarming his enemies. But this failed him at key moments in the Lewinsky scandal, leading right up to floor debate.

Most troubling to the GOP moderates that Clinton had counted on were his responses Nov. 27 to the Judiciary Committee's 81 questions. His answers were carefully crafted in the same legalistic manner that marked his testimony. Many undecided Republicans wanted to hear not just another attempt at a heartfelt contrition from Clinton. They wanted a more open admission of his having lied under oath — regardless of how his opponents might use it, or if it would place him in greater jeopardy of criminal charges after he left the White House.

"What's more important — his presidency or the chance that he might at some time be prosecuted?" asked John Edward Porter, R-Ill.

Clinton may have also miscalculated in relying on public opinion, which for months showed overwhelming opposition to impeachment. A Washington Post-ABC News poll released Dec. 15 showed respondents opposed impeaching and removing Clinton by 61 percent to 38 percent.

But the overall numbers masked the fact that, while Democrats opposed impeachment by 82 percent to 17 percent, Republicans endorsed it by 64 percent to 36 percent. And moderate Republicans began hearing from an increasing number of hard-core supporters demanding impeachment.

The approaching end of the 105th Congress at first appeared to hamper any GOP hopes of impeachment. Democrats complained about the timing, though Republicans were quick to note that until two months ago, Democrats were just as eager to wrap up the debate.

When Democrats picked up seats on Nov. 3, the roles switched. Democrats urged a go-slow approach while Republicans expressed a new determination to finish.

The result: Clinton's fate was decided by a lame-duck session, including outgoing members.

Many congressional and constitutional experts agreed that impeachment could carry over from one Congress to another, having done so in the cases of three federal judges. But the necessity of doing so was in some dispute.

Outgoing members, who had already lost their office space on Capitol Hill and were herded into temporary quarters, expressed disbelief at the action. "The idea of having your last vote be on impeachment is almost surrealistic," said Glenn Poshard, D-Ill., who lost a gubernatorial bid. "I can't believe it's gotten to this point."

Judiciary Committee

The historic vote came one week after the Judiciary Committee finished up work on the fourth and final article of impeachment. The fourth charge,

approved 21-16, said that Clinton "willfully made perjurious, false and misleading sworn statements" when responding to the committee's questionnaire. *(1998 CQ Weekly, p. 3364)*

"At every turn when he was faced with the choice of answering questions honestly or deceitfully, the president has chosen deception," said Christopher B. Cannon, R-Utah.

But committee Republicans scaled back the final article of impeachment by dropping charges that Clinton had lied to the American people, his Cabinet and staff, and frivolously asserted executive privilege when seeking to block testimony by Secret Service agents and White House lawyers.

An amendment by George Gekas, R-Pa., approved 29-5, jettisoned charges related to executive privilege and lying to the nation and his Cabinet. Several panel Republicans said those charges had not been sufficiently proved, especially the executive privilege claim.

After voting the final article, committee Republicans easily killed the Democrats' resolution to censure Clinton for making "false statements concerning his reprehensible conduct" with Lewinsky. It also said that he had "violated the trust of the American people, lessened their esteem for the office of the President, and dishonored" the presidency.

Clinton's misconduct, though "reprehensible," said Rick Boucher, D-Va., did not rise to the level required for impeachment. "In adopting this resolution of censure, we will give voice to the widely held public view that the president should not be removed from office but that he should be admonished by the Congress for his conduct."

Republicans countered that impeachment was the only appropriate step to condemn presidential misconduct and that there was no provision in the Constitution for censure.

Republicans defeated the censure resolution, 14-22. Robert C. Scott, D-Va., voted "nay," and Waters voted "present."

Announcements

Clinton's prospects for avoiding impeachment dwindled steadily in the ensuing days.

Livingston, who had lain low on impeachment for weeks, wrote Gephardt Dec. 12 to notify Democrats that they would not have an opportunity to offer

a censure resolution on the floor.

"Censure of the president would violate the careful balance of separation of powers and the scheme laid out by the Framers to address the issue of executive misconduct," Livingston wrote.

A number of Republicans who had not previously declared their intentions did so Dec. 14. None had been regarded as likely candidates to oppose impeachment, and none did.

The news got worse for Clinton the following day, when several GOP moderates — including Jack Quinn of New York, who had previously opposed impeachment — announced they would vote to impeach. They included some of the White House's top prospects: Nancy L. Johnson, R-Conn.; Sue W. Kelly, R-N.Y.; and Fred Upton, R-Mich.

Clinton, Johnson said, "does not have the right to commit perjury when it is convenient or when he thinks the charges against him are frivolous."

By Dec. 16, Clinton's outlook had gone from critical to grave. Almost hourly, undecided Republicans stood before television cameras and microphones to say they would vote to impeach Clinton.

Porter, another GOP moderate who had once spoken against impeachment, switched in favor. The announcements of others, such as iconoclast Jim Leach of Iowa, as well as Sherwood L. Boehlert and Rick Lazio, both of New York, seemed to seal Clinton's fate. Lazio, who had just returned from a trip to the Middle East with Clinton, had earlier leaned against impeachment.

Debate Begins

The debate formally began at 9 a.m., Dec. 18, a cool, crisp day in Washington. Ray LaHood, R-Ill., widely respected for his fairness, wielded the gavel. *(CQ Weekly, p. 3280)*

Members easily defeated a Democratic motion to adjourn, offered in protest of the GOP leadership's decision to vote on impeachment while the airstrikes against Iraq were under way. An almost full chamber then sat somberly as the clerk read the four articles of impeachment.

Hyde laid out the GOP position, saying, "The nation's chief executive has shown himself incapable of enforcing its laws, for he has corrupted the rule of law by his perjury and his obstruction of justice."

Gephardt attacked Republicans for staging the debate during the military action against Iraq and for blocking a vote on censure. "I can only conclude that this may be about winning a vote, not about high-minded ideals," he said.

Many members took pains to polish their words. Some spoke from notes or handwritten speeches they had revised on the floor.

Vic Fazio, D-Calif., said he was "sad that a reckless president and a Republican Congress driven by blind animus for him have brought us to this moment in history."

On the next morning, Democrats caucused to hear Hillary Rodham Clinton thank them for standing with her husband. Some members emerged from the meeting with moist eyes. For Democrats, the tumultuous week meant a full range of emotions: sadness, anger, frustration and defiance.

The decision by GOP leaders to block their effort to censure Clinton provoked genuine outrage among Democrats, who said that they had allowed the GOP, when it was in the minority, to present alternatives on momentous issues.

From a strictly partisan standpoint, said Chet Edwards, D-Texas, "We think it's going to thrust Democrats into the majority in the House and possibly the Senate in 2000."

Castle agreed that the Republicans were more downcast than Democrats after the vote and said that impeachment "has huge political ramifications." He predicted that people will revise their thoughts about the parties and individual lawmakers in ways "that will never go away." ◆

Against the Grain

Republicans who voted against impeachment:

Amo Houghton of New York: Houghton, a Rockefeller Republican, said on the House floor Dec. 18: "I'm proud of my party, but I'm opposed to impeachment. . . . When all the arguments are done and when the votes are taken, this is what we must work for: the humanity, the healing of this nation."

Peter T. King of New York: King has long tangled with the Republican Conference on leadership issues. Speaking on the House floor Dec. 18, he said, "I strongly believe that for a president of the United States to be impeached... for an election to be undone, there must be a direct abuse of presidential power. . . . How many of our former presidents would we have lost?"

Constance A. Morella of Maryland: Morella, who represents the affluent Washington-area Maryland suburbs, said in a written statement that the president would be remembered "not for the many accomplishments that have occurred during his term in office but for his sordid behavior and his failure to take responsibility for that behavior. However, putting the country through the turmoil and tumult of a Senate trial . . . is wrong."

Christopher Shays of Connecticut: Perhaps the highest-profile House GOP moderate, Shays announced on the House floor Dec. 19 that "the impeachable offenses have not been proven, and the proven offenses are not impeachable. . . . We've all tried to do our best, and we'll all have to live with our vote for the rest of our lives."

Mark Souder of Indiana: Souder, a steadfast conservative, considered changing his position under heavy pressure from constituents, but ultimately voted against all but the third article of impeach-

ment. "My preference would be to combine the Starr report with additional evidence, when complete, of the campaign finance violations which the Justice Department continues to investigate," he said. "Impeachment is a rarely used, and extremely divisive, procedure."

Democrats who voted for impeachment:

Virgil H. Goode Jr. of Virginia: A freshman from southern Virginia's rural tobacco country, Goode supported the first three articles of impeachment. He said he "was always concerned about lying under oath by the president."

Ralph M. Hall of Texas: One of the few remaining old-style Southern Democrats, Hall voted for three articles of impeachment. "You just have to vote your conscience, and I did that," he said.

Paul McHale of Pennsylvania: After news of Clinton's relationship with Monica Lewinsky broke, McHale became the first Democrat to call for the president to resign. He said he voted in favor of the first three articles of impeachment after deciding "the evidence is overwhelming" that Clinton lied under oath and tried to obstruct justice.

Charles W. Stenholm of Texas: A well-liked fiscal conservative, Stenholm voted for the first three articles of impeachment. "The consequences of the president's actions go well beyond the details of perjury. They go to the heart of our national character."

Gene Taylor of Mississippi: Taylor, a renegade entering his sixth full term in the House, said he voted for all four counts of impeachment because "I think perjury is a very serious crime. And I believe it was intentional."

The 13 House Republicans Making the Case Against Clinton

All 13 Republicans managing the House case against President C.inton are attorneys. Ten have some prosecutorial experience; three have been managers in previous Senate impeachment trials; three have been United States attorneys; and four have been military prosecutors. Here is a look at their legal backgrounds, in order of Judiciary Committee seniority.

■ Henry J. Hyde

Prior to electoral politics, he defended law enforcement officers. He became an icon for conservatives in his freshman House year by pushing enactment of a ban on federal funding of most abortions. He helped win the 1986 conviction in the Senate of Harry E. Claiborne, who was stripped of a federal judgeship in Nevada while serving a prison sentence for tax fraud. He has long been respected for even-handedness, but under his chairmanship the Judiciary Committee's impeachment deliberations were marked by partisanship. When his five-year extramarital affair in the 1960s was reported last year, he dismissed it as a "youthful indiscretion." **Biography:** 74 years old; took 67 percent to win 13th term in November representing Illinois' 6th District (Chicago suburbs); J.D., Loyola University, Chicago, 1949.

■ F. James Sensenbrenner Jr.

He practiced law for less than a year before winning his first election, to the state Assembly. In Congress, he says his most memorable moment was his prosecution of the impeachment of Walter L. Nixon Jr., convicted by the Senate in 1989 and stripped of a federal judgeship in Mississippi for lying to a grand jury. He says he has a "knack for cutting to the quick," but his sometimes abrasive personality has rankled members of both parties. An heir to the Kimberly-Clark fortune, he won $250,000 in the District of Columbia lottery in 1998. **Biography:** 55 years old; took 91 percent to win 11th term in November representing Wisconsin's 9th District (Milwaukee suburbs); J.D., University of Wisconsin, 1968.

■ Bill McCollum

As commander in the Navy Judge Advocate General Corps, he prosecuted a variety of cases, from drug possession to military infractions; in the reserves, he did defense work and served four years as a military judge. As Judiciary's Crime Subcommittee chairman, he has pushed

Hyde

Sensenbrenner

McCollum

Gekas

Canady

Buyer

for tough crime packages with lengthened sentences. Despite contributing more than $900,000 to colleagues' campaigns, he finished third when he ran for majority whip in 1994. **Biography:** 54 years old; took 66 percent to win 10th term in November representing Florida's 8th District (Orange County; part of Orlando); J.D., University of Florida, 1968.

■ George W. Gekas

He spent six years as an assistant district attorney for Dauphin County, Pa., which includes the state capital. He helped manage the impeachment of Alcee L. Hastings, convicted by the Senate in 1989 and stripped of a Florida federal judgeship on charges of conspiracy to accept a bribe, perjury and leaking wiretap information. Hastings won a House seat three years later. **Biography:** 68 years old; unopposed for ninth term in November representing Pennsylvania's 17th District (Harrisburg area); J.D., Dickinson School of Law, 1958.

■ Charles T. Canady

He has no prosecutorial experience. He practiced real estate, commercial and administrative law with two firms for 13 years before he entered the House. He was first elected to the Florida Legislature in 1984 as a Democrat and lost in 1990 after switching parties. **Biography:** 44 years old; unopposed for fourth term in November representing Florida's 12th District (Lakeland area); J.D., Yale University, 1979.

■ Steve Buyer

After serving as a liaison to federal prosecutors in Virginia while in the Army Judge Advocate General Corps, he served as a deputy to the Indiana attorney general and then opened a civil litigation practice. As an Army reservist, he served as counsel to the 22nd Support Command during the Persian Gulf War, where he provided legal advice on treatment of enemy prisoners of war and refugees. **Biography:** 40 years old; took 63 percent to win fourth term in November representing Indiana's 5th District (northern rural, Kokomo); J.D., Valparaiso University, 1984.

■ Ed Bryant

As the U.S. attorney in Memphis, he won convictions in the state's largest mass-murder case and in the nation's first civil rights case for sexual harassment against a sitting judge. But a hung jury resulted from his prosecution of Rep. Harold E. Ford, D-Tenn. (1975-97), on bank, mail and tax fraud charges; after a jury was seated for the second trial, Bryant resigned in protest when his Justice Department superiors backed Ford's request for a different panel. Ultimately, Ford was acquitted. Bryant also taught law at West Point and served in the Army Judge Advocate General Corps. **Biography:** 50 years old; unopposed for third term in November representing Tennessee's 7th District (west central); J.D., University of Mississippi, 1972.

Bryant

■ Steve Chabot

He has no prosecutorial experience, but while running a solo law practice he gained some trial experience handling domestic disputes and defending accused criminals. In five years on the Cincinnati City Council, he advocated making criminals on probation contribute to public works projects. **Biography:** 45 years old; took 53 percent to win third term in November representing Ohio's 1st District (Western Cincinnati and suburbs); J.D., Northern Kentucky University, 1978.

Chabot

■ Bob Barr

In four years as the U.S attorney in Atlanta, he managed the prosecution of Rep. Pat Swindall, R-Ga. (1985-89), who was convicted for lying about a scheme to launder illegal drug profits; key evidence included secretly made tape recordings. In November 1997, before the independent counsel's inquiry was expanded to include the Monica Lewinsky affair, he introduced legislation to start an impeachment inquiry against Clinton. On Jan. 11, Hustler magazine publisher Larry Flynt accused Barr of hypocrisy for refusing to answer questions in his divorce case from his second wife about his relationship with the woman now his third wife. Barr helped draft the impeachment article, rejected by the House, accusing Clinton of abuse of power for "evasive" answers to questions from the House. **Biography:** 50 years old; took 55 percent to win third term in November representing Georgia's 7th District (Rome; part of Marietta); J.D., Georgetown University, 1977.

Barr

■ Asa Hutchinson

As the U.S. attorney in Fort Smith from 1982 to 1985, he prosecuted Roger Clinton on cocaine charges; the president has credited the conviction with turning his half-brother's life around. Some Democrats say Hutchinson should be disqualified as a manager because his brother, Tim, is a GOP senator from Arkansas. Rep. Hutchinson worked for Rep. John Paul Hammerschmidt, R-Ark. (1967-93), in 1974, when he won re-election over Clinton. And

Hutchinson

Cannon

Rogan

Graham

Hutchinson was state GOP chairman during Clinton's final two years as governor. **Biography:** 48 years old; took 81 percent to win second term in November representing Arkansas' 3rd District (Fayetteville, Fort Smith); J.D., University of Arkansas, 1974.

■ Christopher B. Cannon

He has no prosecutorial experience but spent four years as criminal defense lawyer for corporations. After three years as an associate solicitor at the Interior Department and a brief stint as a Commerce Department consultant, he bought the Geneva Steel Co. in Utah in 1987. His success led him in 1990 to start Cannon Industries, a venture capital firm; he is still its head. **Biography:** 48 years old; took 77 percent to win second term in November representing Utah's 3rd District (Provo, state's eastern half); J.D., Brigham Young University, 1980.

■ James E. Rogan

While Los Angeles County deputy district attorney, his closing argument in a 1990 drunken-driving case consisted of pouring 10 cups of beer and setting them before the jury to show the defendant's consumption, snapped his fingers to show how fast the victims died and sat down. He has said he felt he had one more big case in him but told the Los Angeles Times the impeachment was not what he had in mind. Both as a prosecutor and as a municipal judge in Glendale, he favored allowing both sides to agree that previous sworn testimony could be considered evidence without recalling witnesses. **Biography:** 41 years old; took 50 percent in November to win second term in California's 27th District (Pasadena, Burbank); J.D., University of California, Los Angeles, 1983.

■ Lindsey Graham

In his most celebrated case as a military defense attorney, he won an officer's acquittal by exposing flaws in Air Force drug tests; the Pentagon tacitly acknowledged these by overhauling the program. Soon thereafter, he was transferred to Germany and was chief prosecutor for the Air Force in Europe from 1984 to 1988. Returning home to a private practice, Graham spent four years as an assistant attorney in Oconee County and was city attorney for Central, S.C. In Congress, he played a pivotal role in the 1997 attempt by disgruntled Republicans to oust Rep. Newt Gingrich, R-Ga. (1979-99), as Speaker. **Biography:** 43 years old; took 99 percent of the vote in November to win third term in South Carolina's 3rd District (Anderson, Aiken); J.D., University of South Carolina, 1981.

Senate Rules for Impeachment Trials Are Alternately Precise and Vague

The Senate's rules for judicial and presidential impeachment trials are, by turns, excruciatingly precise and frustratingly vague. They were first written for the trial of President Andrew Johnson in 1868 and have been modified only slightly since, most recently in 1986.

These 26 rules constitute an imperfect road map for what might happen in a trial of President Clinton. For instance, a trial could be ended immediately with a motion to adjourn, if the motion received a majority vote. That scenario is not explicitly provided for under the impeachment rules, though legal scholars say such an action would be permitted.

Like other Senate rules, those covering impeachment can be changed by a two-thirds majority vote.

Following are excerpts from the Senate's rules for impeachment trials, followed by brief explanations where applicable.

• 1) *"Whensoever the Senate shall receive notice from the House of Representatives that managers are appointed on their part to conduct an impeachment against any person and are directed to carry articles of impeachment to the Senate, the Secretary of the Senate shall immediately inform the House of Representatives that the Senate is ready to receive the managers, for purpose of exhibiting such articles of impeachment, agreeably to such notice."*

The House "managers" act as prosecutors of impeachments. In the case against Clinton, Judiciary Committee Chairman Henry J. Hyde, R-Ill., will be the lead manager. The new House that convenes Jan. 6 will have to do an official reappointment, which could reopen the impeachment matter in the 106th Congress, in which Democrats gain five seats.

• 2) *"When the managers of an impeachment shall be introduced at the bar of the Senate and shall signify that they are ready to exhibit articles of impeachment against any person, the Presiding Officer of the Senate shall direct the Sergeant at Arms to make proclamation, who shall, after making proclamation, repeat the following words, viz: 'All persons are commanded to keep silence, on pain of imprisonment, while the House of Representatives is exhibiting to the Senate articles of impeachment'. . . . after which articles shall be exhibited, and then the Presiding Officer of the Senate shall inform the managers that the Senate will take proper order on the subject of the impeachment, of which due notice shall be given to the House of Representatives."*

The Senate must inform the House when it is ready to formally receive the articles of impeachment. The presentation of those articles will occur in an elaborate ceremony that will highlight the gravity of a Senate impeachment trial and the archaic language that will be used. The admonition by the sergeant at arms to keep silent comes straight from the Johnson trial.

• 3) *"Upon such articles being presented to the Senate, the Senate shall, at 1 o'clock afternoon of the day (Sunday excepted) following such presentation, or sooner if ordered by the Senate, proceed to the consideration of such articles and shall continue in session from day to day (Sundays excepted) after the trial shall commence (unless otherwise ordered by the Senate) until final judgment shall be rendered . . ."*

The key phrase here is "unless otherwise ordered by the Senate." The Senate has a long tradition of modifying rules, by agreement, to adapt to circumstances. The trial would likely commence at 1 p.m. on the day after the articles are presented. But the Senate would then probably delay further proceedings. That would provide the president's attorneys time to respond to the charges in the articles. The Senate granted Johnson 10 days to prepare a response.

• 4) *"When the President of the United States or the Vice President of the United States . . . shall be impeached, the Chief Justice of the United States shall preside; and in a case requiring the said Chief Justice to preside notice shall be given to him by the Presiding Officer of the Senate of the time and place fixed for the consideration of articles of impeachment, as aforesaid, with a request to attend. . . ."*

William H. Rehnquist, chief justice of the United States, would preside over the Senate during Clinton's trial, a role prescribed in the Constitution. The rules state that the Senate's presiding officer — Vice President Al Gore — would swear in Rehnquist. But Gore could avoid that politically awkward situation and let Strom Thurmond, R-S.C., the president pro tempore of the Senate, swear in Rehnquist. The chief justice, in turn, would swear in senators, who pledge to "do impartial justice according to the Constitution and laws."

• 5) *"The Presiding Officer shall have power to make and issue, by himself or by the Secretary of the Senate, all orders, mandates, writs, and precepts authorized by these rules or by the Senate, and to make and enforce such other regulations and orders in the premises as the Senate may authorize or provide."*

Rehnquist's authority is akin to that of a trial judge, though it is constrained in key areas (see Rule 7 below).

- 6) "The Senate shall have power to compel the attendance of witnesses, to enforce obedience to its orders, mandates, writs, precepts, and judgments, to preserve order, and to punish in a summary way contempts of, and disobedience to, its authority. . . ."

The Senate has the authority to subpoena witnesses, and it would be up to the sergeant at arms to enforce the subpoenas. While it is not provided for under the rules, the Senate may also direct the sergeant at arms to request and, if necessary, compel the presence of absent senators.

- 7) "The Presiding Officer of the Senate shall direct all necessary preparations in the Senate Chamber, and the Presiding Officer on the trial shall direct all the forms of proceedings while the Senate is sitting for the purpose of trying an impeachment. . . And the Presiding Officer on the trial may rule on all questions of evidence including, but not limited to, questions of relevancy, materiality, and redundancy of evidence and incidental questions, which ruling shall stand as the judgment of the Senate, unless some Member of the Senate shall ask that a formal vote be taken thereon. . . ."

The Senate would be Rehnquist's courtroom, but senators could overturn his rulings on evidence and the like with motions that would carry on a majority vote. But Rehnquist would not rule on pretrial motions that might be brought by attorneys for the White House. The Senate would vote on such motions, after oral arguments by Hyde and White House attorneys.

- 8) "Upon presentation of articles of impeachment and the organization of the Senate as hereinbefore provided, a writ of summons shall issue to the person impeached, reciting said articles, and notifying him to appear before the Senate upon a day and at a place to be fixed by the Senate and named in such writ, and file his answer to said articles of impeachment and to stand to and abide the orders and judgments of the Senate thereon. . . ."

After the articles of impeachment are presented, the Senate would take up a resolution, which would issue a summons to the president to appear and outline a schedule for the trial.

- 9) "At 12:30 o'clock afternoon of the day appointed for the return of the summons against the person impeached, the legislative and executive business of the Senate shall be suspended, and the Secretary of the Senate shall administer an oath to the returning officer. . . ."

This action confirms that the accused, in this case the president, has received a summons to appear.

- 10) "The person impeached shall then be called to appear and answer the articles of impeachment against him. If he appears, or any person for him, the appearance shall be recorded. . . ."

Again, the president's attorneys would represent him at the trial. The elaborate steps taken to inform the president of the charges and call him to appear underscore how humiliating this process is for the accused.

- 11) "That in the trial of any impeachment the Presiding Officer of the Senate, if the Senate so orders, shall appoint a committee of senators to receive evidence and take testimony at such times as the committee may determine..."

Under this rule, which was adopted in 1935, the Senate can appoint a committee to review evidence and take testimony. Such committees have been used during judicial impeachments. But it would be almost inconceivable that the Senate, in a case as important as the president's, would offload the task of gathering evidence to a committee.

- 12) "At 12:30 o'clock afternoon, or at such other hour as the Senate may order, of the day appointed for the trial of an impeachment, the legislative and executive business of the Senate shall be suspended, and the Secretary shall give notice to the House of Representatives that the Senate is ready to proceed to the impeachment of [the president] in the Senate chamber."

A trial of Clinton would likely prevent the Senate from accomplishing anything else. But Senate Majority Leader Trent Lott, R-Miss., and other senators have suggested that the Senate could "dual-track," perhaps by conducting the trial in the afternoon, while taking up legislative business at other times.

- 13) "The hour of the day at which the Senate shall sit upon the trial of an impeachment shall be (unless otherwise ordered) 12 o'clock [noon]; and when the hour shall arrive, the Presiding Officer upon such trial shall cause proclamation to be made, and the business of the trial shall proceed. The adjournment of the Senate sitting in said trial shall not operate as an adjournment of the Senate; but on such adjournment the Senate shall resume the consideration of its legislative and executive business."

A motion to adjourn, if approved by a majority, would shut down the trial. A Democratic effort to adjourn the trial would almost certainly be linked to a proposal to censure the president.

- 14) "The Secretary of the Senate shall record the proceedings in cases of impeachment as in the case of legislative proceedings, and the same shall be reported in the same manner as the legislative proceedings of the Senate."

- 15) "Counsel for the parties shall be admitted to appear and be heard upon an impeachment."

- 16) "All motions, objections, requests, or applications whether relating to the procedure of the Senate or relating immediately to the trial (including questions with respect to admission of evidence or other questions arising during the trial) made by the parties or their counsel shall be addressed to the Presiding Officer only, and if he, or any Senator, require it, they shall be committed to writing and read at the Secretary's table."

• 17) *"Witnesses shall be examined by one person on behalf of the party producing them, and then cross-examined by one person on the other side."*

One of the more intriguing questions in a Senate trial of the president is whether Hyde or the White House attorneys would call the major figures in the Monica Lewinsky saga — Lewinsky herself, Linda R. Tripp, Betty Currie and others. Those witnesses would face cross-examination for the first time.

• 18) *"If a Senator is called as a witness, he shall be sworn, and give his testimony standing in his place."*

• 19) *"If a Senator wishes a question to be put to a witness, or a manager, or to counsel of the person impeached, or to offer a motion or order (except a motion to adjourn), it shall be reduced to writing, and put to the Presiding Officer. The parties or their counsel may interpose objections to witnesses answering questions propounded at the request of any Senator and the merits of any such objection may be argued by the parties or their counsel. Ruling on any such objection shall be made as provided in Rule 7. It shall not be in order for any Senator to engage in a colloquy."*

Senators would have to remain quiet through the proceedings. They must write down their questions to witnesses and submit them to Rehnquist, who would then ask them. The big exception would permit senators to offer motions to adjourn the trial. The counsels for each side, by contrast, are allowed to question witnesses and raise objections, just as in a criminal trial.

• 20) *"At all times while the Senate is sitting upon the trial of an impeachment the doors of the Senate shall be kept open, unless the Senate shall direct the doors to be closed while deliberating upon its decisions. A motion to close the doors may be acted upon without objection, or, if objection is heard, the motion shall be voted on without debate by the yeas and nays, which shall be entered on the record."*

In the 1990s, this is taken to mean that television cameras would be permitted to record the proceedings, unless the Senate votes to go into closed session. TV cameras were first installed in the Senate chamber in 1974 for the possible trial of President Richard M. Nixon, who resigned rather than face impeachment.

• 21) *"All preliminary and interlocutory questions, and all motions, shall be argued for not exceeding one hour (unless the Senate otherwise orders) on each side."*

• 22) *"The case, on each side, shall be opened by one person. The final argument on the merits may be made by two persons on each side (unless otherwise ordered by the Senate upon application for that purpose), and the argument shall be opened and closed on the part of the House of Representatives."*

Hyde would be the lead House manager and would prosecute the case. As such, he would make opening and closing statements. But it is expected that he would be accompanied by attorneys with courtroom experience.

• 23) *"An article of impeachment shall not be divisible for the purpose of voting thereon at any time during the trial. Once voting has commenced on an article of impeachment, voting shall be continued until voting has been completed on all articles of impeachment unless the Senate adjourns for a period not to exceed one day or adjourns sine die. On the final question whether the impeachment is sustained, the yeas and nays shall be taken on each article of impeachment separately; and if the impeachment shall not, upon any of the articles presented, be sustained by the votes of two-thirds of the Members present, a judgment of acquittal shall be entered; but if the person impeached shall be convicted upon any such article by the votes of two-thirds of the Members present, the Senate shall proceed to the consideration of such other matters as may be determined to be appropriate prior to pronouncing judgment . . . the Presiding Officer shall first state the question; thereafter each Senator, as his name is called, shall rise in his place and answer: guilty or not guilty."*

That final roll call, with each member pronouncing the president guilty or not guilty, provides a dramatic conclusion to impeachment trials. The Constitution requires a two-thirds vote for conviction. Rehnquist would announce the judgment of conviction and removal from office. No formal vote is needed for removal, although the rules and the Constitution are silent on this.

The provision calling for the Senate to continue voting until the articles of impeachment have been disposed of, or to adjourn, is intended to prevent a recurrence of the delays in voting that delayed resolution of Johnson's case. After failing to convict Johnson on the first article, the Senate waited two weeks to consider the other articles.

• 24) *"All the orders and decisions may be acted upon without objection, or, if objection is heard, the orders and decisions shall be voted on without debate by yeas and nays, which shall be entered on the record, subject, however, to the operation of Rule 7, except that when the doors shall be closed for deliberation, and in that case no member shall speak more than once on one question, and for not more than 10 minutes on an interlocutory question, and for not more than 15 minutes on the final question, unless by consent of the Senate, to be had without debate. . . ."*

Senators would debate all procedural matters — as well as the ultimate question of the president's guilt or innocence — behind closed doors.

• 25) *"Witnesses shall be sworn. . . . Which oath shall be administered by the Secretary, or any other duly authorized person. . . ."*

• 26) *"If the Senate shall at any time fail to sit for the consideration of articles of impeachment on the day or hour fixed therefor, the Senate may, by an order to be adopted without debate, fix a day and hour for resuming such consideration."*

First Impeachment Offers Insight On Framers' Intentions

The first case of impeachment in Congress has been curiously ignored by American historians — despite the fact that many of the participants in the 1798-99 Senate trial helped to write the Constitution. In fact, the defendant, William Blount, had been a delegate to the Constitutional Convention, and so had his attorney.

Thomas Jefferson drafted the rules of Jefferson's Manual under which Congress still proceeds while watching over the trial as Senate president.

The case has been given short shrift because the questions on which it turned have not been at issue in the succeeding 200 years. These included whether a jury was required in addition to the senators, whether someone out of office could be impeached, whether the defendant must be present and whether a member of Congress could be impeached. While the answer in each case is now "no," it was not clear at the time.

A 1998 book on the case gives some insight on how the Founding Fathers approached impeachment in practice as well as in theory. Many of the framers were in Congress, then meeting in Philadelphia, while the case was proceeding through the House and Senate.

"The First Impeachment," by Buckner F. Melton Jr., an assistant professor of law at University of North Carolina, examines the Blount scandal, which resulted not only in the first impeachment trial, but also the first expulsion of a member from Congress.

Blount was a North Carolina entrepreneur who had served in the Continental Congress as well as the Constitutional Convention, where he was a sporadic participant. George Washington named him governor of the new territory of Tennessee, and he became one of its first senators after it became a state in 1796.

The next year, Blount's land dealings led him into a conspiracy with the British, in which an Indian attack was planned to gain Spanish Florida and Louisiana for Britain. A remarkably indiscreet letter from Blount to an acquaintance he was trying to recruit fell into the wrong hands and made its way to Philadelphia, where Congress was meeting.

President John Adams forwarded the letter to Congress on July 3, 1797, and it caused an uproar. Four days later, the House voted unanimously to impeach Blount. The Senate, not to be outdone, expelled him the next day.

But that was not the end. The Senate went ahead the next year and opened an impeachment trial, even though Blount had skipped bail after it was reduced from $50,000, a fortune at the time, to $2,000.

At the trial, he was skillfully represented by a framer from Philadelphia, Jared Ingersoll. The sporadic trial lasted a year, ending in early 1799 with a 14-11 vote to dismiss the charges. It is not clear, however, whether this was because he was no longer in office, or because the Senate opposed making its members subject to impeachment by the House — or perhaps the Senate was simply fed up with the long, contentious proceedings.

The record is filled with debate on the meaning of impeachment, but little bears directly on the crucial question of what constitutes "high crimes and misdemeanors" — mostly because Blount's actions were so high-handed as to border on treason.

"If you're looking for a magic moment when they said something to solve the riddle of impeachment, it isn't there," Melton said in an interview.

But the book does make several points that are relevant today:

• A trial can indeed be stopped by a majority vote — the same strategy that may be attempted to end the trial of President Clinton.

• Partisanship lay behind every move. The factions in those days were known as Federalists and Republicans, and they scrapped over procedural issues in predictable groups — switching sides depending on how they saw their advantage.

• The House did no evidence-gathering before voting to impeach Blount, leaving it to the Senate to collect the facts. Democrats accused the House of rushing to judgment in the Clinton case, but the framers who watched the Blount trial were perfectly comfortable with the haste and lack of evidence in the House.

Melton said the members were following the English Parliament's practice of "impeachment by clamor" in which "the notoriety of the offense was so great that there was no need for evidence at an early stage."

The House Judiciary Committee's long investigation of Watergate in 1973-74 was laudable, Melton said, but unnecessary.

"The Blount impeachment, however, strongly indicates that were we to follow the framers' lead, the House could properly invoke the impeachment power with much more abandon."

Political crisis ends with president in office but his reputation severely tarnished

Senate Acquits Clinton

The second presidential impeachment trial in U.S. history has ended with Bill Clinton still in the White House — and still enjoying the phenomenal popularity ratings that have become the hallmark of his tenure. While the Senate's lopsided verdict in the president's favor was entirely predictable long before its formal declaration on Feb. 12, it hardly represented a victory or vindication for the nation's 42nd president.

As he emerged from the congressional crucible that has consumed him for the past year, his character and integrity were impugned by political allies and opponents alike. His personal conduct was condemned in the harshest terms possible. A leading Democratic senator said the president had behaved like "a pig." A Republican said the name "Clinton" will eventually become synonymous with liar.

The president launched a bid for rehabilitation when he appeared in the White House Rose Garden two hours after his acquittal and offered his most abjectly humble apology of the past year.

Yet for all that, his presidency was never seriously imperiled. It had been clear for weeks that the Senate would not even approach the two-thirds majority the Constitution requires for conviction on impeachment articles and removal from office.

"The Founders really didn't want us to be France," said Bob Kerrey, D-Neb., referring to a nation where regimes once fell with frequency. "They made it extremely hard to remove a popularly elected president."

For three long days, senators deliberated behind their chamber's closed doors on the twin articles of impeachment brought by the House, which alleged that Clinton committed perjury and obstruction of justice in trying to conceal his relationship with Monica Lewinsky, a former White House intern. (*1999 CQ Weekly, p. 47*)

Then, shortly after noon on Feb. 12, the senators served notice that they

were ready, the Senate's doors were opened and Chief Justice William H. Rehnquist posed the final question of the trial: "Senators, how say you? Is the respondent, William Jefferson Clinton, guilty or not guilty?"

When their names were called alphabetically, senators stood at their desks and delivered their verdicts. It was a moment last seen in 1868, when President Andrew Johnson survived equally fateful roll calls by a single vote.

In this case, by sharp contrast, the only real suspense centered on whether either article would garner a simple majority of Senate support. That would have provided a legally meaningless but symbolically important victory for the Republicans who pushed the House to impeach Clinton in December. (*1998 CQ Weekly, p. 3320*)

But the House prosecutors, who had chafed under limitations imposed by senators during the trial, failed to achieve even that modest goal. Article I, alleging Clinton committed perjury before a federal grand jury, steadily lost support as the trial progressed and was defeated, 45-55. Ten Republicans joined with all 45 Democrats in rejecting the charge. (*1999 CQ Weekly, p. 409*)

Lott puts the best Republican face on the Senate verdict after Clinton's acquittal on Feb. 12, as Rehnquist departs after presiding over the first presidential impeachment trial in 131 years.

Investigating the Investigator

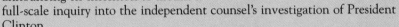

Attorney General Janet Reno has long treated complaints against Independent Counsel Kenneth W. Starr with a kind of steely silence. Allegations were normally met with mild statements of how they would be reviewed or referred to U.S. District Judge Norma Holloway Johnson.

That position changed dramatically the week of Feb. 8, with the disclosure that the Justice Department had sent Starr a letter in January announcing its intention to mount a full-scale inquiry into the independent counsel's investigation of President Clinton.

The move is further evidence that Starr will not simply fade into the night with the end of the Senate impeachment trial. With the potential of a high-profile investigation, partisan arguments on Capitol Hill over the propriety of his probe — and a debate over whether to continue the independent counsel statute (PL 103-270) after it expires June 30 — Starr will likely be a polarizing figure for some time to come.

Starr has not yet commented on the inquiry, which would probably look into the way his aides confronted former White House intern Monica Lewinsky in a Virginia hotel on Jan. 16, 1998, five days before the first reports of her alleged affair with Clinton surfaced. It would also examine how Starr first came to know of Lewinsky, what contacts his office had with lawyers for Paula Corbin Jones, and whether the independent counsel violated any laws by not disclosing any such contacts as part of his request to Reno for authority to investigate whether Clinton unlawfully concealed his affair with Lewinsky from lawyers in the Jones case.

All these allegations were raised by Democrats during the Nov. 19 Starr hearing that was part of the House Judiciary Committee's impeachment inquiry. Starr denied any wrongdoing. (*1998 CQ Weekly, p. 3154*)

The disclosure of the Justice Department probe prompted the same partisan spats that Starr himself elicits. Senate Judiciary Committee Chairman Orrin G. Hatch, R-Utah, said the Clinton administration was running "the most partisan Justice Department this century." He charged that the investigation is a way of laying the groundwork for firing Starr.

Democrats, who see Starr as having an anti-Clinton vendetta, responded that the time was ripe for the investigation. "It would have been a mistake to do that while Bill Clinton's fate was hanging in the balance," said Rep. Barney Frank, D-Mass. "That would have looked like coming to his rescue."

Article II, which alleged a scheme by the president to obstruct justice, was regarded by most senators as the far stronger count. But it was defeated on a vote of 50-50. Five Republicans, all of them moderates from the Northeast, joined unanimous Democrats in rejecting the charge. (*1999 CQ Weekly, p. 409*)

That means that the high water mark for conviction on either count was 17 votes short of conviction, so the House prosecutors won only three of every four votes that they needed.

The result still spared the prosecutors a measure of embarrassment by enabling them to claim they swayed half the Senate, if not a majority. Prosecutors themselves accepted defeat with resignation and a hint of bitterness. "We all have our opinion of the president," said Rep. Lindsey Graham, R-S.C. "But under our system, impeachment is hard. It was meant to be hard. And it's over."

The Fallout

In the immediate aftermath of the votes, senators were left to ponder a series of political and legal questions that will take months, if not years, to answer. Among them:

Will the five Republicans who voted against removing Clinton from office face retaliation from the party's conservative base? Will Democrats find it a mixed blessing to have voted unanimously to keep this president in office? How long will it take Washington, which has been preoccupied with Clinton's fate for months, to return to normal?

But as the curtain descended on the five-week proceeding, trial-weary senators were mostly focusing on a one-week Presidents Day recess and the chance to trade their special hybrid roles as judges and jurors for their more familiar jobs as politicians and legislators.

The trial itself was a quasi-judicial proceeding firmly fixed in the political milieu. That was made clear when senators, after voting Feb. 9 to conduct final deliberations in secret, resorted to their favored practice of speaking at length, both in the chamber and to waiting reporters outside.

It was hardly the freewheeling deliberations hoped for by Senate Majority Leader Trent Lott, R-Miss. "We're just droning through these speeches," Jeff Bingaman, D-N.M., said Feb. 10.

When it was all over, however, senators felt as if they were entitled to a pat on the back, if for no other reason than for resisting the rigid partisanship that marked the House impeachment proceeding. Senators shook hands across the aisle, with lawyers for the president and with House prosecutors.

The Senate earned the warm praise of Rehnquist, who presided over the 20-day trial with a quick wit and an even quicker gavel. Repaying the compliment, senators awarded Rehnquist a ceremonial gavel and passed by voice vote a resolution (S Res 37) praising his work as the presiding officer in the trial.

The camaraderie was soon halted, however, by a bomb threat that forced the evacuation of the Capitol for 75 minutes of the usually balmy winter afternoon.

Attention quickly turned to the president for his statement on the trial. For his part, Clinton defied predictions by Republicans that he would be less than gracious in victory. "I want to say again to the American people how profoundly sorry I am for what I said and did to trigger these events and the great burden they have imposed on the Congress and on the American people," he said.

Harsh Rhetoric . . .

In all likelihood, the Senate's twin votes acquitting Clinton will stand as Congress' last statement on the presidential scandal that exploded onto the national scene 13 months ago. A bipartisan group of senators, most of them Democrats, were rebuffed in an attempt to force an up-or-down vote in a proposal to censure the president. That effort was rejected on a procedural vote moments after the trial ended. (*1999 CQ Weekly, p. 367*)

But while the notion of an official censure might have died, the statements that senators delivered — either during the secret deliberations, or to the worldwide media throng waiting outside — left no doubt of their distaste for Clinton's behavior.

In some cases, that might have been at least partly designed for political effect. Those who voted to acquit, particularly Democrats, appeared determined to create some political distance from the president. Still, the vehemence with which Democrats denounced the president was surprising.

"The president has disgraced himself and dishonored his office," said Jack Reed of Rhode Island, a reliable ally of the president. Clinton's actions were "boorish, indefensible, even reprehensible," said Richard H. Bryan of Nevada. (*1999 CQ Weekly, p. 366*)

And Kerrey accused the president of intentionally placing Lewinsky in legal jeopardy by permitting her to file a false affidavit in the Paula Corbin Jones sexual harassment lawsuit. That charge was not part of the impeachment articles.

"Removing him because he's a pig, that's not on our list," Kerrey remarked to reporters Feb. 10.

Republicans were not to be outdone in questioning the president's character and morals. Olympia J. Snowe of Maine voted to acquit because, she said, in some instances evidence was lacking and in others charges that were proved to her satisfaction still failed to meet the constitutional standard of "high crimes and misdemeanors." But Snowe also was withering in her criticism.

"As a woman who has fought long and hard for sexual harassment laws, I resent that the president has undermined our progress," she said. Referring to Clinton's White House affair with Lewinsky, she added: "No matter how consensual this relationship was, it involved a man with tremendous power, with authority over a 21-year-old sub-

How Senators Voted

Republicans voting guilty on both articles:

Abraham, Mich.
Allard, Colo.
Ashcroft, Mo.
Bennett, Utah
Bond, Mo.
Brownback, Kan.
Bunning, Ky.
Burns, Mont.
Campbell, Colo.
Cochran, Miss.
Coverdell, Ga.
Craig, Idaho
Crapo, Idaho
DeWine, Ohio
Domenici, N.M.
Enzi, Wyo.
Fitzgerald, Ill.
Frist, Tenn.
Gramm, Texas
Grams, Minn.
Grassley, Iowa
Gregg, N.H.
Hagel, Neb.
Hatch, Utah
Helms, N.C.
Hutchinson, Ark.
Hutchison, Texas
Inhofe, Okla.
Kyl, Ariz.
Lott, Miss.
Lugar, Ind.
Mack, Fla.
McCain, Ariz.
McConnell, Ky.
Murkowski, Alaska
Nickles, Okla.
Roberts, Kan.

Roth, Del.
Santorum, Pa.
Sessions, Ala.
Smith, N.H.
Smith, Ore.
Thomas, Wyo.
Thurmond, S.C.
Voinovich, Ohio

Republicans voting not guilty on both articles:

Chafee, R.I.
Collins, Maine
Jeffords, Vt.
Snowe, Maine
Specter, Pa.

Republicans voting not guilty on Article I, guilty on Article II:

Gorton, Wash.
Shelby, Ala.
Stevens, Alaska
Thompson, Tenn.
Warner, Va.

Democrats voting not guilty on both articles:

Akaka, Hawaii
Baucus, Mont.
Bayh, Ind.
Biden, Del.
Bingaman, N.M.
Boxer, Calif.
Breaux, La.
Bryan, Nev.
Byrd, W.Va.
Cleland, Ga.

Conrad, N.D.
Daschle, S.D.
Dodd, Conn.
Dorgan, N.D.
Durbin, Ill.
Edwards, N.C.
Feingold, Wis.
Feinstein, Calif.
Graham, Fla.
Harkin, Iowa
Hollings, S.C.
Inouye, Hawaii
Johnson, S.D.
Kennedy, Mass.
Kerrey, Neb.
Kerry, Mass.
Kohl, Wis.
Landrieu, La.
Lautenberg, N.J.
Leahy, Vt.
Levin, Mich.
Lieberman, Conn.
Lincoln, Ark.
Mikulski, Md.
Moynihan, N.Y.
Murray, Wash.
Reed, R.I.
Reid, Nev.
Robb, Va.
Rockefeller, W.Va.
Sarbanes, Md.
Schumer, N.Y.
Torricelli, N.J.
Wellstone, Minn.
Wyden, Ore.

ordinate, in the workplace —and not just any workplace."

Perhaps the toughest words of all came from Robert F. Bennett of Utah, who voted twice for conviction. "Bill Clinton will go down in history as the most accomplished, polished liar we have ever had serving in the White House," he said. "The name Clinton is entering the political lexicon . . . it's synonymous for an elegant and well-crafted lie."

Charles E. Grassley, R-Iowa, suggested that Clinton could stumble again into an ethical or moral thicket. "My suspicion is there's plenty of skele-

tons in this guy's closet and they're going to drop out from time to time, and shoes are going to fall and maybe even legs are going to fall."

. . . Followed by Votes To Acquit

For a variety of reasons, the case brought by the House never had a realistic chance of crossing the Constitution's formidable two-third barrier to conviction. Some Democrats challenged the trial's very legitimacy, on the grounds that impeachment was approved by the House on nearly party-line votes. Others maintained the case was flawed because it was based on allegations lodged

House prosecutor Graham holds Senate trial tally sheets at a news conference after the Feb. 12 verdict. 'Under our system, impeachment is hard,' he said. 'It was meant to be.'

by a biased, out-of-control prosecutor, Independent Counsel Kenneth W. Starr, whose conduct of the inquiry is now the subject of a Justice Department inquiry. (1999 CQ Weekly, p. 362)

"Extreme partisanship and prosecutorial zealotry have strained this process in its critical early junctures," said Patrick J. Leahy, D-Vt. "Partisan impeachments are lacking in credibility."

Finally, all Democrats and a number of Republicans were troubled by the particulars of the case itself. (1999 CQ Weekly, p. 376)

The Senate agreed with the president's lawyers, who took the position that Clinton's testimony before a federal grand jury, while clearly evasive, did not cross the high legal threshold to become perjurious.

Senators from both parties agreed that the prosecution had made a much stronger case that Clinton obstructed justice — a charged based primarily on the allegation that he encouraged Lewinsky to file a false affidavit in the Jones case. But several Democrats said the facts laid out by the prosecutors, while compelling, formed only a circumstantial case. To the vast majority of Republicans, such objections amount to legal nit-picking. Many focused on what they regarded as the totality of the president's wrongdoing in the Lewinsky affair. And some accused him of misdeeds that went well beyond the case brought by the managers.

Bennett said he had originally decided to vote to acquit Clinton for perjury but changed his mind because he felt the president's statement before the grand jury fit into what he called a pattern of "habitual mendacity." Underscoring the diverse factors that influenced senators, Bennett said Clinton's "stealth" decision in 1996 to create a national wilderness area in Utah fit into that pattern. He conceded that if this were a standard trial, such issues would not be relevant.

But the nation's founders, he contended, "were not naive enough to think that we would check our understanding of the history of the accused president at the door as we took up this burden."

The Final Test

The final act in the impeachment drama was dominated by the largely symbolic tussle for the minds of a handful of senators who might have been persuaded to create a simple majority for the obstruction charge. As senators went behind closed doors Feb. 9 for final deliberations, very little else was in doubt.

The prosecution and White House lawyers had just spent two days — Feb. 6 and Feb. 8 — largely restating the same arguments for conviction and acquittal they had been making since the trial began.

The Feb. 6 session was considered crucial for the House managers. While the Senate had voted previously against calling Lewinsky as a witness, prosecutors won permission to roll four television monitors onto the Senate floor and show clips from her videotaped deposition, taken Feb. 1, and from the depositions taped in the next two days by presidential confidant Vernon E. Jordan Jr. and White House aide Sidney Blumenthal.

But that presentation appeared to change no one's mind, as the trio generally stuck to previous statements and testimony.

Lewinsky's long-awaited testimony was ambiguous enough to provide ammunition to both sides, but Clinton's lawyers had a clip they were particularly eager to show.

"No one asked me or encouraged me to lie, but no one discouraged me either," she said, repeating for a national television audience the grand jury testimony she gave under Starr's grant of immunity from prosecution.

Then the lawyers for both sides returned for one final round of sparring, as anxious senators fidgeted and showed the strain of sitting silently through the proceedings. Judiciary Committee Chairman Henry J. Hyde of Illinois, the last of the 13 House prosecutors to speak, delivered a passionate, freewheeling address larded with quotes from Shakespeare, Saul Bellow and Charles de Gaulle, among others.

Failure to convict, he pleaded, would "raise the most serious questions of whether the president is in fact subject to the law or whether we are beginning a restoration of the divine right of kings."

Before the Senate could decide Clinton's fate, it had to decide whether to do so behind closed doors, as Senate rules require. (1999 CQ Weekly, p. 142)

A proposal to open the debate drew backing from across a broad ideological spectrum but was defeated, 59-41, eight votes short of the 67

Clinton's Public Reaction: Humility, Regret

President Clinton's public response to the end of his impeachment ordeal was a contrite appeal for "reconciliation and renewal for America." Behind closed doors, he was said to be plotting revenge.

In brief remarks from the Rose Garden after the Senate vote Feb. 12, a somber Clinton made his most direct apology to date for his actions.

"I want to say again to the American people how profoundly sorry I am for what I said and did to trigger these events and the great burden they have imposed on the Congress and on the American people," Clinton said. "Now I ask all Americans, and I hope all Americans here in Washington and throughout our land, will rededicate ourselves to the work of serving our nation and building our future together."

The carefully choreographed response to the long-awaited news of his acquittal came only a day after a New York Times story depicted Clinton as itching for revenge against the House Republicans who impeached him. The story — "Clinton Vows Strong Drive to Win a House Majority, Advisers Say" — quoted unidentified "advisers" who described Clinton as viewing the 2000 elections as payback time.

Republicans, who have watched their political fortunes fall as they pursued Clinton's impeachment, reacted with predictable outrage. "It is deeply troubling that the president views closure of this constitutional process as an opportunity for re-

venge," Senate Majority Leader Trent Lott, R-Miss., said Feb. 11.

Speculation that Clinton would target political enemies such as House impeachment manager James E. Rogan, R-Calif., for defeat in 2000 conflicted with the White House message of the week: Let's get this behind us and get on to doing the nation's work. (*1999 CQ Weekly, p. 376*)

If Clinton was taking any satisfaction from the political misfortunes of his enemies, he was determined not to let it show. Asked after his remarks whether he could "forgive and forget," Clinton paused and said, "I believe any person who asks for forgiveness has to be prepared to give it."

The White House — "a gloat-free zone," according to spokesman Joe Lockhart — took pains to avoid the appearance of celebrating the verdict. "There's nothing to celebrate here," White House aide Paul Begala had told reporters. "Saying that you win this is like saying you win an earthquake. You survive it and you rebuild."

Clinton made his remarks two hours after White House Chief of Staff John D. Podesta informed him of his acquittal. The scene — a humbled president standing alone at a Rose Garden lectern — differed from that of December after the House voted to impeach him. Then, two busloads of House Democrats went to the White House for a pep rally. In retrospect, even Democrats recoiled at the sight of a defiant Clinton amid a sea of Democrats vowing, despite his im-

The GOP was furious that Clinton rallied Democrats to his side at the White House after the House impeached him on Dec. 19.

peachment, to serve "until the last hour of the last day of my term." (*1998 CQ Weekly, p. 3320*)

"I thought it was wrong," said Rep. James P. Moran, D-Va., who did not attend the Dec. 19 event. "What were we celebrating? The fact that he was impeached?"

With Clinton's acquittal assured, Vice President Al Gore, who would immediately have become president if Clinton had been convicted, spent the day at events in Baltimore and Albany, N.Y. Clinton postponed a trip to Mexico to be in Washington for the vote.

Clinton still faces potential criminal charges for his wrongdoings. But even House Judiciary Committee Chairman Henry J. Hyde, R-Ill., relentless in his pursuit of impeachment, said the entire matter should be dropped. "I don't think indicting and criminally trying him, after what we have all been through, is going to be helpful to the country," Hyde said after the vote. "I think we should try to find areas we can agree on and get some legislation passed."

needed to change the impeachment rules. (*1999 CQ Weekly, p. 409*)

Political Context

The intense speculation over whether even one article would draw a 51-vote majority took on heightened political importance, especially for Republicans. Hyde and the managers aspired to that majority as some validation for their efforts. Conservative activists hoped to

cite such a vote as a lasting rebuke that would show most members of both houses of Congress had believed the president's behavior met the constitutional test for removal from office.

"Everyone within the Republican Party understood the dynamics of failing to get a majority," said Marshall Wittmann, director of congressional relations at the Heritage Foundation. "That's the water level."

But GOP support for conviction began draining as moderates began delivering statements announcing their votes.

Not surprisingly, James M. Jeffords, the soft-spoken Vermonter who often finds himself in the cross-hairs of his party's conservatives — and who faces reelection next year — was first to break for acquittal. Removing Clinton on the House's charges would set a precedent that could imperil future presidents, re-

Senators Explain Their Votes

Below are excerpts from the statements by several of the senators who announced their impeachment verdicts on Feb. 10-11, before the secret deliberations were concluded:

Tom Harkin, Democrat of Iowa

A few weeks ago, I used a barnyard term to describe what I thought this case amounted to, and the longer the case has gone on, the more I am convinced that that characterization was correct. . . . I believe it to be one of the most blatant political, vindictive actions taken by the House of Representatives since Andrew Johnson's case was pushed through. . . . The Radical Republicans of 1868 have been replaced by the zealous Republicans in the House of Representatives of 1998.

Chuck Hagel, Republican of Nebraska

After stripping away the underbrush of legal technicalities and nuance, I find that the president abused his sacred power by lying and obstructing justice. How can parents instill values and morality in their children? How can educators teach our children? How can the rule of law for every American be applied equally if we have two standards of justice in America — one for the powerful and the other for the rest of us?

James M. Jeffords, Republican of Vermont

I am gravely concerned that a vote to convict the president on these articles may establish a low threshold that would make every president subject to removal for the slightest indiscretion, or that a vote to convict may impale every president who faces a Congress controlled by the opposing party.

Bob Graham, Democrat of Florida

History should, and I suspect will, judge that William Jefferson Clinton dishonored himself and the highest office in our American democracy. But despite their disreputable nature, President Clinton's actions should not result in his conviction and removal from office. . . . The charges against the president do not meet the high constitutional standards established by the framers.

Slade Gorton, Republican of Washington

I cannot will to my children and grandchildren the proposition that a president stands above the law and can systematically obstruct justice simply because both his polls and the Dow Jones index are high. Our duty in this case is as unpleasant as it was unsought. . . . Because I believe the president obstructed justice, I made the only choice available to me: I voted to remove him.

John H. Chafee, Republican of Rhode Island

This, as I said before, has been a deeply troubling case. Overshadowing all has been the president's reckless, tawdry behavior coupled with misleading statements, that have undermined the dignity of the presidency and brought about a divisive and unpleasant chapter in our history. Absent the proof that I find necessary to justify the removal of a president, I will vote to acquit.

Richard G. Lugar, Republican of Indiana

The crimes committed here demonstrate that he is capable of lying routinely whenever it is convenient. He is not trustworthy. Simply to be near him in the White House has meant not only tragic heartache for his wife and his daughter but enormous legal bills for staff members and friends who admired him and yearned for his success. . . . The president should have simply resigned and spared his country the ordeal of this impeachment trial and its aftermath.

Richard H. Bryan, Democrat of Nevada

Does it rise to the constitutional standard of bribery, treason or other high crimes and misdemeanors? I think not. The president's conduct is boorish, indefensible, even reprehensible. It does not threaten the republic.

Wayne Allard, Republican of Colorado

When President Clinton chose not to "tell the truth, the whole truth, and nothing but the truth," he put himself above the law. He violated his oath and undermined the rule of law which he had sworn to uphold.

Paul Wellstone, Democrat of Minnesota

Let us learn that the subject matter of impeachment must be a matter of gravity, calling into question the president's very ability to lead and endangering the nation's liberty, freedom, security. Let us learn that the case against the president must be a strong and unambiguous one in fact, and in law, for even a president deserves the benefit of our reasonable doubts. The charges against the president do not rise to those levels.

Gordon H. Smith, Republican of Oregon

Political prisoners around the world look to the United States for hope, not because we have a popular president but because we have laws to protect us from a popular president. If the president of the United States is allowed to break our laws when they prove embarrassing to him or conflict with his political interests, then truly some public trust has been violated, a trust which relates chiefly to injuries done immediately to society itself.

Joseph I. Lieberman, Democrat of Connecticut

My disappointment and anger with the president's actions were reawakened as I listened to the evidence the managers have presented. And like many of my colleagues, I am left dissatisfied with the all-or-nothing nature of the choice we have been asked to make in this proceeding, between removing this president from office on the one hand, or not removing him on the other, which could imply exoneration or even vindication. . . . I want it understood that I am saying "not guilty of a high crime or misdemeanor," and that is all I can say.

Senate Blocks Censure, Ending Trial Without a 'Unifying Statement'

For all of the uniqueness of the Senate trial of President Clinton, an effort to follow it with a presidential censure ended in all-too-familiar fashion — the failure of a procedural motion by the minority party on a nearly party-line vote.

That happened Feb. 12 just a few minutes after Chief Justice William H. Rehnquist declared Clinton acquitted and formally gaveled the court of impeachment to a close. When Dianne Feinstein, D-Calif., sought permission to deviate from normal Senate proceedings so she could offer a censure resolution, her effort was effectively postponed indefinitely by the GOP on a 43-56 vote. (*1999 CQ Weekly, p. 409*)

Majority Leader Trent Lott, R-Miss., said afterward that he orchestrated the move to avoid a debate because he considered censure "extra-constitutional" and "we were out of time."

The draft resolution said Clinton engaged in an "inappropriate relationship" with Monica Lewinsky that was "shameful, reckless and indefensible"; that he "deliberately misled and deceived the American people, and people in all branches of the United States government"; and that his conduct "is unacceptable for a president of the United States, does demean the office of the president as well as the president himself, and creates disrespect for the laws of the land."

As House Democrats had last year, Senate Democrats pushed for a harshly worded censure resolution as an alternative to conviction and removal from office. But critics responded that censure would do little more than provide political cover by enabling senators to acquit the president with one pair of votes, then rebuke him with a third vote.

"It's important to end with a unifying statement that reaches across party lines and across the lines of how we voted in the impeachment process," Sen. Joseph I. Lieberman, D-Conn., a censure supporter, said in an interview the day before censure was shelved.

"It's going to be blocked by a classic Senate parliamentary maneuver, which is not a very satisfying way to end this," he said.

Search for Alternatives

Throughout the final days of the trial, Lieberman worked with Feinstein and Robert F. Bennett, R-Utah, to draft a bipartisan censure resolution or a letter of reprimand that could be included as part of the trial record.

"Our intent is not to bind or influence the court one way or another, for good or ill, in making any determinations which it may about the president's conduct," Feinstein said, noting that Clinton could be prosecuted after he leaves office. "Our purpose is to speak to the moral ramifications of the president's conduct, and to the message those actions . . . send to the people of our nation, especially its youth."

Some Republicans who initially dismissed censure said they believed it could politically benefit their party. "Acquittal isn't the best place to leave this matter. . . . No real purpose is made by denying us the vote, and I think there could be something in it for us as well," said Sen. Mitch McConnell, R-Ky.

But many other Republicans countered that censure raised problems with the separation of powers between the branches of government.

"You either remove the president or you have no ability to transcend the line that represents the separation of power," said Sen. Phil Gramm, R-Texas, who made the motion to postpone a censure vote.

Even some Democrats supporting censure acknowledged that they had problems with using strongly worded legal language to pass moral judgment on Clinton's conduct. They said developing an agreement on censure that would prove satisfactory to all sides would simply take too long.

"It would probably have to be taken up in the first week after recess, and I don't think anybody wants to be talking about this in the first week after recess," said John D. Rockefeller IV, D-W.Va.

"When I finish as a juror . . . I'm not going to be for censure," echoed Sen. Arlen Specter, R-Pa., in a news conference two days before the vote. "I'm going to go home."

gardless of party, he said.

A bid to render a unique verdict was contemplated by Arlen Specter, R-Pa. Saying he was citing Scottish legal precedent, he said Feb. 10 he planned to vote "not proven" instead of "guilty" or "not guilty," partly as a way to register his opinion that the trial had been too superficial.

But on decision day, Specter changed his mind, twice declaring, "Not proven, therefore not guilty."

Three other GOP moderates voted to acquit on both counts: Snowe, John H. Chafee of Rhode Island and Susan Collins of Maine.

Five other Republicans, including a quartet of committee chairmen, ended up rendering a split decision, voting to acquit on perjury but to convict on obstruction of justice: Slade Gorton of Washington, Intelligence Committee Chairman Richard C. Shelby of Alabama, Appropriations Committee Chairman Ted Stevens of Alaska, Government Affairs Committee Chairman Fred Thompson of Tennessee and Armed Services Committee Chairman John W. Warner of Virginia.

All are former prosecutors, a final signal that the Senate viewed the House's rationale for impeachment with both legal and political suspicion. ◆

Political Participation

This section reviews current issues in electoral politics.

The first article features the GOP's difficulty in attracting female voters, long a Democratic stronghold. As women have gained prominence in the politics during the past decade, both as candidates and a core voting constituency, both parties have been focusing on issues to attract the female vote. The Democrats have championed issues such as pay equity, child care for working mothers, family leave and increased spending on public education. These are concerns of women, who now vote in larger numbers than men do. Republicans have had to play a game of gender catch-up as the 2000 elections draw closer. House Republicans are keenly aware that their slim six-vote majority could slip, giving control of the House back to the Democrats, and women could be the key to maintaining or losing that control.

The campaign contribution loophole known as "soft money" is examined following the midterm elections. While direct contributions to political parties and campaigns that promote specific candidates are regulated, the gray area of "educating voters" through issue ads, phone banks and get-out-the-vote drives is not regulated. Also, interest groups, political action committees and individuals may advertise for a specific candidate, as long as the advertising is done completely independent of the candidate's campaign.

In interest group politics, the debate over managed health care reform is illustrated by the two opposing sides — the insurance industry and the medical community. The insurance industry, backed by pro-business Republicans, is fighting hard to prevent an overhaul of the health care system. Changes to the current system, they say, would drive up the cost of insurance premiums, resulting in loss of insurance for many consumers. Democrats are seeking changes in the law that would provide a universal "Patients Bill of Rights," which would include, among other provisions, allowing patients to sue their health plans for punitive damages.

These insurance alliances were successful in preventing passage of such legislation in the 105th Congress, and they are moving quickly to build support for their position in the 106th Congress. The medical community, backed by the American Medical Association, is taking the opposite stance. Doctors are arguing that medical decisions regarding care should be determined by the doctor, not the insurance company. Medical practitioners contend that the well-being of the patient is being undermined by the push for profitability by large corporations.

The focus on interest group politics is rounded out with articles on the telecommunications industry and the gaming industry. Currently, telecommunications firms are battling to exploit vague language in the 1996 Telecommunications Act, or pushing to rewrite entire provisions of the law to favor their segment of the market. At stake are billions of dollars as telecom giants fight over access to cable television systems, which could be used to provide high-speed Internet service. Another article illustrates the political clout of the gaming industry. As social conservatives push to limit or eliminate gambling, a coalition of casino and hotel executives have responded with heavy lobbying and campaign contributions. Victories for the coalition included the defeats of David Beasley, the incumbent South Carolina governor who opposed the state's lucrative video poker games, and Alabama governor Fob James, who opposed a state lottery. Both were Republicans who lost to candidates supported by the gambling interest.

Parties plan to win House with economic ideas that attract women without alienating men

Dollars and Sensitivities: Finessing the Gender Gap

After years of searching, politicians think they have found the way to a woman's vote: through her wallet. As Democrats and Republicans prepare for campaigns in 2000 that could shift control of the House, law-

makers are emphasizing bread-and-butter issues such as Social Security, education and health care in an intense effort to woo women. Making up more than half the electorate, women are more likely than men to vote and more likely to vote Democratic.

Democrats are keenly aware that they cannot erase Republicans' six-vote House majority unless they keep women's support. Republicans could lose control of the chamber if they do not broaden their appeal.

Rather than emphasizing civil rights, as Democrats did in 1992, however, or agitating to shrink the size of government as Republicans did in 1994, lawmakers are trying to win the support of female voters by focusing on their economic security. (*1994 Almanac, p. 3*)

The agenda reflects the priorities of women who are struggling to balance work with the needs of children and aging parents. It has the added benefit of appealing to,

rather than alienating, men who face the same challenges.

"The women's agenda is not just abortion and the Equal Rights Amendment," said Celinda Lake, a pollster at Lake, Snell, Perry and Associates. "Congress is realizing these [economic concerns] are not just peripheral issues, but central issues, and you can talk about them and hold your male support."

That task is easier for Democrats — whose agenda coincides neatly with women's political priorities — than for Republicans, who must maintain their strong support among men who appreciate the party's historical emphasis on taxes and other fiscal issues.

"We definitely have a gender gap," said Republican Rep. Jennifer Dunn of Washington, who is leading her party's efforts to appeal to more women. She cited recent polls showing that Republican congressional candidates still lag with female voters. But she thinks the divide can be narrowed.

"Republicans are in a very good position

CQ Weekly April 24, 1999

now, because they do not take women for granted," Dunn said. "That is the beginning."

Democrats' laser-sharp focus on women is reflected in an agenda, framed in President Clinton's Jan. 19 State of the Union address, that emphasizes issues such as pay equity, education and child care — traditionally Democratic strengths among women. Clinton's Social Security plan calls for higher benefits for women, who depend more than men on the system. (*1999 CQ Weekly, p. 201*)

Kennedy, shown in October with Clinton, says the DCCC has developed a "synergy" with EMILY's List, a large PAC that aids Democratic women who support abortion rights.

For their part, Republicans have quickly moved education legislation to the floor, are pushing anew for a managed care overhaul and are promising to protect Social Security in general, though avoiding endorsing major changes.

With women more likely than men to vote — in 1996, 56 percent of women voted, compared with 53 percent of men — gender politics have taken on heightened importance. But the dynamics have changed over the years.

In 1992, which pundits dubbed the "year of the woman," anger over the Senate's handling in 1991 of Anita Hill's sexual harassment charges against Supreme Court nominee Clarence Thomas helped propel four Democratic women into the Senate. (*1992 Almanac, p. 8-A*)

Two years later, Republicans took

back the House and Senate largely on the strength of male support. In 1996 and 1998, Democrats reclaimed House seats partly because women turned out.

Money Matters

Within the feminist movement, there is also a renewed emphasis on economic security.

More than 100 groups, from Church Women United to the National Organization for Women, united formally as the National Council of Women's Organizations last year to elevate their political presence. The council's first national summit, on March 15 and 16, concentrated on how proposed Social Security overhauls would affect women. (*1998 CQ Weekly, p. 1038*)

"Most of the activism of the council is around economic issues. There was a void," said Susan Bianchi-Sand, the council chairman and executive director of the National Committee on Pay Equity.

"There had been very active pro-choice coalitions, sexual harassment protests and activity; but on issues like welfare, affirmative action, pay equity," there was little organization, she said.

Leaders of several women's groups said they have long been out front in trying to secure pension rights, easier credit for women, and time off work for new children or emergencies in the

1993 Family and Medical Leave Act (PL 103-3), which requires employers with more than 50 workers to grant unpaid leave to employees for the birth of a child or a family emergency. Organized labor is very active on women's pay issues. (*1993 Almanac, p. 389*)

But some leaders concede that the more economic-oriented message has been muffled in recent years as they have turned to battling Republicans in Congress on abortion and other issues.

Complicating matters was last year's impeachment debate. Some feminists and Democratic women in Congress were criticized as reluctant to issue a strong reprimand of Clinton in light of his affair with former White House intern Monica Lewinsky. (*1998 CQ Weekly, p. 223*)

"While the women's groups did condemn his [Clinton's] personal behavior, they also understand that the administration in terms of public policy has been very supportive," said Gail Shaffer, chief executive officer of Business and Professional Women/USA.

In an indication of the intricate nature of the politics, the business group did not attend the March 15 summit even though it is a member of the National Council of Women's Organizations. Shaffer said there were scheduling conflicts but also concerns among members that the gathering was weighted too heavily toward Democrats.

Women in Prominent Spots

Gender issues are not confined to the House. On March 25, the Senate voted in support of an amendment to the 2000 budget resolution (H Con Res 68) calling for a $5 billion increase in child care funding. (*1999 CQ Weekly, p. 749*)

In the House, because the margin between the two parties is so slim, concern about the 2000 elections is part of the calculation on issues great and small.

After women failed to secure any Democratic leadership posts in November, Minority Leader Richard A. Gephardt, D-Mo., created an elective position of assistant to the Democratic leader. Rosa DeLauro of Connecticut, who had run unsuccessfully for House Democratic caucus chairman, won.

After Clinton's State of the Union address, Dunn was one of two members who gave the Republican Party's televised response, emphasizing her experiences as a single mother. (*1999 CQ Weekly, p. 208*)

The Wirthlin Group has just completed a major survey for the National Republican Congressional Committee (NRCC) of what voters want. One of the subsets emphasized was women.

Within the GOP, there is some feeling that the gender gap has resulted from the packaging, not the product. Lawmakers argue that many women were turned off by the styles of former House Speaker Newt Gingrich, R-Ga. (1979-99), and 1996 presidential nominee Sen. Bob Dole, R-Kan. (1969-96).

"Our message is fine. Some of the messengers we had would talk in language that was macho, geared more toward fellow men," said Rep. Thomas M. Davis III, R-Va., chairman of the NRCC. "We're going to do just fine with women, a little better with men."

To bolster his case, Davis pointed to recent polls showing that Republican presidential hopefuls Gov. George W. Bush of Texas and former Transportation Secretary Elizabeth Dole were outperforming Vice President Al Gore among women. An April 17 study by the Pew Research Center for the People and the Press found women preferred Bush to Gore, 52 percent to 42 percent. Clinton ran nearly 20 points ahead of Bob Dole among women in January 1996.

In another sign of the emphasis on women, the Democratic Congressional Campaign Committee (DCCC) has as its political director Karin Johanson, a former political director of EMILY's List, which aids Democratic women who support abortion rights.

The group, whose name stands for "Early Money is Like Yeast," delivered $7.5 million in the 1998 election cycle and contacted millions of women in get-out-the-vote activities.

"We're having a very much closer synergy between EMILY's List and the DCCC," said Committee Chairman Rep. Patrick J. Kennedy, D-R.I. "The issues driving the women's vote are all Democratic issues. It's more of a hand-in-glove approach than ever before."

For the Senate, Republican New Jersey Gov. Christine Todd Whitman is planning to run, and first lady Hillary Rodham Clinton is considering a campaign in New York.

Many experts believe that the Democratic Party will have a hard time retaking a majority in the Senate, but many Democrats are hopeful about their chances in the House.

Ellen R. Malcolm, president of EMILY's List, said a change in House leadership is within sight: "In the past two elections, seven of our Democratic women have taken back Republican House seats. We are quite confident we can meet that goal in 2000."

Bruce Oppenheimer, a political scientist at Vanderbilt University in Nashville, Tenn., said that while the number of Democratic women candidates has increased markedly, Republicans have not recruited a lot of women. "In 1996, the same number of women ran in general elections for the House as in 1986," he said.

But Rep. Anne M. Northup of Kentucky, who is heading GOP recruitment this session, said: "I am looking for opportunities. Women sort of wait for an invitation. Politics is a world that's been so traditionally male. Men don't wait for invitations; they go after it."

Economics and More

The emphasis may be on economics, but abortion and family planning will still loom large in 2000, as both parties try to energize core supporters on both the left and right whose vote is based on the issue.

Elizabeth Dole and Bush, both abortion opponents, have been criticized by some conservatives for not taking a hard enough line, although others want the party to cool its rhetoric. The National Abortion and Reproductive Rights Action League in March began running ads in New Hampshire and Iowa accusing the Republican candidates of ambiguity on the issue. *(1999 CQ Weekly, p. 742)*

The Planned Parenthood Federation of America is taking the offensive with a legislative agenda that would require insurance coverage of contraceptives.

Beyond abortion, which is always a divisive issue, the contest for women's votes raises a number of politically difficult questions. Republicans must choose in some instances between the business community and consumer interests.

On health care, for example, Democrats want to allow patients to sue health maintenance organizations, while many Republicans do not. There is support in both parties for requiring managed care plans to allow women to designate their obstetrician/gynecologists as primary care physicians so they would not need referrals to see them.

Last year, the Women's Legal Defense Fund gave itself the more encompassing name the National Partnership for Women and Families. A top issue is managed care. *(1999 CQ Weekly, p. 799)*.

On education, Republicans favor local control, while Democrats want more federal involvement.

The issue of pay equity also has prominence, but no consensus. Clinton's fiscal 2000 budget included $4 million to pay for initiatives aimed at closing the gap between men's and women's pay, including trying to get businesses to hire women in fields in which they are underrepresented.

Top Republicans oppose legislation to set wage guidelines. The U.S. Chamber of Commerce released a study disputing pay inequities, and Concerned Women for America, a conservative group, criticized pay equity legislation.

"Feminists believe women would be better off in an economy where the federal government dictates how much everyone earns," the conservative organization said.

There may be action on smaller measures. One factor is the Congressional Caucus for Women's Issues. A force in the 1980s for expanding rights to pensions, credit and other issues, the group went through a lull after 1994, when Gingrich eliminated staff and funding for all caucuses.

Last year, Co-Chairwomen Del. Eleanor Holmes Norton, D-D.C., and Rep. Nancy L. Johnson, R-Conn., persuaded nearly all House women to join the caucus. The leaders developed an agenda that called for a renewed effort on women's health research and child support, but steers clear of abortion.

This year all but two of the 58 House women belong. Current Co-Chairwomen Sue W. Kelly, R-N.Y., and Carolyn B. Maloney, D-N.Y., are developing an agenda that includes pay issues, women in the military and support for women-owned business.

"The women's caucus has been one of the most bipartisan and the more successful," said Maloney.

There are fissures, however. In March, Maloney, the chief sponsor of a Democratic bill to expand tax credits and subsidies for child care, testified on the measure before the House Ways and Means Subcommittee on Human Resources. *(1999 CQ Weekly, p. 706)*

Subcommittee Chairman Johnson opposed the bill, arguing that states already receive record aid for child care under the 1996 welfare law (PL 104-193). *(1996 Almanac p. 6-3)* ◆

Interest Groups Seek Best Value For Copious Campaign Dollars

Issue ads, phone banks and get-out-the-vote drives attract spending that is largely unregulated

If money talks, voters in this year's elections got an earful. The cost of congressional races for the 1997-98 cycle already tops a record-breaking $1 billion in direct donations to candidates and national political parties.

And that is not the final count. Fundraising numbers for the last three weeks before the Nov. 3 election are still coming in to the Federal Election Commission. And the FEC tracks only the spending that falls under federal regulation. It does not count the millions of dollars spent by outside interest groups on such things as issue advocacy advertising and get-out-the-vote efforts — activities that played major roles in the November outcome.

The $1 billion figure also does not include the millions of dollars spent on independent expenditures — spending by outside groups on ads, phone banks and direct mailings that must be reported to the FEC but that have no cost limits as long as they are not coordinated with the candidates.

When the calculating is done, the 1998 congressional campaigns are expected to be the most expensive for a midterm election in history, according to the Center for Responsive Politics, a nonpartisan group that tracks money in politics.

Where is all the campaign money coming from?

To be sure, much of it is not coming from the average American voter. According to the FEC, 57 percent of the money donated to the general-election campaigns of candidates came from individuals — about $329 million. About $167 million (29 percent) came from political action committees (PACs). The FEC also said $46 million (8 percent) came from the candidates, mostly in loans to themselves.

Money raised by the national parties came primarily from individuals. But much of that money came in unlimited "soft money" donations from a small group of wealthy individuals.

The Center for Responsive Politics says people who donate $1,000 or more to political campaigns and committees make up only one-tenth of 1 percent of the American population.

"There's only a small number of people

AFL-CIO President John Sweeney spoke Sept. 22 at an Ohio convention, urging union members to vote for Democrats. From Oct. 1 to Oct. 14, the AFL-CIO spent $1.3 million on direct mailings aimed at energizing union voters.

who can afford to give the money that makes a difference in elections," said Eric Schmeltzer, spokesman for Public Campaign, a nonpartisan group that promotes fundraising changes and public financing of campaigns. He said he is concerned that "those who pay the piper call the tunes."

Unregulated Money

Under federal law, individuals can donate no more than $1,000 per primary or general election to candidates and no more than $5,000 per year to PACs. There is also a $25,000 annual limit on how much an individual can give to federal candidates or political parties.

But those limits apply only to "hard" money contributions — money that is spent to promote specific candidates. People can give unlimited amounts of "soft" money to national political parties, as long as that money is spent only on "party building" activities and not to help specific candidates.

Soft-money fundraising has increased exponentially in recent years as parties have figured out the most effective ways to use it.

Between Jan. 1, 1997, and Oct. 14, 1998, the Democratic national campaign committees raised $78.8 million in soft money, an in-

Quick Contents

In the 1997-98 election cycle, outside interest groups focused on get-out-the-vote efforts. They sought to energize voters in specific demographic groups and to encourage group members to vote for specific candidates.

The Rules on Spending

Here is a quick guide to campaign contributions and regulations:

● **Hard money.** Individuals are allowed to give up to $1,000 to a candidate for the primary and $1,000 for the general election. They can give up to $5,000 annually to political action committees (PACs) and up to $25,000 per calendar year in total political contributions. These limited donations, which must be reported to the Federal Election Commission (FEC), are called "hard money."

● **Soft money.** Federal law limits the amount of money people can give to political campaigns and bans corporations and labor unions from donating to candidates, but "soft" money provides a way around these restrictions.

Soft money, also called nonfederal money, refers to contributions to political parties that can be used only for "party building" activities such as voter education programs and registration drives.

Individuals and outside interest groups can give unlimited amounts of soft money to national political parties, but all soft money contributions must be reported to the FEC. Donations often come in $100,000, $200,000, or even $500,000 lump sums.

Soft money cannot be used to directly promote the election of candidates. The national parties are more frequently using the money to run "issue ads" that praise the work and stances of candidates without expressly calling for their election.

● **Issue ads.** The Supreme Court ruled in 1976 in *Buckley v. Valeo* that limits on campaign contributions applied only to "communications that in express terms advocate the election or defeat of a clearly identified candidate for federal office." A footnote in the ruling defined express terms to include such phrases as "vote for," "elect" or "support."

Because issue ads do not contain such terms, they are not subject to any reporting requirements or spending limits. Issue ads, however, usually praise or attack a candidate's legislative votes and positions.

Both national campaign committees and outside interest groups have begun to run more and more issue ads using unregulated money.

● **Independent expenditures.** PACs, interest groups and individuals can spend unlimited amounts on independent advertisements that expressly support or oppose a candidate, as long as the spending is not coordinated with the candidate's campaign.

Unlike issue ads, they can use terms such as "vote for" or "support." These expenditures must be reported to the FEC.

crease of 84 percent over the same period in the last midterm election cycle.

Republicans during that same period raised $93.7 million in soft money, a 144 percent increase over the last midterm elections.

Among the top individual soft-money donors this cycle was Bernard L. Schwartz, chairman of Loral Space and Communications Ltd. Schwartz gave more than $950,000 to the Democratic national campaign committees in 1997 and 1998. Schwartz also was the biggest individual donor of campaign cash during the 1995-96 election cycle. He came to the public's attention following allegations that he helped hand over sensitive technology to the Chinese government and tried to buy influence with campaign contributions — a charge he denied. (*1998 CQ Weekly, p. 3304; 1998 CQ Weekly, p. 1376*)

Another big-money giver was David Koch, an oil billionaire and the head of Koch Industries Inc., who gave $180,000 in soft money to Republicans this cycle. Foster Friess, money manager of the Brandywine mutual fund, gave $215,000 this year to Republicans. And Richard DeVos, founder of the Amway Corp. and owner of the Orlando Magic basketball team, and his wife each gave $500,000 in April 1997 to Republicans.

Corporations also poured millions of soft dollars into the national campaign committees this election cycle.

The tobacco company Philip Morris was the No. 1 soft-money donor this cycle, giving more than $2.3 million. That includes a $250,000 soft-money donation to the Republican National Committee on Oct. 22, less than two weeks before Election Day.

The Walt Disney Co. contributed more than $700,000 in soft money over the past two years, including a $150,000 donation to the Democratic National Committee on Oct. 28, five days before the election.

Although soft money cannot be used for candidate advertising, the parties have been spending more and more of these funds on "issue ads" that can extol the virtues or faults of candidates without expressly calling for their election or defeat.

A new study by the Annenberg Public Policy Center of the University of Pennsylvania found that 70 percent of issue ads run in the final two months before the November elections were paid for by the Democratic and Republican national campaign committees.

The study also found that most of those ads — 59.5 percent — were attack ads against candidates.

Issue ads are one of the fastest growing political tactics used by the parties and outside groups. The study found that money spent on issue ads more than doubled this election cycle compared with the 1995-96 cycle.

Annenberg estimates that 77 groups and committees spent between $275 million and $340 million on issue ads this cycle, compared with the $135 million to $150 million spent last time around. That money is unregulated, meaning groups do not need to report how much they spent on the ads, nor where the money came from.

Sen. Russell D. Feingold, D-Wis., a supporter of overhauling the campaign finance system, demanded that outside interest groups, as well as the Democratic Party, not run issue ads in his behalf during his re-election bid this year.

"It's outrageous the money coming from sources that is completely undisclosed," Feingold said in an interview this month. "Independent groups have grown to the point where they're starting to diminish the power of the individual donor. People feel they really don't count any more."

Feingold added: "I know of cases where consultants sat down with candidates and told them, 'You won't have any control over your campaign because of these outside groups.' "

Outside Interest Groups

But outside interest groups say they are merely serving as conduits to allow voters to express their views on issues.

They insist that issue ads educate the public and help to create a better-informed electorate. And they argue that any limits on issue advocacy would impede their constitutional right to free speech.

"Our goal is to locate people of faith, to educate them on the issues and to activate them," Christian Coalition Executive Director Randy Tate, a former congressman, said in an interview.

The Christian Coalition, a conservative nonpartisan group, spent $3.1 million on issue advocacy campaigns this election cycle, including the distribution of 45 million voter guides during the primary and general-election seasons and a half-million automated phone calls in the final days before the Nov. 3 election encouraging coalition members to vote.

It was the most money the group has ever spent during an election cycle, and former Rep. Tate, R-Wash. (1995-97), said he expects his organization to be even more active during the next two years.

Because the guides and phone calls did not explicitly endorse any candidates, the money spent does not fall under any reporting or limitation requirements. Tate said his group's activities made an impact on the 1998 elections in that "our people went out and were informed on the issues."

The Christian Coalition also spent about $250,000 on radio ads this cycle, addressing various legislative issues including school prayer, the "marriage tax penalty" and so-called partial-birth abortions. Tate said the ads did not target congressional candidates, although they did specifically mention the names of incumbents and how they voted on the issues.

Another outside group to make use of issue ads this year was Americans for Job Security, a pro-business trade association established in 1997. It spent $6 million to $7 million on issue ads this year, nearly one-third of that attacking Democratic Rep. Frank Pallone Jr. of New Jersey

and urging voters to tell Pallone to "keep his hands off Social Security."

Pallone, who was ultimately re-elected, charged the group with being a front for health insurers angry with him for supporting changes in health maintenance organizations.

The Sierra Club, an environmental group, spent $1.5 million on issue ads this year. The ads attacked or praised the environmental voting record of incumbents running for re-election, but stopped short of directly expressing political support or opposition to them.

"They are highly effective," said Chris Norman, associate political director of the Sierra Club.

Norman stressed that the ads are not meant to lend political support to candidates but are aimed at "educating voters" on the environmental records of incumbents.

The issue ads were part of a broader $6 million "voter education" campaign over the past two years that included distributing hundreds of thousands of voter guides.

The Sierra Club also participated in political activities that are regulated by federal law. For example, it lent 40 staff members to various campaigns, encouraged its 400,000 members to vote for certain candidates and ran independent expenditure ads in several political races.

"We have a lot of tools in our basket," Norman said. "We had a real impact on the elections. Eighty-eight percent of our endorsed candidates won."

Independent Expenditures

Like issue ads, independent expenditures have no spending limits. Unlike issue ads, independent expenditures must be reported to the FEC. But they can expressly endorse the election or defeat of a candidate. In the final three weeks before Nov. 3, outside groups and political parties spent more than $6 million on independent expenditures.

These costs include mailings, phone banks and advertisements in behalf of candidates. But the expenditures must be made independently of the candidate, without any coordination.

The American Medical Association spent nearly $760,000 in behalf of three GOP House candidates between Oct. 12 and Nov. 2. Its biggest expenditure was $332,935 for radio and television ads for Rep. Greg Ganske, R-Iowa. Ganske, a surgeon, was one of the few Republicans who backed an AMA-supported Democratic bill to regulate man-

aged care health plans. (*1998 CQ Weekly, p. 3109*)

The AMA also spent $140,345 to help Rep. Jon D. Fox, R-Pa., and $286,099 to help Republican Ernie Fletcher, who won Kentucky's 6th District seat.

The National Rifle Association spent the most of any group on independent expenditures during the final weeks of the congressional campaigns.

The group spent more than $1.6 million in behalf of 30 congressional candidates, including $202,975 for GOP Sen. Alfonse M. D'Amato of New York and $227,802 to help GOP Sen. Lauch Faircloth of North Carolina. Both lost their re-election bids.

Another group that made a lot of independent expenditures was Campaign for America, a group that favors a campaign finance overhaul. It spent more than $450,000 to help Democratic Rep. Scotty Baesler's campaign against GOP Rep. Jim Bunning for a Kentucky Senate seat. Bunning won.

The League of Conservation Voters spent $751,476 in the final three weeks of the campaign to defeat nine House and Senate candidates, including $174,611 against Rep. Mark W. Neumann, R-Wis., who lost his Senate bid against Feingold, and $166,169 against Rep. Linda Smith, R-Wash., who lost her bid to oust Democratic Sen. Patty Murray.

Throughout the election cycle, the League of Conservation Voters spent $2.3 million on its "Dirty Dozen" campaign targeting congressional candidates who did not support the group's environmental agenda.

Along with television ads, the group mailed out more than 200,000 pieces of direct mail, distributed 38,000 leaflets and made more than 220,000 get-out-the-vote telephone calls.

The league was rewarded on Election Day. All five Senate candidates targeted for defeat lost their races.

"The Dirty Dozen campaigns are hard-hitting political campaigns that empower voters by giving them factual information they can use in deciding how to cast their ballot," said league President Deb Callahan. "We helped put the environment on the electoral agenda in 1998, and we intend to keep it there in 2000."

Get Out the Vote

Perhaps the most influential use of outside money this year was on get-out-the-vote efforts. Millions of dollars were spent by groups to energize voters in specific demographic groups and to encourage organization members to vote for specific candidates.

The FEC does not regulate money spent by groups on nonpartisan get-out-the-vote efforts. But interest groups must report to the FEC any spending on communications to their members that encourage them to vote for or against certain candidates.

Between Oct. 1 and Oct. 14, the AFL-CIO spent $1.3 million on direct mailings to its union members, including $108,000 in mailings in support of Baesler, an $80,000 mailing to support Sen. Barbara Boxer, D-Calif., who narrowly won her re-election bid, and more than $78,000 in mailings in behalf of Democrat John Edwards, who defeated Sen. Faircloth in North Carolina.

The AFL-CIO, which during the last election cycle spent $25 million on issue ads, this time focused most of its money on energizing union voters.

There are 13 million AFL-CIO members across the country, and 40 million adults live in a home with a union member, so the mailings reached beyond members.

The union also sent volunteers to union sites across the country to talk to members and encourage them to vote.

Heeding dire predictions that the November elections would draw record-low voter participation, the AFL-CIO decided that the turnout of its members would be essential.

Many pundits credit the union's get-out-the-vote effort with giving Democrats the edge they needed to pick up five House seats. Twenty-two percent of those who voted Nov. 3 came from union households, up from 14 percent in 1994. And 70 percent of those union members said they voted Democratic, according to the Voter News Service, an exit polling firm.

About 46 percent of the nation's union membership turned out to vote, compared with only 36 percent of the total voting age population, according to AFL-CIO surveys.

"The major part of our program was turning out union votes," said AFL-CIO political director Steve Rosenthal. "The bottom line was you had an electorate where almost a quarter of the voters came from union households, and we don't represent a quarter of the public. . . . That is an extraordinary accomplishment for our people."

African-American voters were also targeted by outside groups to go to the polls Nov. 3.

The NAACP launched a get-out-the-vote campaign targeting 10 states. The nonpartisan group sent out 45,000 volunteers to knock on doors, register voters at churches, drive people to polls and even baby-sit for mothers who wanted to vote. The group also published about 500,000 voter score cards detailing how incumbents stood on issues important to black voters.

The NAACP, however, did not specifically call for the election or defeat of any candidates. Hilary O. Shelton, director of the group's Washington bureau, said the NAACP reached out to 3 million black voters.

"If you look at who won and look at their agendas, the people who fared best are the ones who were consistent with our issues," Shelton said. "We gave them the information, and African-American voters were really psyched to go to the polls."

Although the share of the black vote did not increase nationally from 1994, it did grow in the politically tumultuous South.

Blacks were an essential factor in electing statewide Democratic candidates in Maryland, the Carolinas, Alabama and Georgia, where the black vote increased from 19 percent of the state's total vote in 1994 to 29 percent in 1998, according to exit polls.

Women's groups also poured big money into energizing female voters this year.

EMILY's List, a group that raises money for Democratic candidates, spent nearly $3 million on get-out-the-vote campaigns in 22 states. It was the same amount of money spent during the 1995-96 presidential election cycle.

The money went to mail 8 million pieces of political literature and make 2 million phone calls. The group targeted Hispanic women, African-American women, seniors and women who have been shown to vote in presidential elections but not in midterm races.

"Personal contact with women voters really makes a difference," said Stephanie Cohen, communications director for EMILY's List.

Cohen said women's votes were essential in several hard-fought Senate races, including Boxer's re-election bid and the successful Senate race of former Democratic Rep. Blanche Lincoln of Arkansas. ◆

By swaying presidential campaigns and the public, advocates see an 'in' on the Hill

Health Care Forces Fight To Frame the Debate

Although the presidential election is more than a year away, a political campaign is already up and running in the key early states of New Hampshire and Iowa. Campaign workers are talking with editorial boards, polling voters and spreading their message.

The campaign, however, is not that of a White House hopeful. Instead, it is being led by the American Association of Health Plans (AAHP) — the country's leading representative of managed care plans.

Fearing that presidential candidates will make managed care a top issue in the 2000 elections, the association has launched a preemptive campaign to block a broad overhaul of the health care system.

"It became very clear that for an association to get its message across, the challenge was to adopt the tactics of a political campaign," said Karen Ignagni, the head of the AAHP. "We're on the offensive rather than the defensive. We're not waiting for 2000. We're building our beachhead before it becomes a runaway political issue."

As Congress prepares to bring a managed care overhaul bill to both floors this summer, the AAHP is joining insurance and business groups to aggressively fight proposals that would create new government mandates on health insurers. They argue that such mandates will drive up costs and force many businesses to drop health coverage for their workers.

On the other side, doctors and consumer groups are intensifying their lobbying efforts in support of such broad legislation. They say that without federal protections, Americans will suffer at the hands of insurance companies who put profits before patients.

Some groups are waging their fights directly with members — running ads in various congressional districts and threatening to withhold political support — while others, such as the AAHP, are targeting presidential candidates and public sentiment in hopes of swaying the national debate on health care.

If her group and others can influence the rhetoric of the presidential races, Ignagni believes, they can have a direct impact on con-

gressional action during the next two years.

Last year, congressional Democrats rallied behind a broad "patients' protection" bill that would have, among other things, allowed consumers to sue their health plans for punitive damages. Republican leaders opposed the legislation, instead crafting a bill extending some federal protections to patients.

After millions of dollars were spent by insurance and business groups, managed care legislation died in the 105th Congress.

"Had it not been for the Health Benefits Coalition and the efforts of its individual members, there absolutely would have been legislation passed last year," said Dan Danner, chairman of the Health Benefits Coalition, a group of insurance and business groups opposed to new health care mandates. "The coalition did a great job of educating members on the issue last year, and that will pay dividends again this year."

But during the 1998 elections, dozens of congressional candidates ran on the promise of enacting major changes in the health care system, and congressional Republicans acknowledge that the issue has become too politicized to ignore.

Quick Contents

Insurers and business groups, as well as doctors and consumer groups, are borrowing a page from the politician's handbook. They are organizing early and attacking often to influence Congress in the managed care debate.

Ganske, who has been targeted by health insurers because of his bill that would increase patients' rights, says their attacks give him an opening to explain his views.

Politics of Policy

The AAHP has decided that if you can't beat the politicians, join them.

"Politicians respond to politics," said Mark Merritt, vice president and chief of strategic planning for the association. "Quality health care is a second tier issue for politicians. The first tier issue is how can they get re-elected."

The association began gearing up its campaign almost immediately after the 1998 congressional elections.

In January, the group commissioned a poll of 300 likely Republican presidential voters in New Hampshire by

Chip Kahn of the Health Insurance Association of America said managed care companies are aiming to influence not only Congress, but also public perception of the companies.

Republican pollster Whit Ayres.

Results showed that managed care legislation is not high on voters' priority lists — a message the AAHP hopes will convince presidential candidates to keep it off their agenda.

According to the poll, conducted Jan. 4-5, 85 percent of the respondents who have managed care plans are satisfied with their coverage. The poll also showed that a candidate's stance on managed care ranks near the bottom of a list of 11 factors likely to have an important influence on voters in the Republican presidential primary.

By shopping the polling numbers around to editorial boards across New Hampshire and Iowa, the association hopes to squelch the issue before presidential candidates seize on it.

"We want to get voters to tell the politicians, 'Don't do this to us,' " Merritt said.

The AAHP also has held numerous media events across the two states, presenting small-business leaders who say federal managed care legislation will make it impossible for them to afford health care coverage for their workers.

"Whatever presidential candidates talk about drives what Congress talks about and how it's debated publicly," said Merritt, a longtime political strategist who handled press for Lamar Alexander's 1996 presidential campaign.

The U.S. Chamber of Commerce is making a more direct appeal to members of Congress not to pass managed care legislation. The Chamber created a "grasstops" program, which goes into districts and identifies members' allies.

As the health care debate heats up, the Chamber will ask these allies to personally lobby the members against the legislation.

"We gauge the issues they most care about and ask them to write the member about it," said Cecelia A. Adams, director of congressional and public affairs with the Chamber of Commerce. "It reaches the members at a different level. Grass-roots letters and calls may not get directly to a member of Congress. These kinds of correspondence go directly to the member."

The Doctors' Spin

Insurance and business groups are not the only ones working behind the scenes to influence the health care debate.

The American Medical Association (AMA), the country's leading doctors' group, is using a tactic similar to that used by the Chamber of Commerce — but seeking the opposite result. The AMA has contacted hometown friends and associates of key senators and House members to ask them to lobby their congressional buddies for managed care legislation.

The AMA is also taking part in a national "Patients' Bill of Rights Day" on April 9 that is being coordinated by a variety of groups that support managed care legislation.

The event will feature news conferences and rallies across the country calling for legislation to extend federal protections to patients. Members of Congress will take part, and organizers say they expect President Clinton to appear at a rally either in Washington or Philadelphia.

"It will reveal the sheer numbers of people who support a patients' bill of rights," said Judith L. Lichtman, president of the National Partnership for Women and Families, one of the organizers of the event. Lichtman's group is working with a variety of labor, women's, medical and religious groups to push Congress to pass managed care legislation this year.

"We think women are a litmus test as to how well our health care system works. We have an enormous stake in this debate," Lichtman said. "This is a major priority for us."

Along with the April 9 event, the groups launched an on-line petition drive in March, asking people to sign a letter calling for congressional action on managed care. The letter will be presented to members of Congress as the House and Senate prepare to vote on any legislation.

Ad Campaign

Doctors, insurance and business groups are also taking to the airwaves to catch Congress' ear.

Various state affiliates of the AMA are expected to start broadcasting radio ads across the country soon. The ads call for Congress to pass a statutory definition of "medical necessity" — a contentious issue because the definition of medical necessity determines whether doctors or insurers have the final say in the kind of care patients receive.

Insurance and business groups have begun their own $2 million campaign on radio and TV during Congress' spring recess.

The Business Roundtable, an association of leading executives, bought more than $1 million worth of radio ads in 20 congressional districts across the country attacking bills introduced by Sen. Edward M. Kennedy, D-Mass., and Rep. Greg Ganske, R-Iowa. The bills (S 6, HR 358, HR 719) include provisions that would allow patients to sue their health insurers under state malpractice laws. The Health Benefits Coalition spent nearly $1 million on TV ads that also attack the Kennedy and Ganske bills, charging the legislation will drive up premiums and leave more Americans unable to afford health insurance.

"Congress is about to change your health insurance, and you'll pay the price," the ads warn, saying the Ganske and Kennedy bills would cost families $200 more a year. Ganske has asked the groups to pull their ads, saying they are inaccurate.

Last year, the Health Benefits Coalition spent more than $2 million lobbying against managed care legislation. The coalition said it may spend at least that much this year.

The AAHP is also running ads in Ganske's home state. The ads, which show a piñata being hit with a stick, attack politicians for "bashing HMOs and other health plans to trick you into voting for them." The ads say that if managed care proposals such as Ganske's bill are enacted, 28,000 Iowans could lose health care coverage.

Ganske, a former plastic surgeon, said he was well aware that the insurance industry would target him this year, and he launched a pre-emptive strike of his own with $22,000 worth of television ads in early March. His ads call for bipartisan support for managed care legislation.

But Ganske said the business and insurance advertising spots attacking his bill have actually helped his cause.

"I love it," Ganske said in an interview. "We're getting calls from across the country asking us about our bill."

Ganske said as viewers of the negative ads call his office to express their opposition to his legislation, his staff is able to explain the details of his bill and convince them to support it.

"I hope they keep running the ads. It gives us the opportunity to get out our message," Ganske said.

But he warned that the GOP leadership could suffer politically if it continues to oppose broad legislation extending federal protections to patients.

"The Republican leadership is playing with fire," Ganske said. "We have a very small majority, and we could be looking at very significant realliances in this next election."

An Expensive Campaign

The millions of dollars being spent on broadcast ads during the congressional recess is just the tip of the iceberg.

During last year's debate, tens of millions were spent by supporters and opponents of managed care legislation. The price tag for this year's lobbying campaigns is likely to be even greater.

During the first six months of 1998, insurance companies and business groups involved in the managed care debate spent $60 million lobbying Congress, according to The Associated Press, which studied spending reports filed with the secretary of the Senate. That amount does not include the $11 million spent on advertising against managed care legislation, nor millions more in campaign contributions during the congressional elections. The AAHP alone spent $1 million during the first half of 1998 as Congress debated managed care legislation.

On the other side of the issue, medical groups, trial lawyers, unions and consumer groups who support a broad managed care overhaul spent more than $14 million lobbying Congress in the first six months of 1998. The top lobbyist on the issue was the AMA, which spent $8.3 million. This year, the AMA is set to spend at least that much on lobbying, according to association spokesman James Stacey.

The AFL-CIO is getting into the action as well, recently announcing that it will spend millions on managed care. During the first six months of 1998, the union spent $1.4 million lobbying Congress. In February, the AFL-CIO announced that it will spend $40 million between now and the 2000 races to help elect candidates who support its positions on managed care, the minimum wage and other labor issues.

The AMA is broadening its tactics by threatening to withhold money from candidates to try to galvanize the debate. The doctors' group has historically given the bulk of its contributions to Republicans, but it warns that could change.

During the 1996 elections, the AMA gave 85 percent of its contributions to Republicans. That dropped to 70 percent during the 1998 election cycle, and the group promises it will drop even more if Republicans do not start voting for a broad managed care overhaul. Already, state AMA affiliates have turned down requests from top Republicans for fundraisers.

Sprucing Up Their Images

Besides impressing members, health insurers are also hoping to burnish their image with the American public.

The Coalition for Affordable and Quality Healthcare, a group of large insurance companies and associations, will spend $10 million this year on an ad campaign aimed solely at shaping their public image.

The ads, expected to hit the television airwaves sometime in April, will not mention any bills or congressional members. Instead, they will simply tout the benefits of managed care plans.

Last fall, the coalition ran $5.5 million worth of television ads during the two months before the November elections.

"Survey after survey shows that our image is not as positive as we would like," said Chip Kahn, president of the Health Insurance Association of America and a board member of the Coalition. "The public has been barraged by anecdotes in the media and political rhetoric. The purpose of the ads is to chip away at what we consider to be an unfair image."

Although Kahn said the coalition and its ads are non-political, he acknowledged that an improved public image can only help the insurance industry during the legislative debate on managed care.

"As policy-makers consider proposals that affect the health care system, it is incumbent upon us to try to move the public's perception and understanding of what we do," Kahn said.

He added: "Health care is a front-page issue, a major political card that's played in every election cycle. The [health insurance] industry is caught up in the whirlwind."

Merritt of the AAHP agreed that health care — and the politics surrounding it — require a new and improved form of lobbying.

"The reality is the nature of lobbying has changed," he said. "The days where you can go have lunch with a member to drive legislation are gone." ◆

Self-employed physicians seek collective bargaining rights to counter managed care's clout

Doctors Look for Union Label

The days of private family physicians — who were free to establish fees and decide which medical treatments all of their patients received — are long gone.

Today, 92 percent of the nation's doctors have contracted with at least one managed care plan, which generally means accepting the insurer's decisions about fees and which treatments are covered.

But doctors, increasingly frustrated with the loss of power, have started banding together to increase their leverage as they negotiate with large health insurance companies. While many doctors are joining unions, more than half the nation's physicians are prohibited from collective bargaining under current labor laws.

Now they are looking to Congress to change that. The medical community is exerting its clout on Capitol Hill to push for legislation that would allow doctors and other health care professionals who contract independently with health insurance plans to form collective bargaining units.

But the doctors are up against another powerful lobbying force, the insurance industry, which says that physicians are looking for a blank-check policy that would undercut the mission of managed care: to provide quality health care in the most cost-effective way.

Independent doctors, the insurance industry says, are private practitioners — many of them already highly paid — who can set their own fees, solicit their own patients and turn down any health plan contracts they find objectionable.

In the coming weeks, the battle is expected to focus on a measure (HR 1304) introduced in March by Rep. Tom Campbell, R-Calif. The bill, which is expected to be the subject of hearings in the House Judiciary Committee in May, would make independent doctors and other health care professionals exempt from antitrust laws that prohibit them from bargaining collectively.

While the Campbell bill is just six pages long, health insurers and doctors say it could have as much impact on Americans' health care as broader managed care overhaul measures because it would shift the balance of power in the health care system.

"Allowing doctors antitrust exemptions,

AP PHOTO / CHARLES KRUPA

such as those contained in Rep. Campbell's bill, would result in collusion on prices, and that collusion will lead to higher health care costs and higher health insurance premiums for consumers," Chip Kahn, president of the Health Insurance Association of America, said after Campbell introduced his bill.

The American Medical Association (AMA), which represents 300,000 doctors, has endorsed the measure and made the issue a top priority on its legislative agenda.

Boston doctors and other medical workers, shown protesting corporate takeovers in health care in 1997, say managed care has limited their fees and flexibility to treat patients.

The AMA has also considered forming a union for its doctors. At its regular meeting in April, the group decided to defer doing so until its delegates debate the issue in full at the June meeting. In the meantime, it plans to keep the pressure on Congress.

"Collective bargaining will be the biggest single item of business at our annual meeting in June," said Dr. Richard F. Corlin, a gastroenterologist in Santa Monica, Calif., and speaker of the AMA's House of Delegates. "We are going to continue to increase pressure on members of Congress in a variety of ways — using media, public relations and direct contact with members. We will steadily and progressively continue to grind away at this issue."

Campbell first introduced a collective bargaining bill in the 105th Congress. The House Judiciary Committee held hearings but did not mark up the measure. This year, more than two dozen members from both parties have cosponsored his legislation, and Campbell's aides say they are hopeful a Senate companion bill will be introduced soon.

'De Facto' Employees

Under the Sherman Antitrust Act of 1890 and the Clayton Act of 1914, only workers who are considered "employees" of health plans, hospitals or other businesses can unionize and collectively bargain. Doctors who run private practices but have contracts with one or more health insurance plans are considered "independent contractors" and are prohibited from collective bargaining.

But an increasing number of self-employed doctors across the country say health plans are asking them to sign contracts that limit payments or treatments or include other provisions they find unacceptable, such as "gag clauses," which prevent doctors from talking to patients about treatments the health plan would not cover. They say the managed care industry has gained leverage as it has grown and consolidated through mergers. Doctors say they have become de facto employees of the health plans with which they have contracts.

The campaign for collectively bargained rights is largely a result of the rapid growth of the managed care system. According to InterStudy, a Minnesota think tank that tracks managed care trends, 79 million Americans were enrolled in HMOs as of July 1998, compared with 34.7 million people in 1990.

According to Campbell, there have been more than 162 health plan mergers in the past 10 years. Since 1994, 18 leading insurers have combined into six, prompting some doctors to fear that a few large insurance companies will monopolize the market and have the power to arbitrarily set fees and standards of care.

In Southern California, six HMOs hold 75 percent of the health care market. In Minneapolis, three HMOs account for 80 percent of the market, according to the journal Health Affairs.

"Sixty-five to 70 percent of my patients, at least, are in managed care contracts," said Dr. George Koenig, a neurosurgeon in Redwood, Calif. "These insurers have such a share of the market that if you want a viable practice you can't walk away from them."

Koenig and other doctors complain that they have no choice but to sign contracts giving health plans blanket authority to set fees and place restrictions on medical service.

"A few years ago, Blue Cross came to me and said, 'You don't have to sign this contract, but if you don't, you'll lose a large number of your patients,'" said Dr. Michael P. Connair, an orthopedic surgeon in Connecticut and president of the Federation of Physicians and Dentists, a national doctors' union.

"Doctors don't have any right at all to speak up against them, and therefore we're divided and conquered."

Insurers argue that individual doctors have tremendous leverage in negotiations.

"We have to have doctors. They do have some influence here," said Bill Pierce, director of public relations for the Blue Cross Blue Shield Association. "These contracts can be and often are negotiated deals. Doctors can exercise some of their weight. We need them. We do have to negotiate with them."

Insurers also question whether doctors who have formed bargaining units would walk off the job — leaving patients without medical care — if they did not get what they wanted.

Campbell's bill would specifically prohibit health care professionals from participating "in any collective cessation of service to patients."

Patient Protections

Self-employed doctors argue that collective bargaining would benefit not just physicians, but also patients, ultimately leading to better care. They say that in negotiating contracts with HMOs, they would insist on many of the same patient protections now being considered by Congress.

"This is a back door to managed care reform for patients, without legislators having to do it themselves," said Connair.

For example, Connair said, contracts often allow health plans to define "medical necessity," giving insurance companies absolute veto power over doctors' medical judgments. Some contracts also limit the type of drugs doctors can prescribe or contain clauses that prevent doctors from recommending treatment the managed care company may deem too expensive.

Health insurers argue that many of the contract clauses doctors oppose are designed to limit costs.

"The purpose of the marketplace is to make plans accountable to patients. It is presumptuous of physicians to say they're the only protectors," said Kahn of the industry association.

Insurance industry officials assert that doctors are interested in collective bargaining simply as a way to make more money.

"The idea of collective bargaining was supposed to be for the little man, trying to amass enough power and clout to ensure they can keep a roof over their heads or food in their mouths," said Jon Comola, vice president of government relations with Blue Cross Blue Shield of Texas. He noted that the average doctor's salary in Texas in 1997 was $187,000.

"The whole idea of collective bargaining was to ensure meat and potatoes, not to ensure your grandchild will drive a Mercedes," he said.

Doctors say their salaries are not the issue.

"I don't care if doctors made half of what they are making now or twice as much as they are making now," said the AMA's Corlin. "The issue is: What is a fair negotiating process?

"Health plans that pay their CEOs what they do have no right to talk about how much doctors make," he added.

Corlin cited the 1996 merger of Aetna Inc. and U.S. HealthCare. In that transaction, U.S. HealthCare founder and CEO Leonard Abramson received more than $800 million in cash and stock options.

Even though they are prohibited from collective bargaining, independent doctors across the country, anxious to exert more control over their managed care contracts, are exploring a variety of ways to gain power at the negotiating table — including joining unions.

They are facing many obstacles, however.

Federal Scrutiny

In New Jersey, a group of several hundred doctors who contract with the AmeriHealth HMO have tried to join the United Food and Commercial Workers Local 56.

The move is being reviewed by the National Labor Relations Board's (NLRB) regional office in Philadelphia.

Union officials argue that the New Jersey doctors are subject to so much control by AmeriHealth that they are de facto employees of the health plan and should therefore be allowed to unionize.

AmeriHealth argues that the doctors are "independent contractors" barred from unionizing under labor laws.

"They contract with a variety of insurers. They are independent business people," said Jim Paynard, senior director of corporate communications for AmeriHealth. "It's an independent business decision they have to make. They can contract with other people if they want."

Paynard added that AmeriHealth payments make up only about 3 percent of the doctors' incomes, showing that the doctors are not dependent upon the health plan contracts.

Although most observers believe the NLRB will reject the union effort, a positive ruling could set a precedent for other doctor unions across the country.

In Delaware, the Department of Justice filed a lawsuit in August against the Federation of Physicians and Dentists, charging it illegally organized a boycott among area orthopedic surgeons against Blue Cross Blue Shield.

The federation, a Tallahassee, Fla.-based organization that represents 8,500 doctors and dentists in 20 states, says it simply served as a conduit for information between doctors and the health plan and did not break any labor laws.

In 1996, the federation recruited nearly every orthopedic surgeon in Delaware. In 1997, when Blue Cross Blue Shield announced it would reduce payments to its contracted doctors, nearly all the Delaware orthopedic surgeons in the federation notified the health plan that they were terminating their contracts.

While the Justice Department charges that the federation violated antitrust laws, federation executives say they did nothing more than advise their members on contractual issues and the doctors independently decided whether to reject or accept the contracts.

Jack Seddon, executive director of the federation, said Campbell's bill is needed to ensure his group can continue to help doctors negotiate fair contracts, and ultimately improve care for patients.

"Managed care companies cannot unilaterally dictate patient treatment," Seddon said. "There is no doubt in my mind that there is no better way to monitor the health care system than through collective bargaining."

But Kerin Hearn, company spokesperson for Blue Cross Blue Shield of Delaware, said collective bargaining will ultimately hurt patients by injecting outside interests into local health care markets.

"Blue Cross Blue Shield of Delaware has been here for 35 years. We have a good relationship with physicians here," Hearn said. "We very highly value our local relationships and ability to talk with physicians. Our company's built on that."

Looking to States

In the meantime, doctors are looking to state legislatures for action on the issue. One possibility is Texas, where the medical community has an active lobbying presence. In March, two Republicans in the Texas Legislature introduced a bill that would allow independent groups of doctors to appoint a representative to negotiate on their behalf when an HMO exceeds 15 percent of an area's market share. Under the measure, the state would be required to supervise the ne-

A bill sponsored by Campbell is scheduled to be the subject of hearings before the House Judiciary Committee in May. Last year, a similar measure died in committee.

gotiating activity.

A proposed merger between Aetna U.S. Healthcare and Prudential HealthCare would give the combined company about 39 percent of the HMO market in the Dallas-Fort Worth area, according to the Texas Medical Association.

The AMA helped draft the bill and has recommended its use in other states. State lawmakers in Florida, New Jersey and Pennsylvania are looking at introducing similar legislation.

Self-employed doctors say they will continue to push for collective bargaining rights even if legislative efforts fail this year.

"If this bill doesn't get passed this year, it will come back," said Koenig. "This issue is not going to go away." ◆

As Hill Considers Law's Failings, Companies See Their Opening

Billions of dollars are at stake as companies lobby against trend toward mergers and try to turn 1996 telecommunications law to their own advantage

FCC Chairman Kennard talks about the telecommunications industry on Jan. 27. "The one thing I've learned in this job is that no one really knows exactly what the future is going to look like."

Quick Contents

As the search intensifies for new markets in the telecommunications industry, America Online, US West and MCI are joining forces to lobby Congress to reopen the Telecommunications Act of 1996. They want access to cable network lines to deliver the Internet more quickly.

Three years after passage of the landmark Telecommunications Act of 1996, America Online Inc., the nation's top Internet service provider, has launched an all-out lobbying campaign with powerful allies to change the law.

The coalition of companies seeking to open access to cable networks — which includes Colorado-based US West Inc., a regional phone company, and long-distance carrier MCI WorldCom Inc. — has quietly made contacts on Capitol Hill. They want legislation to force AT&T Corp. to give competitors access to the vast cable television network that AT&T will acquire in its $48 billion merger with cable giant Tele-Communications Inc. (TCI).

"I think there is a growing political momentum for the changes to provide open or equal access to cable or Internet services, and the need is great," said George Vradenburg, the senior vice president and general counsel for global and strategic policy at America Online, commonly known as AOL.

The fight over access to cable television

systems has become a battleground in a broad debate over proposed changes in the 1996 law (PL 104-104). AOL wants to use cable to provide high-speed Internet connections, bypassing slower telephone networks. *(1996 Almanac, p. 3-43)*

But on Feb. 4, Federal Communications Commission (FCC) Chairman William Kennard signaled that the regulatory agency may become another obstacle for AOL. He said the FCC would not necessarily require AT&T to give its competitors access to the high-speed Internet pipeline.

"At this point, because the Internet is still in its infancy, it's not appropriate today to write such rules," Kennard said.

The fate of the rules will carry high stakes for the cable television industry, which serves 65 million households, and the $110 billion local telephone industry, which serves more than 94 percent of the nation's homes.

"Huge stakes are involved here. The companies account for a sizable chunk of the New York Stock Exchange," said Robert W. Crandall, a senior fellow at the Brookings Institution. They also account for a big lobbying army in Washington: A study by the

Center for Responsive Politics, which tracks campaign contributions and lobbying, found that the top 9 telecommunications companies spent $60 million on lobbying in 1997.

Meanwhile, US West and Texas-based GTE Corp., a regional phone company, have opened another front in the debate over the law, pushing for legislation to clarify provisions so they can compete for lucrative contracts to provide long-distance data transmission services to businesses. The law bars the Baby Bell companies, which provide local phone service, from offering long-distance services until they prove there is competition for local phone service on their home turf. Anger over the refusal of the FCC to permit them to enter the long-distance business has prompted some Baby Bells to seek help from Congress.

In a Feb. 3 speech at a Washington conference, Solomon D. Trujillo, president of US West, sharply criticized the 1996 law and the FCC for creating a "regulatory and legal morass."

Trujillo laid out the company's legislative agenda: It wants open access to cable networks and competition in long-distance data transmission to businesses, and if lawmakers agree, a deadline to allow the Baby Bells to compete for long-distance residential customers.

US West has support from GTE and from its four Baby Bell siblings, created from the breakup of AT&T in 1982, in its efforts to enter the market for long-distance data transmission. (*1982 Almanac, p. 316*)

"We don't expect Congress to legislate broadly on long-distance voice services in the very near future," said Alan Ciamporcero, vice president of regulatory affairs for GTE. "We would like to see them immediately lower the barriers to long-distance data traffic."

While US West, GTE, AOL and their allies are campaigning, AT&T has begun a powerful counter offensive.

"The act should not be reopened. It will discourage the very investment needed to bring local telephone competition," said James W. Cicconi, the senior vice president for government affairs and federal policy at AT&T's Washington office, who previously served as deputy chief of staff to President George Bush. He charged that AOL and its allies were trying to "torpedo" the deal with Tele-Communications Inc.

But one House Republican close to the issue said: "The Baby Bells and America Online are working toward the same goal. They are going against AT&T."

The battle involves lobbying armies with powerful political weapons.

AT&T has its most influential defender in House Commerce Committee Chairman Thomas J. Bliley Jr., R-Va., who echoed his longstanding support of the law and praised a planned joint venture between AT&T Corp. and Time Warner Inc. for delivering home telephone service over cable television wires.

"This important joint venture means that scores of American homes will soon realize the advantages of competition in their local telephone services, including expanded choices and lower costs," Bliley said Feb. 1.

Bliley, whose committee would handle any telecommunications legislation, staunchly opposes reopening the 1996 law, saying that it would rekindle a bitter debate and lead to more litigation. Nonetheless, US West, GTE, AOL and their allies are certain to wield powerful influence over the debate in the 106th Congress, and they are trying to reassure members that they do not want a full-blown rewrite of the law, only narrow revisions.

In addition to Bliley, other key senators include Commerce, Science and Transportation Committee Chairman John McCain, R-Ariz., a sharp critic of the 1996 law; Communications Subcommittee Chairman Conrad Burns, R-Mont., who has said he is concerned about the lack of high-speed Internet access to residents in large parts of the country, including his own state; and Ernest F. Hollings of South Carolina, ranking Democrat on the subcommittee and a staunch defender of the law.

The original seven Baby Bells — since reduced to five by mergers — provided the main impetus for the 1996 law. They sought to be freed from restrictions imposed by the 1982 consent decree that broke up AT&T and gave U.S. District Court Judge Harold H. Greene control over corporate expansion plans. The law put regulation in the hands of the FCC and spun off the seven Bell companies to provide local telephone service, but it left long-distance service in the hands of AT&T and other emerging carriers such as Sprint and MCI.

Reauthorization Battle

The opening for AOL and its allies will come when Congress begins considering the reauthorization of the FCC this year.

House Commerce Telecommunications Subcommittee Chairman W.J. "Billy" Tauzin, R-La. — a champion of the Baby Bells — is threatening to seek a major restructuring of the FCC as part of its reauthorization.

The Baby Bells hope to have another ally to push for legislation and put pressure on the FCC: House Speaker J. Dennis Hastert, R-Ill. Georgia-based BellSouth Inc. has developed close ties to Hastert. The company, which gave $10,500 to his 1998 campaign, employs Hastert's friend and 1986 campaign manager, Daniel J. Mattoon, as a lobbyist. Mattoon's wife is treasurer of Hastert's Keep Our Majority PAC, which raised $128,330 in the 1997-98 election cycle. (*1999 CQ Weekly, p. 38*)

The debate is likely to be fueled in part by sharp criticism of the 1996 law by consumer groups. The Consumers Union blasted the act in a Feb. 3 news conference in Washington.

The group released figures collected by the Bureau of Labor Statistics showing a 21 percent rise in urban cable television rates nationwide between February 1996 and December 1998. Over the same period, rates for intrastate long-distance calls rose 10.2 percent and local telephone rates rose about 3.2 percent. Only interstate long-distance telephone rates showed a slight decline: 1.6 percent.

The Supreme Court ruled Jan. 25 in a contentious case pitting the Baby Bells and state regulators against the FCC. The court ruled against the Baby Bells by reaffirming the authority of the FCC to establish rules to ensure competition in local service — instead of giving that authority to state regulators. The ruling makes it easier for long-distance companies to meet one federal standard if they want access to local telephone networks, instead of complying with rules set by 50 states. (*1999 CQ Weekly, p. 266*)

Model of Ambiguity

In the majority opinion, Justice Antonin Scalia seemed to express sympathy for the FCC, calling the law a "model of ambiguity or indeed of self-contradiction." Scalia said the confusing text is "unfortunate for a piece of

AT&T Chairman Michael C. Armstrong and TCI Chairman John C. Malone on June 24. Above, Rep. W.J. "Billy" Tauzin, R-La.

AT LEFT, AP PHOTO/BEBETO MATHEWS; ABOVE, CQ PHOTO/SCOTT J. FERRELL

legislation that profoundly affects a crucial segment of the economy worth tens of billions of dollars."

Despite the pungent criticism, key lawmakers said they have no stomach for a full-fledged rewrite and contend that the ambiguity in the law was necessary to resolve bitter disputes.

"I've said my mea culpas. We made the law as clear as we could politically," Tauzin said in an interview. "If you had a law that everybody understood completely, nobody would like it."

Nonetheless, some longtime foes of the law, echoing the criticism of Scalia and consumer groups, are calling for revisions well beyond such issues as open access to cable networks.

Two of the five senators who voted against the 1996 act — McCain and Patrick J. Leahy, D-Vt. — both are promoting major revisions.

In the wake of the Jan. 25 ruling, McCain said it is "extremely important for the Congress to re-examine" the law. He has been suggesting revising parts of the law to require reinvigorated competition.

Leahy has proposed a bill to block pending mergers of Illinois-based Ameritech and Texas-based SBC Communications, and of New York-based Bell Atlantic and Texas-based GTE Inc. His proposal would block mergers of any companies that hold more than 5 percent of the total local access telephone lines in the nation.

Leahy has said Congress should

overhaul the 1996 law "before the pieces of Ma Bell are put together like some disfigured Frankenstein."

Republican Mike DeWine of Ohio, the chairman of the Senate Judiciary Antitrust, Business Rights and Competition Subcommittee, plans to hold a hearing this month to examine the spate of recent mergers in the industry.

Though action by Congress to block mergers is not likely, criticism of giant telecommunications companies is continuing to mount.

"We were supposed to get competition, lower prices and better service. Instead, what we got was an oligopoly, and we're heading toward monopolistic practices. Our worst fears were realized faster than I expected," said consumer advocate Ralph Nader.

Meanwhile, cable television networks are quickly emerging as the key battleground in the telecommunications debate in the 106th Congress.

Unlikely Allies

The battle has begun to unify foes of AT&T in an unlikely alliance. The Baby Bells, fearful of AT&T's promise to deliver local telephone service to customers via cable television lines, are adding their lobbying clout to the effort led by AOL.

AOL has launched a new lobbying alliance, the OpenNet Coalition, with other Internet service providers and MCI WorldCom. The coalition has

hired a Democrat and a Republican to plead its case — Greg Simon, former chief domestic policy adviser to Vice President Al Gore, and Rich Bond, a former Republican National Committee chairman.

"The Internet works because it is open," Simon said. "We cannot allow cable companies to change that basic fact by giving their own Internet service providers exclusive access."

FCC Under Fire

While Congress decides whether to make changes to the 1996 law, Kennard has begun considering whether to require open access to the vast wired empire that will be created by the merger of AT&T Corp. and Tele-Communications Inc.

"I would prefer not to add conditions to the merger agreement," Kennard said in an interview Jan. 27. Instead he said he hopes the commission would write a rule dealing with how the merged company would provide access to its cable television network.

The question of access to cable television networks offers just one example of the plethora of difficult decisions pending before the FCC.

"If anybody in this business tells you what the world is going to look like in five years or even three years, they are not being very thoughtful about it," Kennard said.

"We don't know exactly where it's going. But we do know some very important trends," Kennard said.

One trend, he said, is toward a demand for greater speed in telecommunications networks. Cable television networks offer one answer to that demand because they can carry more information more quickly on their cable wires than the telephone companies can over copper wires.

Kennard knows he is under heavy pressure from Capitol Hill.

"Chairman Kennard basically gets a little overenthusiastic in some areas in promoting the policies of the administration," said Burns, whose subcommittee will consider a two-year reauthorization of the FCC.

"They tend to forget at the FCC that they are an arm of Congress, not an arm of the administration," Burns said. He called for better oversight to ensure "a better line of communication between what the intent of Congress is with the particular bureaucracies." ◆

As regulatory efforts intensify, gambling industry steps up lobbying, political donations

Casinos Look To Improve Their Odds on Capitol Hill

Quick Contents

A congressionally commissioned study of the effects of gambling, due in June, is expected to set up a showdown between the gaming industry and moral conservatives, among others. Lawmakers are expected to debate a variety of proposals to tighten regulations on gambling.

SUN HERALD (MISS.) NEWSPAPER / DAVID PURDY

An aerial view of "casino row" in Biloxi, Miss., the home state of Senate Republican Leader Lott, who has opposed legislative action that would hurt the industry.

For the second year in a row, National Republican Senatorial Committee Chairman Mitch McConnell flew to Las Vegas last fall to collect contributions from the gambling industry for GOP candidates.

The Kentucky senator was not alone. A parade of lawmakers traveled to the casino mecca in the 1997-98 election cycle to solicit donations from Stephen A. Wynn, chairman of Mirage Resorts Inc., and other industry honchos.

The other visitors included Vice President Al Gore; Senate Majority Leader Trent Lott, R-Miss.; Senate Minority Leader Tom Daschle, D-S.D.; and Charles B. Rangel of New York, the ranking Democrat on the House Ways and Means Committee. All wanted the same thing — money from the deep coffers of the casino world.

Frank J. Fahrenkopf Jr., the former Republican National Committee chairman who now heads the American Gaming Association, the trade group representing casino operators, made sure that each visitor got a full briefing from casino executives and tours

that included displays of tight security measures.

"We wanted to make absolutely sure they understood our industry and its concerns," Fahrenkopf said. "Historically, for years, members of both parties have had fundraisers, and yet we'd find that very few knew a thing about the industry."

The generous donations and methodical lobbying are part of an all-out campaign by the gambling industry to avoid expanded federal regulations. A loose coalition of anti-gambling advocates, including conservative groups such as the Christian Coalition and consumer watchdogs such as Public Citizen, are pressing for new curbs during the 106th Congress.

The $50 billion-a-year gambling industry has been on a winning streak across the country, doubling its revenues since 1990. There are now lotteries in all but 13 states, and of those 13, 10 offer some other form of gambling, such as casinos or horse or dog racing. Only three — Hawaii, Tennessee and Utah — have not been attracted to gambling by the lure of jobs and new revenues.

But now, the industry faces a daunting challenge as legislators prepare to receive a report from a national commission that is expected to show that legalized gaming carries huge societal costs, including gambling addiction, corruption, prostitution and violent crime.

Gambling: Boon or Burden?

Critics of the industry are hoping the report will provide the impetus for legislative action, such as reintroduction and passage of a proposal first made last year by former Sen. Daniel R. Coats, R-Ind. (1989-99), to eliminate a federal policy that allows gamblers to offset any winnings with losses for tax purposes. Sen. Jack Reed, D-R.I., is considering offering a similar bill in 1999.

Other proposals discussed by anti-gambling advocates include limits on advertising similar to those applying to tobacco companies and financing treatment for gambling addiction. (1998 CQ Weekly, p. 3178)

"First it was tobacco. Next it was guns. Now they are coming after us," said Wayne Edward Mehl, a veteran lobbyist for the Nevada Resort Association. He accused the industry's critics of trying to handcuff a lucrative business that is an important source of revenue for the states.

"Gambling is going to be a major issue in 1999. And frankly, we are very concerned," said Mehl.

The gambling industry has been amassing an army of lobbyists and using campaign donations to try to curry favor with lawmakers of both parties in hopes that it can shape or kill any gambling bills that surface this year.

Showdown in June

The battle over anti-gambling initiatives is expected to begin in earnest in June, when the National Gambling Impact Study Commission will send its long-awaited report to Capitol Hill. The panel was created by Congress three years ago to study the social and economic effects of the gambling industry. (1996 Almanac, p. 5-44)

"I think we're going to find there is a major problem with addiction. And second, there's a problem with corruption," said Rep. Frank R. Wolf, R-Va., a strong opponent of gambling who sponsored the law (PL 104-169) creat-

The Virtual Casino

The Internet has emerged as a key element in the congressional debate over gambling.

Sen. Jon Kyl, R-Ariz., has vowed to renew his efforts to ban Internet gambling in 1999, citing the toll that gambling can take on families and the danger of abuses by unregulated businesses that take bets over the Internet.

Last year, the Senate voted 90-10 to approve Kyl's Internet gambling ban as an amendment to the 1999 Commerce, Justice and State spending bill. But the proposal was not included in the omnibus budget law (PL 105-277), and it died. (1998 CQ Weekly, p. 2817)

Dozens of Web sites offer a chance to bet. The Justice Department estimates that they account for $600 million in illegal sports wagers and millions more in legal wagers on electronic games, which are not specifically barred by federal law.

For the most part, the Web sites are not operated by casino operators, and they often are based offshore, outside the reach of state or federal authorities. Some major casinos regard Internet gambling operators as unregulated rivals and have argued for a ban or tougher regulation, while other casinos are experimenting with the Internet for marketing or intrastate gambling that would be regulated by the states.

"We would support an interstate ban but have no position on intrastate Internet gambling," said Wayne Edward Mehl, a Nevada Resort Association lobbyist representing 100 casino operators.

Democratic Sen. Richard H. Bryan of Nevada, a defender of casinos, has argued that states may have a tough time regulating Internet gambling. He said the "only responsible choice Congress can make is to simply prohibit it."

'You Can't Hide On-Line'

The Justice Department has offered mixed reviews of proposed leg-

islation. In a crackdown last spring, the agency accused 21 operators and managers of electronic gambling services of conspiracy to violate a 1961 wire communications law (PL 87-216). The law makes it illegal for gambling businesses to take wagers on sporting events by phone. The defendants were accused of violating the law by accepting sports wagers over the Internet or from toll-free telephone calls.

"We have a simple message: You can't hide on-line, and you can't hide offshore," said Attorney General Janet Reno.

However, the department also quietly raised concerns that legislation could be difficult to enforce if it created penalties for bettors.

Kyl's proposal would set a $500 fine and three months in jail for Internet bettors and a $20,000 fine and four years in jail for Internet gambling operators.

I. Nelson Rose, a gambling law expert at the Whittier Law School in California, said legislation might clarify confusion about whether the 1961 law applies to sports betting over the Internet and other forms of gambling such as bingo or electronic card games. "It's terribly unclear whether the law bans Internet gambling," Rose said.

But Kyl's proposal is opposed by the Interactive Gaming Council, a trade group for Internet gaming operators. Instead of a ban, the group supports a global regulatory scheme to ensure that games are fair.

The council gained allies among media companies that offer "fantasy" sports leagues that allow people to win prizes based on the performance of imaginary teams — including a Web site sponsored by ESPN, the Walt Disney Co.'s sports news operation.

Kyl's proposal was revised to allow a reasonable administrative fee for such "fantasy" games. But Sue Schneider, chairman of the Interactive Gaming Council, said Kyl's bill remained far too restrictive.

Gambling State by State

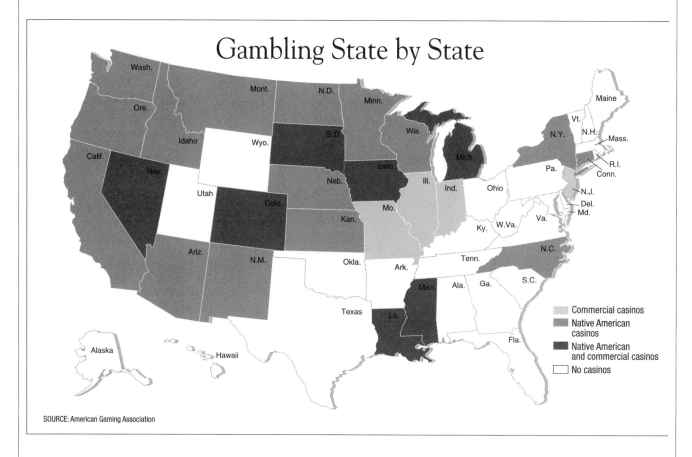

Commercial casinos

Native American casinos

Native American and commercial casinos

No casinos

SOURCE: American Gaming Association

ing the commission.

He fired the first shot in his 1999 campaign against gambling by introducing a bill (HR 316) on Jan. 6 to bar casinos on ships that "cruise to nowhere," unless on-board gambling is specifically permitted by states. These ships, operating in Florida, Georgia, New York, Massachusetts and South Carolina, make day trips outside the three-mile domestic coastal limit to skirt state bans on casino gambling.

Mehl predicted that Wolf's bill would be the first of many anti-gambling proposals in 1999.

Companies that operate or provide equipment for the three major gambling businesses — state lotteries, casinos, and horse and dog racing — are preparing to fend off or try to modify likely proposals aimed at curtailing the growth of gambling through tax code changes, new regulations and addiction treatment financed with fees.

And the industry has demonstrated its clout. Gambling interests supported campaigns that contributed to the defeats of two Republican governors last November — Alabama's Fob James Jr., who opposed a state lottery, and South Carolina's David Beasley, who opposed video poker games.

At the same time, voters in California gave overwhelming support to an initiative that expanded gambling on Indian reservations. It was strongly opposed by Nevada casinos. (*1998 CQ Weekly, p. 2999*)

On the national level, a new study by the watchdog group Common Cause found that the gambling industry gave a total of $1.2 million to federal candidates in 1997-98, with slightly more than half going to Democrats.

Another study, by the Center for Responsive Politics, found that the industry gave about $3.1 million to the two parties, nearly two-thirds of it going to Republicans. The biggest donors to parties included Mirage Resorts Inc. ($291,000), Starwood Lodging Corp. ($205,000), Circus Circus Enterprises Inc. ($205,000) and MGM Grand Inc. ($175,000).

Morality vs. Money

With gambling-related businesses based in nearly every state, members hear from local entrepreneurs who have stakes in the future of the industry. For example, a dozen casinos line the white sand beaches of the Gulf Coast of Mississippi, near where Lott makes his home, in Pascagoula. In the suburban Chicago district of House Speaker J. Dennis Hastert, R-Ill.,

there are two floating casinos, one operated by Circus Circus Enterprises and the other by Hollywood Casino Corp.

For Republicans, the gambling debate threatens to drive a wedge through the heart of the party.

Some conservatives are questioning whether the party known for opposing abortion and pushing family values can be in favor of gambling. GOP presidential and congressional candidates are being warned that accepting contributions from the gambling industry will carry a political price.

Rep. Steve Largent, R-Okla., criticized both parties for taking gambling industry donations. "I don't regard it as being clean money," he said in a Jan. 15 interview.

The Republican National Committee considered but rejected a proposal to shun gambling-related campaign contributions on Jan. 21. Buddy Witherspoon, a committee member from South Carolina who proposed the ban, said the party needs to take a strong moral stand that would be backed by its core constituents.

"This is a pro-family issue. I don't think we should rely on money from gambling," he said.

Mehl, the lobbyist for Nevada's re-

Indian Gambling Operations Find 'Devoted' Advocate in Rep. Kennedy

Rep. Patrick J. Kennedy, D-R.I., represents an urban district far from the native lands of the Agua Caliente Band of Cahuilla Indians and the Viejas Indians of California.

But geography aside, he has become their champion in promoting and defending Indian gambling operations against attacks by anti-gambling advocates and rival casino owners.

The 31-year-old son of Sen. Edward M. Kennedy, D-Mass., is a rising star in the Democratic Party, recently named chairman of the Democratic Congressional Campaign Committee, the candidate recruitment and fundraising apparatus for House Democrats. And he has used his seat on the House Resources Committee to champion Indian gambling.

He plans to offer a bill in 1999 similar to one he pushed unsuccessfully last year that would have permitted the Narragansett Indians to operate a gambling business on their reservation in southern Rhode Island.

The bill has become a focal point in the battle between Indian tribes and Wall Street companies that back casinos in America's biggest gambling meccas — Las Vegas and Atlantic City.

The American Gaming Association, one of the gambling industry's primary trade groups, has not taken a stand on Indian gambling, because some of its members have contracts to manage Indian casinos. But some members of the group argue that Indi-

Kennedy announces his bid for a third term at the Rhode Island statehouse on June 22, 1998.

an casinos are poorly regulated and have an unfair advantage because they pay no state or federal taxes.

About 150 Indian tribes operate casinos across the country. They include the opulent 23-story Foxwoods Resort Casino in Connecticut, which has $1 billion in annual revenues and is operated by one of the nation's smallest tribes, the

Mashantucket Pequots.

A study by the Center for Responsive Politics found that a dozen tribes with casinos donated more than $830,000 to political parties in the 1997-98 election cycle, including $350,000 from the Connecticut tribe.

Increased Oversight

Senate Indian Affairs Committee Chairman Ben Nighthorse Campbell, R-Colo., and Senate Minority Whip Harry Reid, D-Nev., are considering changes in the regulation of Indian casinos, including increased funding for federal oversight.

Kennedy's proposal would reverse an exemption that prevented the Narragansetts from operating a gambling business under the Indian Gaming Regulatory Act of 1988 (PL 100-497) unless they received approval from voters in the state for any new casino. (*1988 Almanac, p. 622*)

One foe of gambling, GOP Sen. John H. Chafee of Rhode Island, fumed that Kennedy seemed "totally devoted" to expanded gambling in Rhode Island. But Kennedy replied that it is "hypocritical" to prohibit an Indian casino in a state that operates a lottery.

While Kennedy refused to take political donations from the Narragansetts for his own re-election campaign, his leadership political action committee got $21,000 from seven Indian casino operators in the final weeks of the 1997-98 election cycle.

sort industry, said his members were concerned about efforts by Witherspoon and other anti-gambling advocates to attack the industry's political donations and lobbying.

"Frankly, it's possible that some candidates won't accept contributions, particularly in the presidential campaign," he said.

He noted that former Senate Majority Leader Bob Dole, R-Kan. (1969-96), was criticized for accepting money from the industry for his 1996 presidential campaign.

But in the 1998 congressional elections, candidates of both parties flocked to Las Vegas. And in Nevada, the industry has already prepared for a

long battle over restricting gambling.

Rep. Shelley Berkley, D-Nev., elected to her first term in November to represent the Las Vegas area, said casino executives and state officials are worried that the gambling issue could become a one-sided battle, with Nevada and other states with private casinos pitted against lawmakers from states without. "I'm prepared to lay down on the tracks right next to our senators," she said, pledging to defend her state's gambling industry.

Berkley knows the gambling industry firsthand. She worked as a waitress at the Sands Hotel and later as the hotel's vice president of government affairs.

Like most casino executives, she said she did not worry much about Washington, but the industry had a rude awakening in 1995 when President Clinton proposed a 4 percent tax on gambling receipts to help finance the welfare overhaul.

The proposal was short-lived, but Mehl said the industry — which had long focused its attention on winning support for casinos, video poker and other businesses in state capitals — began to keep a closer watch on Washington.

After throwing its support behind Dole in the 1996 presidential election in response to the Clinton tax proposal, the industry became more balanced in giving to candidates of both parties, according to Mehl and other lobbyists.

"The industry has gotten a lot more sophisticated in dealing with politics," Mehl said.

Donations have helped to win friends for the industry in Congress. And their help may be needed to try to deflect or reshape anti-gambling proposals in 1999.

A Target for Taxes

The administration's gambling tax proposal never got off the ground and is not expected to be revived, but, because of its rapid growth, the gambling industry could offer an inviting target for politicians searching for sources of revenue to pay for new programs.

The Coats amendment last year would have raised money to pay for education vouchers by preventing gamblers from subtracting losses from their winnings to reduce their income tax bill. And some anti-gambling groups are calling for new fees on the gambling industry to raise money for gambling addiction treatment.

But foes of gambling offer mixed views on proposed taxes.

"I don't want a tax, because I don't want government to depend on gambling money. It would be very hard for government to break that habit," said Tom Grey, executive director of the National Coalition Against Gambling

Expansion.

Last year, Coats' proposal sparked opposition from Mirage Resorts, which contributed $250,000 to the Senate GOP campaign committee soon after the proposal was introduced. Coats withdrew the amendment after Lott opposed it. (*1998 CQ Weekly, p. 1736*)

Both Sen. Jon Kyl, R-Ariz., and Rep. Robert W. Goodlatte, R-Va., have pledged to introduce legislation to attack a rapidly growing form of betting — Internet gambling. (*Box, p. 39*)

Other lawmakers, including Jerrold Nadler, D-N.Y., are considering proposals to enlist help from financial services companies to keep an eye out for problem gamblers. Nadler might renew his proposal from last year that would eliminate priority for creditors in bankruptcy proceedings that want to collect gambling debts charged to credit cards from automated teller machines in casinos.

Jackpot on K Street

While lawmakers consider legislation targeting gambling, the industry has stepped up an aggressive lobbying campaign to go along with its political giving.

The industry's top guns include Dole, now a lobbyist and an adviser to the California Nations Indian Gaming Association; former GOP Chairman Haley Barbour, who represents Powerhouse Technologies, which operates state lotteries; and former Rep. Dennis Eckart, D-Ohio (1981-93), who represents Circus Circus Enterprises Inc.

Gambling interests have also been building bridges to political operatives with ties to the GOP and conservative interest groups.

For example, the American Gaming Association and Mirage Resorts have tapped Republican pollster Frank Luntz to conduct surveys and political research. And the association has also hired the consulting firm headed by conservative tax activist Grover Norquist to follow issues on Capitol Hill.

Gambling critics have responded to the industry's army of lobbyists by urging lawmakers and political parties to shun contacts with gambling interests.

"Gambling is corrupting the political process," Wolf said recently. "Both sides are taking the money, Republicans and Democrats."

As an example, he pointed to the case of former Louisiana Gov. Edwin Edwards, a Democrat who has been

charged by federal prosecutors of taking a $400,000 payment from Edward DeBartolo Jr. in return for awarding the state's last riverboat casino license to his company, DeBartolo Entertainment. Edwards denies it was a bribe.

DeBartolo, who also owns the San Francisco 49ers professional football team, gave $100,000 to federal political action committees from 1988 to 1996, according to a study of federal election records by Common Cause.

Under Pressure

Hoping to short-circuit some of the debate, both sides have been putting pressure on the National Gambling Impact Study Commission in hopes of shaping its report. The panel is assembling data on the scope of gambling-related problems in the nation.

The gambling industry insists that the commission must acknowledge that the industry is an increasingly important economic force. It accounts for more than 1 million jobs in gambling operations and businesses that build, operate or provide supplies to them. And it pays more than $2.9 billion each year in federal, state and local taxes to support public schools and other government services.

Industry leaders also contend that their operations have drawn investors and tourists to previously overlooked towns across the country.

But anti-gambling advocates are pushing the commission to recommend tough new measures to restrict gambling. The critics argue that gambling's success has come at high cost to individual bettors and society.

Studies estimate that there are more than 4 million gambling addicts in the nation, and perhaps 11 million more who are on the verge of becoming addicts.

Earl Grinols, an economics professor at the University of Illinois, said gambling's social costs include lost time and money that could be spent on other activities, the potential for increased crime, and regulatory costs for state, federal and local government.

Bernie Horn, spokesman for the National Coalition Against Legalized Gambling, predicted that the study would favor gambling opponents and harden battle lines in the debate.

"People are going to wonder how somebody can be pro-family and be taking all this money from gambling interests," he said. ◆

Government Institutions

The articles in this section provide insight into the workings of the major institutions of American government: Congress, the presidency, the judiciary and the bureaucracy.

The start of the 106th Congress in 1999 proved to be shaky for the Republican majority. The Congress came into session following the post-election resignation of Speaker Newt Gingrich, R-Ga.; the resignation of Speaker-designate Robert L. Livingston, R-La., who left Congress after admitting to sexual improprieties; and the passage by the lame-duck session of the 105th Congress of two articles of impeachment of President Bill Clinton, passed largely along partisan lines. The first article of this section is in-depth look at House Majority Whip Tom DeLay, R-Texas, who helped spearhead the impeachment effort and currently drives the House GOP. Other articles cover Congress's ability in moving forward following the impeachment and Senate trial, a vote study that reveals partisan voting in Congress is at its highest levels, and Congress's ability to shape policy on key issues such as Kosovo and the China spying allegations.

The section on the presidency examines the relationship between President Clinton and Congress. The first article delves into the impeachment and its effect on the presidency as an institution. Critics of the impeachment declared that it was an attempted political coup d'etat by overzealous House Republicans, who were willing to take losses at the polls and watch their leadership fall, even though the likelihood of a conviction by the Senate was remote. The difficulties between the administration and Congress were further illustrated by the fact that the president's successes were measured not by his own legislative victories but in terms of the Republicans' failures: the loss of Republican House seats during the 1998 election, the resignation of Newt Gingrich following those losses and Republican concessions on the rushed omnibus appropriations bill. The section concludes with an outline of Clinton's agenda for the rest of his presidency.

The sole piece on the judiciary examines a high-profile case: the reauthorization of the independent counsel statute. Critics claim that the statute allows for an unconstitutional fourth branch of government that is not subject to fiscal restraint or oversight. Speaking out in opposition to the law was none other than Independent Counsel Ken Starr, who was appointed to investigate President Clinton and is easily the most controversial person to hold the office of independent counsel. Starr claimed that independent counsels are subject to partisan attack, particularly without institutional support form the Justice Department.

The federal bureaucracy is the part of government that citizens deal with in their daily lives. Currently, a battle is being waged over the method to be used for the 2000 census. Democrats want to use statistical sampling; Republicans want to use the status quo method of actual head counts. For politicians in Congress, the prize is congressional seats. But for the mayors of large metropolitan areas, the stakes are also high: millions of dollars in federal funds. Mayors support sampling, saying that the previous census count was inaccurate, resulting in lost state and federal dollars for municipal projects and programs. Most block grants from the federal government are awarded based on census population counts. Another federal bureaucracy that truly affects every home is the Internal Revenue Service. CQ editors examine the progress made since the IRS overhaul bill was passed in 1998. The law sought to emphasize customer service at the IRS and to give taxpayers more rights during audits.

With Speaker's blessing, the whip is expanding his reach to keep tabs on lobbyists

Tom DeLay: 'The Hammer' That Drives the House GOP

Regarded by both parties as the most effective majority whip in recent memory, the tobacco-chewing Texan has recently expanded his already considerable power base. With the permission of Hastert, his former protégé, DeLay is now the main conduit between House Republicans and K Street. The lobbyists, like many lawmakers, are both impressed and occasionally offended by DeLay's methodical carrot-and-stick approach to building legislative victories. Come-from-behind wins, he says, are an especially "huge rush."

Every good politician knows that power abhors a vacuum. No one in the House has a sharper sense of that axiom than Majority Whip Tom DeLay.

Consider the way he worked the House floor on April 28, when the new Speaker, J. Dennis Hastert of Illinois, signaled to his troops that they could "vote their consciences" on a resolution supporting the U.S. airstrikes in Yugoslavia. While Hastert waited until the last moment to cast his own "yea" vote, DeLay saw the opportunity to strike another blow against President Clinton and bent just enough Republican arms to defeat the measure.

Or look what happened last fall when John A. Boehner of Ohio lost his bid for reelection as chairman of the House Republican Conference. DeLay immediately persuaded the new leadership team to allow him — the third-ranking man in the leadership, behind Hastert and Majority Leader Dick Armey of Texas — to become the new liaison to business and trade groups. J.C. Watts Jr. of Oklahoma, Boehner's replacement as conference chairman, simply did not move quickly enough to thwart DeLay.

It was the same with impeachment. When no other top Republican wanted to trumpet the president's sexual indiscretions and alleged deceptions, DeLay made it his cause to insist that ouster from office, not congressional censure, was the only just punishment.

"If you give Tom the opportunity to assert himself, he will," said Rep. Peter T. King, R-N.Y. "If there's a power vacuum, he fills it."

Authoritatively grabbing the reins like some mythical cowboy, and letting people know it, is part of how the native Texan De-Lay works. He cultivates a tough-guy mystique as someone to be feared, and not to be trifled with. He perceives himself as quite able to deflect the arrows of critics. He always expects to win. He will cut the deals and raise the money he needs for victory. He takes matters into his own hands if he thinks he can do the job better. He relishes his nickname — "The Hammer" — and keeps a long leather

bullwhip in his Capitol office.

To all this, he brings potent mixtures of anger and persuasiveness, partisan fervor and political practicality. Sometimes combative while rounding up votes, he wants it known that he will do most anything to keep fellow Republicans happy, from plying them with Texas barbecue during late votes to ensuring they are not cheated out of their share of pet projects in appropriations bills. Despite his conservative zeal, which has prompted him to push the GOP against the popular tide on an array of issues, one of DeLay's new campaign 2000 projects is designed to help reelect GOP moderates in order to hold or expand the party's narrow House majority.

Now, with Hastert's blessing, the whip is aggressively expanding his reach outside Congress. Already known for his open eagerness to leverage K Street money and influence to achieve party goals — most recently the midyear boost in defense spending — he has broadened his boiler-room vote-counting operation by taking responsibility for keeping tabs on the influential business and ideological groups that are Republicans' natural allies.

DeLay's grasp on so much authority has led many to suggest he is the House's most powerful man. That may be too simplistic.

The Speaker has a comparable base of support, with his own network of lobbyists, fealty from a GOP rank and file eager for him to succeed, and stature as the highest legislative official under the Constitution. In addition, DeLay is showing respect for his former protégé by following Hastert's lead on two issues — gun control and campaign finance — that DeLay would rather throw in the trash.

Rather, DeLay seems clearly to be the second-most powerful lawmaker in the House, a reputation he does little to discourage while Armey struggles to rebuild from a slide in GOP confidence that spawned a bid to oust him from the leadership last year. *(Armey, p. 48)*

Asked recently how he managed to become what Republicans and Democrats alike consider to be the most effective whip in recent

memory, DeLay, who began his career as an exterminator, flashed an "aw shucks" grin and confidently replied: "That would be like braggin' on myself. Let other people evaluate me on how I do it."

Deploying the Lobbyists

One way he has done it is by capitalizing on just about every advantage inherent in the job or given him by Hastert. And under the guidance of his chief deputy whip, Roy Blunt of Missouri, business lobbyists this year have become a de facto extension of DeLay's 67-member whip operation.

Brought together in clusters based on common interests, the lobbyists are deployed from the very beginning of a legislative push, and they are used both to identify members' positions and to pressure them to vote the leadership's way. At most strategy sessions, DeLay steps into the meetings just long enough to deliver a rallying pitch, then leaves while subordinates hone in on the details.

"He's efficient. He knows his stuff. He doesn't like to fool around," said Lonnie Taylor, senior vice president for congressional affairs at the U.S. Chamber of Commerce. "We take on assignments and provide updates or feedback on an as-needed basis."

The marching orders given defense contractors during the drive to enact the $14.5 billion fiscal 1999 supplemental spending measure (HR 1141 — PL 106-31) were typical of DeLay's methods. *(1999 CQ Weekly, p. 1071)*

While others regularly present themselves as the public face of the House Republican leadership — Watts, Hastert and Armey are shown above at a March 25 news conference on the Capitol steps — DeLay often works the legislative levers from behind the closed doors of his whip's suite in the Capitol. He sat for an interview there on May 27, the Ten Commandments and a bust of George Washington behind him.

Several weeks before the initial May 6 House vote, lobbyists from such major defense contractors as the Boeing Co., Lockheed Martin Corp. and Northrop Grumman Corp. were called to meeting with Susan Hirschmann, DeLay's chief of staff, and top aides from the Appropriations Committee.

The message, according to participants, was that the defense industry must actively push the bill, designed principally to finance U.S. participation in the NATO mission in Kosovo, or risk losing coveted payouts in the fiscal 2000 defense spending bill, which had not yet begun to move.

The lobbyists were each given a form and told to return it to the whip's office indicating what efforts they had made to identify wavering members and to obtain their votes. Headed "Progress Report," the document asked for such details as whether the lobbyists had used letters, telephone calls or personal contacts.

Highly motivated to help out, the defense contractors targeted House groups seen to be wavering on the bill, including GOP fiscal conservatives and members of the Democratic "Blue Dog" group. In the end, the House passed the bill by 206 votes.

"It was very smart tactically and also from a policy standpoint," said defense consultant Pete Rose. "It absolutely was effective and contributed to the success of the bill."

Democrats briefly tried to ignite public sentiment against DeLay's tactics. Once again, they lamented, the Hammer was pounding heads, and they implied that such conduct was unbecoming of a leader of the House.

But longtime observers of Congress recognized not a new approach to vote getting, but a road-tested strategy borrowed from the Democrats in their majority days. One of DeLay's role models, in fact, is former Rep. Tony Coelho, D-Calif. (1979-89), now the new chairman of Vice President Al Gore's presidential campaign but in the 1980s a House majority whip known for hardball tactics — and a sometimes questionable merging of public policy with private enterprise and political consideration.

The Democrats' continuing success at getting unions, women's groups and other interests to mobilize for one another's issues has prompted DeLay to take the opposite tack: He organizes business groups around shared concerns.

Under Boehner, a compact group of lobbyists from an array of businesses generally met once a week. A drawback of that system, GOP aides say, was that executives at telecommunications companies, for example, would resist lobbying for the Republican health care plan out of concern that they would lose support for their own special interests if they started meddling in other controversies.

The Price of Doing Business

The strategy used for the defense supplemental bill was copied to win initial passage in March of the budget resolution (H Con Res 68) for fiscal 2000. (*1999 CQ Weekly, p. 749*)

In that case, DeLay deployed representatives from two GOP-leaning powerhouses, the Chamber of Commerce and National Federation of Independent Business (NFIB), as well as from such smaller groups as the Food Marketing Institute, which represents supermarkets.

Again, the whip's orders were designed to appeal to the lobbyists' self-interest: Participants got the message that anyone interested in a tax cut down the road was expected to help out with the budget resolution.

John Motley, senior vice president of the Food Marketing Institute, said it made good political sense for his group to support a budget that could pave the way for tax legislation later in the year. A reduction in estate taxes is especially important to the association's many family-owned grocery chains.

Mark Isakowitz, a Republican lobbyist formerly with the NFIB, said DeLay's practice of checking on the commitments made by the groups keeps them on their toes.

"There is always a sense of accountability with Tom," he said. "But that's the way it ought to be. The truth of the matter is people respond if they are asked later, 'Did you do what I asked you to do?' He is very serious and task-oriented."

Not all move along so cheerfully, however. One May meeting of business lobbyists was marked by Republicans' frustration with polls showing gun control to be more important to voters than tax relief, the GOP's strong suit.

The DeLay operation told the business representatives that it was time to repay past favors by helping Republicans raise the public profile of their push for tax cuts. They were to report back on activities undertaken to meet

this goal, said two lobbyists.

"If that was not an intimidation, then it's a failure of the English language to cover that," said one, who spoke on condition of anonymity. What was more galling, he added, is that his clients have little interest in helping on tax cuts, "because every time there's a targeted tax cut vote for some, it's the business community that has to pay."

That some lobbyists prefer to keep their complaints to themselves speaks volumes about the respect and occasional fear that DeLay engenders.

Under Hastert, power is much more decentralized than it was under the previous Speaker, Newt Gingrich, R-Ga. (1979-99), who seemed to have a finger in every legislative pie. When the party's business allies wanted to appeal a decision by a committee chairman during the 104th or 105th Congresses, they turned to Gingrich as a court of last resort. Hastert has signaled that he will not routinely open his Speaker's office doors to such entreaties, so lobbyists now are taking their appeals to those in the leadership with whom they have pre-existing relationships — or to Tom DeLay. (*1999 CQ Weekly, p. 458*)

This is all part of doing business with DeLay, said former Rep. Steve Gunderson, R-Wis. (1981-97), a moderate who was once DeLay's chief deputy whip and lavishes praise on him as the "ultimate political and power broker."

"If you approach Tom DeLay, you have to be willing to play his game of politics in Washington, and that's everything from networking to fundraising," Gunderson said in an interview. "I don't know that Tom DeLay gives anyone . . . a free ride."

Clinton's Nemesis

The person in Washington least likely to get easy treatment from DeLay is the president.

Almost from the start of the Clinton scandal early in 1998, the whip positioned himself on the House floor and in network television talk shows as the conscience of conservatives angered by what they saw as moral decay in the White House. By year's end, DeLay was the only Republican leader willing to lead the congressional excoriation of Clinton. The election had cost the GOP five House seats and driven Gingrich to announce his resignation. Before quitting in the face of disclosures about his own sexual affairs, Robert L. Livingston, R-La. (1977-99), had been reluctant to make impeachment the hallmark of his tenure as Speaker-designate. And Armey was still recovering from a narrow escape from losing his post as majority leader. (*1998 CQ Almanac, p. 7-4*)

DeLay led the Republicans to spurn a congressional censure as an alternative to impeachment, a move that catapulted him to national prominence and gave him folk hero status among social conservatives. Soon, his "in" box was stuffed with invitations to address local and state GOP groups. (*Impeachment, 1998 Almanac, p. 12-44*)

"Tom DeLay walks into rural America and people come up to him and call him their hero," said Ed Buckham, DeLay's former chief of staff.

This year, the fight against Clinton has played itself out in the ongoing debate over U.S. involvement in Kosovo.

DeLay's first visit to the White House after Clinton's acquittal occurred in early spring, when Clinton and his top advisors briefed congressional leaders on the Balkans. The GOP leader said he listened quietly for a couple of hours, then gave the president a piece of his mind.

"I told him that my daddy taught me how to use a gun when I was . . . 8 years old, and he told me that if I ever pointed that gun at anybody I better be ready to kill him," DeLay recalled in an interview May 27. "Then I told the president, 'You're about to go bomb Kosovo, but you're not committed to go all the way. It may get so bad that you have to go all the way, and it scares me because you don't know what you are doing.'"

Nothing personal against the president, DeLay said; they even politely shook hands. It is just that, in his view, the president "doesn't have the moral authority to lead" on either Kosovo or any other issue.

DeLay reinforced his point a few weeks after that White House briefing, when he sensed imminent defeat for a resolution supporting the military operation and talked to just enough members to ensure its defeat on a tie vote. (*1999 CQ Weekly, p. 1038*)

Raising Money and Controversy

DeLay earned the sobriquet "The Hammer" soon after Republicans won control in 1994. Having won a three-way election for whip, he worked quickly to acquire more contributors from K Street and to press trade associations to hire only Republicans for top positions. (*Box, this page*)

The DeLay File

Rise in Texas

Born in Laredo on April 8, 1947 . . . Spent much of his childhood in Venezuela with his father, an oil drilling contractor . . . Married Christine Ann Furrh in 1967; they have one child and two foster children . . . B.S., University of Houston, 1970 . . . Opened his own exterminating business, Albo Pest Control Co., in 1973 . . . Served in Texas House from 1979 to 1984 . . . Elected to the U.S. House to represent Texas' 22nd District (southwest Houston and suburbs; Fort Bend and Brazoria counties) in 1984 . . . Re-elected to eighth term with 65 percent in 1998 . . . George Bush carried the 22nd by 18 percentage points over Bill Clinton in both 1992 and 1996.

Up Leadership's Ladder

Won appointment to the House Republican Committee on Committees, which makes panel assignments, as a freshman in the 99th Congress . . . Named assistant regional whip and appointed to Appropriations Committee in 1987 . . . Elevated to deputy whip in 1989 . . . Managed unsuccessful campaign of Edward Madigan of Illinois for GOP whip in 1989 . . . Lost deputy whip's job when Newt Gingrich of Georgia was elected whip instead . . . Elected chairman of Republican Study Committee, a conservative policy group, in 1990 . . . Elected Republican Conference secretary, fifth-ranking position in House GOP hierarchy, in 1992 . . . Elected majority whip after Republicans won control of the House in 1994, defeating Robert S. Walker of Pennsylvania (1977-97) and Bill McCollum of Florida.

Conservative Voting Record

Voted to authorize the Persian Gulf War . . . Voted for balanced-budget constitutional amendment . . . Voted against Family and Medical Leave Act . . . Voted against banning some assault weapons . . . Voted to ban almost all federal abortion funding . . . Voted against lifting ban on gays in the military . . . Voted to approve GATT and NAFTA trade accords and to revive presidential fast-track trade negotiating power . . . Voted to relax clean water act standards and to impose limits on federal environmental regulatory powers . . . Voted against campaign finance overhaul . . . Voted for all four articles of impeachment against President Clinton . . . Average annual support scores of 97 percent from the American Conservative Union, 92 percent from the U.S. Chamber of Commerce, 2 percent from the AFL-CIO and 2 percent from Americans for Democratic Action.

Life in Power

In January 1996, when the GOP abandoned its government shutdown strategy, he said: "This president has jerked us around for 46 days; we'd better accept the reality that there's not going to be an agreement." . . . In May 1997, he advocated impeaching federal judges "who stray beyond the Constitution." . . . In April 1997, when Democrats alleged that business lobbyists helped write a deregulation bill in his office, he shoved Rep. David R. Obey, D-Wis., on the House floor . . . In July 1997, he participated in the coup attempt against Speaker Gingrich, but he later earned respect for publicly admitting his complicity and apologizing to fellow Republicans . . . In November 1997, the ethics committee dismissed complaints alleging he improperly helped clients of his lobbyist brother, Randy, and had linked legislative favors to lobbyists' campaign contributions . . . In July 1998, his Capitol Police bodyguard, Detective John Gibson, was slain in the whip's Capitol office suite by a man with a record of mental illness . . . In May 1999, the ethics committee admonished him for threatening a trade group for hiring a Democrat as its president.

Armey Finds Rehabilitation On the House Floor

Now in the second tier of House GOP leaders, Armey looks on at a Capitol lunch May 19, as Jordan's King Abdullah chats with Hastert and Minority Whip David E. Bonior, D-Mich.

It was a little odd that the second-ranking House Republican would have to pound the podium and demand the attention of his party caucus.

"I will be heard!" Majority Leader Dick Armey of Texas commanded after a fellow Republican tried to interrupt his speech at the May 26 meeting of the GOP Conference.

Armey was angry and frustrated. His fellow conservatives, led by Tom Coburn of Oklahoma, were messing up the floor schedule — the principal purview of majority leaders — insisting on debating more than 100 amendments to an agriculture spend-

ing bill. At that moment, Armey was less concerned with Coburn's complaint — that the GOP is disastrously close to busting statutory budget caps — than he was about keeping the legislative trains on schedule. Passing the fiscal 2000 appropriations bills quickly is essential to preserving GOP negotiating room in the fall, Armey told the rank and file.

They did not heed Armey's advice. Unable to instill discipline in the ranks, later that night the GOP leadership pulled the agriculture bill (HR 1906) off the floor. *(1999 CQ Weekly, p. 1271)*

While that failure was not solely Armey's responsibility, it underscored what many members say is his diminished standing. "I think people have had the sense to work with him, but realistically, there's not much substance there," said one colleague who — like other Armey critics — declined to be quoted by name.

But Armey and his allies said that under Speaker J. Dennis Hastert, R-Ill., Armey has welcomed the chance to focus on managing the floor — not an easy task with what effectively is a six-vote majority — and leaving the political machinations and message delivery to others. "I don't think he's really got the time to be the spokesman" for the party, said John T. Doolittle, R-Calif.

Still, Armey's move to the second tier of GOP leaders is a big change from five years ago, when he co-wrote the winning "Contract With America" campaign manifesto and then was unopposed for election to the No. 2 job in the new majority. *(1994 Almanac, p. 570)*

Since then, however, rhetorical gaffes, policy misstatements and a falling-out with some fellow conservatives have come to the brink of forcing him from the leadership. In the 106th Congress, he sounds far less confrontational and has even sound-

His tactics have gotten him into trouble on occasion. In May, he was criticized by the House Committee on Standards of Official Conduct for attempting last year to pressure an electronics trade association to hire a Republican as its president. *(1999 CQ Weekly, p. 1141)*

In the past six years, DeLay's re-election effort and Americans for a Republican Majority (ARMPAC), his leadership political action committee (PAC), have raised a combined $5.5 million — the vast majority to help elect House GOP candidates. DeLay was the first member of the current majority hierarchy to begin raising money for a leadership PAC. While the com-

bined fundraising total of his leadership and personal political groups through the end of last year is less than either Gingrich's or Armey's, it dwarfs that of the Speaker. And DeLay's totals do not include the unregulated "soft money" that ARMPAC is raising for activities not explicitly linked to a candidacy. *(Chart, p. 50)*

A new fundraising group DeLay is backing has stirred more controversy. Called the Republican Majority Issues Committee, it has a goal of raising $25 million to help elect House Republicans in two dozen competitive races in 2000. It is run by a former top aide to DeLay, Karl Gallant, who ran ARMPAC for

three years. And it is using the party's top draws at fundraising events. Organizers say Hastert, Armey, DeLay and Watts all boarded the yacht of the DeVos family, the founders of Amway and longtime GOP contributors, for a fundraiser last month.

But even though the new group will act much like a campaign committee, it will neither register with the Federal Election Commission (FEC) nor disclose the names of its contributors.

Gallant said in an interview May 21 that the group need not register because it does not plan to expressly endorse candidates, give them money or coordinate with their campaigns.

ed accommodating to moderate Republicans on issues such as raising the minimum wage and overhauling campaign finance law. (*1999 CQ Weekly, pp. 1073,1265*)

"It's a different Dick Armey," said Paul M. Weyrich, president of the conservative Free Congress Research and Education Foundation. At an April meeting of conservative activists, he said, Armey "did not jump over the bridge on issues, but he was very soft and non-confrontational. . . . This is a guy who used to get into fights with some people. . . . He was not as feisty as he had been in the past."

Armey's less ostentatious political life even extends to his wardrobe: He recently retired his crusty armadillo cowboy boots in favor of a pair fashioned of common calf leather.

More Mechanics

Unlike the days when Speaker Newt Gingrich, R-Ga. (1979-99), would prod him and other leaders to show what they were doing to advance the "revolution," Armey said in a brief interview May 18, Hastert has let the majority leader concentrate on legislative mechanics.

"Denny is a legislator; he's like me," Armey said. "He's more legislative and less political, and you don't pay as much attention to the big picture, broad vision" as under Gingrich.

Armey may relish the new role, but many GOP lawmakers say it was forced upon him as a kind of purgatory in which he might rehabilitate his standing. The trust that Armey once commanded from members was shattered in 1997, when he joined the attempted coup against Gingrich. Armey denied his involvement, in contrast to his sometime rival, Majority Whip Tom DeLay, R-Texas, whose candid admission of complicity earned colleagues' respect. (*1997 Almanac, p. 1-11*)

The lingering enmity almost boiled over in November, when Armey was not re-elected majority leader until the third ballot. (*1998 Almanac, p. 7-7*)

After the voting, a red-faced Armey emerged from the Cannon Caucus Room and offered a humble message with which to begin his comeback: "I was fortunate enough that I have been provided an even more keenly honed opportunity to learn and understand the needs and interests of this majority."

His fortunes improved a few weeks later, when Robert L. Livingston, R-La. (1977-99), spurned the speakership. So bitter had their relationship become that Livingston's staff briefly considered doing away with Armey's post and managing House floor action themselves, GOP aides said.

Less Tension

Republicans say the anger against Armey has subsided. "There's less hard feelings; there's less tension. And he looks happy," said W. J. "Billy" Tauzin, R-La.

Some conservatives who opposed Armey's re-election say he is not always a factor in their legislative strategy. Moderates, meanwhile, appear to have become the main beneficiaries of Armey's promise to listen to all sides. One of them, Rick A. Lazio of New York, is one of Armey's two deputies.

Until this year, "I never felt that my point of view was given an open airing" by the leadership, said Sherwood Boehlert, R-N.Y. "Some of his statements this year have been very gratifying."

In one such pronouncement, Armey declared May 11 that campaign finance legislation (HR 417) supported by some moderates should be debated on the floor in July. That conflicted with a less specific commitment that had been made at the time by Hastert, who the next day let it be known that Armey was not speaking for the leadership. Still, Armey is said to have a good working relationship with Hastert.

He rarely speaks at leadership meetings, and when he does he often cites a Texas-style aphorism, a tale of bass fishing or a country-Western lyric. Instead, he is noticed more than ever before conversing with members on the House floor and inviting them to strategize with him over a meal. Last month, he broke his own ban on overseas travel and led a congressional delegation to Yugoslavia.

Armey also is trying to improve his performance on news talk shows by asking more telegenic members to critique his television appearances.

"I would pick up a newspaper and read a story and often times wince at a statement," Boehlert said. "I have more confidence now."

Rather, he said, it plans to copy the on-the-ground techniques that the AFL-CIO used to spur Democratic turnout last year, including sophisticated voter identification and get-out-the-vote efforts.

But on May 26, the Democratic Congressional Campaign Committee (DCCC) called on Attorney General Janet Reno to have the Justice Department's Campaign Finance Task Force investigate. The new GOP effort, said DCCC spokesman Erik Smith, "is pushing beyond all known legal boundaries."

A DeLay spokesman said that while the congressman is helping the organization by appearing at its fundraising events, he is not otherwise involved.

DeLay also has asked each of his whips to contribute $3,000 to an effort called Retain Our Majority Program, organized in late March, to help re-elect 10 House Republicans targeted by the Democrats. Lobbyists and business PACs also have been tapped for gifts.

DeLay bristles at any suggestion that money corrupts the political process. "People [call] us prostitutes and the mud splashes right back on them. I don't know of a dishonest member of Democrats or Republicans that allows money to affect their ultimate decision-making," he said.

Fighting Campaign Finance Bills

Efforts to overhaul the campaign finance law — to tighten reporting requirements and curb soft money — are adamantly opposed by DeLay, who calls the proposals a threat to free speech.

Last year, the whip was in charge of blocking such efforts from reaching the House floor. Once the debate began on the bill sponsored by Christopher Shays, R-Conn., and Martin T. Meehan, D-Mass., DeLay went to the floor day after day to push one GOP amendment after another in a bid to stop the bill. (*1998 Almanac, p. 18-3*)

This year, in deference to Hastert's decision to allow a House debate on

House GOP Leadership Fundraising — DeLay's Rise

	1993-94	1995-96	1997-98	Total receipts
NEWT GINGRICH				**$18,242,697**
Monday Morning PAC *(1)*		$1,354,897	$1,791,330	$3,146,227
House election committee	$2,012,572	$6,252,069	$6,831,829	$15,096,470
DICK ARMEY				**8,073,111**
Majority Leader's Fund		1,659,947	1,925,488	3,585,435
House election committee	1,177,630	1,248,706	2,061,340	4,487,676
TOM DeLAY				**5,529,741**
Americans for a Republican Majority *(2)*	312,178	681,895	905,434	1,899,507
House election cmmittee	669,010	1,620,227	1,340,997	3,630,234
JOHN A. BOEHNER				**4,617,052**
The Freedom Project		319,681	1,032,116	1,351,797
House election committee	709,466	1,322,349	1,233,440	3,265,255
J.C. WATTS Jr.				**3,698,909**
American Renewal PAC *(3)*	0	0	320,609	320,609
House election committee	477,582	1,374,562	1,526,156	3,378,300
J. DENNIS HASTERT				**2,888,450**
Keep Our Majority PAC	None	100,172	130,600	230,772
House election committee	689,729	948,369	1,019,580	2,657,678

NOTES: (1) GOPAC is not shown here. Although associated with Gingrich, it raised money almost exclusively for state and local Republican candidates. The leadership PACs shown here were created principally to support congressional candidates. (2) DeLay also has started the House Managers PAC, to aid the 13 GOP prosecutors in the Clinton impeachment trial, which will file its first FEC report in July. His leadership PAC also raises "soft money," which it does not report to the FEC. (3) Called the Black Congressional Fund until November 1996.

SOURCES: Public Disclosure Inc.; Federal Election Commission, CQ Research by Derek Willis

campaign finance legislation in September, DeLay said he plans to take a slightly lower profile. But only slightly. "Don't get me wrong. I will be fighting as hard as I can to kill" this year's Shays-Meehan measure (HR 417).

Not only has Shays been pressing fellow Republicans to defy the leadership and sign a discharge petition to force an earlier House debate, but he also is attacking leadership PACs such as those of DeLay for "purchasing influence over their colleagues." At a news conference May 26, Shays predicted some of that PAC money would find its way into the coffers of a GOP primary challenger in his district next year.

DeLay said in a later interview that he does not intend to work for Shays' defeat, even if his actions are "disappointing."

"I can't explain why members make such comments," said DeLay. "I try to deal with the issues. . . . We have a very different philosophy. I try my best not to make it personal."

Another GOP renegade, King of New York, took it personally when he suspected DeLay of trying to strip him of his chairmanship of the Banking Subcommittee on Oversight. King —

who with Shays and just two other House Republicans voted against every article of impeachment — had frequently criticized DeLay for his efforts to try and remove the president from office. But as the impeachment issue has faded, so has King's fear of retribution.

"Even with any trouble I have had, I walk up to him and say 'Hello,' and he says 'Hello,' " King said. "It's not that he has a mean streak. It's political. I have never heard people talk about a dark side, a nastiness. There is no dark side."

Fear or Trust?

Many members say that DeLay does not use fear tactics to instill loyalty. Rather he tries to cultivate a bond of trust with every member of the Republican Conference.

He respects a difference of opinion on issues but has little use for a member who promises to vote as the leadership wants and then switches sides without warning, current and past members said.

"Tom DeLay has a lot of personal and professional pride," Gunderson said. "He does not want to be embarrassed. He will at least respect you if you tell him where you are at. That's what makes vote counters good vote counters."

Several Republicans said the mutual trust between DeLay and his GOP colleagues was cemented in 1997, when DeLay plotted with restless conservatives in an unsuccessful attempt to remove Gingrich from the Speaker's chair. Unlike Armey, who also was involved, DeLay publicly apologized to the rank and file and subtly pointed the finger at others who also were involved but had denied complicity.

Afterward, DeLay retreated with his allies to his offices and prayed. He was interrupted by Rep. Ray LaHood, R-Ill., a Gingrich defender, who wanted to shake DeLay's hand and congratulate him for telling the truth. "He didn't try and weasel his way out of it. He really didn't," LaHood said recently.

In day-to-day matters, DeLay has made sure that his office is useful to members with problems, whether it is a pet provision in an appropriations measure or an out-of-town travel arrangement.

At the 1992 Republican Convention in Houston, just up the road from his home in Sugar Land, DeLay helped lawmakers with such seemingly trivial matters as hotel reservations, restaurant choices and arrangements for rental cars. "He was a full-blown concierge service," Robert Rusbuldt, a senior vice president of the Independent Insurance Agents of America, recalled appreciatively.

Such an accommodating style defies DeLay's reputation as a tart, tobacco-chewing conservative with no time for nonsense. But it was exactly that image that charmed Lindsey Graham, R-S.C., when he visited DeLay in 1994 to seek support for his first House campaign.

"He was talking about the 'Contract With America' and raising money," Graham recalled. "He would spin around in his chair, get all excited and spit. And I said, 'This will work. I can do this too.' "

Just how long DeLay intends to play the political game is uncertain. Those close to him say his goal is not to become Speaker, but to enjoy the legislator's luxury of being the majority whip working with a Republican in the White House.

For now, he just enjoys the victories.

"All I can remember is time and time again, getting up in the morning and being 50 to 60 votes behind, and five or six hours later having the votes to pass," he said. "It's a huge rush, a huge rush. I'm very competitive, and I love winning." ◆

Ideological battle impedes bills, but some members welcome chance to play up differences

Partisan Voting on the Rise

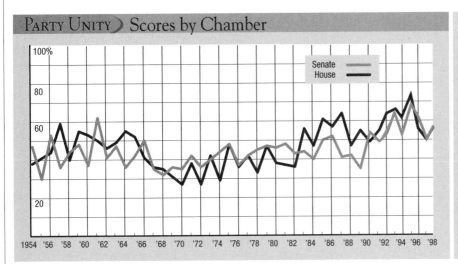

PARTY UNITY ▶ Scores by Chamber

Senate
House

Definition
The percentage of recorded floor votes in each chamber on which a majority of one party voted against a majority of the other party.

1998 Data

	Partisan Votes	Total Votes	Percent
Senate	175	314	55.7%
House	296	533	55.5%

The end-of-session decision in the House to impeach the president on a pair of party-line votes brought an emotionally draining end to a year marked throughout by a rise in partisan voting.

An analysis of 1998 roll-call votes compiled by Congressional Quarterly found that 56 percent of the votes in each chamber (55.7 percent in the Senate; 55.5 percent in the House) pitted a majority of one party against a majority of the other. That is an increase of about 5 percentage points over 1997 party-unity vote ratios, reversing a two-year decline in the proportion of such votes.

Roger Davidson, a congressional scholar at the University of Maryland, says even those figures did not fully reflect the depth of differences between the two parties, because Congress passed relatively few major bills.

"It was a low workload year. You could argue that both parties were distracted by impeachment in 1998," he said. Yet the parties continued to have passionate differences on emotional issues such as abortion, school vouchers, gay rights, affirmative action and the minimum wage.

In fact, Davidson argues, Congress is in the midst of the most partisan era

since Reconstruction at the end of the Civil War. "There is a very deep chasm between the parties," he said.

Whether the emotions unleashed in the impeachment fight will spill over into other issues in 1999 is unclear. While members of both parties decried the acrid tone of the impeachment debate, there were differing views on whether the rising tide of party-unity votes in 1998 was a troubling development or a welcome one.

For moderates such as Rep. David E. Price, D-N.C., the increase in partisanship was worrisome because it could hinder agreement in 1999 on key issues including education funding and a Social Security overhaul.

"Partisan feelings have been rubbed raw. We're just going to have to see what will happen in 1999," Price said in an interview. "Voters want issues resolved. There is not a lot of sympathy for excessive partisanship."

But for some lawmakers who had partisan political objectives, and less compromising legislative goals, 1998 was, if anything, not partisan enough.

"We failed to put bills on the floor with more of a partisan pattern to define differences," said Rep. Tom Coburn, R-Okla. Coburn said it was important for parties to stake out positions in 1999 on abortion, proposals to cut government and other issues.

Reversing a Trend

Partisan voting spiked in 1995, when more than two of every three votes were party-unity votes, but it declined over the next two years. In 1997, party-unity votes accounted for 50 percent of votes in either chamber, the lowest level since 1990 in the House and 1991 in the Senate. (1997 Almanac, p. C-7; 1995 Almanac, p. C-14)

The balanced-budget agreement of 1997, in which Democrats and Republicans agreed on a plan to eliminate the deficit in five years, was emblematic of the spirit of bipartisanship that marked the first year of the 105th Congress. But that tone changed quickly in 1998.

Joseph Cooper, a Johns Hopkins University political scientist, says Independent Counsel Kenneth W. Starr's investigation of Clinton's sexual relationship with a White House intern prodded both parties to form battle lines in 1998. "Republicans thought the Monica Lewinsky case would be a silver bullet," he said. "They became rigid in their policy goals."

In one of the first floor votes of the year, Republicans on Feb. 5 backed legislation to rename Washington National Airport after a GOP hero, former President Ronald Reagan. Democrats were strongly opposed to the measure in the House, and evenly split in the Senate. Supporters said the legislation would honor Reagan, but opponents said it was a blatant political act.

Skirmishing continued to erupt periodically through the rest of 1998.

Bitter disputes over policy "riders" contributed to long delays in the passage of major appropriations bills, culminating in the late-October rush to wrap eight unfinished spending bills into a huge omnibus measure (PL 105-277). (*1998 CQ Weekly, p. 3081*)

Battle Over Riders

Typical of the partisan trench warfare on spending bill riders was the dispute over the Census Bureau proposal, supported by Democrats, to use statistical sampling in the 2000 census in order to improve the accuracy of the count and include citizens who might otherwise be missed because of poor English, the lack of a permanent residence or other reasons. Results of the census will determine House district boundaries for the 2002 election.

In a party-line floor vote Aug. 5, Republicans defeated a Democratic amendment to permit sampling. The omnibus spending bill ultimately provided funding for the departments of Commerce, Justice and State only through June 15, 1999, in order to provide more time to work out the sampling dispute. (*1998 CQ Weekly, p. 3108*)

Social issues, such as abortion, provided fertile ground for other disputes in 1998. The House voted to override Clinton's veto of a bill (HR 1122) to ban "partial birth" abortion, but the Senate failed by three votes to follow suit.

Republicans elected to cut short some other abortion battles to clear the way for the omnibus spending bill. For example, they agreed to strip from the agricultural appropriations bill a House floor amendment approved along party lines that would have barred the Food and Drug Administration from using funds to test or approve the French abortion pill, RU-486.

Despite the increase in partisan voting in 1998, Congress reached bipartisan agreement on significant legislation, including the $217.9 billion surface transportation reauthorization law (PL 105-178), an overhaul of housing programs (PL 105-276), Internal Revenue Service reforms (PL 105-206), and reauthorization of Head Start (PL 105-285).

Some of the biggest partisan battles were fought over bills that were de-

signed to delineate clear political differences. For example, Republicans forced a showdown on education policy and won passage of a bill (HR 2646) to create tax-preferred savings accounts for elementary and secondary school expenses, including private school tuition — a bill that Clinton vetoed. (*1998 CQ Weekly, p. 3102*)

Democrats also sought confrontation. For example, Sen. Richard J. Durbin of Illinois said Democrats wanted Republicans to take a stand on managed care. While a House-passed GOP bill (HR 4250) encouraged increased patient protections, it stopped short of a Democratic proposal to allow patients to sue health plans in state courts. The House bill was tabled, or killed, in the Senate. "We wanted there to be a clear message showing what the parties were for in the election," Durbin said. (*1998 CQ Weekly, p. 3109*)

A $368.5 billion settlement reached by state attorneys general with cigarette makers to resolve tobacco-related lawsuits fell apart in the Senate, after the two parties staked out divergent positions. A number of Democrats joined John McCain, R-Ariz., to support a broad bill (S 1415) to raise the price of a pack of cigarettes by $1.10 and require "look-back" penalties if cigarette companies failed to meet youth smoking reduction targets. GOP leaders backed a narrower approach for reducing teen smoking. The Senate fell three votes short of invoking cloture on the McCain bill. (*1998 CQ Weekly, p. 3110*)

Campaign finance was another battleground. Reps. Christopher Shays, R-Conn., and Martin T. Meehan, D-Mass., overcame obstacles erected by the leadership to win House passage of legislation (an amended version of HR 2183) to ban "soft money" contributions in federal elections and expand regulation of advertising. But the drive foundered Sept. 10 when the Senate came eight votes short of ending debate on a proposal to attach a bill (S 25) sponsored by McCain and Russell D. Feingold, D-Wis., to the Interior appropriations bill (S 2237). (*1998 CQ Weekly, p. 3096*)

The lack of a broad consensus on partisan issues such as campaign finance changes gave a minority of members a powerful tool to block legislation in the Senate. Of 29 cloture motions considered — including the failed attempt to end debate on McCain's campaign finance bill — only 11 were approved.

On the 18 defeated cloture motions, Democrats cast 755 votes in line with their own caucus, and 30 votes in agreement with Republicans.

While Democrats were often a frustrated minority in Congress, they won enough Republican support to win 61 of 175 party-unity votes in the Senate, and 80 of 296 such votes in the House. Many of the votes amounted to Pyrrhic victories, however. For example, while Democrats were able to marshall enough GOP support to defeat two the four articles of impeachment against Clinton Dec. 19, they could not attract enough Republicans to defeat the other two.

In recent years, both parties have shown a high degree of loyalty on votes when the parties disagree, and that pattern continued in 1998 as Republicans succeeded in keeping an average of 86 percent of their conference in line on party-unity votes in both the House and Senate. Democrats kept an average of 87 percent of caucus members unified on these votes in the Senate, and 82 percent in the House.

Crossing Party Lines

Lawmakers who voted most often against their caucus tended to be Republican moderates, mainly from the Northeast, and conservative Democrats, typically from that party's former stronghold in the South.

In the Senate, no Republican voted with Democrats more often than any Democrat. And no Democrat voted against his party more often than any Republican did.

Republicans who voted in agreement most often with the other party were James M. Jeffords of Vermont and Arlen Specter of Pennsylvania in the Senate, and Constance A. Morella of Maryland and Christopher Shays of Connecticut in the House.

Democrats who voted most often with Republicans were Robert C. Byrd of West Virginia and John B. Breaux of Louisiana in the Senate, and Ralph M. Hall of Texas and Virgil H. Goode Jr. of Virginia in the House.

While the ongoing impeachment proceeding may spawn further division in the Senate this year, in the House, some members said emotions may cool. "We are at the point where we hit rock bottom, and I now hope we are coming back," Appropriations Committee Chairman C.W. "Bill" Young, R-Fla., said Dec. 19. ◆

As big initiatives fall by the wayside, party may settle for a record of cautious competence

GOP's Great Expectations For '99 Fade to Modest Hopes

All year, Republicans have known that they would have only a narrow window of opportunity through which to push major policy initiatives and thereby change the topic from impeachment. By the start of summer, an especially complicated season of appropriations would be in full swing; by autumn, the eyes of the public and the attention of Congress would be turning to the 2000 elections.

Now that window is beginning to close — Memorial Day is just two weeks hence — and GOP aspirations for engineering a handful of headline-grabbing legislative triumphs appear to be fading fast.Eager to erase their image as the party preoccupied with punishing President Clinton, the Republicans wanted to charge out of the blocks as soon as the impeachment trial was over in February. They hoped to enact a significant cut in taxes and work with the president on a history-making plan to save the Social Security program. But their optimistic agenda is clearly wobbling, overtaken by the war in Kosovo and shaken by the conflicting pressures inherent in the GOP promises.

Gone is the 10 percent across-the-board tax cut, the glittering star atop the GOP's legislative agenda during the winter. Gone, too, is just about any realistic hope of overhauling Social Security.

Certainly, Republicans have some legislative accomplishments. Last month, Clinton signed a modest bill that they crafted to give states more flexibility to waive federal education rules. The House and Senate have passed legislation calling on the president to deploy a national missile defense program, a GOP priority since the Reagan administration.

On time, Congress adopted the Republican budget resolution (H Con Res 68) for fiscal 2000 — a marked change from last year, when the fiscal blueprint was never finished because it triggered so much internecine warfare among Republicans.

But frequently this spring, Republicans seem to have been forced into fighting defensive battles on the Democrats' turf — over issues ranging from Social Security to education, medical insurance, the minimum wage and, most recently, gun control. Indeed, the Senate GOP suffered self-inflicted damage the week of May 10 when, in an embarrassing reversal, it tried to give ground in agreeing to new curbs on the sale of firearms at gun shows. The president, seeing Republicans in open retreat, dismissed their proposal as insufficient. (*1999 CQ Weekly, p. 1142*)

The target for adjourning the first session of the 106th Congress is at the end of October, after 18 more scheduled legislative weeks, and many Republicans believe that much of that time will be devoted to meat-and-potatoes issues, with appropriations dominating the agenda. The start of 2000 will be when the presidential campaign is at its most intense, with the nominations likely to be determined in the winter. By then, pivotal maneuvers in the House and Senate races that will determine partisan control of the 107th Congress will also be at a fever pitch. All that means that dramatic breakthroughs on Social Security and other thorny matters will more than likely have to wait until 2001 — and even then only if they are pushed in the first legislative agenda of the next president.

"We'll get done what we can get done rationally and reasonably with a narrow majority," said Rep. Robert L. Ehrlich Jr., R-Md.

Democrats are already preparing to hang the "do-nothing" label on the 106th Congress — a strategy that they see as having worked for them in last November's elections.

"This Republican Congress is about letting time pass, not about achieving an agenda," said Sen. Robert G. Torricelli of New Jersey, chairman of the Democratic Senatorial Campaign Committee.

A Low-Key Year

A low-key year of modest accomplishments may not be such a bad thing for the GOP, many Republicans say. Ever since he took over in January as the unexpected House Speaker, J. Dennis Hastert, R-Ill., has been struggling to project an image of cau-

Quick Contents

To change the subject from impeachment, Republicans wanted to jump into tax cut and Social Security bills this spring. But they have been stymied by the war in Kosovo, pressure from Democrats and the conflicts inherent in their own promises. And next comes appropriations — a consuming task that has troubled them since their takeover in 1995, and one made especially complex this year by the politics of the new budget surplus.

The gun control debate
arranged turned on the GOP

Hastert's role in the Kosovo
debate came under fire

tious competence that he hopes will represent his party's style of governing at the Capitol.

Under his leadership, House Republicans vowed, people would be able to forget the crisis-a-day style of the previous Speaker, Newt Gingrich, R-Ga. (1979-99); there would be no clever campaign slogans, and no GOP promises would go unfulfilled.

Such an approach made sense, said Thomas E. Mann, the director of governmental studies at the Brookings Institution, because Republicans "made such a hash of their party image during the last Congress" with what many people saw as their single-minded pursuit of the president.

"It is presenting the party in a way that, rather than scaring voters, they show they can be trusted," he said in an interview May 11.

As the minority party, Democrats face far less pressure to produce. For House Republicans, their very standing as the majority — secured at the moment with just four votes votes to spare — may be riding on their ability to claim credit for some legislation with appeal to middle-income voters.

In the image wars, at least, the Republicans are gaining. Since impeachment began receding from the public's consciousness in the spring, Republicans have made slow and steady gains in public opinion polling. Two polls conducted April 17-19, one for Reuters and one for NBC and The Wall Street Journal, showed the GOP ahead — albeit by a single percentage point — on the so-called generic ballot question of whether those surveyed would vote for a Republican or Democratic congressional candidate if the election were held now. Two weeks after this Congress convened, at the height of the impeachment trial, the Democrats were 7 to 10 points ahead.

Still, pursuing a scaled-back agenda — currently premised on strengthening national security and finding a way to fence off surplus Social Security revenues — carries certain risks. Some Republicans and conservative activists are already grumbling that the party is setting its sights too low. Impatient House conservatives are preparing their own agenda built around a major tax cut. "We don't see a plan to get to the end of the year," David M. McIntosh of Indiana, the chairman of the Conservative Action Team, complained May 12. "We don't see tax cuts."

A moderate House Republican, who asked not to be identified, echoed those sentiments. "I'm about ready to start speaking out that we don't have an agenda," she said.

Another potential problem exists with the three-yards-and-a-cloud-of-dust strategy: Any fumbles automatically become big news. Hastert discovered that when, as he has admitted, he mishandled his participation in the most recent debate on the mission in Kosovo. He supported, but did not promote, a resolution endorsing the ongoing air-strikes, which was defeated on a tie vote. (*1999 CQ Weekly, p. 1038*)

The next — and by far the biggest — test for the leadership will be to enact the 13 spending bills that are supposed to fund about one-third of the federal government for fiscal 2000. Facing the extraordinarily tight limits imposed by the 1997 balanced-budget law (PL 105-33), senior Republicans candidly admit that the party has yet to come up with a strategy for enacting those bills — the most mundane yet essential task Congress performs each year. (*Budget law, 1997 Almanac, p. 2-18*)

Senior Republicans argue that 1999 will be judged a successful year if they can avoid a train wreck on appropriations. Ever since Republicans took control of Congress four years ago, the spending measures have been their Achilles heel. They have either overreached in year-end negotiations with Clinton — prompting a pair of partial government shutdowns at the end of 1995 — or caved in to the administration's spending requests, undercutting their carefully cultivated image of fiscal conservatism.

"If we can complete them in a timely fashion, that's a considerable achievement," Larry E. Craig of Idaho, chairman of the Senate Republican Policy Committee, said May 4 of the appropriations bills.

That promises to be a tall order, said Rep. Sam Johnson, R-Texas. "I think we are getting behind the power curve again without any real need to," he said in an interview May 12.

The overall pressure on spending will

be eased somewhat if, as expected during the week of May 17, Congress clears and the president signs a $14.6 billion supplemental appropriations measure (HR 1141). It was assembled principally to pay for the war in Kosovo, but Republicans and Democrats alike loaded it up with billions of dollars in additional spending. (1999 CQ Weekly, p. 1135)

That pumped-up spending bill might make the task of the Appropriations committees slightly easier, but most lawmakers still expect a long, hot summer of wrangling over spending priorities for the next year. And by autumn, GOP budget hawks are dubious that the leadership will be able to live up to its pledge not to dip into the Social Security-generated budget surplus to fund regular government operations.

The process got under way the week of May 10, when three bills were marked up with minimal initial controversy by House Appropriations subcommittees. (1999 CQ Weekly, pp. 1141, 1152, 1153)

"Trouble is coming, and it's going to create a showdown over breaking the budget caps," said Rep. Mark Sanford, R-S.C. "Based on what we've seen with the supplemental, we'll smash right through them."

Crisis After Crisis

Ever since it convened, the 106th Congress has been buffeted by a series of unexpected, and in some cases historic, events. Until Feb. 12, the Senate was consumed by the first presidential impeachment trial in 131 years. The House had no role in that drama, except for the team of House members prosecuting the case against the president, but the start of the session had already been slowed by the House's leadership transition.

Just six weeks after Clinton's acquittal, NATO launched an aerial bombing campaign against Serbia to halt the Serbs' drive to "ethnically cleanse" in Kosovo. That overshadowed Washington's domestic policy debate and submerged the agendas of both parties. And the high school shootings in Littleton, Colo., shocked the nation and prompted Senate Majority Leader Trent Lott, R-Miss., to arrange the Senate debate on gun control.

That tumultuous sequence also wreaked havoc on the Democrats' legislative plans. They had hoped to trumpet issues such as new funding for school construction and restrictions on managed care health insurers, but they were hamstrung as well. Still, Democrats already appear to be on the verge of an important triumph; Hastert and other senior Republicans have signaled that a rise in the minimum wage — a cornerstone of the Democratic agenda — is all but inevitable. (1999 CQ Weekly, p. 1073)

Banking on Social Security

Still, Republicans insist they have made important strides this year, in spite of the many distractions and detours. Perhaps most important, they say, their plan to set aside Social Security revenues in a "lock box" — to be used only for retirement benefits and for paying down the $5.5 trillion national debt — will have important political implications, even though it stands virtually no chance of becoming law. (1999 CQ Weekly, p. 957)

"It takes it off the table, politically," Ehrlich said. "Bill Clinton hasn't demagogued us at all for four months on Social Security, and that's got to be some kind of record."

"Even if it doesn't happen, we can go to people and say we are trying to save the program," said Sen. Olympia J. Snowe, R-Maine, a member of the Budget Committee.

But the Balkans conflict undermined that theme, because Congress was forced to tap Social Security reserves to underwrite both the military expenses and all the other items lawmakers added to the supplemental bill.

In the long run, Republicans believe that the lock box will make it less politically risky for them to push for deep tax cuts. In the past, Clinton has scored points by accusing the GOP of being willing to erode Social Security's foundation in pressing for tax reductions.

But several barriers stand before the GOP's hopes of enacting a significant tax cut. First, because the entire near-term surplus is generated by Social Security revenues — which the Republicans have vowed not to touch — there are no resources available to underwrite a meaningful loss in tax revenue in 2000. So the most that the GOP can hope for this year is to extend a host of relatively small, business-related tax provisions, which are due to expire.

And Republicans are far from unified over which taxes should be cut. While some still trumpet the 10 percent across-the-board tax cut, others have joined with Democrats to support narrower, targeted cuts. Still other Republicans have shown interest in a proposal (S 274) by Torricelli and Sen. Paul Coverdell, R-Ga., to expand the bottom 15 percent bracket to include more taxpayers.

Those ideas, and several others, were aired at a recent Senate Republican meeting on taxes, which reached no consensus. "There was a strong sense of purpose, but no unanimity," Snowe said. "Everybody had a different idea."

Beyond the lock box proposal, the GOP is similarly divided over the Social Security system. GOP leaders have proceeded cautiously, chiding the president for failing to provide leadership on the issue while making it clear they do not want a full-scale congressional debate this year. But House Ways and Means Committee Chairman Bill Archer, R-Texas, and Social Security Subcommittee Chairman E. Clay Shaw Jr., R-Fla., have come forward with a plan to replace a portion of Social Security benefits with individual retirement accounts. (1999 CQ Weekly, p. 1023)

Though chances for a broad bipartisan deal on Social Security are just about nil — in part because liberal Democrats vehemently oppose the concept of allowing people to invest their own retirement funds — some Republicans say the party will miss a golden opportunity if it sits on the sidelines and lobs criticism at the president.

"You can't just sit here and whittle away your time, just because you're afraid the president will demagogue the issue," said Rep. Mark Foley, R-Fla.

Touting National Security

While Kosovo is being blamed by Republicans for slowing their legislative momentum, there is a sense among GOP lawmakers that it could burnish the party's credentials on national security.

The administration's handling of the war will "be one of the decision points that people are going to make when they vote for president and for the Congress" in 2000, Sen. Kay Bailey Hutchison, R-Texas, told a convention of women GOP activists May 11. "The reason it's going to be so important is because it's been botched in the last two terms."

After jousting with Democrats on issues such as education and Social Security, some Republicans seem relieved to shift the conversation to national security and foreign policy. "It's our traditional strong suit," Snowe said.

Foreign affairs have historically been more important in presidential contests than in House and Senate races. And congressional action on Kosovo to date has been marked more by confusion than coherence, which could undercut the GOP's effort to seize political advantage. That Congress is about to cut a nearly $15 billion check to pay in part for a military operation that the House declined to endorse is one element of this.

Still, Republicans are trying other ways to illustrate administration weakness on international matters, particularly relations with China. Several committees are probing reports that lax security at U.S. nuclear weapons labs led to compromises of the nation's nuclear secrets. Congressional concern over Chinese espionage will be in the spotlight with the release of a declassified House report on the issue. That long-awaited report may be released the week of May 17. (*1999 CQ Weekly, p. 1161*)

Summer of Discontent

Aside from spending, the summer will be highlighted by partisan battles over education, health care and campaign finance. For the most part, the parties are expected to use these debates to road-test political themes rather than seek common ground.

After Memorial Day, the Senate will debate proposals to regulate managed care plans. But Democrats are pressing for far more federal regulation of health insurance — backed by the threat of court action — than Republicans can accept. (*1999 CQ Weekly, p. 701*)

Campaign finance advocates are pressing for a House vote on legislation to eliminate unrestricted contributions of "soft money" to political parties. They appeared to get a boost May 11 when Majority Leader Dick Armey, R-Texas, said it would be his preference to schedule a campaign finance debate by the end of July. The Speaker later reiterated his plan for a debate in September, which may anger GOP moderates. Either way, Senate opponents of altering campaign finance law still appear to have enough votes to sustain a filibuster.

Republicans and Democrats are jockeying for tactical advantage in advance of this year's showdown over reauthorizing the law (PL 103-382) setting elementary and secondary education policy. After taking a beating at the hands of

Moving to refine their legislative agenda, Republican leaders from the House and Senate met May 12 to promise a joint effort for a bill that would create a "lock box" to shield the Social Security trust fund from other uses — and, perhaps, to shield the GOP from criticism that they are willing to cut into Social Security to pay for tax breaks. Among those attending were Lott, above, and Senate Majority Whip Don Nickles, R-Okla., left.

Democrats on education, House Republicans have decided to break the authorization bill into several smaller ones in order to create a drumbeat of floor action throughout the summer and fall. That could showcase GOP interest in an issue that is a top voter concern. But the partisan divide remains wide over administration proposals for hiring new teachers and underwriting school construction.

In the end, most analysts believe that this session of Congress might not be any more productive than the last, when lawmakers were distracted by election-year politics and the looming impeachment debate.

"It will take presidential leadership in 2001 to break the logjam," said Marshall Wittman, director of congressional

relations at the Heritage Foundation, a conservative think tank.

Wittman said the slow progress of legislation to limit lawsuits arising from the year 2000 computer glitch is instructive. The bill is generally regarded as one of the few this year that bears the "must-pass" label, because of fears of a tidal wave of post-millennium litigation. The Senate version (S 96) has bipartisan support — and the backing of the high-tech community — but it has been stalled by a filibuster. The House bill (HR 775) was approved May 12 but is facing a veto threat. (*1999 CQ Weekly, p. 1151*)

"Under any normal legislative environment, it would have been fairly easy to pass the Y2K bill," Wittman said. "But look at what's happened." ◆

GOP wants quick action to stop espionage, while Democrats warn of micromanagement

With Cox Report's Release, Struggle for Consensus Begins

A House committee report on China's theft of U.S. technology drew immediate cries for action on Capitol Hill and touched off a wave of proposed solutions. But Republicans learned that implementing the report's recommendations will be trickier than reacting to its revelations.

GOP attempts in the House and Senate to amend pending defense bills to tighten security stalled May 27 after Democrats objected.

"This does not bode well for us being able to deal with the China problem and security in a bipartisan way," said Senate Majority Leader Trent Lott, R-Miss., after withdrawing one proposal when Democrats threatened a filibuster.

The long-awaited declassified version of the House report — a 1,016-page, seven-and-a-half-pound document in three volumes, complete with color photographs — confirmed a stream of earlier newspaper revelations that China has used a network of spies, front companies and visitors to the United States to obtain nuclear secrets and other military technology over several decades. The report said the stolen secrets "give [China] design information on thermonuclear weapons on par with our own."

The thefts occurred at least as early as the late 1970s, according to the report, with significant secrets stolen in the mid-1990s and espionage "almost certainly" continuing today. It also said China "has stolen or otherwise illegally obtained" U.S. missile and space technology that has improved its military and intelligence capabilities.

The report of the bipartisan House Select Committee on U.S. National Security and Military/Commercial Concerns with the People's Republic of China contained 38 recommendations, including tightening export control laws, strengthening counterintelligence at the Department of Energy, sharpening oversight of U.S. satellite launches in China, improving the domestic U.S. space launch industry, and requiring more prompt notification of future security lapses to Congress and the executive branch. (*1999 CQ*

NEWSMAKERS PHOTO / ATOMIC ENERGY COMMISSION

Los Alamos National Laboratory in New Mexico, a center of nuclear weapons research, is the focus of congressional and administration efforts to tighten security after allegations of decades of spying by China. Here scientists prepare for nuclear testing in 1974. Some lawmakers have called for more security screening of employees; others want to halt visits by scientists from certain countries.

Weekly, p. 1252)

"What we are doing here today, I hope, will be a beginning and not an end," said Rep. Christopher Cox, R-Calif., the committee's chairman, in releasing the report May 25. "I hope that we will be able to cooperate with the administration and with the committees in the Senate as well as in the House to enact our recommendations."

President Clinton echoed earlier statements by administration officials that by and large, the recommendations were acceptable. "The overwhelming majority of those recommendations we agree with and are in the process of implementing," Clinton said May 25.

Though Congress and the administration agree that security at nuclear weapons laboratories needs to be tightened, they are at odds over whether it should be done by the administration or Congress.

In addition, the report's calls for tightening export control laws have provoked fears among high-technology companies that have been campaigning for looser controls.

"There's a collective holding of the breath," said Marc Pearl, senior vice president of government affairs and general counsel for the Information Technology Association of America, a Washington group representing 11,000 high-tech companies. "This controversy has nothing to do with anything private companies have done. It would be unfortunate if there was a crackdown on exports."

Reviewing Relations

Political rhetoric over the report stayed hot. Some Republicans called for the resignations of Attorney General Janet Reno or national security adviser Samuel R. Berger, while Democrats countered by noting that security problems dated back to the Reagan and Bush administrations. (*1999 CQ Weekly, p. 1248*)

Some lawmakers said the report was a rationale for a fundamental re-examination of relations with China. House International Relations Chairman Benjamin A. Gilman, R-N.Y., called the Clinton administration's policy of "strategic partnership" with China "naive and misguided" in the wake of the report's revelations.

But other lawmakers foresaw little dramatic change in relations between the two countries. "There's too much mutual interest, too much mutual need, too much at stake," said Joseph R. Biden Jr. of Delaware, the Senate Foreign Relations Committee's ranking Democrat. "You can't ignore a billion people, and they can't ignore us."

Chinese officials denounced the House report as an inaccurate and misguided attempt to demonize their country. Their comments came three weeks after the accidental U.S. bombing of China's embassy in Belgrade further poisoned relations between the two nations. (*1999 CQ Weekly, p. 1161*)

Some experts, however, predicted that Beijing is aware enough of the impact of the report to seek to repair ties with the United States.

"There's a floor under this relationship in that neither side wants to let this thing deteriorate," said Peter W. Rodman, director of national security programs at the Nixon Center, a Washington think tank specializing in foreign policy. "What's happening is

Inside the Espionage Report

Following are major findings of the special House committee investigating China's acquisition of U.S. technology:

● "The People's Republic of China has stolen design information on the United States' most advanced thermonuclear weapons."

● "Elements of the stolen information . . . will assist [China] in building its next generation of mobile ICBMs, which may be tested this year . . . [and] could have a significant effect on the regional balance of power."

● "Security at our national nuclear weapons laboratories does not meet even minimal standards."

Key Recommendations

● The Energy Department should implement as quickly as possible and then sustain an effective counterintelligence program.

● Key agencies should assess the national security risks of continued scientific exchange programs between the United States and China that involve the national laboratories.

● Congress should examine whether the Energy Department should remain in charge of nuclear weapons development and maintenance.

● The United States should insist that China adhere to and abide by the Missile Technology Control Regime, a multilateral pact to limit the spread of missile technology.

● The United States should work to establish new, binding international controls on technology transfers and improve the tracking of technology.

● The State Department should have the sole authority, and adequate resources, to license the export of satellites.

● Congress should give the satellite industry tax credits to cover licensing costs.

● The Defense Department should arrange for security at overseas launches of U.S. satellites.

● Export-control laws should apply to communications among satellite manufacturers, buyers and insurance companies.

● Congress should pass legislation to stimulate expansion of the U.S. space launch industry.

● The Energy and Defense departments should review the national security implications of exporting high-performance computers to China. Legislation should grant export licenses only with the condition that China disclose the end-user of each machine.

● Congress should re-enact the Export Administration Act, which expired in 1994. The most sensitive technologies should be subject to more extensive review. Licensing for others should be streamlined.

● U.S. companies with national security interests should notify the government of mergers with foreign-controlled companies.

● Congress should enact legislation requiring the Justice Department to share national security information with other, concerned federal agencies.

● U.S. agencies should conduct a broad intelligence analysis of China's aims, goals and objectives in acquiring technology.

that the tone is souring and there's no new advances being made, but there's still a basic dialogue."

Agreeing to Disagree

In Congress, initial hopes of establishing a bipartisan consensus that might mirror the spirit in which the Cox committee operated proved elusive in both chambers. (*1999 CQ Weekly, p. 1253*)

The problems were first illustrated

in the House on May 27, when Republican leaders abruptly pulled from the floor the rule governing debate on the fiscal 2000 defense authorization bill (HR 1401). (*1999 CQ Weekly, pp. 1289, 1291*)

The move came after the China committee's ranking Democrat, Norm Dicks of Washington, joined party colleagues in arguing that the rule would not allow consideration of a proposed amendment stemming from the report and intended to shore up security at nuclear weapons labs.

The rule for the legislation did contain other proposed Republican amendments offered in reaction to the Cox report. Among them was a controversial initiative by Armed Services Committee Chairman Floyd D. Spence, R-S.C., to have the Defense Department prepare a plan to assume control of Energy Department national security programs, including weapons production sites and national laboratories.

Energy Secretary Bill Richardson has strenuously objected to what he sees as congressional micromanagement of security at his agency's labs, saying that he has moved aggressively to implement a series of reforms in recent months. But some Republicans contend such measures do not go far enough.

The House Science Committee also weighed in on the Energy Department's management. It approved, by voice vote, on May 26 an amendment to a bill (HR 1656) authorizing Energy Department projects dealing with commercial applications of energy technology.

The amendment, by Jerry F. Costello, D-Ill., and George Nethercutt, R-Wash., would put a moratorium on access by citizens of certain countries to classified areas of Energy labs, but would allow case-by-case waivers.

A New Agency?

In the Senate, a more ambitious security initiative faced a difficult struggle. Jon Kyl, R-Ariz., offered an amendment to the fiscal 2000 defense authorization bill (S 1059) to reorganize the Energy Department's Office of Defense Programs and create a new agency, the Nuclear Security Administration, to oversee nuclear weapons production.

The new agency would be a separate "stovepipe" within the department, insulated from normal bureaucracy and its procedures, accountable directly to the Energy secretary to ensure more accountability of nuclear weapons activities, Kyl said.

His amendment also would write into law the department's office of counterintelligence, whose director would report any security breaches directly to the president and Congress.

But the proposal provoked a rare public dispute between two of the Senate's leading voices on nuclear matters: Pete V. Domenici, R-N.M., chairman of the Energy and Water Appropriations Subcommittee, and his home-

state colleague Jeff Bingaman, ranking Democrat on the Energy and Natural Resources Committee.

Domenici joined Kyl in supporting the amendment, saying the Energy Department suffers from a "one-size-fits-all syndrome" in which nuclear programs must work within the demands of other agency priorities. Bingaman said the amendment was being offered too hastily and would produce "substantial unintended consequences."

Richardson wrote in a letter to Bingaman that he would recommend that Clinton veto the bill if the amendment was included. "The security mission cuts across the entire department, not just defense programs facilities," Richardson wrote.

After Democrats threatened a filibuster over the amendment, Lott called a break for negotiations that stretched into several hours. Eventually, he announced that the proposal will be offered as an amendment to the fiscal 2000 intelligence authorization bill (S 1009 — S Rept 106-48), which aides said would come up in early June.

"Shame on us because our secrets were stolen, and shame on Democrats," a frustrated Domenici told reporters.

Lott did persuade senators to pass, by voice vote, a relatively modest amendment to the defense bill to strengthen U.S. export control laws, increase counterintelligence training and require greater monitoring of satellite launches and better notification to Congress of security breaches.

Apart from the intelligence bill, Lott said he still anticipates major legislation later in the year dealing with the issues raised by the report. "There's got to be some balance between commercial desire, trade and national security," he told reporters May 27.

Security Guard Lapses

Congress began investigating the administration's dealings with China after reports that two satellite companies — Loral Space & Communications Ltd. and Hughes Electronics Corp. — might have compromised national security in helping Beijing determine the causes of rocket failures in 1995 and 1996.

The report found shoddy monitoring of U.S. satellites launched in China, with private security guards sleeping on the job, reporting for work under the influence of alcohol and even consorting with prostitutes. It recommended a se-

ries of steps to improve security, including making the Defense Department responsible for hiring and screening security officers for the launches.

The report also called for giving the State Department enough workers and money to handle the processing of export licenses for companies sending satellites to China. In the fiscal 1999 defense authorization law (PL 105-261), Congress shifted oversight authority for satellites from the Commerce to the State Department last summer because of national security concerns. (*1998 Almanac, p. 8-3*)

The export control situation has led many business groups to call on Congress for action on long-stalled legislation to regulate "dual use" exports with both military and commercial value. The most recent Export Administration Act (PL 103-10) expired in 1994, and industries contend that a better legal framework is needed to reflect the end of the Cold War — a finding echoed in the Cox committee's report. (*1999 CQ Weekly, p. 268*)

Past attempts to rewrite the legislation have become bogged down in a maze of committees with jurisdiction over the issue. Businesses also have tried to ensure their interests overseas remain protected.

"It is a very, very tough issue to deal with," said Willard A. Workman, vice president of the international division at the U.S. Chamber of Commerce. "It only seems we're able to come to a conclusion when the debate is precipitated by a crisis."

Michael B. Enzi, R-Wyo., chairman of the Senate Banking, Housing and Urban Affairs Subcommittee on International Finance and Trade, has been working for months on a bipartisan reauthorization of the act. He said he hopes to introduce legislation soon that will reflect about half of the 38 findings of the Cox committee.

Enzi said the bill will reflect the committee's conclusion that there should be multilateral rather than unilateral controls over exports. Cox said reauthorizing the act in such a way is probably the most important of the committee's recommendations.

"We need to talk, one nation at a time, to each of our allies and solicit support for a multilateral regime," he told the House International Relations Asia and the Pacific Subcommittee May 26. "This requires American leadership." ◆

Congress

Members face unparalleled opportunities to engage — or alienate — the public

How Will Congress Navigate The New Media Maelstrom?

Quick Contents

The public is deluged with more information about government, from more sources, than ever before. But interest in Washington news continues to decline, a trend that the impeachment saga appears to have done nothing to reverse. Some media analysts say that the new media landscape will do little if anything to change the way lawmakers operate.

Last September, the House set a dubious standard in open government when it released Independent Counsel Kenneth W. Starr's report on President Clinton, in all its tawdry detail, directly and instantaneously to the public over the Internet. Five months later, as the impeachment drama reached its climax, the Senate moved to the other extreme. It retreated behind closed doors to debate Clinton's fate — shutting out the press and public — just as senators had in the previous presidential impeachment trial 131 years earlier, when information moved at the speed of a steam engine.

Since Clinton's acquittal on Feb. 12, Congress has turned gratefully from the Monica Lewinsky sex and cover-up scandal to much more familiar subjects, such as education policy and the budget. And what seemed like an occupying army of journalists has decamped from the Capitol, leaving its hallways passable once more.

But the exhausting, enervating saga of impeachment has raised troubling questions for both the media and Congress. And, as the seemingly schizophrenic congressional attitude toward openness demonstrates, lawmakers are struggling to come to grips with a new and dizzyingly complex media environment — and one that still appears to prefer sizzle to substance.

The 24-hour news cycle, the range of nightly political talk shows on the airwaves and, of course, the Internet, were not even known to politicians just a few years ago. Today, they are an integral part of the political and legislative process.

Lawmakers who harbor embarrassing personal secrets used to fear exposure only by their opponents, by a small cadre of muckraking journalists — and by the mainstream press when private behavior had a manifest impact on public conduct. Today, Larry Flynt's millions of dollars and Matt Drudge's Web site present new reasons to worry.

Indeed, the notion of keeping anything secret these days, aside from highly classified national security information, strikes many as ludicrous. That made the decision to debate Clinton's guilt behind locked doors, with sen-atorial expulsion the prescribed punishment, seem all the more anachronistic.

Paradoxically, Americans are deluged with more information about government, from more sources, than ever before. But it has done little to galvanize the electorate; interest in Washington news seems on a perpetually downward arc. So, in the impeachment's aftermath, politicians stand at a crossroads in their relationship with the media and the public.

Will members of Congress use their expanding opportunities to communicate with the public through the media to encourage civic involvement by focusing on issues that matter? Or will they allow the new media universe to be dominated by the governmental trivialities and scandalous tidbits that turn off voters?

Politicians universally express a desire to use their media access more constructively, but there is little optimism that the current pattern will change. Some political scientists say that most incumbent lawmakers from both parties are uncomfortable with the notion of using the media to mobilize a disinterested citizenry.

"Neither side has much need for or interest in political tactics that might, in effect, stir up trouble from below," Benjamin Ginsberg of Johns Hopkins University and Martin Shefter of Cornell University write in their newly revised book, "Politics by Other Means." "Both sides prefer to compete for power without engaging in full-scale popular mobilization."

Following are some features of the new media landscape that members of Congress are confronting:

Enduring Culture of Scandal

The Lewinsky affair has prompted intense soul-searching among print and broadcast journalists about how far to go in investigating politicians' personal lives.

The debate intensified this month when many mainstream news organizations — after considerable internal debate — reported the claim of Juanita Broaddrick, an Arkansas

Dozens of reporters filled the Senate Press Gallery each day of the Clinton impeachment trial. Above, they were briefed Jan. 25 by John Czwartacki, Lott's spokesman. But six weeks later, on March 10, the room was far less crowded for debate on a bill to give states latitude in spending federal school aid.

CQ PHOTOS / DOUGLAS GRAHAM

nursing home operator, that she was sexually assaulted by Clinton in 1978. Conservatives complained that Broaddrick's story should have been disclosed long before the end of Clinton's trial. Many media critics complained that the unproven charges should never have been aired at all.

"We are moving toward a journalism of assertion rather than a journalism of verification, and the cost for society is high," Tom Rosenstiel and Bill Kovach wrote in The Washington Post. Rosenstiel directs the Project for Excellence in Journalism, funded by the Pew Charitable Trusts; Kovach is the curator of Harvard University's Nieman Foundation for Journalism.

But despite all the reservations that many news organizations harbor about running such stories — and despite the public's growing antipathy toward the media — Washington's culture of scandal is likely to endure. (*1999 CQ Weekly, p. 680*)

"I laugh every time I hear someone say it will change," said Larry J. Sabato, a University of Virginia professor and the author of "Feeding Frenzy," a book about the way the press covers scandalous behavior by politicians. "After a few months, a decent interval, it all will happen again."

It may not take that long. Flynt, the Hustler magazine publisher, has set an April 6 publication date for his special report on the

Mr. Wexler Goes to Washington — And To Every Media Outlet

Anyone who had even a passing interest in impeachment and has even modest skill at operating a television remote control knows Rep. Robert Wexler.

Though his name might remain unfamiliar, his face is not.

Click, and he is in your face on "Rivera Live," delivering another in his series of impassioned defenses of President Clinton. Click again, and Wexler's high-decibel warning of the apocalyptic consequences of impeachment is replayed on "Upfront Tonight," another CNBC program: "So wake up, America! Our government is about to shut down."

His staff estimates that the sophomore Democrat from Florida was interviewed on television about 100 times during the six months when the impeachment wars raged in Congress. That is more TV face time than many lawmakers get in a lifetime.

"We did 'em all," Wexler recalled a bit wistfully, referring to the growing menu of cable programs that thrive on verbal combat. His personal favorite, though, remains a progenitor of the genre: CNN's "Crossfire."

But as he analyzed the recent surge in his media profile, Wexler's calm and reflective demeanor belied his extroverted and sometimes emotional television persona. There was none of the Queens-accented bombast that

prompted political writer Ronald Brownstein of the Los Angeles Times to label Wexler "the human advertisement for the mute button."

The experience was almost entirely positive, Wexler said. "I got to do in one term what it might have taken 10 terms to do."

Wexler's was a multifaceted crusade on behalf of the president; he did not restrict himself to TV — or even to targeting a voting-age audience. In January, he wrote a brief article for the magazine Time for Kids, explaining why "Clinton should stay." Tailored to the PG-13 crowd, it never mentioned sex or even Monica Lewinsky, only a "private matter" that, while serious, did not warrant Clinton's removal. "What else are you going to do for Time for Kids?" he asked with a shrug.

Gramm, R-TV

Certainly, Wexler is not unique among members of Congress in his unabashed willingness to play to the cameras. On Capitol Hill, the show-horse quotient has been rising in recent years, as more and more members try to replicate the success of such media-savvy lawmakers as John McCain, R-Ariz., Charles E. Schumer, D-N.Y., and Phil Gramm, R-Texas, each of whom used his understanding of the press to stage high-profile tenures in the House

that became launching pads for election to the Senate.

When Gramm was a mere freshman senator, ABC News correspondent Cokie Roberts said that "no camera, microphone, or notebook could be too inconveniently located for Phil Gramm."

But that was back in the days before Rivera and his cable TV competitor Chris Matthews, before televised political discourse expanded from the polite world of the Sunday interview shows on the Big Three broadcast network to the panoply of prime-time cable slugfests. Television, it is said, loves a fight. Throughout the Lewinsky scandal, senators and representatives from both parties were not shy about joining the fray.

Sen. Robert F. Bennett, R-Utah, who appeared several times on "Larry King Live" and other programs, is still basking in his new status as a celebrity. On a recent trip to Mexico, Bennett had an experience familiar to anyone who has had a brush with fame. Climbing up a narrow staircase inside an ancient Mayan pyramid, he encountered a woman who was certain she had seen him before — but was just not quite sure where.

"People are not used to seeing me on TV, they're used to seeing Orrin," Bennett said, referring to his home-

"extramarital exploits" of pro-impeachment Republican lawmakers, reports that are fueled by a promise of payments of $1 million for credible information. Flynt says his motive is to expose hypocrisy at the Capitol. His threat of exposure prompted Rep. Robert L. Livingston, R-La. (1978-99), last year to renounce the speakership and leave Congress altogether. *(1998 CQ Weekly, p. 3333)*

When such allegations surfaced in the past year, however, they did not usually mean the political death penalty. House Government Reform Committee Chairman Dan Burton, R-Ind., and Judiciary Committee Chairman

Henry J. Hyde, R-Ill., survived disclosures of long-running affairs. Flynt's allegation of hypocrisy by Rep. Bob Barr, R-Ga., has caused barely a ripple.

Lawmakers are sometimes the most aggressive promoters of such stories. House Majority Whip Tom DeLay, R-Texas, has accused the White House of encouraging the circulation of negative personal stories about Republicans. But DeLay and other conservatives were clearly interested in seeing Broaddrick's story publicized. And many Democrats took private glee when the scandal spotlight turned on the GOP.

In the House impeachment debate, Minority Leader Richard A. Gephardt,

D-Mo., declared to warm bipartisan applause that "the politics of slash and burn must end." But it seems that too many — in Congress and in the media — have a stake in its continuing. Part of the reason is that while the vast majority of the public has been turned off by the nonstop scandal news coming out of Washington, millions continue to seek it out. In January, "Rivera Live," hosted by Geraldo Rivera on CNBC, earned its highest ratings in nearly two years when Flynt appeared as a guest.

Television Rules . . . for Now

Even in an era when broadcast television faces increasingly stiff competi-

Wexler, left, and Barr were two House members whose media profiles expanded the most during impeachment. They appeared together Sept. 20 on 'Meet the Press.'

state colleague, Republican Orrin G. Hatch. "All of a sudden, I'm on 'Larry King' and 'Face the Nation,' and they're saying 'Wow.' "

Pluses and Pitfalls

But Wexler and a handful of others, such as Rep. Bob Barr, R-Ga. — whose passion for impeachment was just as ardent as was Wexler's opposition to it — rose beyond being TV regulars in the months after Independent Counsel Kenneth W. Starr's report arrived at the Capitol. They were practically ubiquitous, night after argument-filled night.

The question is whether all the exposure did Wexler any good, either back home or in his efforts to rise in Congress. Conventional wisdom suggests that few lawmakers, if any, enhanced their careers with

their performance on impeachment. Two House managers in the Senate trial, Republicans Asa Hutchinson of Arkansas and Lindsey Graham of South Carolina, have earned the most plaudits.

The jury is still out on impeachment's residual benefits for Wexler, an ambitious but still low-ranking minority member on the Judiciary and International Relations committees — hardly power posts, barring the outbreak of war or another impeachment.

Yet he sees almost nothing but good things flowing from his recent fame. Even before Sen. Connie Mack, R-Fla., announced his retirement, Wexler was conducting statewide polls, just in case. The results, he said, were encouraging, and he is now among the 10 House members from

Florida weighing a race for the Senate next year. Two others were on the House GOP team of impeachment managers. (*1999 CQ Weekly*, p. 605)

Now that he is well-known among the bookers who set the guest lists for programs, he has been invited back to discuss intervention in Kosovo and other foreign policy topics.

"That is the stuff I love talking about," he said, adding that in his district — which includes the heavily Jewish communities of Boca Raton and Palm Beach — Middle East policy is virtually local politics.

Yet there has been a downside as well. In December, Wexler was threatened with death in a single-page, handwritten letter sent to his Washington office. The Secret Service and FBI took the threat seriously enough to find him extra security for a Florida speaking engagement just as the House was voting to impeach the president.

Moreover, Wexler's efforts to portray himself as a moderate — virtually a requirement for Democrats running statewide in Florida — have probably suffered by his immoderate support of the president. If he runs for the Senate, his "Wake up, America" line is not likely to be recalled too warmly in the Panhandle or the state's other conservative redoubts. Wexler admits he has made some enemies, though he was not opposed for election to his second term.

"In my first race, I won 66-34," he said. "Now I guess the 34 percent knows why they didn't vote for me."

---

tion, it endures as the most important medium for political communication.

"I'm still struck by the fact that the lowest-rated show on CBS still has six times the audience of the highest-rated show on CNN," said Rep. Christopher Cox, R-Calif.

Former Rep. Lee H. Hamilton, D-Ind. (1965-99), said that early in his career he never gave a second thought about appearing on television. "But then I found that the old saying was true: 'If you're not on TV, you're not there for a lot of folks,' " said Hamilton, now director of the Woodrow Wilson International Center for Scholars. Hamilton's challenge was to get coverage by the local

stations, which stretched from Cincinnati to Indianapolis, that broadcast to his mostly rural constituents. His reputation as a foreign policy expert already gave him extensive air time on national television.

There are still a handful of camera-shy lawmakers, mostly venerable veterans, who subscribe to the dictum of former House Appropriations Committee Chairman Jamie L. Whitten, D-Miss. (1941-95), that "you do your job best when you do your job quietly."

But there are fewer such members all the time. And several junior members of Congress used hot rhetoric on television during impeachment to heighten their

profiles in the capital. (*Story, pp. 62–63*)

Substance Seldom Sells

For the past several years, the public relations contest between Clinton and Congress has been a rout in the president's favor, largely because of his skillful use of television.

"Impeachment proved again that Congress is no match for the president, at least this president, in the television age," Sabato said.

In their infrequent legislative triumphs, Republicans have successfully tailored their message to the TV audience. In 1997, for instance, the Senate Finance Committee hit a public relations home run with three days of emotional hearings showing how taxpayers were being victimized by bureaucrats at the IRS. Propelled by public outrage over those abuses, a sweeping overhaul of the agency (PL 105-206) was enacted last year. *(1998 CQ Weekly, p. 1756)*

But politicians from both parties say it is difficult to attract TV attention to most policy-related issues. It is a familiar refrain from policy-makers at every level: Broadcast news prefers flash to facts and scandal to substance.

"It's been that way for a while," said Sen. Richard G. Lugar, R-Ind. "You can make a good case that those things that seriously affect us, like the crisis in Kosovo, receive only tangential attention."

"It reflects the national media's boredom with Washington, No. 1, and its boredom with Congress, No. 2," said Stephen Hess, a senior fellow at the Brookings Institution and the author of "Live from Capitol Hill," a book about the congressional press corps.

After impeachment, the appetite for Washington news may be further diminished. And while the networks allot at least some time to Kosovo and the budget debate, cable TV news programs that for months staked their ratings on the impeachment story appear to have no interest in anything but scandal-related news from Washington.

Coming of Age?

Media critic Jon Katz believes that the Internet came of age during the Lewinsky scandal. "Big stories always change media," he recently told the Boston Globe. "The death of Elvis created the tabloid culture. The gulf war legitimized cable as a medium."

The Lewinsky scandal erupted in January 1998 after Drudge reported on his Web site that Newsweek was reporting a story revealing the president's relationship with Lewinsky. Eight months later, the House voted to release the Starr report. Millions searched for the report on the Web sites of the House and others that carried it — including Congressional Quarterly.

While this scandal gave the Internet new credibility, even lawmakers who are Web aficionados say Katz's claim is extravagant. For one thing, there are still relatively few on-line news organizations that generate original material, a fact underscored by the circumstances of Drudge's scoop.

That may be changing. More news organizations are establishing separate

on-line news operations, and many are covering Capitol Hill. "About 90 percent of the new organizations seeking press credentials are Internet-related," said Robert E. Petersen, superintendent of the Senate Press Gallery.

Still, several recent studies show that while the Internet audience is growing rapidly and becoming less elitist, it is not clamoring for news about Congress or politics. "Today, with 41 percent of adults using the Internet, the weather is the most popular news attraction," said a survey by the Pew Research Center.

So lawmakers are not yet inclined to revise their TV-oriented communications strategies in favor of a Web-only approach. But they cannot afford to ignore the Internet, either.

"It just means we have to cover more bases," Cox said.

The long-shot victory in Minnesota last fall of Reform Party Gov. Jesse Ventura was helped immeasurably by his use of the Internet. His campaign went on-line to raise money, organize volunteers and deliver "rapid response" to an opponent's charges that he favored legalizing prostitution.

Ventura ultimately may have more to do with putting the Internet on the political map than Drudge or Lewinsky. "He showed it's the next thing," said Sen. Robert F. Bennett, R-Utah.

Members of Congress use the Web largely to assess the views from constituents or "as a vehicle to advertise themselves," writes Brigham Young University Professor Richard Davis in his new book "The Web of Politics."

For most lawmakers, however, the Internet is not yet an important part of the political arsenal. Senate Republicans have been promoting their agenda for the year in a series of old-fashioned town hall meetings — an approach former President Harry S Truman would have been comfortable with. The Web site of Senate Majority Leader Trent Lott, R-Miss., who has been speaking at the meetings, includes virtually no specific proposals. For example, it says only that "tax reductions will be a key component of my agenda."

And while electronic mail has become a means for lawmakers to take the pulse of their constituents, the volume of computer missives can be overwhelming. During the impeachment trial, there were e-mail system crashes across the Hill.

As with everyone else in America, Congress is being buffeted by rapidly

changing technological and sociological forces that it can only dimly understand, much less control.

When Orrin G. Hatch, R-Utah, was first elected to the Senate in 1976, "he stunned everyone by sending an audiocassette to every GOP delegate at the state convention," Bennett recalled. "In '92, when my opponent sent a promotional videocassette to every delegate, it was yawn time. . . . But I used a computer to phone answering machines with a personal message, and that was a hit."

Sunshine and Shadows

After the widespread criticism of the Senate's closed deliberations in the Clinton trial, one might think that secrecy is still passé on Capitol Hill. But the reality is far different.

Lawmakers did not raise a peep last fall when Clinton administration officials and GOP leaders closeted themselves for days in a Capitol conference room to carve up a half-trillion dollars in the omnibus appropriations package (PL 105-277), continuing a recent end-of-the-year ritual of high-stakes horse-trading. *(1998 CQ Weekly, p. 2885)*

In those cases, there is usually no great clamor from the public or the media for openness. It would probably be impossible for such a deal to coalesce if all sides played to the cameras. And lawmakers are not eager to shed light on pet projects that they typically squirrel away in massive spending bills.

Far different rules apply when what has been called the "scandal industrial complex" is revved up. When the media descends en masse on Congress to cover an explosive story — whether impeachment or the 1991 confirmation hearings for Supreme Court Justice Clarence Thomas — there is immense pressure to open up everything.

Surprisingly, the Senate was able to resist those pressures when it retreated to the privacy of the Old Senate Chamber in early January to hash out ground rules for the Clinton trial.

But the final deliberations on the president's fate were devoid of any real debate. It was as if the cameras were never turned off, as senator after senator, knowing their statements would eventually be made public, stuck cautiously to their prepared scripts.

The Senate's experience with secrecy "was not the be-all and end-all some had hoped for," Lugar said. "Don't expect it to happen again any time soon." ◆

Congress Set To Provide Money, But No Guidance, for Kosovo Mission

After the House refuses to either support or disown Clinton's policy, Senate leaders maneuver to block a similarly divisive debate

Forced to vote on U.S. strategy in the Balkans, the House found no strategy of its own April 28, demanding congressional approval for sending ground troops but neither endorsing nor condemning the current NATO air campaign against Yugoslavia. The Senate is likely to duck the issue altogether the week of May 3.

Senate Majority Leader Trent Lott, R-Miss., and Minority Leader Tom Daschle, D-S.D., will move to table, and thus kill, a resolution that would give President Clinton authority to use all necessary force to pursue NATO success in the Balkans. They said a divisive debate might send the wrong signals.

While lawmakers cannot make up their minds on Clinton's strategy, they feel no ambivalence about his soldiers. A supplemental fiscal 1999 defense spending bill ostensibly to cover operations in the Balkans could be twice the amount Clinton requested.

House appropriators on April 29 approved a $12.9 billion measure, and the Senate is all but certain to approve at least the $6 billion Clinton requested, if not substantially more. (*1999 CQ Weekly, p. 1013*)

The Senate will vote on the defense spending only after it has been attached to the conference report on an earlier supplemental (HR 1141) that would provide disaster relief for Central America and U.S. farmers. That vote may come the week of May 10.

Administration officials dismissed the significance of the House votes on the Balkans. "They seemed to take all sides of the issue without taking responsibility for promoting one policy," White House spokesman Joe Lockhart told reporters April 29.

Speaker J. Dennis Hastert, R-Ill., drew a different message from the House debate. Clinton, he told reporters, should "come to the Congress and lay out . . . why we are there, what his plan is, and what our end game on

this thing is. . . . The rank and file need to have confidence that the vote yesterday shows they don't have."

An overwhelming majority of Republicans voted against Clinton's Balkans policy, goaded by Majority Leader Tom DeLay, R-Texas, who warned his colleagues not to "take ownership" of Clinton's policy by "voting to continue an unplanned war by an administration that is incompetent of carrying it out." (*1999 CQ Weekly, p. 1038*)

Among the 31 Republicans who broke with DeLay were leading members of defense committees who appealed to the party's traditional support for presidential discretion in the use of force.

"The principle of the commander in chief having the power to move quickly . . . will outlast the Clinton administration," warned Duncan Hunter, R-Calif.

War Powers

With NATO planes pounding targets in Serbia for a sixth week, congressional leaders had not been eager to debate Clinton's policy or, as some GOP lawmakers have taken to calling it, "Clinton's war."

But Rep. Tom Campbell, R-Calif., by invoking a section of the 1973 War Powers Resolution (PL 93-148), forced the House to take up two resolutions — H Con Res 82, ordering a withdrawal of U.S. forces, and H J Res 44, declaring war on Yugoslavia. Two others were added to the agenda to give members a broader policy choice — S Con Res 21, to authorize the current air operations, and HR 1569, to require authorization for any ground troops.

As it happened, only the measure on ground troops passed the House, 249-180. (*1999 CQ Weekly, p. 1042*)

The other resolutions were defeated, including the endorsement of the air war, which lost on a tie vote, 213-213. (*1999 CQ Weekly, p. 1042*)

The Senate, meanwhile, may have been trapped accidentally into taking

up a resolution (S J Res 20) that would authorize the president to use "all necessary force" to achieve NATO's goal of forcing the Serb-dominated government of Yugoslavia to halt its persecution of ethnic Albanians in the province of Kosovo.

That resolution was designed by a bipartisan group led by John McCain, R-Ariz., to express support for NATO to begin planning how it would use ground troops to occupy Kosovo in case the current bombing campaign does not induce Yugoslav President Slobodan Milosevic to give in. There was no mention of the War Powers Resolution.

Senate Parliamentarian Bob Dove announced April 28, however, that the resolution fit the criteria for triggering the War Powers Resolution, even though it was not designed with that in mind.

A Foreign Relations Committee meeting to vote on the measure, scheduled for April 29, was canceled to allow time for Senate leaders to negotiate a compromise under which action on the McCain measure would be deferred until May 10.

Lott is one of many Republicans who do not want either to endorse what they see as a badly flawed Clinton policy or to cast a vote that could be taken as encouragement by the Milosevic regime. So the real meat of the negotiations concerned what other options senators would be offered, besides McCain's proposal, whenever the Senate took up the issue.

But the negotiations broke down, leaving the Senate on the procedural autopilot set by the War Powers Resolution. Under that timetable, the McCain resolution would have been discharged from the Foreign Relations Committee on May 1, if the panel had not reported the measure by then.

On April 30, the committee voted 14-4 to report McCain's resolution to the Senate without a recommendation.

U.S. Apache helicopters arrive in Tirana, Albania, for possible use against Serbian forces in neighboring Kosovo. NATO forces have stepped up their air assaults in an effort to cripple Serbia's war machine.

Campbell's Gambit

The War Powers Resolution was passed to force presidents to get congressional approval for overseas missions longer than 60 days, though no chief executive has acknowledged its authority. The resolution requires expedited congressional consideration of war-related measures during that period. (*1999 CQ Weekly, p. 970*)

Campbell set out deliberately to force a court test of the act, and on April 30 he led a bipartisan group of 17 House members in filing suit against Clinton, asserting that his commitment of forces to the NATO campaign violated the War Powers Resolution.

The suit seeks to force Clinton to either withdraw forces from the NATO mission or seek congressional authorization.

When the House International Relations Committee considered Campbell's two resolutions on April 27, it reported each to the floor with a recommendation that it not be passed:

● H Con Res 82, requiring the president to withdraw forces from combat against Yugoslavia was reported negatively by a vote of 30-19;

● H J Res 44, a declaration of war against Yugoslavia, was reported negatively by a vote of 49-0.

When the House took up the two Campbell resolutions April 28, it also considered the two other measures — HR 1569, cosponsored by Republicans Bill Goodling of Pennsylvania, Tillie Fowler of Florida and John R. Kasich of Ohio on ground troops, and S Con Res 21, endorsing the air campaign.

Clinton's Promise

At a White House meeting on April 28, with a bipartisan group of Senate and House leaders, Clinton insisted that he had no plans to use troops and that he would consult with Congress before committing them. However, like all of his recent predecessors, he refused to be bound by Congress on this point.

Minutes before the House voted on HR 1569, Clinton's assurances, embodied in a letter to Hastert, were circulated to all members. However, some administration allies said this came too late to make a difference. "That letter should have been here this morning, on the desk of every member," complained John M. Spratt Jr., D-S.C.

Shortly before the House refused to endorse the current air war, it rejected, 139-290, Campbell's resolution calling for withdrawal of U.S. forces — including air units — from the conflict. It also rejected, by a vote of 2-427, H J Res 44, which would have declared war on Yugoslavia. (*1999 CQ Weekly, p. 1042*)

Although the troop-authorization measure would be binding law if enacted, the House vote to pass it was essentially symbolic. There is little prospect that it would be passed by the Senate and even less that Congress could override the certain presidential veto.

Moreover, when Rep. Ernest Istook, R-Okla., tried April 29 to add a similar provision to the draft supplemental appropriations bill that would fund military operations against Yugoslavia through the rest of fiscal 1999, the House Appropriations Committee brushed him aside, refusing even to take a roll call vote on his amendment.

Military Spending

As for the supplemental funding bill, which is the lifeblood of U.S. operations against Yugoslavia, the only question seems to be how much money the House will add to the $6 billion Clinton requested to replenish the missiles and bombs, fuel and spare parts used up in the air war.

Most indications are that the House will approve the enlarged bill during the week of May 3.

Some House members who backed the administration on the key votes warned that even a symbolic repudiation of the administration's war policy might embolden Milosevic and encourage dissent within other NATO countries.

"This will encourage [Milosevic] to hunker down," said Eliot L. Engel, D-N.Y. "This will encourage him to think that, somehow or other, the Congress will step in and deny the president the right to win this war."

Defense Secretary William S. Cohen echoed that view during an April 29 press conference, commenting that the vote not to endorse the air campaign was "counterproductive." ◆

Will impeachment usher in an era of legislative branch primacy?

The Presidency in the Balance

The House Judiciary Committee's report that accompanied the articles of impeachment against President Clinton began, curiously, with the phrase "equal justice under law."

The curious element is that this phrase is not generally associated with the legislative branch of government. Rather, it is a credo of the judicial branch. It was penned in 1935 by architect Cass Gilbert, and etched into the Supreme Court building he designed.

In the impeachment report (H Rept 105-830), the words commence an argument that Clinton committed impeachable offenses, namely that he may have acted to pervert that equality of justice by lying under oath, obstructing justice and lying to Congress in an attempt to conceal his relationship with former White House intern Monica Lewinsky.

But "equal justice under law," as well as "the rule of law," a phrase favored by committee Chairman Henry J. Hyde, R-Ill., strike many constitutional scholars as odd in the context of impeachment. The prevailing, though not universal, view is that impeachment is primarily a political function, rather than a legal one.

In a presidential impeachment, most constitutional experts agree, lawmakers are asked whether they wish to claim a popular mandate to remove a popularly elected official. They are not called upon to don robes or wigs, or play jurors or grand jurors. They are not supposed to judge their political adversaries. They can set their own standards of evidence and are not required to follow the legal definition of crimes such as perjury. (*1999 CQ Weekly, p. 3328*)

To many experts, the Clinton impeachment has a deeply troubling element — an overreaching Congress taking on a quasi-judicial function from one branch of government to mount a political challenge to another. This, they say, could erode the separation of powers doctrine and make impeachments more common, especially in light of the voters' demonstrated pref-

For the impeachment report, Republicans borrowed the words, "Equal Justice Under Law," which are etched into front of the Supreme Court building. In the foreground is "Guardian or Authority of Law" by sculptor James Earle Fraser.

erence for divided government.

"This concerns me a great deal, and it has nothing to do with who is president," said Thomas Sargentich, law professor at American University. "My concern is that for the integrity of a government, for a workable system of checks and balances, impeachment should largely stay in the background. Otherwise, we are changing our system of government and moving toward something that is more like a parliamentary system."

Lowering the Bar

If the Clinton impeachment appears as an overreach by Congress, it may also be seen as something of an act of desperation. One of the most unavoidable ironies of the year is that it was Clinton who was caught in an affair with a subordinate and a series of lies, but it was the House Republican leadership that imploded and the GOP that took losses at the polls in November.

Four years ago, when Republicans gained control of the House, they elected as Speaker a man who once spoke of making the House a "co-equal" to the

White House. That vision, articulated by Newt Gingrich, R-Ga., in 1979, has all but vanished. (*1999 CQ Weekly, p. 3333*)

Yet, the Clinton impeachment may be the last desperate grasp at that dream. As it was done at great political risk to the party and at great damage to the House civility, the effort to impeach Clinton had an almost kamikaze element to it — as if House Republicans were so determined to bring the president down, they were willing to go down with him. The quintessential expression of this was Speaker-designate Robert L. Livingston, R-La., announcing his resignation in the well of the House, and demanding Clinton's as well.

In terms of audacity, this impeachment is unprecedented. There have been sixteen impeachments in all, including 13 judges, one president, one cabinet secretary and one senator.

Not since 1868 has a president been impeached. Not since then has a government official been impeached on a party-line vote. With the possible exception of Judge Harry E. Claiborne, who was found unfit for office in 1986

— he was in jail serving a sentence for tax fraud — no one has been impeached for something so far removed from his official duties.

No one has been impeached as the result of an independent counsel report to Congress. No one has been impeached in a lame duck session of Congress. And never before has an impeachment advanced on the argument that it is an end in itself — the ultimate censure, as Rep. Bill McCollum, R-Fla., termed it.

These precedents have already sparked a fierce debate over whether the action against Clinton will "lower the bar" for future impeachments.

"If we move from 'high crimes and misdemeanors' to 'we don't like the president; we think he lied,' we're going to have these things all the time," said Paul Finkelman, a University of Akron law professor and co-author of "Impeachable Offenses: A Documentary History from 1787 to the Present."

Because Clinton is a polarizing figure, there is a natural tendency for people to view the constitutional issues through the prism of Clinton. But Kathleen Clark, a Washington University law professor and critic of Clinton, says the two must be separated out, now matter how difficult that is.

"I'm of two minds on this," she said. "As it affects Clinton there's a kind of justice in this. It's not a very beautiful justice. It's a kind of retributive justice. But it's a justice."

On the other hand, she said, as this affects the institution of the presidency, it is a highly inappropriate, antidemocratic action.

The anti-democratic element is that not only was Clinton elected and reelected, he was elected by people fully aware of his history of half truths and sexual peccadilloes, Clark said. If they elected him under those circumstances, what right does Congress have to try to un-elect him?

Part of the trickiness of the Clinton case is that it was brought by Independent Counsel Kenneth W. Starr. It started out as a purely legal exercise, and when it was fully developed, it was thrust into the political arena.

Had it started in a more public way, it likely would not have advanced as far. It would have been politically difficult for congressional committees to play major roles in the investigation, as they did in Watergate. The pressure on them not to delve into such tawdry affairs would have been great.

But Starr was shielded from such pressures. He was not himself accountable to voters. He gathered his information in private and was able to pressure Clinton before his grand jury. When he had gotten what he needed, he went to Congress.

'A Sorry Mess'

Many Republicans say broader arguments about the presidency miss the fundamental point that the Clinton impeachment is laced with allegations of serious violations of law — something most of Clinton's successors would presumably avoid.

Charles T. Canady, R-Fla., agreed that there is an "element of truth" to the argument that future presidents would always be "looking over their shoulders" in fear of an impeachment.

But, he said, if future presidents lie under oath and obstruct justice, "I would like for them to be looking over their shoulders."

A number of Republicans make the argument that potential violations of law, even those limited to personal conduct, are impeachable since they undermine the president's authority as the chief law enforcement officer. The central premise behind the Clinton impeachment is that a president, who has great powers under his control, must demonstrate that he is accountable to the same justice that others are.

This is not universally accepted, even among Republicans, some of whom do not think any of the charges against Clinton warrant impeachment. And some see a mixed bag among the individual charges.

George Van Cleve, chief minority counsel on the committee that investigated the Iran-Contra scandal in 1987, said that of the two articles approved by the House, the obstruction of justice charge arising from the sexual harassment suit brought by Paula Corbin Jones is not "even in the zone" of an impeachable offense. But, he argues, the perjury charge stemming from Starr's investigation may well be.

"This whole thing is kind of a sorry mess," Van Cleve said. "I think personally I wish it hadn't come to this. But it's difficult for me to criticize people who say they are not going to tolerate [Clinton's] behavior."

An Emboldened Congress

If future presidents could be weak-

ened by this impeachment, future Congresses may be emboldened.

The 105th Congress has shown a great deal of interest in expanding its prerogatives at the expense of other branches. Many of the same people who were early advocates of impeaching Clinton — most notably Majority Whip Tom DeLay, R-Texas — are advocates of widespread use of the impeachment process for judges whose rulings they do not favor.

Even those members with more restraint have backed restrictions on the powers and scope of the judicial branch that have provoked some unusually vocal complaints from judges. In April, the House passed a "judicial reform" measure (HR 1252) that would have limited judges' ability to overturn laws created through ballot initiatives. The Senate did not take up the measure.

Over the last four years, Congress has passed, or attempted to pass, a series of laws restricting judges from ruling in areas where civil liberties organizations frequently litigate — such as immigration and prison overcrowding — and forced them into areas favored by conservative groups, most notably adjudicating crime issues at the federal level. (*1999 CQ Weekly*, p. 1660)

On the presidential front, in addition to the impeachment, congressional Republicans have shown a new willingness to challenge the president on foreign policy issues, breaking a longtime America tradition that politics ends at the water's edge.

Angered by Clinton's decision Dec. 16 to bomb Iraq on the eve of an impeachment vote, delaying the vote, several Republicans, including Senate Majority Leader Trent Lott, R-Miss., and House Rules Committee Chairman Gerald B.H. Solomon, R-N.Y., expressed open dissension. DeLay announced in advance, on NBC's "Meet the Press" three days before the bombing, that he could not be supportive.

The dispute only intensified in the days that followed, as Republicans and Democrats fought bitterly over whether the debate should go forward with American troops in harm's way.

The Senate's Role

How the Senate treats the articles will bear heavily on the question of whether the impeachment bar will be lowered for future presidents.

"The Senate disposition will have a huge impact," said Michael Gerhardt, a law professor at the College of William and Mary in Virginia and an expert on impeachment. He said the acquittal of President Andrew Johnson in 1868 essentially "wiped the slate clean."

Particularly if Clinton is acquitted in trial, or if there is a bipartisan move to stop the proceedings before a full-blown evidentiary portion of the trial, the impact on future presidents could be mitigated. This would reinforce previously held views that impeachment should not be used for unlawful conduct that is private and does not subvert the government.

If the process ends in a harsh censure, the conclusions could be blurred. Would the lack of a conviction be a repudiation of the impeachment, or would the censure be a vindication of them? There would surely be a vigorous debate on this among the partisan interests on Capitol Hill, particularly if the impeachment trial was used as a tool to persuade Clinton to volunteer for some kind of penalty beyond censure.

The 2000 election also could be a determining factor on whether the Clinton impeachment is seen as vindicated or repudiated, or neither.

Damaging the Institution

In making the argument that removing Clinton from office would damage the presidency, Clinton supporters could gain backing even from senators who do not much like him personally.

They could combine that with an interest in averting the embarrassing spectacle of a Senate trial in winning the support of moderate Republicans who want an early way out. If this happens, Clinton should count himself lucky, say many experts.

"If a bipartisan Senate group spares the country from a six-month trial by arranging a censure deal, they'll do it for institutional respect for the presidency more than personal feeling for Bill Clinton," said Charles Tiefer, a University of Baltimore law professor and former House Democratic counsel.

Support for the institution of the presidency also provides a powerful counter-argument to those who say Clinton should resign now to spare the nation a Senate trial.

This analysis is rejected by many Republicans, who view appeals to the institution of the presidency in much the same way as writer Samuel Johnson saw patriotism: as the last refuge of

scoundrels — or in this case the refuge of the defenders of scoundrels. During Watergate, many Republicans point out, President Richard M. Nixon made similar arguments about the impact of impeachment on future presidencies.

So far, Clinton himself has not made public appeals in behalf of the presidency. If he did, his sincerity

During Watergate, Nixon, shown saying goodbye after resigning in 1974, warned that impeaching him would make it easier to impeach future presidents.

would be in question, since his personal interests would coincide so neatly with his statements of principle.

"It's pretty tough to take as unbiased the position of a person who is literally in the position of saving his own skin," said Van Cleve.

The Andrew Johnson Legacy

Many historians believe Johnson's impeachment in 1868, even though it did not lead to a conviction, had a palpable impact on the presidency and Congress for years to come.

"The impeachment of Andrew Johnson in 1868 led to the most intense period of congressional domination and presidential weakness in American history," said Tiefer. "We may well move in that direction now."

The argument for this is the string of undistinguished presidents that followed Johnson and lasted until Theodore Roosevelt breathed new life into the office at the outset of the 20th century.

That argument may be a bit sweeping. In truth, the mediocre presidents may have started with Martin Van Buren in 1837 and lasted through the century, with the one stellar exception of Abraham Lincoln. But many scholars argue that the impeachment played a role.

In an ironic sense, however, the Johnson example may prove a boon to Clinton. The crisis could bring down the Clinton presidency. He could become a disgraced ex-president who lost the trust of an American public exhausted by months of scandal.

But in another sense, the impeachment could enhance his legacy.

Today, Johnson is not known as one of the most miserable presidents in American history. He is not remembered for his drunkenness during his swearing-in ceremony in 1865 as vice president, or his considerable lack of intellect. He is not remembered for his tolerance of slavery or his defiance of Congress. Rather, he is known as the president who weathered an unfortunate and ill-founded impeachment attempt.

By the same process, Clinton could be remembered as a persecuted president who withstood an onslaught, and defended the prerogatives of his office, even as he brought its dignity into question through his dalliances. For Clinton's harshest critics, this could be the ultimate indignity. ◆

Presidency

Clinton's agenda has dim prospects on Hill, but it offers his party an attractive platform

A Manifesto for 2000

Bill Clinton's remarkable up-and-down presidency would end on a positive note if he obtained even a modest fraction of the ambitious agenda he laid out in his State of the Union address.

Clinton delivered the speech Jan. 19 in front of House members who impeached him and senators who are now sitting in judgment. It was the second address in two years given under unusual circumstances. Never before has an impeached president appeared before Congress.

Clinton gave last year's State of the Union speech only a week after the scandal over his relationship with former White House intern Monica Lewinsky had led many political pundits to declare his presidency on the brink of extinction. This year's pep rally came only hours after his defense began its case in the Senate trial. (1999 CQ Weekly, p. 183)

Clinton did not mention impeachment in his 77-minute speech. Instead, he focused on the themes that have led the American people to elect him twice and give him extraordinary job approval ratings despite his alleged wrongdoings. At the heart of the roster of initiatives was a call to "save Social Security now." Clinton then outlined new — and old — proposals on health care, education, crime, trade, the environment and campaign finance reform.

For example, he suggested setting aside trillions of dollars over 15 years to bolster Social Security reserves, investing some of the set-asides in the stock market, creating subsidized retirement accounts to supplement Social Security, allowing tax credits to help families care for the elderly, shoring up Medicare, improving schools and raising the minimum wage. (1999 CQ Weekly, p. 176)

"With our budget surplus growing, our economy expanding, our confidence rising, now is the moment for this generation to meet its historic responsibility to the 21st century," Clinton said.

But it is difficult to see how an ad-

Clinton, who revels in the annual State of the Union ritual, shakes hands with lawmakers and Cabinet members as he leaves the House on Jan. 19 after giving his speech.

ministration under siege, a House in which Republicans hold a razor-thin majority and much contempt for the man they impeached, and a Senate hog-tied by Democrats can come together to pass much at all — despite vows by all three not to let impeachment get in the way of doing the nation's business.

Many if not most of the politically pleasing initiatives that studded Clinton's speech are legislative long shots. But they give Democrats a poll-tested agenda to present to voters in the 2000 elections. Relatively little of it appears likely to become law, but it is the platform that Democrats hope will return control of Congress to them — and keep the White House in their hands.

Clinton's speech earned predictable plaudits from Democrats and grudging admiration from Republicans. "The president gave another good speech under difficult circumstances," said House Speaker J. Dennis Hastert, R-Ill.

Even the Rev. Pat Robertson, chairman of the conservative Christian Coalition, said Clinton "hit a home run" and that "from a public relations standpoint he's won." Then he added: "They might as well dismiss the impeachment hearing and get on with something else because it's over as far as I'm concerned."

Indeed, opinion polls conducted im-

mediately after Clinton's address showed Clinton still riding high. His job approval rating was 66 percent in an ABC News poll and a record 76 percent in an NBC News poll.

Polls notwithstanding, Clinton's agenda landed with a resounding thud among the Republicans he called on to help pass it. The president's wish list of new programs was not accompanied by details on how to pay for them. And Clinton did not press for tax cuts, despite the escalating size of projected annual federal budget surpluses.

"A $4 trillion surplus and not a penny for tax cuts," said House Majority Leader Dick Armey, R-Texas, who, along with Majority Whip Tom DeLay, R-Texas, declined during the speech to clap even for the most obvious applause lines. "I welcome the president's admission that not all of the surplus is needed to save Social Security," Armey said. "He proposes to spend the rest on Washington programs, and we propose to return it to working Americans as tax relief."

A Clinton Favorite

Republicans also laid out their agenda Jan. 19 and in subsequent days, though they struggled to be heard over the din of impeachment, the publicity surrounding Clinton's address and the follow-up White House road show that rollicked in Democratic strongholds such as Buffalo, N.Y. The annual State of the Union ritual is clearly a Clinton favorite, and he resisted calls from Republicans and even some in his own party to delay the address or submit it in writing.

But his speech — filled with applause lines that prompted standing ovations and close to 100 interruptions — raised hackles with some Republicans, especially the senators weighing his fate. "It's kind of awkward to be in the Senate one afternoon talking about impeachment, hear a rah-rah speech that should have been made to the Democratic National Committee and then be back in tomorrow going over impeachment," said Majority Whip Don Nickles, R-Okla.

Republicans continued to try to show that they were not being sidetracked by impeachment. But their pursuit of impeachment against the wishes of a clear majority of Americans has taken its toll: The same polls that show Clinton remains popular show Republicans faring poorly among voters.

Central to reviving the party and at the core of the GOP's agenda is a 10 percent across-the-board cut in marginal income tax rates.

"Washington demonstrated last year that unless the surplus is given back to the taxpayer, it will be spent," said Senate Finance Committee Chairman William V. Roth Jr., R-Del. "The broad-based tax cut in our package will be the simplest, fairest and, I believe, the most productive way to give the money back."

As he did last year with his call to "save Social Security first," the president sought to use the sacrosanct retirement system to foil the GOP's tax cut plans.

"What I said last night is not as popular as what others can tell you," Clinton said Jan. 20 in Buffalo. "Others can say, 'We have got this surplus now. I just want a big tax cut. I'll give it back to you.'. . . But I believe, if we save 60 percent of this surplus for Social Security . . . we can protect Social Security for 55 years."

The budget surpluses over the next 15 years are anticipated to total about $4.5 trillion. Republicans quickly embraced Clinton's plans to save roughly 60 percent, or $2.8 trillion, for Social Security. What to do with the remaining $1.7 trillion — which may or may not accrue, depending on economic performance and federal spending — is at the core of the philosophical chasm separating Democrats and Republicans.

The public seems to be with Clinton, consistently supporting use of the surplus for Social Security and Medicare instead of for tax cuts. The ABC News poll found 62 percent of the public supporting Clinton's call to dedicate the bulk of the surplus for Social Security and Medicare vs. only 24 percent in favor of

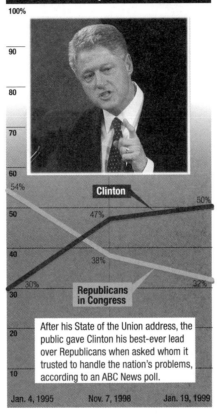

Who do you trust to handle the nation's main problems?

Clinton

Republicans in Congress

After his State of the Union address, the public gave Clinton his best-ever lead over Republicans when asked whom it trusted to handle the nation's problems, according to an ABC News poll.

Jan. 4, 1995   Nov. 7, 1998   Jan. 19, 1999

dedicating it to tax cuts. The public also gives Clinton a 50 percent to 32 percent edge over congressional Republicans when asked who it has more faith in to handle the nation's agenda.

Gridlock on the Horizon

The immediate outlook is gridlock of the kind that gripped last year's session, during which high-profile bills on taxes, a campaign finance overhaul, tobacco regulations and patients' rights all stalled.

"Ninety-some percent of his proposal was all more government," Nickles said of Clinton's plans. "I don't think you'll see this Congress pass it. Most of it I'll be working very aggressively to see it doesn't pass."

But Republicans know they cannot be content to kill Clinton's popular agenda. They must offer voters other op-

tions and at least get their bills to Clinton's desk. Last year, divided Republicans failed to get a tax bill through Congress when a five-year, $80 billion House-passed tax cut measure died in the Senate. (*1998 CQ Weekly, p. 3094*)

At no point last year did Republicans and Clinton engage in substantive negotiations on how to bridge their differences and agree on a budget plan. Instead, in the session's waning days, Clinton and Congress hammered out a budget-busting omnibus spending bill (PL 105-277) that tapped $21 billion of the surplus for "emergency" spending that, in effect, broke the 1997 budget agreement — and presented appropriators with enormous problems as they contemplate this year's round of spending bills. (*1998 CQ Weekly, p. 3081*)

Conspicuously absent during last year's budget debate was any realistic effort to strike a deal that could become law. The basis for such a deal would involve Clinton trading tax cuts for additional spending increases. With such a huge surplus, there is plenty of money to finance such an arrangement.

There is also plenty of incentive. Republicans do not want the 106th Congress and their party going into the 2000 elections with nothing to show except that they impeached Clinton and blunted his agenda.

Clinton's Senate trial adds uncertainty to the mix. On one hand, both the White House and Republicans want to demonstrate that they can do the "people's business" at the same time that the Senate debates whether to remove Clinton from office. The White House and most lawmakers assume that Clinton will not be removed, and both sides have expressed confidence that they will be able to work together once the debacle is over. "We must put aside the rhetoric and get down to work," Hastert said.

Others fear that the repercussions of impeachment may be impossible to shake. "If we spend several more weeks on [impeachment], I think the atmosphere is going to be so poisoned that even people with good friends across the aisle are going to have a hard time working together," said Sen. Patrick J. Leahy, D-Vt.

Something for Everyone

The speech carried no direct reference to impeachment, although in an oblique reference to his troubles, Clinton said: "Perhaps, in the daily press of events, in the clash of controversy, we

Clinton's Initiatives

President Clinton outlined numerous budget and tax proposals in his State of the Union address, many of which had been released in the days leading up to the Jan. 19 speech. Details will be officially unveiled Feb. 1 when Clinton sends his fiscal 2000 budget proposal to Congress. Highlights include:

• **Social Security.** A proposal to set aside 62 percent — or about $2.8 trillion — of projected budget surpluses over 15 years to shore up Social Security's cash reserves. Surpluses in the next 15 years are expected to total about $4.5 trillion. One-quarter of the set-asides would be invested in stock markets, marking the federal government's first investment in the markets. Clinton said his plan would extend Social Security's solvency by more than 20 years, to 2055. The New Deal retirement plan is now expected to run out of money after 2032 as Baby Boom retirees grow in number and live longer than previous generations.

Clinton proposed setting aside another 11 percent of surpluses – averaging about $33 billion a year, or $500 billion — to create subsidized retirement accounts, to be known as Universal Savings Accounts, similar to the 401(k) plans offered to employees by many businesses. These accounts would supplement but not replace Social Security. The government would provide a certain dollar amount to most Americans, and would match individual contributions to the accounts, with larger matches going to people with lower incomes. (1999 CQ Weekly, p. 178)

• **Medicare.** A call to use 16 percent of surpluses to ensure the solvency of Medicare, the federal health insurance program for the elderly and disabled, until 2020. Clinton also revived last year's proposal to allow people between ages 55 and 65 who lose their health insurance to buy into Medicare, and said the program should cover prescription drugs.

• **Long-term care.** An annual tax credit of up to $1,000 for expenses of the elderly, ailing and disabled, and the families that care for them.

• **Family assistance.** A tax credit of up to $250 a year per child under one year old for parents who stay home to care for children.

• **Education.** Redirecting the $15 billion in annual federal spending on public schools to emphasize, as Clinton put it, "what works and to stop supporting what doesn't." Clinton said he would send Congress an "Education Accountability Act" later this year that would, among other things, require that states and school districts end automatic grade promotions, improve the worst schools or close them, administer teacher competency tests, and improve school discipline.

• **Labor.** Raising the minimum wage by $1 an hour over two years, to $6.15. Clinton also called for women and men to get equal pay for equal work through enforcement of equal pay laws. He has requested tax credits of up to $1,000 a year, and other assistance, for the working disabled.

• **Trade.** A call to expand trade and open markets, starting with legislation to renew the president's fast-track trade negotiating authority.

• **Defense.** Spending an additional $12 billion in fiscal 2000 and $110 billion over the next six years to improve military readiness, reversing the decade-long decline in defense spending. (1999 CQ Weekly, p. 181)

• **Crime.** A request for $6 billion over five years to support police hiring subsidies, including up to 50,000 new officers in high crime areas. Clinton also called for expanded drug testing and treatment of prisoners, safe school programs, and restoring the five-day waiting period for handgun purchases.

• **Conservation.** More than doubling the money (to $1 billion) for land purchases and other conservation purposes, and $700 million in tax credits to finance bond initiatives to preserve open spaces.

do not see our own time for what it truly is — a new dawn for America."

Instead, Clinton focused on proposals new and old, offering something for everyone.

For senior citizens, Clinton proposed to extend the solvency of Social Security by using regular tax revenues to help shore up the program, which traditionally has been financed solely by a dedicated payroll tax and interest on bonds in the program's trust funds. (1999 CQ Weekly, p. 178)

For the first time, the government would invest some trust funds in the stock market, an idea that fell flat with Republicans who do not want the government holding stock in private companies. "No, no, a thousand times no," said House Ways and Means Committee Chairman Bill Archer, R-Texas.

In a bow to Republicans, Clinton proposed to eliminate the limit on earnings that seniors from ages 62 to 70 can make without losing their Social Security benefits.

In addition to strengthening the core Social Security program, the president said he wanted to use about $33 billion a year to create subsidized retirement accounts.

Clinton also proposed to use 16 percent of surpluses to extend to 2020 the solvency of the equally sacrosanct Medicare health insurance program for the elderly and disabled. He also wants a second chance for last year's failed plan to allow retirees as young as 55 to buy into Medicare. And he proposed to add coverage of prescription drugs to Medicare's basic benefits package.

Some criticized Clinton for proposing the new benefit and for promising part of the surplus to shore up Medicare, saying it undercut deliberations of the National Bipartisan Commission on the Future of Medicare, which is scheduled to report to Congress in March on ways to make the program stronger for future generations. (1999 CQ Weekly, pp. 51, 65)

Clinton also urged both parties to work with him to pass legislation that would give patients more leverage with their health care insurers. "Last year, Congress missed that opportunity and we must not miss that opportunity again," Clinton said. "For the sake of our families, I ask us to join together across party lines and pass a strong, enforceable patients' bill of rights."

Concerning tobacco, Clinton announced that the Justice Department was preparing to take the tobacco companies to court over the medical costs of caring for smokers, with any recovered funds to be dedicated to Medicare. He also promised to put in place new federal regulations governing medical record privacy if Congress did not act by August 1999. (*1998 CQ Weekly, p. 1986*)

The president's proposals drew instant ire from the business community, which assailed him for again seeking unnecessarily to expand the federal government's role in the nation's health care system.

In proposals likely to win favor among both Republicans and Democrats, Clinton asked for tax credits for long-term care (up to $1,000 annually), for parents who stay home to care for children ($250 per child under age 1) and to help disabled people who work (up to $1,000 per year). Republicans have signaled that they like this menu of small tax breaks — though they want to go further.

Congressional Republicans are less likely to support Clinton's call to raise the minimum wage over two years by another dollar per hour, to $6.15. They displayed no fear on that issue last year, although they caved to Clinton during the 1996 campaign and raised the minimum wage by 90 cents. (*1996 Almanac, p. 7-3*)

Clinton's reiteration of his request for fast-track trade negotiating authority left most of his fellow Democrats sitting on their hands, though his call to pass an Africa free trade bill won approval from his allies in the Congressional Black Caucus. (*1998 CQ Weekly, p. 3130*)

Passing the so-called Brady bill to reimpose a five-day waiting period for the purchase of handguns is a dead letter in the GOP-led Congress. Republicans are also likely to resist his call for additional police hiring subsidies. The chances for a campaign finance overhaul remain dim, and prospects for a 55 cent-per-pack increase in cigarette taxes are uneven at best.

"It isn't enough that he spends the whole surplus," grumbled Senate Budget Committee Chairman Pete V. Domenici, R-N.M. "Now he has a cigarette tax — going to collect that and spend that too."

Clinton's speech marked the opening salvo for GOP lawmakers who have already seen their share of turmoil and surprise, from their disappointing showing in the November elections, to the resignation of House Speaker Newt Gingrich, R-Ga., to the stunning announcement

by his presumed successor, Robert L. Livingston, R-La., that he, too, would step aside. The shake-up in GOP ranks leaves Republicans with an untested Speaker and a narrow House majority that promises to be an unrelenting headache to manage. (*1999 CQ Weekly, p. 8*)

Moreover, Republicans are struggling to gain traction with an agenda of limited government that is more difficult to sell in an era of budget surpluses.

With the departure of Gingrich, Republicans are seeking to put a fresh face on their party. So it fell to the telegenic

Reps. Dunn, left, and Largent helped Republicans attach fresh faces to their agenda when they delivered the Jan. 19 GOP response to Clinton's State of the Union address.

Reps. Jennifer Dunn, R-Wash., and Steve Largent, R-Okla., to present the official GOP response to Clinton.

"Next year, there will be a $63 billion surplus. Mr. President, give it back," Dunn said. "Last year, a typical mother and father who both work paid nearly 40 percent of their income in taxes . . . . That's the highest percentage of income ever paid in taxes by American families."

Added Largent: "We will continue our efforts to control Washington's wasteful spending and its insatiable appetite for your money."

Surplus Estimates

The next step in the annual budget ritual is the submission of Clinton's fiscal 2000 budget on Feb. 1. With it will come new surplus estimates. The Congressional Budget Office (CBO) will al-

so issue revised surplus and economic forecasts Jan. 28.

But preliminary estimates by the Senate Budget Committee give Republicans hope that they can advance a budget blueprint with plenty of room for tax cuts. The unofficial numbers forecast that an on-budget surplus (as opposed to the larger unified budget surplus that includes Social Security revenues) would materialize in fiscal 2002. That would make cutting taxes much more politically palatable because Democrats could not cast it as an attack on Social Security. (*1998 CQ Weekly, p. 1999*)

When Clinton says he wants to dedicate the bulk of the surplus to Social Security, he is actually proposing to pay down a portion of the nation's $5.5 trillion national debt, which would help the economy by putting downward pressure on interest rates and boosting national savings.

Under Clinton's plan, the normal flow of Social Security surpluses into the system's trust funds would continue. Additional bonds equal to the $2.8 trillion influx into the system would be added to the trust funds.

"You are double-counting for a good cause — paying down the debt," said former CBO Director Robert D. Reischauer, now a senior fellow at the Brookings Institution. "If you didn't wrap that up in Social Security and Medicare, it wouldn't be politically viable." ◆

Success score droops as White House priorities make scant headway

Clinton's Biggest Prize Was a Frustrated GOP

President Clinton set out an ambitious agenda in his 1998 State of the Union address, but most of his priorities fell by the wayside. He succeeded mainly in blocking conservative initiatives.

President Clinton's historic defeat on two articles of impeachment in the House on Dec. 19 dwarfs all other votes when it comes to assessing his success in the 1998 session of Congress.

In fact, even without the votes that made him the first elected president in U.S. history to be impeached, Clinton's legislative year has to be scored as a failure — if the goal was to advance a policy agenda. Virtually all of his major proposals died.

But if — as cynics would have it — the main thing in politics is to triumph over one's political adversaries, then Clinton performed rather well. He effectively shut down the Republican agenda, including tax cuts and reduced regulations, helped deliver unexpected Democratic victories at the polls in November and, indirectly, contributed to the stunning downfall of then-House Speaker Newt Gingrich, R-Ga.

On paper, Clinton ended the year with a 51 percent success score, according to Congressional Quarterly's annual study of voting patterns. This means he prevailed on 51 percent of the 154 House and Senate floor votes on which he took a position.

That is, on the surface, a fairly low score. It is lower than the scores of Presidents Dwight D. Eisenhower (76 percent) and Ronald Reagan (56.1 percent) in their sixth years in office. It is lower, even, than President Richard M. Nixon's (59.6 percent) in his sixth year — the year he resigned rather than face impeachment.

In fact, Clinton's score was the sixth lowest of any president since Congressional Quarterly began keeping track of such things at the beginning of the Eisenhower administration 46 years ago.

Almost none of the priorities that Clinton set at the beginning of the year became law, and few of them even got a floor vote. Tobacco legislation, campaign finance overhaul, "fast track" trade legislation and a "bill of rights" for patients in managed health care all fell far short of enactment.

But Clinton seems to resist being judged by ordinary standards.

Like a clutch quarterback in the final seconds of play, he came through when he had to. After losing a series of House appropriations floor votes, he managed to recover most of his losses when eight of the measures were folded into a massive end-of-session omnibus bill.

The resulting package (PL 105-277) funded

PRESIDENTIAL SUCCESS ❯ History

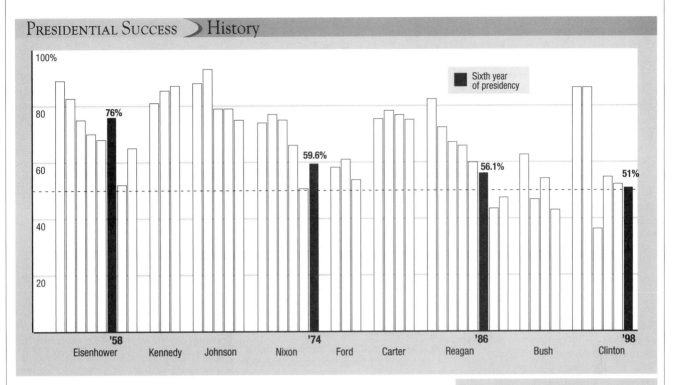

several Democratic priorities, including increased spending for teachers, while excluding most of the conservative policy "riders" added in the House.

And with the Republicans in postelection disarray, it was Clinton — despite his lame-duck status — who set much of the legislative tone for this year. His call to save Social Security first, for example, continues to undercut Republican efforts to cut taxes.

In that sense, Clinton fared better than Eisenhower and Reagan, both of whom suffered big congressional setbacks at the polls at this point in their presidencies and saw their power wane.

"Given the partisan tensions that culminated in the impeachment vote, it's quite surprising that Clinton did as well as he did in Congress," said Norman J. Ornstein, a congressional scholar at the American Enterprise Institute, a Washington think tank.

Personal Scandal

For Clinton to merely survive the year in office, let alone win enactment of any major initiatives, was a kind of victory. He was haunted by charges of lying under oath about a sexual liaison with a White House intern, leading members of both parties to support an impeachment inquiry.

Although Clinton took no formal position on early House votes related to the scandal, such as a Sept. 11 vote to publicly release a sexually explicit

report by Independent Counsel Kenneth W. Starr, the issue dominated the landscape, giving Clinton scarce chance to pursue his vigorous agenda.

On the other hand, it meant he had nothing to lose by battling GOP initiatives, thereby turning the subject away from scandal. By threatening vetoes on a battery of issues from tax cuts to restrictions on overseas family planning funds, the president stymied congressional conservatives just when it seemed that they should be piling up political points.

When threats were not enough, Clinton wielded his veto pen to stop five bills. The measures would have expanded the tax benefits of education savings accounts (HR 2646); created school vouchers in the District of Columbia (S 1502); punished countries that offered technical assistance to Iran's missile program (HR 2709); appropriated less money than Clinton wanted for agriculture programs in fiscal 1999 (HR 4101); and tied reauthorization of State Department programs to anti-abortion restrictions in international family planning (HR 1757).

In a year marked by sharply drawn partisan lines, House Democrats supported Clinton 74 percent of the time; Senate Democrats averaged 82 percent support. Regionally, Clinton fared best with Eastern Senate Democrats (84 percent support) and worst with Southern House Republicans (22 percent support).

Definition
How often the president won his way on roll call votes on which he took a clear position.

1998 Data

Senate	48 victories
	24 defeats

House	30 victories
	52 defeats

Total Clinton success rate: **51%**

His most reliable Republican supporters in the Senate were John H. Chafee of Rhode Island (77 percent) and James M. Jeffords of Vermont (69 percent). In the House, the most GOP support came from Constance A. Morella of Maryland (71 percent) and Sherwood Boehlert of New York (60 percent).

Domestic Setbacks

In his 1998 State of the Union address, Clinton laid out an ambitious domestic agenda. He called for a health care bill of rights to protect consumers; comprehensive regulation of tobacco; tightened campaign finance laws; expanded Medicare benefits; an increased minimum wage; expanded child care programs; and the hiring of 100,000 new teachers.

He got virtually nothing.

Most of his proposals, such as permitting uninsured people as young as 55 to enroll in Medicare, never made it out of the gate. Other plans, including tobacco and campaign finance legislation, were extensively debated in Congress before falling to Senate procedural motions. (*1998 CQ Weekly, pp. 3110, 3096*)

Clinton also failed on environmental issues. Proposals to create tax credits to promote energy efficiency and launch clean water initiatives received scant attention on the Hill, and the administration was unable to generate enthusiasm for ratifying a global warming treaty.

The president did somewhat better on his proposal for $7.4 billion over five years to hire 100,000 new teachers. After an extensive appropriations battle, he won the $1.2 billion needed for the first year — but no authorizing language that would give momentum for additional funding.

"Clinton had a big agenda, and it just didn't happen," said George C. Edwards III, director of the Center for Presidential Studies at Texas A&M University. "It's very difficult to point to a very important piece of legislation that has Bill Clinton's stamp on it."

Overall, on domestic issues, Clinton lost on 43 of 69 House votes, and 19 of 36 Senate votes, not counting nominations. Many of his defeats came on conservative-backed policy riders to appropriations bills, such as proposals to limit access to abortion or create vouchers for private schools.

In the end, however, most of those riders fell by the wayside. Demonstrating that even an embattled White House wields considerable clout, Clinton carried the day on much of the end-of-session negotiating on fiscal 1999 spending.

The omnibus appropriations bill opened the gates for a flood of new spending, giving the president victories for such items as funding for the Bosnia peacekeeping mission, Year 2000 computer fixes, anti-terrorism efforts and farm relief. (*1998 CQ Weekly, p. 3081*)

Although Republicans also scored a few victories, they never recovered from the eleventh-hour negotiations, which took place just weeks before their Nov. 3 electoral setbacks. "We have failed in this process," said a disheartened Rep. Jon Christensen, R-Neb.

President Clinton's patients' "bill of rights" was among the casualties of the session.

Foreign Policy

Presidents traditionally do best in the foreign policy and defense arena, and Clinton has been no exception.

In 1998, he prevailed in the Senate on 15 of 20 foreign policy and defense votes. In the House, however, which proved more difficult terrain for the president across the board, Clinton won on just four of 13 votes.

One of Clinton's biggest victories came when the Senate voted to open the doors of the North Atlantic Treaty Organization, allowing Hungary, Poland and the Czech Republic to join the strategic alliance (Treaty Doc 105-36). (*1998 CQ Weekly, p. 3126*)

Clinton also won on repeated votes to fund the U.S. mission in Bosnia. And after a yearlong battle, he prevailed upon lawmakers to appropriate $18 billion for the International Monetary Fund, which he considered an essential step in staving off a global economic downturn.

Yet the president failed to win ratification of a comprehensive nuclear test ban treaty. Lawmakers also refused his repeated requests to pay off debts to the United Nations.

The House twice voted to restrict technology transfers to China, despite administration opposition. It also rebuffed Clinton by passing a bill (HR 2709) that would have punished overseas research laboratories and compa-

nies that provided missile technology to Iran. Clinton vetoed the measure.

Taxes and Trade

Clinton may have scored his most resounding victories on an issue that Republicans had hoped to convert into Election Day gains: tax cuts.

By urging Congress to set aside the budget surplus for the Social Security trust fund, rather than use it for tax reduction, he divided conservatives and ultimately paralyzed GOP efforts to cut taxes by $100 billion or more.

To some GOP leaders, it was Clinton's use of the Social Security debate, as much as any issue, that fueled Democratic gains at the polls. "We should have been more aggressive," Gingrich said after the elections.

But for Clinton, the tax issue proved a rather hollow victory. He failed to stir much debate about ways to ensure the future solvency of Social Security, meaning that both he and Congress will have to wrestle with the "third rail" of politics this year.

The president could also point to victories on other tax-related issues. The House failed to pass a constitutional amendment, opposed by the White House, that would have made it more difficult for Congress to impose new taxes. And the Senate turned back a plan that would have terminated the internal revenue code.

In addition, Clinton claimed victory when Congress cleared a measure (PL 105-206) to overhaul the IRS. However, GOP lawmakers also took credit for the bill, which was one of the few concrete achievements that elected officials of either party could point to in 1998.

Clinton's biggest economic setback may have come Sept. 25, when the House voted overwhelmingly against giving him fast-track trade negotiating authority. The White House took no formal position on that vote because of unusual political currents, but urged GOP leaders to hold off until early 1999 before bringing the top administration priority to the floor. (*1998 CQ Weekly, p. 3130*)

With many House lawmakers opposing the plan, GOP leaders are skeptical about reviving the issue before 2001. That would leave Clinton with greatly reduced leverage when he tries to negotiate overseas trade agreements in his final two years in office. ◆

Independent Counsel Holds No Brief For the Law That Empowered Him

Starr tells Senate panel the statute unconstitutionally creates a fourth branch of government that is 'especially vulnerable to partisan attack'

Had there been even a slight chance that the independent counsel law would be reauthorized by its June 30 expiration deadline, it was eliminated April 14 when Kenneth W. Starr — the most controversial personification of the statute in its 21-year history — told Congress of his opposition to the law.

Although he opposed the statute as long ago as the 1980s, while working in the Justice Department during the Reagan administration, Starr's testimony was portrayed by some on the Senate Governmental Affairs Committee as one of the great ironies of recent years. With his characteristic air of dispassion, the lawyer who has spent nearly five years leading the inquiry that imperiled Bill Clinton's presidency told the committee, in effect, that he never should have had the powers he has.

"I don't know if it was an act of repentance or reflection," said Joseph I. Lieberman, D-Conn.

Richard J. Durbin, D-Ill., said it appeared that Starr had come to Capitol Hill to beg Congress to "stop me before I prosecute again."

Starr formally announced his opposition two days after another event that did not bode well for the future of independent counsels. On April 12, U.S. District Court Judge Susan Webber Wright found Clinton in contempt of court for his deposition testimony in the Paula Corbin Jones sexual harassment lawsuit — the very statements at the heart of the groundwork that Starr laid for the president's impeachment. (*1998 CQ Weekly, p. 2387*)

Critics of the independent counsel law (PL 103-270) cited that ruling as evidence that misconduct by high government officials can be appropriately punished without using the unwieldy and blunt instrument of an independent counsel inquiry.

But it was Starr's testimony that appeared to foreclose the last chance that the measure's defenders would even start to push to renew the law before it lapses in 11 weeks. Starr has been one of the most assertive independent counsels ever. His probe, which is now estimated to have cost $39.2 million, started in 1994 with a look at the Whitewater land deals that Clinton engaged in while governor of Arkansas. It peaked with a referral to the House in which he said Clinton committed 11 separate impeachable offenses stemming from his affair with former White House intern Monica Lewinsky, which Clinton denied in his testimony in the Jones case. The House impeached the president, but the Senate acquitted him. (*1999 CQ Weekly, p. 361*)

Reauthorization Draft

"I fully expect the current independent counsel statute will expire on June 30," Lieberman told reporters after Starr's testimony. "Perhaps when it expires we will get a little distance from all the passions and partisanship that were aroused."

Still, Lieberman has joined with three others on the panel — Susan Collins, R-Maine, Arlen Specter, R-Pa., and Levin — to begin drafting a reauthorization bill. The details remain largely unformed, he said, but the measure would create some sort of special prosecutor who could not be fired at will by the attorney general. Lieberman said it had not been decided whether this person would operate within or independent from the Justice Department. He did say the group had decided to propose dropping the law's current requirements that independent counsels tell the House about any "substantial and credible information" that may warrant impeachment and to submit a final report on every inquiry.

These changes would not be enough to win the support of the administration. The Justice Department on March 2 urged Congress to let the law expire. (*1999 CQ Weekly, p. 542*)

"This committee, at least in one regard, has been able to bring about perfect harmony between you and the administration," Senate Governmental Affairs Committee Chairman Fred Thompson, R-Tenn., told Starr.

Joining the law's bipartisan roster of opponents was former Speaker Newt Gingrich, R-Ga. (1979-99), who was forced into retirement after being blamed when a GOP electoral strategy that emphasized impeachment resulted in a loss of House seats last year. (*1998 CQ Weekly, p. 2989*)

"Not modified. Not improved. Not partial. Kill it," he said at a dinner in his honor April 14. "Get rid of it. Go back to the system we had before 1978."

Starr's Testimony

Starr's appearance was, by and large, far more congenial than his testimony to the House Judiciary Committee on Nov. 19, at the height of the House's impeachment inquiry, when he faced a barrage of hostile questions from Democrats. (*1998 CQ Weekly, p. 3154*)

Democrats Durbin, Carl Levin of Michigan and Robert G. Torricelli of New Jersey criticized Starr for his conduct of the probe. Other Democrats confined their participation at the hearing to comments or questions on Starr's views of the law. On the Republican side, only Judd Gregg of New Hampshire served up the kind of questions that gave Starr easy opportunities to defend his record.

Absent institutional support from the Justice Department, Starr said, independent counsels "are especially vulnerable to partisan attack. In this fashion, the legislative effort to take politics out of law enforcement sometimes has the ironic effect of further politicizing it."

He enumerated a number of problems with how the statute is triggered: The attorney general must initiate an internal inquiry after finding "sufficient and credible evidence" that a high-level official may have violated the law; and appointment of an independent counsel by a panel of three federal judges must be sought if the internal inquiry finds "reasonable grounds" of wrongdoing. (*1994 Almanac, p. 295*)

"Rarely if ever had Congress tried to regulate so specifically such unquantifiable matters," Starr said. "And rarely had Congress sought to tell the attorney general precisely how, and how not, to reach a professional judgment."

Most broadly, Starr concluded, the law unconstitutionally tries to "cram a fourth branch of government into our three-branch system."

The White House joined Senate Democrats in expressing amazement that Starr opposes the law. "It is still somewhat difficult to see how you reconcile the investigation that took place with the constitutional views that he expressed," spokesman Joe Lockhart told reporters.

But in his testimony, Starr said he saw no inconsistency in opposing the law while at the same time exercising its powers, because it had been upheld by the Supreme Court. *(1988 Almanac, p. 123)*

Starr is now prosecuting his indictments of former Associate Attorney General Webster L. Hubbell — ruled valid by a federal judge on April 14 — and Julie Hyatt Steele, a friend of Kathleen Willey, a former White House worker who alleged that Clinton groped her.

Asked whether he believed he had statutory authority to indict Clinton after the president leaves office in 2001, Starr pointedly answered with one word: "Yes." But later in the questioning he raised doubts about how long he will continue. Although the statute has a grandfather clause allowing Starr and the other four existing independent counsels to continue their work even if it lapses June 30 — and to spend whatever they need unless Congress moves to cut off funding — Starr said he would use "professional judgment" in assessing whether and how to proceed. *(1999 CQ Weekly, p. 473)*

Sentelle on the Stand

Starr was followed to the stand by the three judges now assigned to choose independent counsels: David B. Sentelle of the U.S. Court of Appeals for the District of Columbia Circuit, Peter Fay of the 11th Circuit and Richard D. Cudahy of the 7th Circuit.

Sentelle and Fay were on the panel that selected Starr in 1994, and Sentelle spent much of his time defending the selection. Starr's selection was controversial from the outset because he was seen by many Democrats as too closely associated with Republican causes to be fair.

Sentelle was active in GOP politics

"Not once have we been found to have conducted ourselves inappropriately," Starr said in defending his five-year inquiry.

CQ PHOTO / DOUGLAS GRAHAM

before being nominated to the federal bench by President Ronald Reagan in 1985. Shortly before Starr's selection, he had lunch with his home-state senators, North Carolina Republicans Jesse Helms and Lauch Faircloth (1993-99), and Democrats have accused Sentelle of making an inappropriate selection at their behest. Sentelle vigorously denied this in his testimony.

"There was no substantive discussion about the independent counsel process whatsoever" at that lunch, Sentelle said. Had they been conspiring, he said, they would not have done so in a Senate restaurant: "We're not that dumb."

Contempt Citation

Wright's civil contempt citation was the first ever against a sitting president,

and in it she ordered Clinton to compensate the federal court and Jones for expenses incurred as a result of his false deposition. The citation could result in Clinton's disbarment. The matter will be referred to the Professional Conduct Committee of the Arkansas Supreme Court. The judge had signaled soon after the president's Senate acquittal that her ruling was coming. *(1999 CQ Weekly, p. 436)*

"The record demonstrates by clear and convincing evidence that the president responded to plaintiff's questions by giving false, misleading and evasive answers that were designed to obstruct the judicial process," she wrote.

Some Democratic opponents of the president's impeachment said the ruling showed that Clinton could be held accountable for his behavior like any other citizen, without the work of an independent counsel. "It's what we said all along," said Rep. Thomas M. Barrett, D-Wis. "There are mechanisms in place to deal with individuals who defy the courts."

Some Republicans said the ruling gave credence to their view that Clinton's behavior merited removal from office. "It counts as a strong reaffirmation of our work," said Sen. Larry E. Craig, R-Idaho.

But the major Republican sentiment was one of weary unease in revisiting the issue that caused so much political damage. "I'm not going there," said Sen. Mike DeWine of Ohio, when asked to comment about the ruling. He had been one of the most vigorous supporters of a full airing of evidence and witness testimony in the Senate trial.

The same day as Wright's ruling, a federal jury in Little Rock acquitted former Clinton business partner Susan McDougal of an obstruction of justice charge brought by Starr after she refused to cooperate with his probe. The jury deadlocked on two counts of contempt of court, prompting a mistrial.

"If anything should put a stake through the heart of Ken Starr, this should be it," said McDougal's attorney, Mark Geragos, who argued that his client was being unfairly prosecuted by the independent counsel. ◆

Campaign Finance Overhaul's Supporters Hope for a Boost From Clinton-Dole Audits

Supporters of a campaign finance overhaul are holding their breath to see whether the Federal Election Commission (FEC) will force Bill Clinton and Bob Dole's 1996 presidential campaigns to repay millions of dollars in public funding.

Although the commission may not reach a decision for months, overhaul proponents say the case could have broad implications for the future of campaign fundraising. It is unlikely, however, to affect the House Judiciary Committee's impeachment hearings against President Clinton.

Preliminary audits by the FEC charge the Clinton and Dole camps with wrongfully coordinating political advertisements with their national party committees and violating federal spending limits.

The audits, released Dec. 1, recommend that Clinton's campaign pay back $7 million in public funding that it received during the election, and that the campaign of former Sen. Dole, R-Kan. (1969-96), hand back more than $17 million it received in public financing.

The reimbursements are the largest ever recommended by the FEC.

"The commissioners have an obligation to adopt these findings," said Donald Simon, executive vice president of Common Cause, a political watchdog group. "If they don't, if they find the money spent by the parties was not subject to the law, they will be authorizing similar schemes to evade the law. Unless somebody says it's illegal, this will be the wave of the future."

At issue is whether the Dole and Clinton campaigns illegally benefited from millions of dollars in "issue ads" paid for by their respective national party committees. Issue ads do not expressly call for the election or defeat of candidates, and therefore fall outside federal regulation.

Because the 1996 ads run by the Democratic and Republican parties proclaimed the virtues or faults of Dole and Clinton — rather than calling for their election or defeat — the presidential campaigns contend the cost of the ads should not count against the strict spending limits imposed on them if they accept federal matching funds.

But FEC auditors say the ads crossed the line and contained a clear "electioneering message." They said the ads should be considered "in kind" contributions that count against campaign spending limits.

The auditors showed that several ads paid for by the Democratic National Committee were identical to ads run by the Clinton campaign.

The auditors also pointed out that the Dole campaign used the same media firms as the Republican National Committee and that the RNC's issue ads were meant to "influence the outcome of the presidential election."

"This is just one more example that the system is more loophole than law," said Eric Schmeltzer, spokesman for Public Campaign, a group that supports fundraising reforms. "It's symptomatic of the problem of issue advocacy."

If the issue ads' costs are counted as in-kind contributions, the Dole and Clinton campaigns would be well over the spending limits to which they agreed when they accepted matching public funds.

But many doubt the two camps will ever be forced to pay back the public money. The FEC has a history of rejecting or scaling back the recommendations of preliminary audits.

Advocates for campaign finance changes say they hope that regardless of the outcome, Congress will come under pressure to overhaul the system.

"It would be a clarion call for massive reform if the FEC does not follow through," Schmeltzer said. "They would be saying there is little law, and what law there is is barely being enforced."

The FEC's six-member board of commissioners held a hearing Dec. 3 to decide what to do with the audit's recommendations. Commissioners appeared reluctant to accept the auditors'

harsh penalties. The commission will meet again Dec. 9-10 before voting on whether to accept, deny or modify the recommendations. The Dole and Clinton parties can then appeal the ruling.

"We're probably six months from a decision," said commissioner David Mason, a Republican. "This isn't the end; this is maybe the beginning of the end."

At the Dec. 3 hearing, acting commission Chairman Scott E. Thomas, a Democrat, said the alleged violations in the audit were very complex. "The law in this area is hardly clear," Thomas said. "The commission itself over the years has had a great deal of difficulty grappling" with this issue.

Judiciary Committee

The audit comes as Attorney General Janet Reno is set to decide by Dec. 7 whether to name an independent counsel to investigate Clinton's 1996 fundraising. Reno initiated a review of the Clinton campaign in September based on an early draft of the FEC audit. *[Reno ruled against the investigation]*

The audit is unlikely to give Republicans additional ammunition for impeachment. On Dec. 1, the House Judiciary Committee voted along party lines to expand its impeachment investigation to include Clinton's fundraising activities. But on Dec. 3, committee Chairman Henry J. Hyde, R-Ill., held a conference call with Republican committee members to say he no longer wanted to include alleged fundraising violations in the impeachment probe.

Many Democrats have argued that both Clinton and Dole should be investigated for their fundraising activities. "It's quite apparent to me that both parties are playing fast and loose with the law," said Judiciary panel member Jerrold Nadler, D-N.Y. "There's no reason to believe the Democrats are any worse than the Republicans."

Judiciary Committee member Barney Frank, D-Mass., said the FEC audit "deprives Republicans of any political leverage they could get from the campaign finance investigation." ◆

Localities lobby for accuracy, but will Hill-White House census fight make it harder?

Mayors Aren't Sitting Down For the Count

Even before it began, the news conference held by Houston Mayor Lee P. Brown promised to be unusual. Standing solidly with Brown last September 29 were representatives of a coalition as diverse as it was powerful: the United Way, the Houston area Urban League, the Bangladesh Association of Greater Houston, the Baptist Ministers Association of Houston and Vicinity, the Coalition for the Homeless, and even the Houston Apartment Association.

More than 40 groups in all. And the force pulling these disparate groups together was nothing so typical as an economic development coup or a downtown revitalization plan. It was the census.

"An accurate census 2000," Brown declared, "will ensure that Houston receives its fair share of federal and state funding to implement vital city programs and projects."

Houston is by no means unique. From Oakland, Calif., to Richmond, Va., mayors and other local officials are locking arms for one goal — to improve chances that each of their residents will be counted in the 2000 census.

The reason: Lots of money is at stake. They want their share of the $180 billion a year that is distributed from the federal government to communities across the country based on their populations.

Many mayors are worried, however, that the Republican-led Congress and the Clinton administration will not be able to resolve the deep and bitterly partisan differences that have plagued census discussions for the past three years. They worry that political differences will translate into a census riddled with problems. Most of all, they want to avoid a repeat of the 1990 census count, which missed 4 million people nationally — a large percentage of whom lives in cities.

As problematic as the 1990 census was, the 2000 count could prove to be even more so. And some of the toughest questions will not wait for the year 2000 to be answered.

A showdown over using statistical sampling for the census count could cause a partial shutdown of the government in mid-June, when funding will run out for the departments of Commerce, Justice and State, including the Census Bureau, which is part of Commerce.

Lawmakers must decide by June 15 whether to fund sampling, which uses a mathematical formula to estimate population, or stick strictly with the traditional method of an actual head count, which historically has missed people. (*1998 CQ Weekly, p. 2824*)

Complicated Process

It sounds so simple — counting every nose in America every 10 years. But as mayors well know, very little is easy when it comes to the census. The debate over how to conduct the count gained notoriety in 1997, when Republicans inserted provisions in a flood relief bill prohibiting the use of sampling in the 2000 census. President Clinton defied Republican predictions and vetoed the measure, forcing Republicans to back down to allow the legislation to pass (PL 105-18). It has been a sticky, partisan issue ever since. (*1997 Almanac, 1-7*)

Statistical sampling is an estimation of population derived from a physical count of 90 percent of the populace. It has never before been used to the degree proposed by the Census Bureau, which is supported by the National Academy of Sciences and other independent experts in arguing that sampling would improve census accuracy and avoid a repeat of the problems experienced in 1990. (*1990 Almanac, p. 415*)

In addition to dividing Republicans and Democrats, the sampling matter has pitted big cities against smaller ones. Generally, big-city mayors support statistical sampling to augment the census, and mayors of smaller cities oppose the technique because they say it is unconstitutional and will not improve accuracy.

Yet there is one worry that largely unites the mayors, and that is this: Will Congress

Mayor Brown of Houston says he wants his city to have its share of federal money — and sees sampling as a way to ensure that.

help provide for the most accurate census count possible, or will it stand in the way?

Eyes on the Prize

No matter what method is used, there is an enormous amount of money up for grabs.

According to the General Accounting Office, 22 of 25 large grant programs "rely, at least in part, on data derived from the decennial census to apportion funding among states and units of local government." In fiscal 1998, 15 programs gave out $147 billion of the $180 billion distributed annually using census data.

But local officials are not sitting idly by while Congress debates the issue. Mayors are on the march, mobilizing, strategizing and lobbying, all in the hope of making the 2000 census more accurate. They say it is important to avoid the mistakes of the past, and they are citing figures:

• Los Angeles estimates it will have lost $120 million over 10 years because its population was underestimated in the 1990 census.

• New York officials complain that the last census missed from 400,000 to 500,000 residents of their city, at a cost of $45 million a year.

• Houston's Brown estimates that 66,000 people in his city do not officially exist according to census records. While he has not calculated the financial loss for his city, he estimates, "Texas stands to lose an additional $2.18 billion in population-based federal funds" in the decade between the 1990 and 2000 censuses.

• In 1990, officials say Denver was undercounted by more than 40,000, resulting in a loss of federal funding of more than $120 million.

Mayors are frustrated that Congress is locked in a political battle while the issue to them is more basic.

"This is not about politics, it is not about congressional seats and districts; it is about getting money to those states and localities where it is needed," Detroit Mayor Dennis

A Range of Undercounts

The following table shows the total population from the 1990 census and the estimated undercount for sample cities. The undercount figures were provided by the mayors of the respective cities.

City	Population	Number Undercounted	Percent Undercounted
Anaheim, Calif.	282, 133	7,334	2.6%
Charleston, S.C.	80, 414	2,500	3.1
Chicago, Ill.	2,731,743	159,000	5.8
Covington, Ky.	43,264	3,800	8.8
Fayetteville, Ark.	52,662	1,477	2.8
Los Angeles, Calif.	3,553,638	138,878	3.8
Plano, Texas	200,000	1,000	0.5
St. Joseph, Mo.	71,711	5,000	7.0
St. Petersburg, Fla.	240,000	3,497	1.5
Youngstown, Ohio	95,732	4,424	4.6

SOURCE: U.S. Conference of Mayors

W. Archer said.

And consequences are long-lasting. To mayors' vexation, results, once finalized, remain for 10 years. "It bothers us, just being a victim of whatever decisions are made in Washington," said Bill B. Owen, the mayor of Roswell, N.M. "They can move on, but we're forced to live with their mistakes."

Tackling the Problem

Answers should begin emerging over the next few weeks as Congress copes with the census on several fronts.

Soon after the House returns from the spring recess, it is expected to consider HR 472, a Republican-backed bill that would give local governments time to review and challenge census numbers before they become permanent. Republicans say such a mechanism would ensure an accurate count.

Democrats insist that the 45-day delay stipulated in HR 472 for local governments to respond would upset the delicate timetable for completing the census on time and would not provide for a more accurate count. (1999 CQ Weekly, p. 761)

The bill's sponsor, Dan Miller, R-Fla., chairman of the House Government Reform Committee's Census Subcommittee, insists that local input is critical if the census is to be accurate.

"I know that there are two words that local government officials hate to hear from the federal government," Miller said March 17. "And they are, 'trust us.'"

In Miller's view, the Census Bureau needs as many eyes peering over its shoulder as possible. "On one hand, [the Census Bureau tells] local governments how important the census is and how important it is to partner with them to get everyone counted. Then, on the other hand, they are saying, 'We don't want you to check our work.' . . . That type of attitude does not breed confidence in the census. It breeds distrust."

Democrats disagree, and if they are unable to defeat HR 472 on the floor, the Clinton administration has threatened a veto.

An even hotter flare-up will come in the weeks before June 15, when Congress must agree on the fiscal 1999 appropriations for the Commerce, Justice and State departments. If an agreement is not reached, legislators and congressional aides believe there is a real possibility for a partial government shutdown. Congress funded those agencies for six months because of differences over Census Bureau plans for the 2000 count. The unique arrangement was also created to give the Supreme Court time to rule on a challenge to sampling. But on Jan. 25, the court ruled that sampling could not be used to apportion congressional seats but could be used for all other purposes, including distributing federal funds. (1999 CQ Weekly, p. 259)

House Republicans have promised to insert language in the appropriations bill prohibiting the use of sampling for any purpose. Democrats insist that Clinton will veto any bill with such a restriction, leading some to believe that a partial government shutdown this summer is possible.

Meanwhile, Democrats underscore their contention that Republicans are unlikely to compromise on the census by pointing to disclosures that House Speaker J. Dennis Hastert, R-Ill., has enlisted former Republican Rep. Bill Paxon of New York (1989-99) to prepare a strategy for explaining a possible government shutdown. In recent weeks, Paxon has met with Republican media strategists and House leadership aides to forge a blueprint for such a situation.

In addition to explaining the issue to House Republicans, Paxon and others are considering broadcasting advertisements sponsored by the GOP to explain the matter to the public to blunt a backlash such as the one that hurt Republicans when a budget impasse shut down the government in 1995 and 1996 for 27 days. (1995 Almanac, p. 1-11)

With the 1995 experience still fresh in their minds, Democrats are eager for a showdown, believing they will benefit if the government closes over the census, and Republicans are blamed.

"I actually look forward to the fight with Republicans," Rep. Charlie Gonzalez of Texas said March 24, echoing other Democrats. "How can you be part of American democracy when the government doesn't know you exist?"

Khuyen Thi Pham of Amelia, La. The nation's immigrant population has been undercounted, say supporters of statistical sampling.

Cities vs. Towns

There is no shortage of voices in the debate.

The U.S. Conference of Mayors, which represents the biggest cities, is lobbying Congress to support the Census Bureau's sampling plan.

The National Association of Towns and Townships, which speaks for smaller municipalities, however, opposes sampling.

Lurking in the background are groups such as the conservative Southeastern Legal Foundation Inc., based in Atlanta, which opposes sampling. It has vowed to file suit if the Census Bureau goes forward with its plan for a two-number census, one that uses traditional methods for reapportionment and another based on statistical sampling for all other purposes.

Republicans have denounced plans for a dual count, but Census Bureau officials insist it would be the best approach and would yield the most accurate results.

Meanwhile, some mayors threaten to file suit if sampling is not used.

"It will either get resolved in Congress and sampling will be allowed, or it will be resolved in court," said Brian S. Currey, a Los Angeles lawyer who represented 20 major cities and counties that challenged the 1990 census.

"Without sampling," Currey said, "the 2000 census will be less accurate than the one in 1990."

Given the history of the census and the continuing stalemate in Congress, mayors have little room to maneuver.

Indeed, many mayors still remember when 20 large cities and counties won a court order to force an adjustment of the official 1990 population because their cities were significantly undercounted.

Census officials acknowledged the problem, but the Supreme Court ruled in 1996 that former Commerce Secretary Robert A. Mosbacher was not required to adjust the numbers, even though everyone agreed the 1990 census was off by more than 4 million people. (*1996 Almanac, p. 5-52*)

No End in Sight

Democrats and the administration say that Republicans oppose sampling because the people most often missed in traditional head counts are immigrants and the poor, populations that are more likely to vote for Democrats.

Republicans, though, show little sign of giving up. Hastert, asked if there was a way to avoid a confrontation over the census, said in a statement, "We want to make sure that we get a full count of everybody who is physically inside this country at the time of the census. That is important to do. I think we can do it accurately."

Whatever method is used, cities will feel the impact.

"You're talking about real people and real money that can be translated into local services," said Democratic Rep. Grace F. Napolitano of California, who began her political career in 1986 as a member of the Norwalk City Council. "But they cannot do it if they are not counted properly," she said.

Monica Lamboy, assistant to the city manager in Oakland, estimates that her city loses $4 million a year because the 1990 census underestimated its population by 20,000. The extra money, she said, would have been used for transportation projects, the Head Start educational program, and grants to poor and underserved parts of the city.

With the design of the 2000 census in flux less than a year before it is to begin on April 1, 2000, and with Republicans and Democrats no closer to resolving their differences, mayors and other city officials are grimly pressing on, keeping an eye on Washington even though there is a growing worry that the 2000 census may become the flawed 1990 effort all over again.

"In some ways, I'm not even paying attention to Washington because we have so much work to do here," Lamboy said. "We're not going to throw up our hands and quit just because . . . Washington is making things more difficult." ◆

Can the troubled agency restructure itself while staying effective?

Congress Still Skeptical Of 'Kinder, Gentler' IRS

IRS Commissioner Charles O. Rossotti, shown in an interview April 29, is enjoying a long honeymoon with Congress, in part because he tells lawmakers what they want to hear. He says the IRS must change its structure, upgrade its technology and emphasize customer service instead of tax collection. But it is unclear whether Congress' respect for Rossotti will carry over to the troubled agency.

IRS Commissioner Charles O. Rossotti appeared before four congressional committees the week of April 12 as millions of American taxpayers scrambled to file returns. He heard no crying witnesses, no tales of strong-arm tactics and little gnashing of members' teeth.

Rossotti received almost as many compliments as complaints and questions — no mean feat for the head of the often-bashed tax-collection agency, the subject of emotional and highly critical hearings in 1997 and 1998. (1998 CQ Weekly, p. 1145)

It seems Congress has largely decided to give the agency a year to recover from the wounds inflicted by the damaging testimony and time to begin making the changes mandated in the IRS overhaul law (PL 105-206) that Congress cleared and President Clinton signed after the hearings. The measure requires a top-to-bottom IRS revamp to improve customer service and give taxpayers more rights during audits and subsequent court cases. (1998 CQ Weekly, p. 1756)

But the potential for Congress to turn again on its frequent whipping boy does not seem to have diminished. Rossotti may be popular with lawmakers, but many seem to separate him from the career employees blamed for many of the agency's problems. Most say the jury is still out on whether the IRS' notoriously insular culture will absorb the changes mandated by the 1998 law. And many still want to use the IRS as a punching bag. The Senate Finance Committee is considering holding further IRS hearings this fall, spokeswoman Ginny Flynn said, to examine such issues as allegations of retaliation against former committee witnesses.

"A very easy way to get an applause line and to get a vote . . . is to rail against the tax collector," said Armando Gomez, former chief counsel for the National Commission on Restructuring the IRS, a congressional panel that disbanded after recommending many of the changes put in place by the overhaul law.

Commissioner Rossotti said it does not have to be that way. "I don't buy the idea that you're the tax collector so everybody's always going to hate you," said Rossotti, a self-made millionaire whom Clinton brought in to run the agency 18 months ago, to some extent stealing Congress' thunder in remaking the agency. In an interview April 29, Rossotti said it is paramount that the nearly 100,000-employee IRS change its structure, its technology and its attitude if it is to become the kinder, gentler agency that Congress has demanded. It is a task he likens to rebuilding New York City's infrastructure without displacing any residents.

To be sure, there are signs that the IRS' public face is changing. For instance, the service touted its quick decision to correct the 1998 returns of taxpayers who paid too much because they forgot to claim the new up-to-$400-per-child tax credit.

And the percentage of audits continues to fall, reflecting a 20-year trend.

But there is still much to do. The General Accounting Office (GAO) recently reported 15 cases of improper "snooping" into taxpayers' files and, in a 1998 financial audit, said deficiencies in the IRS accounting system had cost the government millions of dollars, including $17 million in refund checks to people who did not deserve them. Recent allegations that officials in the IRS' Houston office retaliated against a whistleblowing employee who spoke at last year's Senate Finance Committee hearings allowed members to criticize the service anew.

Rossotti immediately sent Washington investigators to Houston, and the regional director was placed on administrative leave. Observers say such quick action has helped build Rossotti's cachet with Congress. "He's not making excuses. I think that's politically astute and reflects good judgment," Leslie B. Samuels, former assistant Treasury secretary for tax policy and a partner in the New York law firm of Cleary, Gottlieb, Steen & Hamilton, said in an interview.

But "kinder and gentler" comes with a price. The IRS hearings may have made good theater, but a softer IRS with fewer audits and fewer fraud prosecutions will not produce the maximum amount of government revenue. It is an irony that Congress is still grappling with.

Margaret Milner Richardson, IRS commissioner from 1993 to 1997, said Congress ultimately must decide where it wants the IRS to focus: on friendly taxpayer service or on being the most effective tax collector possible.

"Congress has really not come to grips with what they want them to do," she said in an interview. "All we need is a slight downturn in the economy and I think questions will get louder and louder" about whether the IRS should be collecting more revenue.

Pay Your Taxes — Please

The IRS overhaul is still in its infancy, but there are signs that the agency is softening its fearsome image. Many of the changes were envisioned in the 1998 law and in a 1996 Taxpayer Bill of Rights (PL 104-168). (*1996 Almanac, p. 2-41*)

As expected, the agency has begun to focus on customer service. It even left the phrase "collecting taxes" out of its new mission statement.

During the recently completed tax season — which Rossotti and most experts judged largely successful for its lack of major errors — some IRS offices hosted "Problem Solving Days" to help taxpayers through the tax-filing maze. The IRS also studied phone patterns and scheduled workers to come in at the times when the IRS received the most requests for help. As a result, the IRS says, the number of calls answered quickly increased from 51 percent to 70 percent in the last year.

The IRS produced public service spots for television and radio to alert taxpayers to the child credit and to remind them that they could file for a tax return extension.

A concrete sign that the IRS is baring its teeth less often is a Syracuse University study showing that taxpayers' chances of facing an audit are declining.

According to the university's Transactional Records Access Clearinghouse, the IRS audited 551,420 out of 120.3 million individual income tax returns filed in 1997, or 0.46 percent. That was down from 0.60 percent for 1996 returns and 1.59 percent for 1980 returns. The percentage of individual income tax audits has been falling steadily, while the number of returns has increased steadily. (*Chart, p. 87*)

Besides falling audit rates on individual returns, the clearinghouse found that audits of corporate tax returns had also declined, "dropping to just a shade more than two out of 100" in fiscal 1998. And it found that the number of tax fraud prosecutions is also down, from 1,190 in fiscal 1989 to 766 in fiscal 1998.

The declining rates, the clearinghouse said, are largely due to the loss of more than 4,000 revenue agents and tax auditors from fiscal 1989 to fiscal 1998. The IRS lost many of those employees through attrition, but also shifted about 400 agents to customer service last year.

This has caused some angst in Congress.

At a Ways and Means Subcommittee on Oversight hearing April 13, Chairman Amo Houghton, R-N.Y., asked Rossotti how many audits were too few. And in February, Rep. Jim Kolbe, R-Ariz., chairman of the Treasury-Postal Service Appropriations Subcommittee, which funds the IRS, expressed concern that the IRS had strayed too far from its original mission of collecting taxes.

Rossotti said no one is sure how many audits are too few, but added, "I know one thing — we don't want to get a whole lot lower than where we are."

Yet the fiscal 2000 budget that Rossotti and the Clinton administration submitted to Congress requests funding for 95,767 employees, 220 fewer than in fiscal 1999. The total budget request is $8.11 billion, $2 million more than in fiscal 1999, reflecting small increases in administration, law enforcement and information systems.

Former Commissioner Richardson said the proposed budget is really a "net decrease," given increases in salaries, rents and other expenses. She and Donald Alexander, IRS commissioner during the Ford administration and parts of the Nixon and Carter administrations, said Rossotti, like other commissioners before him, likely argued unsuccessfully for more.

Rossotti maintains that the proposed budget would be sufficient to stabilize the agency and begin to rebuild. In addition to the budget, the IRS can draw on $506 million placed in a technology replacement account that Congress created in the fiscal 1998 Treasury-Postal Appropriations bill (PL 105-61) and increased in the fiscal 1999 omnibus spending bill (PL 105-277). (*1998 CQ Weekly, p. 3081; 1997 Almanac, p. 9-75*)

Work Left To Do

Some members of Congress are concerned that the IRS is becoming too soft, but a good number still worry that it has not remade itself.

Among those is Sen. Connie Mack, R-Fla., who said he is "a little concerned that everybody was just willing to accept any answer given" when Rossotti testified before the Finance Committee on April 14.

Mack says the IRS has not resolved enough of the specific allegations raised during last year's hearings. But IRS officials and Finance Committee Chairman William V. Roth Jr., R-Del., point out that the GAO, not the IRS, is supposed to investigate some of those allegations.

And Rossotti said that as a result of the hearings, which began in September 1997, 12 IRS managers and executives and two employees were disciplined, and several left. The IRS also

Sequel With a High-Tech Twist: Customs Service Hearings Ahead

As with a well-grossing Hollywood movie, certain elements must be present to craft a congressional hearing that grabs the public's attention. Allegations of discrimination and corruption can be a start.

The Senate Finance Committee — progenitor of the popular IRS hearings of 1997, featuring whistle-blowing workers and irate taxpayers telling of alleged strong-arm tactics — may have found another subject with all the elements needed to attract public attention: the U.S. Customs Service.

Customs has been sued over allegations that it targets minorities for drug searches and women for body searches, and that it does not do enough to stop illegal drugs from flowing across the border.

But unlike its IRS hearings, the panel's hearings on the Customs Service, set to begin May 13, are likely to focus on the more staid issue of computer systems.

"These will not be the block-buster-type hearings the IRS hearings were," said committee spokes-woman Ginny Flynn. "We don't want people to go in there with expectations of people crying on the witness stand."

Why not?

At least in part because the Customs Service, unlike the IRS, has the backing of industry groups that are lobbying Congress to help the agency through its troubles.

Willard A. Workman, vice president of the international division at the U.S. Chamber of Commerce, said that while his organization welcomes congressional oversight of Customs, it has encouraged straight-forward hearings.

In part, the Customs Service may also be able to avoid more high-profile hearings because it has a new commissioner — former New York City Police Commissioner Raymond W. Kelly — who, like IRS Commissioner Charles O. Rossotti, is largely saying what members of Congress want to hear. *(IRS, p. 84)*

At a recent speech before the Chamber, Kelly, nine months into his job, outlined plans for remaking Customs — the nation's oldest law enforcement agency and its second-largest producer of government revenue after the IRS.

"Any agency, no matter how proud its past, can develop weaknesses over time," Kelly said April 29. Among the weaknesses he outlined: failure to deal swiftly with cases of corruption, failure to adequately inform arriving passengers about what to expect during a Customs check and a potential technological failure that could leave the agency "simply not equipped to handle the trade of the future."

Kelly is developing plans to address those shortcomings, but in some cases, particularly in replacing the collapsing computer system that Customs uses to process goods coming in and out of the country, he will need help from Congress and the Clinton administration.

Groups Lobbying Congress

More than 200 corporations and organizations have joined a group, known as the Coalition for Customs Automation Funding, to lobby Congress to begin appropriating the $1 billion Customs estimates it needs to replace the system. The agency already has spent $47.8 million on upgrading its computers, with costs running higher than expected.

In his fiscal 2000 budget proposal, President Clinton suggested adding a fee on imported goods to pay for the new computer system, a proposal vehemently opposed by U.S. and foreign businesses, which already pay $22 billion a year in duties and $800 million in processing fees, according to the coalition.

Hearings could help corporations' efforts if testimony highlights the need for more Customs funding without convincing members that the agency could not handle the money if it got it.

Still, it is unlikely all lawmakers will refrain from quizzing the agency on the sordid issues it has faced this year.

At least 12 individuals and groups are suing Customs, alleging that inspectors single out racial minorities for drug checks when they arrive from abroad. And about 100 African-American women from Chicago have filed a class-action suit alleging that inspectors singled them out for body searches because of their sex and race.

In a 1999 report, the General Accounting Office (GAO) faulted Customs for inadequate checks of employees' connections to drug runners or susceptibility to bribery. The GAO, Congress' investigatory arm, said employees living beyond their means should have tipped off the Customs Service and its partner in border control — the Immigration and Naturalization Service — to suspicious activity.

But perhaps the most far-reaching problem, if not the most sensational, is the one on which the committee intends to focus. The main customs-tracking system, which records about $1 trillion in trade annually, is so overloaded that it is occasionally subject to partial breakdowns.

Importers, exporters and Customs Service officials fear it may give out entirely one day. A new system was mandated by the Customs Modernization Act of 1994 (PL 103-182), a section of the legislation implementing the North American Free Trade Agreement. But because it is far from operational, Customs is training its employees to file paper customs reports.

has established central complaint and adjudication units to handle allegations made by employees.

Roth came to Rossotti's defense on those issues. But he and House Ways and Means Committee Chairman Bill Archer, R-Texas, derided the IRS on April 16, the day after Jennifer Long, a 16-year employee of the IRS' Houston office and a star witness at the Finance Committee's September 1997 hearings, learned she might be fired.

"It looks like the new-and-improved IRS that we heard so much about this week is up to its old tricks again," Archer said in a statement. Roth called it a "clear act of retaliation."

Rossotti quickly sent Deputy Commissioner for Operations Bob Wenzel to Houston to investigate allegations of retaliation against Long, and the district's top officials were put on paid leave.

Long testified before the Finance Committee in 1997, telling members that IRS employees routinely violated taxpayers' rights and focused on a quota system. After her testimony, she filed a lawsuit alleging that the IRS had discriminated against her on the basis of age and gender. Long's story was one of several Roth featured in a book — "The Power to Destroy" — that he and his top aide, William H. Nixon, wrote and released in March. It chronicled the Finance hearings and Roth's decision to hold them.

Houston IRS officials allege in recently filed documents that Long's service had long been substandard, which was the reason for her potential dismissal. Long disputes that, as does the Finance Committee. "Jennifer's ratings were the highest they could be before the hearings," said panel spokeswoman Flynn. "All of a sudden these files are popping up saying she also got these lower ratings."

Congress' Job

Sen. Bob Kerrey, D-Neb., said the Long matter highlights the need for Congress and the White House to put in place portions of the 1998 act that apply to them.

Under the law, three members of each of the six committees with jurisdiction over the IRS are required to meet annually by June 1 each year to provide a unified direction to the agency. Ways and Means spokesman Trent Duffy said the committee chairmen are still planning to convene such a meeting, though it is unclear if they

IRS Audits and Tax Returns

Senate Finance Chairman William V. Roth Jr. wrote a book, far right, chronicling the IRS hearings. After the hearings, Commissioner Charles O. Rossotti outlined his plans for a kinder, gentler, more efficient IRS in a report known as "Rossotti's Book." The charts below show that as the number of income tax returns has risen in the past two decades, the number and percentage of audits has fallen — with a marked drop in 1998.

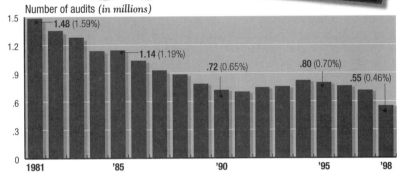

Number of audits *(in millions)*

1.48 (1.59%)
1.14 (1.19%)
.72 (0.65%)
.80 (0.70%)
.55 (0.46%)

1981   '85   '90   '95   '98

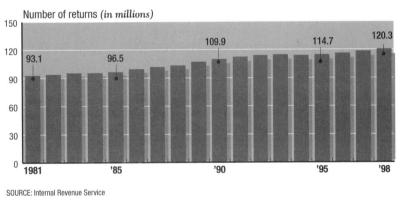

Number of returns *(in millions)*

93.1   96.5   109.9   114.7   120.3

1981   '85   '90   '95   '98

SOURCE: Internal Revenue Service

will do so by June 1.

The White House has already missed a deadline. Under the measure, Clinton had until Jan. 22 to submit to the Senate nominations for a nine-member IRS oversight board. He still has not done so, largely because the candidates are undergoing lengthy searches of their tax records, White House spokesman Barry Toiv said. He added that the deadline was "unrealistic."

Republicans recall that the administration, particularly Treasury Secretary Robert E. Rubin, was never pleased with the idea of an oversight board, even when Republicans modified it to

include the Treasury secretary, IRS commissioner and IRS employee union representative as permanent members. "Their heart's not in it," Mack said.

But Kerrey, who with Rep. Rob Portman, R-Ohio, chaired the restructuring commission that recommended many of the changes included in the overhaul bill, said the Long incident, in which Rossotti seemingly had little choice but to meet congressional demands, shows the need for such a board.

"It will provide some political cover that I think is very much needed," Kerrey said, adding that now Rossotti and other IRS officials must "sit politely while Congress kicks the bejesus out of them."

An oversight board could assure Congress that it had the situation under control, Duffy said. "Treasury and the IRS can say, 'Oh yeah. We're doing great,' but Congress has no way of knowing" now, he said.

But former commissioners and others who frequently deal with the IRS say that the board will just add another layer of bureaucracy and sap much of Rossotti's time.

Entrepreneurial Challenges

Over his Christmas break, Rossotti penned a 60-plus page report, dubbed "Rossotti's Book" by IRS workers, explaining the reasons for his proposed changes. The publication focuses largely on why the agency must reorganize, modernize technology and emphasize customer service.

When front-line employees cannot provide what taxpayers expect, Rossotti says, it is often because they do not have on-line access to a taxpayer's updated file (a fault of technology), and because in the absence of specialists, they must know the entire multivolume tax code (a fault of structure). They may still feel allegiance to the service's old focus on collecting taxes instead of providing customer service.

Rossotti has attempted to fix such problems before, though not on such a grand scale. Before becoming commissioner in November 1997, he founded and ran American Management Systems, a business and information technology consulting firm. It made him an expert in structuring a technology-dependent business.

Even so, he faces challenges in restructuring the IRS.

Geographically, the IRS is a system of 33 district offices and 10 service centers spread across the nation. Each center must administer the tax code to all taxpayers in its district. Four regional offices and the national headquarters oversee the districts.

Rossotti plans to replace that structure with a more specialized set of four operating divisions: wage and investment, covering about 88 million taxpayers filing returns; small business and self-employed, covering about 40 million filers; large and midsize business, covering 170,000 filers; and tax-exempt organizations, covering 1.9 million filers. The latter do not pay income taxes but do pay employment

Recent allegations that the IRS retaliated against Long, right, shown testifying before the Finance Committee in 1997, allowed lawmakers to renew their criticism of the agency.

taxes and withhold taxes from employee checks.

Richardson and Alexander are concerned about this new structure, in part because it would leave some cumbersome issues, such as international taxation, subject to more than one division. And they fear that taxpayers might begin lobbying those in charge of particular issues. But Rossotti said safeguards would be put in place.

Technology changes also may prove difficult. Each IRS district office has been somewhat autonomous, making some of its own purchasing decisions about computers. As a result, the IRS has 13 different e-mail systems, 74 computer operating systems and at least 13,000 vendor software products, Rossotti said.

Access to taxpayers' files, recorded on tape, is through a 1960s-era computer system, a setup that is operable only because longtime IRS employees know how to use it, Rossotti said. Updates to those records cannot be made directly, so employees are not updated on a taxpayer's status for up to a week to 16 days after a change is made. That has often confused taxpayers who thought they had fixed a problem but were sent new letters by employees who did not know the situation had been resolved.

The IRS has a contract with a consortium of private firms to find a new technology system — a challenge for one of the world's largest data processors.

Though Congress has appropriated funding to begin paying for a new system, many members are still troubled that the IRS spent $3 billion to update its computer system before Rossotti arrived. The update was widely judged a failure.

Members are not holding that against Rossotti. His background and straightforward demeanor make him a favorite on Capitol Hill.

At the recent Finance Committee hearing, Max Baucus, D-Mont., said, "I do have a sense that things are progressing, we're turning the corner. . . . Finally, there is a positive change."

Former commissioners, who were most often tax lawyers with some IRS background, did not often get such receptions. "Many have been able to develop good working relationships but were never able to really get past the fact that they were tax lawyers and their job was to go and collect taxes from all the voting Americans," said Gomez, the IRS commission counsel. Most of those commissioners stayed on the job for about three years, according to the IRS.

Rossotti has three and a half years left in his five-year term.

Even his sometime critics, such as former Commissioner Alexander, hope that he will continue to improve IRS relations on the Hill. "He's had the longest honeymoon anybody's ever had," Alexander said. "I hope he stays every minute." ◆

Politics and Public Policy

The term *public policy making* refers to action taken by the government to address issues on the public agenda; it also refers to the method by which a decision to act on policy is reached. The work of Congress, the president and the federal bureaucracy, and the judiciary is to make, implement, and rule on the policy decisions. Articles in this section discuss major policy issues that came before the federal government in 1999, many of which are likely to remain unresolved into 2000.

Social policy initiatives are always a cornerstone of the legislative agenda for both political parties. The first article in this section focuses on progress made since the Welfare Reform Act was passed in 1996 and discrepancies between the various state-run programs. The future of the Medicare system is examined, along with proposals to merge the two-part system, which would cut administrative costs. Other proposals to reform Medicare include raising premiums, increasing the role of private managed care in the system or raising payroll taxes.

Another medical issue examined is the allocation of organs for transplants. Under the current system, donated organs are given to recipients living within the community or state of the donor. A proposal by the Clinton administration would allocate organs to the sickest patients first, regardless of where the patient lived. Because donated organs are scarce, the organ transplant system is not only a matter of life and death, but a high-stakes grab for financial resources by the organ transplant centers and the states where the transplant surgeries are performed.

Financial services overhaul is another area of contention that is pitting pro-business Republicans against socially concerned Democrats. Congress is considering legislation that would remove restrictions on banks that would allow financial institutions to offer banking, insurance and brokerage services. The key sticking point is the Community Reinvestment Act, which requires banks to invest in the communities they serve. The law was passed to end the practice of red-lining — the refusal of banks to lend in communities that were economically depressed. Senator Phil Gramm, R-Texas, the chair of the Senate Banking and Financial Services Committee, is insisting that the requirements of Community Reinvestment Act are loosened and small, rural banks are exempted.

One of the final issues is the passage of a juvenile crime bill. In the wake of the massacre at Columbine High School in Littleton, Colorado in April 1999, the debate over gun control measures erupted in the Senate, and the flames were further fanned in the House. Under heavy public scrutiny, the Senate passed its version quickly, with Republicans giving ground to gun control provisions, including background checks at gun shows. In the House, however, pro-gun Republicans were not as conciliatory. The House version watered down many of the Senate-approved gun control measures, instead adding other amendments aimed at promoting cultural morality. The most notable difference was the provision for background checks at gun shows. The Senate version would require a background check for any show where more than 50 guns were being sold; the House bill required background checks only if there were more than ten vendors at the show. The differences will have to be worked out when the two bills move to conference committee.

As caseloads drop, politicians debate how to boost the earning power of the working poor

Pushing the Limits Of Welfare Overhaul

SALEM, Ore. — Despite a telltale crowd of anxious families milling about its waiting room, this warren of gray desks is no longer a welfare office. It has been transformed into a "self-sufficiency and opportunity"

STATE OF THE UNION
WELFARE

center with one overriding mission — to steer people toward jobs and away from government assistance. From the day individuals apply for welfare at this state social services agency, officials make it clear that most are expected to find a private sector paycheck instead.

Lecturing at a near-shout in one of the center's job training classrooms, case manager Dave Van Wormer warns his somber audience that they, not the government, bear the burden for improving their lot.

"Is unemployment hard?" he asks.

A dozen men and women nod their heads.

"Is it hard all the time?" he continues, providing his own, pointed answer: "Not on a Friday when the sun is shining and you want to go fishing. That's the problem."

The combination of "tough love" and a booming state economy have had an immense impact. Fully 85 percent of those who come into this north Salem office seeking monthly cash benefits never get on the rolls. Most are directed to jobs, though nearly all get some state or federal aid including child care, food stamps and Medicaid health care.

Oregon, which independent studies show has one of the nation's most effective systems for moving people into jobs, has cut its welfare caseload nearly 60 percent since 1994.

The progress has generated much satisfaction but has also sparked a debate about the next step. State officials argue that one of the keys to further reductions in welfare is for Washington to give them more authority. The state has asked the Clinton administration to let it impose work requirements under the federal food stamp program, which is currently an individual entitlement.

Advocates for the poor suggest that the focus on caseload has masked the hard fact that many moving off welfare into minimum wage jobs are still in poverty. They want Congress to provide more money and closely monitor states.

Welfare rolls across the country have fallen 44 percent from 1993 to September 1998. The drop has politicians crowing that wide-ranging state experiments and a landmark 1996 federal welfare law (PL 104-193) have brought about fundamental change. (*1996 Almanac, p. 6-3*)

"Here's some good news: In the past six years we have cut the welfare rolls nearly in half," President Clinton boasted in his Jan. 19 State of the Union address. (*1999 CQ Weekly, p. 201*)

The results are clearly better than predict-

Linda Hernandez, 23, a former welfare recipient, now works at the Oregon Health Plan in Salem.

ed when Clinton signed the law, which ended a six-decade entitlement to welfare and limited benefits to five years. They are so good, in fact, that it sometimes seems the biggest welfare controversy is over who should get credit.

Oklahoma Republican Gov. Frank Keating, in a Jan. 30 radio address, complained that GOP governors, not Clinton, deserved plaudits. "Welfare reform comes from the states, not Washington."

Beneath the applause can be heard some rumblings of unease and disagreement. While they are not proposing changes in the basic structure of the 1996 law, Clinton and many Democrats believe the government must do more not just to reduce caseloads, but to increase recipients' income.

In a sign the welfare issue may play in unexpected ways, former New Jersey Sen. Bill Bradley (1979-1997), seeking the 2000 Democratic presidential nomination, has criticized the Clinton administration for ending the entitlements.

To improve earnings, Clinton's fiscal 2000 budget proposes $1 billion to extend a welfare-to-work training program and focus on fathers who agree to pay child support. It would provide hundreds of millions in new funds for transportation and housing subsidies and tax credits to companies that hire welfare recipients. The White House wants to further restore health and cash benefits to legal immigrants cut off the rolls under the 1996 law and is also proposing to increase child care tax credits for low-income workers. *(1997 Almanac, p. 6-31; CQ budget coverage, p. 290)*

"The area where the administration believes additional investment is needed is child care for working families. Not so much for those leaving the rolls, but low-income struggling families holding on to jobs," said Olivia A. Golden, assistant secretary for children and families at the Department of Health and Human Services.

House Republicans, pulling together their own package of welfare changes, agree with some White House recommendations, but generally seek more flexibility for states and are mulling a change in the amount of money governors are required to put up to receive federal funds. Some, such as Ways and Means Committee Chairman Bill Archer, R-Texas, want to focus on programs that teach conservative values such as abstinence from premarital sex.

Others dismiss Clinton's call for additional money, complaining that states are sitting on billions in unspent funds. House Republicans in 1998 considered cutting welfare assistance.

"There are more than $7 billion in federal funds still available to states for welfare-to-work activities," said House Education and the Workforce Committee Chairman Bill Goodling, R-Pa.

The 1996 law gave states an annual $16.4 billion block grant and broad latitude to design their own programs. To move welfare mothers to work, it provided $13.9 billion in annual child care funds through fiscal 2002. Participants were required to work after two years. By fiscal 2002, 50 percent of recipients are to be in jobs. Nearly all participating states have met the work requirements for single-parent families.

The results to date are optimistic, but analysts caution against reading too much into the numbers. The extent to which the caseload decline is due to a soaring economy is still an open question. Experts also ask whether states have "diverted" needy recipients from welfare by making them endure long waiting periods or by simply giving them one-time cash payments.

"One of the things the [available data] is telling you is that half the people leaving welfare are leaving with earned income. It does make you wonder what's the situation of the others," said Sandra H. Venner, program director of family economic security at the Tufts University Center on Hunger, Poverty and Nutrition Policy.

Caseload reduction is beginning to slow as states get down to hard-to-place individuals.

Further, the welfare changes may have had side effects, such as discouraging people from applying for food stamps and Medicaid. Advocates for the poor and Agriculture Department officials are battling New York City Republican Mayor Rudolph W. Giuliani, charging the city has not complied with laws designed to quickly move poor people onto the food stamp rolls.

"The concern was that states, in their zeal to implement welfare reform, were actually preventing people from applying," said Phil Shanholtzer, spokesman for the Agriculture Department's Food and Nutrition Service.

Looking to States

Oregon has been experimenting with welfare for years. Through trial and error, the state has developed a system that moves individuals into full-time jobs that pay an average $7 per hour.

A May 1998 study by the Manpower Research Demonstration Corp., which analyzes social programs for the disadvantaged, found Portland's welfare-to-work program was among the best it had evaluated in terms of getting people to work at higher than minimum wages and keeping them there. Because the state passed its current welfare law in 1995, before the federal act took effect, it does not fall under the five-year time limit. Oregon imposes a maximum 45-day "assessment" period before recipients can receive monthly benefits, which average $503. Individuals can lose welfare in as little as five months if they do not cooperate.

It is unclear how much Oregon's welfare law has reduced poverty. Studies say that as much as 55 percent of the state's success can be attributed to the buoyant job market.

But it has clearly changed the system. The north Salem welfare office, on the outskirts of the capital city, combines the zeal of a revival tent with the experimentation of a start-up firm.

Caseworkers no longer simply check income data to determine whether applicants qualify for benefits. Describing themselves as employment counselors, they design "work strategies," have formed a team to develop new training programs and are marketing workers to nearby businesses.

Like a business focusing on its bottom line, there is constant attention to the caseload figures. Staffers worry that any unexpected surge in applications might increase the numbers.

Karen Frackowiak, north Salem operations manager at the Adult and Family Services branch, said that until recently the state concentrated on helping welfare recipients who seemed most likely to succeed, ignoring those who were difficult to place or who might end up as "drawer people," a name given to individuals whose cases might languish in the files for years.

"In the past we designed all these programs to fix people's barriers. We gradually learned the labor market could fix many of them," she said.

Now the office functions as a recruiting center for nearby companies, such as Telemark Inc., a telemarketing firm in Wilsonville, 35 miles away. The company, which has a high turnover, has even joined with other firms to provide free bus services.

One who moved from welfare to Telemark is Donna McKeever, 45, a mother of two who had a college degree but no recent work history. She has been with the firm more than a year and has been promoted.

"Welfare to me was a secure cushion," she said, explaining her initial reluctance to leave the system.

Along with the success stories come horror stories of people who say that instead of being flexible, Oregon's system is confusing and gives caseworkers too much autonomy.

Dennis and Rebecca Schaefer and their two children were temporarily camped in a hotel room in the Portland suburb of Beaverton in November after both lost their jobs and their home.

They moved five times in a month. Expecting the state to step in with aid, they instead found themselves lost in a bureaucracy, unsure what help was available or how to apply.

"The main thing we're concerned about now is getting our life back. This life is doing what people tell us to do so we can be together as a family," Dennis Schaefer said. They have since found an apartment, and Dennis Schaefer now works part-time at a grocery store.

Stories such as the Schaefers' give rise to skepticism about the success of welfare "reforms." Kathy Bethel, program director of the Snow-Cap Community Charities in east Portland, said aid requests doubled in the past year.

"We've just shifted it. We have people off food stamps, we have people back to work, but we're losing," Bethel said. "The overwhelming boost [is among] families that have left welfare and are going to work."

As the rolls decline, officials are focusing on treatment for drug and alcohol abuse — a problem affecting half of those in the system. About a third of those left on welfare are children living with relatives or parents who are disabled or unlikely to work.

"The next step for me is . . . what can we do to enable people who've moved into their first job, to get them a better job," said Gary K. Weeks, director of Oregon's Department of Human Resources.

An example of that push is Linda Hernandez, 23, a mother of four, who has moved from welfare to a job answering phone queries at the Oregon Health Plan, the state's Medicaid program. After state officials saw her and other welfare recipients struggle, they assigned a special caseworker to work in the office.

The intensive supervision has

Karen Frackowiak, north Salem operations manager at Oregon's Adult and Family Services, stands by boxes that hold the files of thousands of welfare cases that have been closed.

helped her advance in her job. Hernandez, however, is finding out what other former welfare recipients already know. As the income of a typical family of three increases above $8 an hour, it begins to lose eligibility for government subsidies. Even though wages increase, families may end up with less income.

Officials in Oregon and other states admit even the best programs are no guarantee that individuals who move off welfare will move out of poverty.

Some experts said the nation must discuss new steps for attacking poverty, but said the welfare law should not be expected to carry the burden.

"I don't think it's fair to expect welfare reform to end poverty," said William Waldman, executive director of the American Public Human Services Association, which represents state social service agencies. "But a lot of the evaluations that are being done are being based on that criteria." ◆

Judge Blocks Internet Smut Law, Reopening Child-Access Debate

With no federal protections in place, members may look with more urgency at other proposals, including McCain bill for classroom computers

A federal judge's preliminary injunction Feb. 1 blocking enforcement of the Child Online Protection Act (PL 105-277) spurred new debate on Capitol Hill over how to keep children away from pornography on the Internet.

U.S. District Judge Lowell A. Reed Jr. in Philadelphia extended a two-month temporary ban on enforcement of the 1998 law and expressed strong concern that it would violate the constitutional protection of free speech. (*1998 CQ Weekly, p. 3144*)

Reed expressed "personal regret" for the delay in enforcement caused by the preliminary injunction. But he said in a memorandum, "Perhaps we do the minors of this country harm if First Amendment protections, which they will with age inherit fully, are chipped away in the name of their protection."

Supporters of the law on Capitol Hill said they are disappointed with Reed's decision but remain confident that the law will survive legal review.

"It was a surprising decision in light of case law," said one Republican legislative aide. "Frankly, it was a slap in the face of Congress."

House Commerce Committee Chairman Thomas J. Bliley Jr., R-Va., and two other backers of the new law — Reps. Michael G. Oxley, R-Ohio, and James C. Greenwood, R-Pa. — issued a joint statement, expressing "steadfast support" for the law.

"We seek only to apply the same, common-sense standard to the World Wide Web as prevails in the rest of our free and democratic society," they said. "We look forward to a favorable judgment at the appellate level."

New Legislation

The preliminary injunction prompted discussion on Capitol Hill about what kind of legislation could prevent children from getting access to pornographic Internet sites.

Supporters of the Child Online Protection Act said it was too early to consider revisions to the law, but one Republican legislative aide confirmed that several ideas were being discussed in case it is declared unconstitutional.

The aide said one proposal would require installation of filtering software on any new computer sold to a buyer with children at home. In addition, the aide said, protection from foreign-based Web sites could be achieved with legislation encouraging international agreements on age-verification systems.

Several aides said Congress would probably accelerate consideration of a bill (S 97) by Sen. John McCain, R-Ariz., to require schools to install filtering software on classroom computers to block access to pornographic sites. Schools would need to install software to qualify for grants from a fund that distributes fees paid by long-distance telephone companies to schools to pay for telecommunications services. (*1998 CQ Weekly, p. 1610*)

"The court's decision has certainly increased the urgency of passing the McCain bill," said an aide to McCain. "The bill would at least put filtering software on school computers, until courts can decide" on the legality of the law.

Opposition

McCain's bill is likely to face opposition from some of the same free speech advocates that opposed the law, including the American Civil Liberties Union (ACLU).

While Congress considers the McCain bill, the Child Online Protection Act will face a possible full trial in Reed's court, and whatever the outcome, virtually certain appeals.

Reed's decision came after a weeklong trial pitting 17 plaintiffs, including the ACLU, against the Justice Department. A spokeswoman for the department said it was reviewing the decision and had no comment on it.

The plaintiffs argued that the law would violate the free speech rights of Web site operators and that it might restrict access to information on issues such as abortion and sexual orientation.

For supporters of the law, Reed's ruling represented a setback. The law was designed after a standard used in state laws that bars access by children to sexually explicit material that is "harmful to minors." Reed's written analysis of the law raised doubts about whether the "harmful to minors" standard, applied in the past to bookstores, could include the Internet.

Reed expressed doubt about the effectiveness of the law, noting that it does not cover foreign Web sites. And he said age-verification systems required under the law might drive away adult customers that do not want to furnish their age or name to gain access to pornography. The law set criminal penalties of six months in prison and $50,000 in fines for operators of commercial Web sites that fail to set up age-verification systems to keep children under the age of 17 away from material that is "harmful to minors."

Reed said there was "a substantial likelihood" that the plaintiffs will be able to show that the law imposes a burden on speech that is protected for adults.

Former Sen. Daniel R. Coats, R-Ind. (1989-99), a sponsor of the law, and three House members — Bliley, Oxley and Greenwood — defended the law in a legal brief filed Jan. 14. They argued that the court should adopt the "historical precedent and limitations recognized by Congress" and thus avoid the potential for "overbreadth or vagueness" in the new law.

Justice Department attorney Karen Stewart said in her closing argument Jan. 26 that the "Internet is not a private playground. It can be regulated."

The law replaced the Communications Decency Act, which was contained in the Telecommunications Act of 1996 (PL 104-104).

In 1997, the Supreme Court found that the ban on "indecent" material in that law was too broad. (*1997 Almanac, 5-25*) ◆

Calling community lending act too burdensome, Sen. Gramm seeks relief for small banks

The House That CRA Built: Redlining Law Revisited

Quick Contents

Supporters say the 1977 anti-redlining law known as the Community Reinvestment Act encourages banks to invest in communities they might otherwise overlook. But critics say the law is an unwarranted government intrusion into private business. The debate threatens to stall legislation to overhaul the financial services industry.

MARIN CITY, Calif. – The intersection of Terrace Drive and Drake Avenue in this small, serene neighborhood just north of San Francisco is a place where the arcane world of bank regulation takes root in reality.

Once ruled by menacing youths peddling cheap drugs, the corner today is the gateway to a bright cluster of new town houses. A few blocks away, the town houses give way to rows of new apartments nestled around a bustling retail center with well-lit stores that draw customers from miles around.

Just five years ago, this area was a field where the only notable events were weekend flea markets drawing bargain hunters who picked through goods of sometimes legally questionable origin, police say. Nondescript, high-rise public housing dotted the hills above the dusty valley.

This woeful enclave was in stark contrast to the rest of Marin, one of the wealthiest counties in the nation, a place with a median home price of $395,000. Police, residents and community activists agree that amid all the wealth and beauty of the Bay Area, Marin City was a depressing dust bowl with little to offer the people who lived there, much less outsiders. "You only went there if you were going to buy cocaine," said community activist Carol J. Galante.

A major reason that Terrace and Drake is no longer a forbidding place, according to Galante and others, is a banking law called the Community Reinvestment Act (CRA). It requires banks to document efforts to invest in all segments of the communities where they collect deposits. It might sound like a measure with rather limited consequences, but the law's supporters and opponents are arguing fiercely over its future, and the debate threatens to stall major legislation to overhaul the financial services industry.

The reinvestment law was enacted in 1977 to curtail "redlining," the systematic refusal of lenders to issue loans in deteriorating neighborhoods. It had a modest impact until the early 1990s, when the value of reinvestment commitments shot up from $2.4 billion in 1991 to $680 billion in 1998. This has been attributed to the increased sophistication of community housing groups and increasing pressure from federal regulators who started making their evaluations of bank performance public, among other factors. Supporters say the law does not force banks to make bad loans; rather, it encourages them not to overlook good ones. *(Chart, p. 96)*

But critics such as Republican Sen. Phil Gramm of Texas say the law is an unwarranted government intrusion into private business that creates a paperwork nightmare for banks — especially small banks — and that community groups have learned to abuse the law to "extort" grants and loans from banks. It is in a sense a classic, party-defining dispute between Republicans, who favor deregulation, and Democrats, who believe government policy can help spur economic rejuvenation.

Gramm and his supporters strongly believe that government should not be telling banks how to make loans. "This has become very big business," Gramm, chairman of the Banking, Housing and Urban Affairs Committee, said in an interview March 22. "The regulatory burden on these small banks is overwhelming." And Gramm has the constituents to back him up: Texas is home to about 840 state and nationally chartered banks, more than any other state in the nation.

The reinvestment law's future has been a key issue in legislative efforts to overhaul the nation's antiquated laws governing the financial services industry. Lawmakers and the affected industries generally agree that Congress should repeal Depression-era restrictions on the cross-ownership of banks, brokerages and insurance firms. Bills to do that (HR 10, Senate draft) have been approved by committees in both chambers. *(1999 CQ Weekly, pp. 611, 548)*

The legislation would dramatically change the industry by allowing the creation of financial conglomerates offering customers one-stop shopping for securities, insurance and banking services. But the House and Senate differ on the reinvestment law. The Senate bill would limit its reach, and the

Devaughn Ervin, 10, and Jaelyn Darden, 3, play March 29 in the courtyard of the Richmond City Center Apartments in Richmond, Calif. Community activists say this development, as well as the mixed-use development, below, in what was once a dust bowl in Marin City, Calif., was helped along by the 1977 Community Reinvestment Act. The Marin City renewal project includes town houses, apartments and a shopping center.

CQ PHOTOS BY SCOTT J. FERRELL

House bill would expand it slightly. The dispute over how the law is to work in the new financial world could sink the entire effort.

How the Law Works

The Community Reinvestment Act, signed by President Jimmy Carter in 1977, was part of a sweeping urban aid bill (PL 95-128) that included reinvestment language written by Sen. William Proxmire, D-Wis. (1957-89). A report by the Senate Banking Committee said the law was needed because of "amply documented cases of redlining in which local lenders export savings despite sound local lending opportunities." Views filed by five senators who opposed the measure said the law could create a "paperwork nightmare" that might not achieve the intended goal. (*1977 Almanac, p. 126*)

Then-Federal Reserve Board Chairman Arthur F. Burns opposed the measure, but the Fed has since changed positions. In testimony Feb. 11 before the House Banking and Financial Services Committee, current Fed Chairman Alan Greenspan said the law has worked well overall, although it has problems that need fixing. He did not offer specifics. "It's very significantly increased the amount of credit that's available in the communities, and if one looks at the detailed statistics, some of the changes have really been quite profound," Greenspan testified.

Under the law, bank regulators check for patterns of lending in low- and moderate-income neighborhoods where the banks do business. If they determine that a bank is passing up sound loan opportunities in relatively poor neighborhoods while collecting deposits from those areas, the result can be a poor rein-

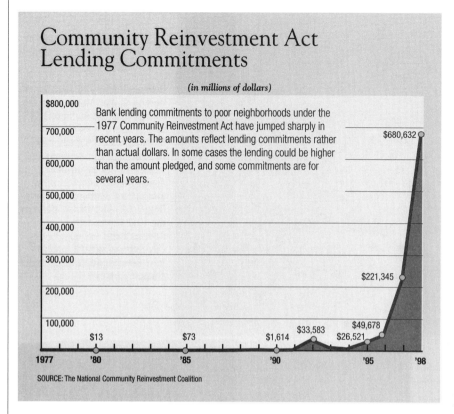

Community Reinvestment Act Lending Commitments

(in millions of dollars)

Bank lending commitments to poor neighborhoods under the 1977 Community Reinvestment Act have jumped sharply in recent years. The amounts reflect lending commitments rather than actual dollars. In some cases the lending could be higher than the amount pledged, and some commitments are for several years.

$800,000
700,000
600,000
500,000
400,000
300,000
200,000
100,000

$680,632
$221,345
$49,678
$33,583
$26,521
$1,614
$73
$13

1977 '80 '85 '90 '95 '98

SOURCE: The National Community Reinvestment Coalition

vestment rating. Banks tagged with an unsatisfactory community lending record face the threat of having applications for mergers or new branches denied — although such actions rarely occur. Besides bank loans, outright cash grants to community groups can help banks reach settlements in reinvestment disputes to help pave the way for the approval of merger or branch applications.

Community groups can play a key role in the rating process by praising banks for specific efforts or criticizing them for ignoring certain areas. Investing in places like Marin City is a way for banks to win favorable reinvestment ratings. Several large California banks have been restructured in the last decade through mergers and acquisitions, and both require good reinvestment ratings to win government approval. Marin City and dozens of other communities have benefited from banks looking for opportunities to establish good community lending records.

Large revitalization projects require architects, contractors, union laborers, real estate companies and other for-profit entities. As a result, some organizations that generally oppose government interference in private business support the reinvestment law. For example, the California Association of Realtors, which opposes a long list of state and federal proposals for land use

regulation, supports the CRA.

Community activist Galante is president and CEO of BRIDGE Housing Corp., a non-profit group that has helped coordinate many community development projects in the Bay Area and elsewhere in California by working with the public and private sectors. Galante said Union Bank was instrumental in the Marin City project, providing much of the lending needed for the retail center, apartments and town houses. Bank of America and World Savings and Loan Association also participated. With Marin City's reputation, it was a risky move for the banks, Galante said. "Many people said the shopping center will never work. People will never go to Marin City," she said. "People were scared of building in Marin City."

Galante said she believes the 1977 law had a lot to do with getting lenders to take a chance on Marin City. Perhaps not coincidentally, Union Bank's interest in Marin City came around the same time the bank was considering a merger. Construction on the Marin City project began in 1993. In 1995, Union Bank merged with the Bank of California to form Union Bank of California, one of the state's largest banks, now with more than 240 offices statewide. "They definitely got some CRA credit, and they definitely should have," Galante said.

Union Bank Vice President Henry Tiedemann said the housing in Marin City sold faster than projected and the bank's loans for retail and commercial development were a success. "It went very well," he said. "We were paid as agreed and it went very smoothly."

Galante's predecessor at BRIDGE Housing was I. Donald Terner, who died in the 1996 plane crash that killed Commerce Secretary Ronald H. Brown. Terner helped BRIDGE establish strong ties with California banks, especially Wells Fargo & Co., which helped finance a development in a troubled neighborhood in Richmond, Calif., among other projects. When Wells Fargo sought to acquire First Interstate Bank, Terner testified in favor, Galante said. The merger went through in 1996. (*1999 CQ Weekly, p. 943*)

Community Groups Converge

In the past two decades, a nationwide network of hundreds of community housing groups have honed their expertise in making use of the 1977 law. National People's Action, a coalition that takes credit for working with Proxmire's staff to create the law, says its membership now includes more than 300 community groups nationwide. Coalition spokeswoman Cris Pope said the law has provided a common theme and a rallying point for community groups from around the country with diverse memberships. On April 11, the group hauled bus loads of protesters to Gramm's home in Washington to protest his efforts to scale back the CRA. (*Gramm, p. 100*)

Another prominent umbrella group, the National Community Reinvestment Coalition, says its membership includes more than 650 dues-paying, non-profit organizations. The coalition tracks CRA-related investments across the nation. Since its enactment, the law has spurred more than $1 trillion in community investment commitments, most of it within the last seven years, according to the coalition.

The coalition says the surge has occurred because community groups are becoming more sophisticated in developing partnerships with banks, and because of structural changes in the banking industry. As more banks have grown into large regional and national operations, they have struck correspondingly larger multistate reinvestment agreements with community groups.

Another reason is that federal regulators, facing increased public pressure from community groups and some legislators, started taking the law more seriously in the last decade, said John E. Taylor, president and CEO of the reinvestment coalition. Regulators also started making their reinvestment evaluations public, Taylor said.

A key function of the CRA is to make sure that banks continue performing their traditional community lending role, said Rep. Bruce F. Vento, D-Minn., a Banking Committee member. "I think it has led financial institutions in a sense back to where their roots are, and doing the job that needs to be done in terms of extending credit," he said at a hearing Feb. 11.

Gramm Takes Aim

The law has come under heavy fire in recent months from Republicans who want to scale it back or even eliminate it. They see it as a heavy regulatory burden, particularly for smaller banks, as well as an intrusive, ham-handed government effort at social engineering.

Gramm goes even further, saying the law is a lever used by community groups to pry money from banks. Gramm said he will hold hearings this year that will highlight instances in which the CRA has been abused. Gramm has emerged as the law's most prominent and relentless critic. Last year he was instrumental in sinking financial services overhaul legislation over reinvestment issues. (*1998 CQ Weekly, p. 2733*)

The Senate Banking Committee approved an unnumbered financial services overhaul bill March 4, but the 11-9 vote broke down cleanly along party lines, in large part because of the bill's provisions on reinvestment.

Gramm's bill generally seeks to ease compliance for banks in two ways.

First, it would make it harder for community groups to challenge a branch opening or bank merger if the bank had a satisfactory reinvestment rating for three years in a row. To mount a successful challenge, the community group would have to provide substantial, verifiable information showing that the bank was not complying with the law. Current law contains no such pre-emptive standard for a re-examination and challenge of a bank's past reinvestment record.

Gramm said he has heard of "no serious challenge" to this provision. However, community groups have said

it is fair to re-examine and raise questions about a bank's past lending practices when plans for a merger or expansion are announced, and they object to making it more difficult to challenge a bank's prior reinvestment ratings.

Small Banks, Big Impact?

The second, more controversial

Galante, right, shown March 29 with Tricia Davis, manager of the Richmond City Center Apartments, helps coordinate community development projects throughout the Bay Area.

change that would be made in Gramm's bill would exempt rural banks with $100 million or less in assets from reinvestment requirements. Gramm said this would have little impact on lending patterns, because most of the affected banks are in such small communities that they take advantage of every lending opportunity or face going out of business.

"A bank with seven or eight employees having to designate a CRA [compliance] officer is just crazy," Gramm said. The provision would not exempt large, big-city banks that do most of the lending in poor, urban areas.

Only one committee Democrat, Tim Johnson of South Dakota, supported the amendment to create the exemption for rural banks. He issued a statement explaining that he supported the reinvestment act generally, but he also favored a narrow exemption for small, rural banks. Johnson joined his Democratic colleagues on the committee in voting against the overall bill.

Gramm said he has met many times

with Senate Democrats, including the committee's ranking member, Paul S. Sarbanes of Maryland, but he has been unable to sway votes among Democrats, whose major objection is to the reinvestment provisions. "I hope we can reach a consensus and have a bipartisan bill," Gramm said. "But I'm beginning to work to line up my 51 votes" for the floor.

Gramm's bill has drawn an unequivocal veto threat from President Clinton. "The bill would undermine the effectiveness of the Community Reinvestment Act, a law that has helped to build homes, create jobs and restore hope in communities across America," Clinton wrote in a March 2 letter to Gramm. The letter cited additional objections to the bill and concluded, "I will veto the bill if it is presented to me in its current form."

Gramm says he is surprised at the level of opposition to what he considers relatively small, common-sense changes to the 1977 law. Community groups strongly disagree that the proposals are minor adjustments. Gramm's proposal to exempt rural banks with $100 million in assets or less would apply to 40 percent of lenders nationwide and 72 percent of rural lenders, according to the reinvestment coalition.

Even if bank loan redlining is less of an issue in small rural communities than in cities, country banks can still shortchange their communities by us-

A Modest Renaissance
For Two Faded Boom Towns

In many ways, Richmond and Marin City are classic examples of what happened to blue-collar communities across the country when fundamental economic changes rattled the job market: painful job losses and income uncertainty followed by a struggle to find new ways to fit into the world.

In these two San Francisco-area communities, the economic upheavals were particularly jarring. During World War II, Richmond and Marin City became booming centers for shipbuilding. Workers arrived by the hundreds from the South to fill a burst of newly available jobs. Residents helped build hundreds of cargo ships for the war effort, but when the war ended the job market crashed as quickly as it had sprouted.

Richmond never quite recovered from this employment jolt, said Police Chief Edward R. Duncan. The city has only 93,000 residents, but there is a large swath of poverty and decay normally associated with much larger cities. Poor economic condi-

tions combined with a rising drug problem drove the number of homicides to a peak of 62 in 1991 — more than six times the 1991 national rate of 9.5 homicides per 100,000 people. The worst place in the city was an area known as the Iron Triangle, so-called because it is surrounded by railroad tracks. It accounted for up to 80 percent of the murders, Duncan said.

Marin City, a smaller enclave surrounded by some of the most expensive homes in the country, did not have the extreme violence of Richmond but did suffer from concentrated poverty and drug abuse. During the war, Marin City was a bustling enclave with hastily erected housing intended for the influx of shipbuilders.

After the war, many workers wandered away in search of work, and the wartime housing came down. In the hills overlooking the site of the wartime city, public housing went up to help shelter those who stayed, and these projects remain in use today as

a reminder that Marin City has a way to go.

In the 1980s, BRIDGE Housing Corp., a nonprofit community group based in San Francisco, began working on deals to sprout multi-use projects in Marin City and the Iron Triangle of Richmond.

The results in both cases — a $75 million development in Marin City and $20 million in Richmond — were complex business deals involving several private and public entities to create a mix of dense residential and retail development. The housing is a blend of market-rate and subsidized units, and it involved California banks that needed favorable community reinvestment reviews to get pending mergers approved. Banks are subject to reviews under the Community Reinvestment Act (CRA), a 1977 anti-redlining measure (PL 95-128). BRIDGE officials say the reinvestment act was a crucial factor in forcing banks to take a hard look at development opportunities in such troubled neighborhoods.

ing deposits to purchase securities rather than make local loans, community activists say.

On a more fundamental level, community groups are concerned that Gramm's proposals would mark the first step in a long march to undo the 1977 law. Gramm offers them little comfort in that regard. He said his proposals would not significantly undermine requirements, but he is noncommittal on whether he believes the law should eventually be eliminated. "Should the federal government, using capital controls, reallocate capital in a private market based on political judgment rather than based on economic judgment?" Gramm asked. "That's a question to ask another day."

For now, Gramm said he is trying to "bring some integrity to the process and deal with what are clearly defined abuses." In particular, he is concerned with what he calls "cash payments" to

community groups. Such payments are sometimes expected in exchange for a community group's silence or support when a bank needs a good reinvestment review, Gramm said.

"Ask these community groups if they take cash payments, and would they oppose banning cash payments," Gramm said. "Any bank that is getting ready to go through a CRA evaluation knows that it needs to build support among various community groups for its application, and so the question is, what role do cash payments play in a process where the objective in law is to promote loans?"

Galante said bank grants to community groups are no different from any other corporate gifts to local causes, and there is nothing sinister or inappropriate about them. BRIDGE Housing received grants of $125,000 from Wells Fargo this year and $100,000 in 1997, and Union Bank recently made a two-

year, $70,000 pledge to BRIDGE. "CRA or no CRA, I don't see it as extortion," Galante said.

House, Senate Differences

House Banking Chairman Jim Leach, R-Iowa, took a more conciliatory approach to financial services overhaul legislation than Gramm. The result was a bipartisan bill (HR 10) approved by the committee, 51-8, on March 11. A Federal Reserve analysis says HR 10 would expand the reinvestment act in three ways:

● It would apply reinvestment requirements for the first time to institutions that are not federally insured. HR 10 would allow the creation of "wholesale financial institutions," a new type of uninsured bank that cannot receive initial deposits of less than $100,000.

● It would make bank expansion into non-banking activities subject to satisfactory reinvestment reviews. Current-

Construction worker Leevester Hall, 43, stands March 30 in front of mixed-use development in Marin City, Calif., where he rents an apartment.

where Richmond lies, the median home price is $192,500, according to the California Association of Realtors. Marin County has a median home price of $395,000, one of the highest in the state.

The Realtors association, which supports the reinvestment law, agrees that the law encourages banks to spread their lending around to all segments of the community, said Marcia Salkin, a lobbyist and director of public policy for the association. "Affordability here has always been a concern," Salkin said. "We've seen CRA as a tool to make sure that money that comes out of that community goes back into those communities."

Leevester Hall, a construction worker who helped rebuild Marin City and has lived in the area all his life, said the development has given people pride and the retail center is providing jobs.

From a hillside overlooking Marin City, Hall pointed to the neighborhood where he rents one of the new subsidized apartments and said he would like to buy a town house when one becomes available. "I saw this place really change," Hall said. "It's one of the best things that happened . . . . I'm really proud of it."

Few would call the resulting developments paradise. Today's urban planners might turn up their noses at the retail centers' strip mall banality and at the simplistic homogeneity of the residential designs. But crime is down in both areas because of improved economic conditions and community-oriented law enforcement, police say. Duncan said the number of murders in Richmond dropped to 18 in 1998, the lowest in 19 years. Both developments include on-site police substations. The banks have gotten solid returns on their investments, according to BRIDGE officials, and there is a waiting list for the housing.

Affordable housing is of particular concern in the Bay Area, where housing prices in even the most modest neighborhoods can be eyepopping. In Contra Costa County,

ly, a bank's attempts to expand into non-banking activities are not subject to such reviews. Banks have crept into limited non-banking activities because of a series of regulatory and court decisions, and HR 10 would facilitate that trend on a broader scale.

● It would allow bank regulators to impose civil or criminal penalties on banks that have poor reinvestment ratings and fail to take corrective action. Current law provides only for denial of a merger or expansion application.

Gramm, who has criticized HR 10 as an unwieldy mass of compromises, said these measures are unacceptable. "The untold story here is that the House bill, just like the bill last year, would vastly expand CRA," Gramm said.

Whatever the difficulties for banks in dealing with the law, compliance rates have generally been high. A researcher for the reinvestment coalition said he knew of no merger or branch

application in recent years that was denied because of poor reinvestment performance. Often, a bank with a questionable record can get an application approved by working out agreements with federal regulators and community leaders to do better in the future.

The banking industry has been low-key about Gramm's efforts. Banks have the most to gain from relaxed reinvestment requirements, and big banks in particular also have much to gain from financial services legislation. They are reluctant to join a push for reinvestment rollbacks that could scuttle progress on the overall bills.

The Independent Community Bankers of America, which represents small banks, is opposed to the House bill because of an issue related to unitary thrifts, and its March 15 statement of opposition makes no mention of the reinvestment provisions.

The American Bankers Association

also has kept the issue at arm's length. If Gramm wants to make reinvestment changes a part of the financial services legislation, "that's his business," said association lobbyist Edward L. Yingling. "We would not tell Sen. Gramm to drop his concerns."

So what is driving Gramm to push so hard for reinvestment changes in the face of veto threats?

Yingling said he believes the disagreement over reinvestment is a matter of strong philosophical beliefs on both sides about the proper role of government. Gramm and his supporters strongly believe government should not be telling banks how to make loans, while Democrats want government to play an active role in making sure that credit is allocated fairly.

Besides philosophical concerns, Gramm has home-state constituents to push reinvestment changes as well. As many as 200 of the state's banks would

Where Gramm Draws the Line

What makes Phil Gramm fight the Community Reinvestment Act?

Gramm sounded eager a few months ago to prove he could get things done as the new chairman of the Senate Banking, Housing and Urban Affairs Committee. But Gramm, R-Texas, now appears willing to sink the biggest bill on the committee's agenda in a clash over an anti-redlining measure.

Banks, brokerages and insurance companies are pushing for financial services legislation (HR 10, Senate draft) that would establish a clearer set of rules for the cross-industry consolidation that is already under way.

Yet Congress finds itself hung up — again — on the 1977 Community Reinvestment Act (PL 95-128), which requires banks to document efforts to invest in all segments of the communities in which they collect deposits. Last year the Senate failed to take a final vote on a House-passed overhaul measure in large part because of Gramm's protests against the bill's reinvestment provisions. Gramm wants to loosen the requirements, especially on small banks. *(1998 CQ Weekly, p. 3099)*

This year Gramm has said he is willing to deal on the issue, but he also has said that he can live without a financial services overhaul if enactment requires too many compromises on key issues. Gramm has staked out positions on the reinvestment act that would draw a presidential veto on the underlying bill and that so far have helped prevent even a whiff of bipartisanship from emerging in the Senate. The banking industry, which is eager for financial services legislation, has remained relatively quiet

Gramm wants to loosen reinvestment requirements, especially on small banks.

CQ PHOTO / DOUGLAS GRAHAM

on the 1977 law. So have most of Gramm's GOP Senate colleagues.

Observers say Gramm's passionate stand on the reinvestment issue is a logical component of his free-market conservatism. Government-forced credit allocation is anathema to conservatives such as Gramm, said John Heasley, general counsel and lobbyist for the Texas Bankers Association. American Bankers Association lobbyist Edward L. Yingling agreed, and said relatively little pressure was coming from interest groups or constituents.

Nevertheless, Gramm has plenty of home-state motivation to push for changes. Texas is home to about 840 state and nationally chartered banks, more than any other state in the nation and about 10 percent of the nation's total, Heasley said. Under Gramm's bill, about 150 to 200 of the state's banks would qualify for exemption from reinvestment require-

ments because they are rural banks with less than $100 million in assets.

Gramm has used the words "bribery" and "extortion" to describe how he believes some community housing groups abuse the law. When it comes to examples, Gramm and his staff generally have held their fire, saying they want to wait until the Banking Committee holds as-yet-unscheduled hearings this year.

But in committee hearings earlier this year, Gramm spoke of a case involving a small Southern bank company that invested heavily in efforts to reach out to a growing Spanish-speaking population. For example, Gramm said, the bank employed bilingual tellers and provided a free wiring service for bank customers to send money to Mexico. Gramm said bank regulators told the bank "they were doing the right things, but doing it the wrong way," and the only way to get a good reinvestment rating was to give money directly to community groups.

Gramm said the hearings will provide evidence that the law needs to be modified. "I find that in debating community groups, they don't take on these issues head on," Gramm said. "It's basically that if you're willing to stop any abuse, any one abuse, that you're against the CRA."

Community groups have few warm feelings for Gramm. On April 11, the National People's Action coalition, in Washington for its annual conference, sent 15 bus loads of members to Gramm's home to protest his efforts to scale back the reinvestment act. Gramm called police, and the crowd broke up with no arrests, leaving Gramm's lawn littered with fliers.

qualify for Gramm's $100 million rural bank reinvestment exemption.

Gramm insists he is ready to push ahead on his overhaul bill, despite the veto threat and lack of progress in lining up the handful of Democratic votes needed to overcome Senate procedural roadblocks. Majority Leader Trent Lott, R-Miss., has pledged floor time for the bill, tentatively set for May.

In the House, the Commerce Committee has joint jurisdiction with Banking on HR 10. A Republican Commerce staff member said hearings have been set for April 28 and May 5 but no markup has been scheduled yet.

Meanwhile, the people of Marin City move about their daily lives largely oblivious to the debate that rages in Washington. Marin County Sheriff's

Sergeant Dan Gallagher, on duty at a police substation in the shopping center on a recent spring day, sounded like the lonely appliance repairman who wishes he had a little more to do. Gallagher said things have changed remarkably in Marin City in just a few years. Drug dealing has dropped off, he said, and his most serious calls lately have been about shoplifting and broken store windows. ◆

Question of whether to give priority to the sickest patients may be decided by Congress

Can Congress Cure Disparities In Organ Transplant System?

As Robert M. Hoffmann works quickly but methodically, doctors and nurses gather around the end of the operating table to glimpse a procedure few ever get a chance to watch. Some perch on stools to get a better view of Hoffmann preparing the pancreas for removal. Like a skilled tailor, he detaches each vessel from the intestine so the pancreas can be easily removed.

Hoffmann, who directs a group that will remove the pancreas and kidneys, finishes his prep work, then a second team of surgeons takes over. They first remove the still-beating heart and then the lungs, which have been inflated with air, and place them immediately into a special solution to preserve them for transplantation. Hoffmann then lifts the pancreas and kidneys from the donor, a 40-year-old man who collapsed at work and could not be revived.

The organs, wrapped in sterile bags, are packed into picnic coolers and surrounded with ice bags for the 100-mile flight back to the University of Wisconsin Hospital and Clinics in Madison, Wis., where Hoffmann is procurement director. Within 24 hours, doctors at the center will transplant these organs into patients whose lives depend on them.

While procuring the organs is both physically and emotionally demanding — in this case, it involved flying in a six-passenger propeller plane to a small town in northern Wisconsin, then several hours of operating — having an organ transplanted into one of the center's patients is, in the words of one Madison surgeon, "our bread and butter." Center officials say that reward keeps them motivated and is integral to their success. Local pride in the institution, they say, also encourages residents in the region to donate their family members' organs and contributes to the center's success in achieving the third-highest donation rate in the nation.

The Clinton administration and critics of the nation's organ allocation system do not see it that way. Arguing that there are wide disparities in waiting times for organs across the country, the Department of Health and

Human Services (HHS) last year proposed that the nation move to a new policy of allocating organs on the basis of medical criteria, rather than geography. The changes would mean that organs harvested by Hoffmann would go to the sickest patients first, no matter where they lived, replacing the current system in which organs are allocated first to people on each transplant center's waiting list, then regionally and then nationally. (*1998 CQ Weekly, p. 1691*)

The administration's proposal sparked an intense and high-stakes national debate over the best way to allocate the already short supply of organs to Americans who most need them for transplantation. Ultimately, the fight will probably land in the hands of Congress, putting lawmakers in the position of having to make sensitive medical ethics policy on an issue that is infused with regional political biases and complicated by highly technical scientific issues.

Already, members of Congress representing areas with regional transplant centers have lined up against those from states with larger centers that stand to gain from a system of national allocation. As regional centers have grown in popularity, they have taken patients — and revenue — from the larger centers.

Congress in the fiscal 1999 omnibus spending law (PL 105-277) delayed the new regulations until October and asked the Institute of Medicine, a division of the National Academy of Sciences, to study whether there are inequities in the current system. The results, which were expected to be completed May 1, may not be ready until the fall. (*1998 CQ Weekly, p. 2822*)

Disparities in Waiting Times

In announcing the administration's policy last year, HHS Secretary Donna E. Shalala, who was chancellor of the University of Wisconsin-Madison before being appointed to the Clinton Cabinet, argued that under the current system, patients in some areas are dying because they must wait five times as long for a liver as patients who live elsewhere. Critics say the current system has had the perverse effect of forcing sick people to uproot their already disrupted lives and travel to centers where the wait may be shorter.

"We believe that medical necessity, not geography, should be the No. 1 criterion for who receives organs for transplantation," Shalala said at a joint House-Senate committee hearing on the issue last June. "And we believe that most Americans would be shocked to find out that under our current system, if they or a loved one needs a transplant, they could lose out to a less sick patient just across the state line."

Currently, people who need an organ choose a transplant center or centers where they want to have the operation. People may list themselves at the center closest to their home, opt for another center in another state, or join waiting lists at several centers to boost the chances they will receive an organ. Critics say the current system, therefore, favors wealthy people who can afford to travel to another region and stay there for recuperation and follow-up care.

The current system stems from a 1984 law, the Organ Procurement and Transplantation Act (PL 98-507), which gives HHS jurisdiction over the national organ allocation program. The department pays for half the transplants performed each year through the federal Medicare and Medicaid programs, which provide medical care to the nation's elderly, disabled and poor. *(1984 Almanac, p. 476)*

Congress enacted the law because there were no national standards covering transplant centers and organs often went to the highest bidder. The law prohibited the buying and selling of organs and called for a creation of a system to distribute them fairly.

In 1987, the United Network for Organ Sharing, the Richmond, Va.-based private contractor that runs the organ allocation program for HHS, established the current system in which the country is divided into 11 regions.

The HHS regulation proposed last year would direct the network to

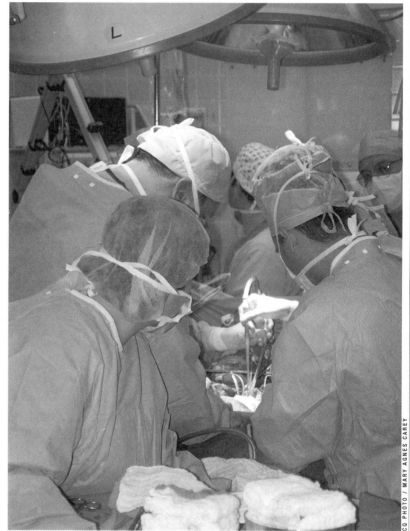

A team led by Hoffmann, left, removes the organs of a donor. The heart and lungs are taken first, then flown to Madison for transplantation within 24 hours.

develop a policy that relies on medical criteria, rather than geography, to determine how organs are distributed for transplant. It calls for those criteria to be standardized and for medical urgency to be the main criterion.

Officials of smaller and midsize regional centers such as Wisconsin's say that dismantling the current system would undermine their success and instead benefit a handful of larger, more nationally known programs, such as

those at the University of Pittsburgh Medical Center and Mount Sinai NYU Medical Center in New York.

The organ network opposes the plan, saying the regulations give them no choice but to turn the current system into one where the sickest patients — who, they say, are not always the best recipients — will have priority for organs over others who stand a better chance of survival.

Underlying the debate is a chronic

shortage of donated organs. Currently, 61,000 people are on waiting lists for kidneys, hearts, livers and other organs, and about 4,300 patients die each year waiting. Both sides agree that increased organ donation would help alleviate the shortage, but the number of donors has remained steady for the past several years, at about 5,500 annually.

The recent announcement by former Chicago Bears running back Walter Payton that he needs a liver transplant has brought renewed attention to the organ shortage. Payton, who is suffering from a rare liver disease called primary sclerosing cholangitis, will die unless he gets a liver transplant. Officials at the Mayo Clinic in Rochester, Minn., where Payton would receive his transplant, have said he will not get preferential treatment over other patients. Payton will join a list of thousands of people who are waiting for a liver.

Payton lives in Barrington, Ill., a suburb of Chicago. According to his spokeswoman, Susan Ward, he selected the Mayo Clinic on the recommendation of a friend who received a transplant there. Payton has decided not to list with other centers because he is pleased with the care he is receiving at Mayo.

An Emotional Experience

From the point at which organs become available until the transplant operation on the recipient, the process is an intense experience. Once a donor becomes available, specially trained hospital personnel must begin the delicate process of talking to grief-stricken families about donating their loved ones' organs. Even when donors have indicated their willingness to contribute their organs for transplantation, family members must approve of the procedure.

In the Wisconsin case, a Congressional Quarterly reporter was allowed to accompany Hoffmann and his team to a town in northern Wisconsin — officials requested that it not be identified because of the strict anonymity surrounding organ donation — to observe the organ procurement.

A little more than three hours after hearing that a donor had become available, Hoffmann and his team arrive at the hospital and wait for anesthesiologists who will watch the donor's heart rate and other indicators to ensure the organs remain viable.

A cautery is used to burn through the skin on the donor's chest, a procedure that avoids excessive bleeding but

Shalala, above, testifying last year before a joint House-Senate committee examining the transplant issue, said that the new regulations will bring much-needed equity to the system of organ allocation. Wisconsin's D'Alessandro, left, argues that the medical community, not politicians, should make the call.

creates a pungent odor in the operating room. Next, a surgical saw slices through the breastbone to expose the heart and lungs, which will be removed first. The kidney and pancreas are removed last. In this case, the donor's liver was damaged by cirrhosis and cannot be used. But the man's tissues and eyes will help dozens of other patients.

As Hoffmann works on the donor, the university's heart and lung surgeons look at X-rays of the donor's heart and lungs to check for tumors or excess fluid.

Less than four hours after the operation begins, the heart and lung recovery team is on a flight back to Madison. Meanwhile, Hoffmann stays behind because a second donor, a 59-year-old man,

has died of a heart attack, and his family has approved donation of his liver and kidneys, if they are deemed acceptable. Hoffmann and his team are exhausted, but they quickly board another plane to reach the donor, who is 30 miles away.

Dr. Hans W. Sollinger, chief of transplant surgery for the Madison program, said such enthusiasm for flying out at a moment's notice to procure organs from a donor — the most physically and mentally demanding part of a transplant surgeon's job — will diminish if the team knows that the hearts, lungs and livers will be given to patients across the country instead of those in their own facilities.

"We come home triumphantly with

our liver, our heart, and you see our patients feeling better. . . . That incentive would go down. We're only human," he said.

Critics of the current system say that fear is unjustified.

"I think that is the most self-serving, bogus argument I've ever heard," said Dr. Charles M. Miller, director of the Recanati/Miller Transplantation Institute at Mount Sinai.

In fact, Miller argues, once a national sharing system is in place, transplant centers such as Madison's will receive as many organs — if not more — than they procure for other programs.

Claude Earl Fox, administrator of the Health Resources and Services Administration, the HHS division that handles organ allocation, said fears that a national system would unfairly redistribute organs between centers are unfounded.

Opponents of the regulations point to an article published last October in the New England Journal of Medicine in which Dr. Peter A. Ubel of the Philadelphia Veterans Affairs Medical Center and Arthur L. Caplan of the University of Pennsylvania Center for Bioethics wrote that allowing the organ allocation system to be based on geography is "ethically indefensible."

Ubel and Caplan said studies of donors' motivation show no evidence that donors or their families ask whether organs will be distributed locally or nationally.

"There is no longer a medical justification for giving priority to candidates who live close to the donor," they wrote.

Miller of Mount Sinai said a fairer allocation system would stimulate organ donation because people would be more inclined to donate if they knew organs were distributed fairly across the country.

Ubel and Caplan said the current policy is rooted in the early days of transplant technology, when surgeons were urged to take organs out of donors and get them into recipients as quickly as possible. But preservation techniques now allow livers to be stored for up to 20 hours without serious damage, permitting safe transport across the country, they said.

Those who prefer the current system argue that switching from a local to a national system means that more people will die. Transporting organs vast distances across the country will drive up costs and cause organs to travel farther, making them less likely to be suit-

able for a transplant.

Dr. Michael E. DeBakey, renowned heart surgeon and chancellor emeritus at Baylor College of Medicine in Houston and director of the DeBakey Heart Center, wrote in an opinion piece in The Washington Post last month that the proposed policy would result in more deaths.

"There is . . . a vital medical reason why the very sickest patients should not always be first in line. Some patients are so sick that their bodies would reject a transplant, and they would require a second or even a third transplant to survive," he wrote. "This would reduce the number of organs available to other patients and, over time, cause hundreds more to die."

Wisconsin's Hoffmann, a procurement transplant coordinator who is certified with the Board of Transplant Coordinators, agreed.

"Everybody knows if you're not critical, the chances of you doing well with a liver transplant are much better," said Hoffmann, who has been procuring organs for transplant since 1964. "Why do patients have to become critically ill and practically dead to get a transplant? That's mind-boggling."

But Miller, Fox and others have said that changing the current system does not mean that the sickest patients will always get the available organ; the change is designed to get the organ to the neediest patient who has the best chance of survival. Supporters of a new system also say it will not drive up transportation costs because most of the broader sharing will be done regionally, with likely candidates being in nearby states rather than across the country.

Examining Allocation Criteria

The strongest argument in favor of changing the system is that there are wide disparities in waiting times. According to a study released last month by HHS, patients who need organ transplants wait nearly two years in some parts of the country but less than two months in others. The study, produced by the organ sharing network, was based on data from 1993 to 1996.

Dr. William W. Pfaff, president of the organ sharing network, said the transplant community has already made changes to the allocation network to accommodate the sickest patients, and it will make additional improvements as needed.

For example, when a kidney be-

comes available anywhere in the country, it is given to the patient whose tissues and antigens constitute a perfect genetic match. Last year, the group also established regulations requiring centers to use the same medical criteria when adding their patients to waiting lists for liver and heart transplants as part of an effort to help equalize waiting times around the country.

"We've always continued to mature and change," Pfaff said.

At Wisconsin, Dr. Anthony M. D'Alessandro, associate professor of surgery at the university's medical school, said waiting times are not the best criteria for judging inequities in the current system because there are vast discrepancies in how centers add patients to their waiting lists and how the seriousness of their medical conditions are determined.

John Fung, director of transplantation surgery at the University of Pittsburgh Medical Center, disagreed that there are wide discrepancies in listing criteria, but said such concerns would be resolved within a new national system.

HHS officials say they want the system to be fairer and not necessarily one that mandates the sickest patients always receive organs first.

"We want a system where the organ goes to the patient, not one where patients go to the organs," Fox said. While the proposed policy must place medical urgency as a key factor in deciding which patients receive organs, HHS does not want organs to be wasted, he said.

Shalala declined to be interviewed. At Wisconsin, university officials say they understand that she must represent the administration's position, but they are surprised their former chancellor is such an adamant supporter of the proposed change.

"I wonder in her heart of hearts what she's thinking when she's brushing her teeth," said Susan Pearsall, a Madison resident whose husband received a liver transplant.

Patient's Perspective

Pearsall's husband, David McCarthy, 62, received a transplant two and a half years ago and now publishes a newsletter, called The Borrowers, for organ recipients. The college professor believes the proposed change will hurt the transplant system because sending organs across the country will weaken them, making them less likely to be used in a transplant. He also believes that success rates for transplants will be lower.

McCarthy knew he was ill when he began to accumulate fluid in his abdominal region. A more ominous sign came in the summer of 1993, when McCarthy could not control his bowel. He went to his doctor for a physical and was told "quit complaining; you're getting old," McCarthy said.

By that October, a specialist diagnosed him with hepatitis C, which McCarthy believes he contracted in a 1957 blood transfusion he received when he injured his spleen while playing football in college. Over time, the condition weakened his liver to the point where it was failing and he needed a transplant.

McCarthy's condition was treated with medication at first, but as his liver weakened, he joined a waiting list at the Madison transplant facility. His second chance at life came on Aug. 10, 1996, when a liver became available from a 43-year-old. At first, his wife did not know what to think as she watched McCarthy in the recovery room. Pearsall thought her husband had a fever, then realized his complexion was returning to its natural color after years of looking pale.

Political Positioning

In Wisconsin, Republican Gov. Tommy G. Thompson led the drive last year in the state legislature to pass a law mandating that Wisconsin residents get priority for organs procured in that state.

If a national allocation policy is implemented, "I know we as a state will not be as aggressive" in procuring organs, Thompson said in an interview at his official residence in Madison.

Wisconsin is one of five states that have passed laws regulating organ allocation. But a new federal regulation would likely supersede any state laws.

Various interest groups have already begun lobbying. The American Liver Foundation favors a national list for organ allocation, arguing that it may prevent organs from being wasted and also would improve medical outcomes. Other patient groups supporting the change include the Transplant Recipients International Organization and the Minority Organ and Tissue Transplantation Education Project. Centers such as Wisconsin that oppose the change have formed their own coalition, the Patient Access to Transplantation Coalition.

Wisconsin Gov. Tommy G. Thompson, shown in 1996, argues that the proposed regulations would hurt states such as his.

In Congress, the battle lines are not readily apparent. The issue is certainly not a partisan one. Some Democrats who live in areas with regional centers that oppose the policy have invoked the traditional Republican argument in favor of states' rights. Some Republicans, such as Sens. Arlen Specter and Rick Santorum of Pennsylvania, are supporting federal intervention. The University of Pittsburgh Medical Center supports the HHS proposal.

Democrats pushing to keep the current system include Sen. Robert G. Torricelli of New Jersey and Rep. Thomas M. Barrett of Wisconsin. Rep. David R. Obey, D-Wis., wants to review the Institute of Medicine study to determine what effect a national system would have on Wisconsin before deciding his position.

The dynamics of the debate have also changed considerably with the announced departure of GOP Rep. Robert L. Livingston of Louisiana. He has been a key defender of the current system because organ transplant centers in his district do not want it changed. House Speaker J. Dennis Hastert, R-Ill., has not yet decided what stance to take in the organ allocation debate.

The lawmaker who probably best understands the issue, Sen. Bill Frist, R-Tenn., who performed over 200 heart and lung transplants before join-

ing the Senate in 1995, said he doubted any legislation would be passed until the study is completed. He has not taken a position on the issue, saying he would prefer to wait for the report.

Frist and others say that Congress would be happy to let the transplant centers resolve the controversy, but the centers — which have their own rivalries — may not be willing to compromise if they feel a deal will benefit other centers more than their own.

Fung is skeptical that Congress will take any action should the report's findings not be known until late summer or early fall.

"I wouldn't be surprised" if Congress declined to act and instead continued the moratorium for another year, he said.

Meanwhile, transplant experts are skeptical that Congress could devise a better system for organ allocation than the medical community.

"Who's better equipped to deal with those problems? Is it the bureaucracy in Washington or those who work day-to-day dealing with patients in the field?" asked D'Alessandro.

But Miller, of the Mount Sinai program, said the federal government needs to intervene in order to even out the waiting times.

"It gets turned into a center argument, but I think it's a patient thing," he said. "Patients should be able to go where they want to go" for a transplant, he said, arguing that while wealthier patients can afford to join waiting lists at several centers, others cannot.

Pittsburgh's Fung agrees. "People are not looking at what's best for the transplant community," he said, but instead are looking out for their own programs.

Some medical professionals warn that unless the transplant community develops its own system in the next three or four months, it may get stuck with a congressional solution that meets the test of political palatability but is unworkable in the field.

Hoffmann believes any sort of compromise would be difficult to broker because "nobody trusts each other. It has become in many ways, survival of the fittest of these programs."

And there is no guarantee that the independently minded medical community would follow a congressional mandate.

"We can't even agree among ourselves," said Hoffmann. "Do you think they'll listen to a bunch of politicians who don't know anything about medicine?" ◆

Lawmakers Envision a Medicare System Greater Than the Sum of Its Parts

Combining the two trust funds would streamline program administration, supporters say, but effect on taxpayers and patients is less clear

As lawmakers wrestle with the future of Medicare, the discussions usually take place in the context of two parts: Part A, which covers hospital stays, and Part B, for doctor visits and outpatient care.

But now, there is relatively widespread agreement among members of Congress who have worked on Medicare that the historical division no longer makes sense. Since the federal health insurance program for the elderly was created in 1965, the traditional lines between hospital care and doctor visits have become blurred. Medical procedures that once required hospital stays can now be handled in outpatient settings. If Medicare were under construction today, experts say, there would be little reason to bifurcate the system.

"In a world where health care is more integrated in delivery, it makes much more sense to have combined funds," said Gail Wilensky, chairman of the Medicare Payment Advisory Commission, which reports to Congress, and former administrator of the Health Care Financing Administration (HCFA), which runs the Medicare program.

If Medicare continues to expand its use of managed care, which has increased significantly among the privately insured population, the two-part system will be even less relevant. Congress in the 1997 balanced-budget law (PL 105-33) encouraged new types of managed care in Medicare. Managed care uses a combined system that coordinates all treatment, whether in the hospital or on an outpatient basis. *(1997 Almanac, p. 6-3)*

Many lawmakers have suggested tearing down the walls between Part A, which is funded by payroll taxes, and Part B, which receives three-fourths of its financing from general revenues and one-fourth from beneficiaries' monthly premiums. Currently, the solvency of the Part A trust fund is used as the main measure of the system's financial health. However, a merger would require a new benchmark for the financial health of the system as a whole.

Critics of the current system say that the rigid division of the program hampers the government's ability to make the system more efficient. A combined system, they say,

Health care has changed significantly since 1965 when President Lyndon B. Johnson, shown with former President Harry S Truman, signed legislation creating Medicare.

could eventually reduce administrative costs and simplify the payment system. And beneficiaries would have a more straightforward cost-sharing structure, although some would likely pay more than under the current program.

The Medicare overhaul debate will resume in a five-week series of hearings beginning April 21 in the Senate Finance Committee. Among the proposals to be discussed is one sponsored by Sen. John B. Breaux, D-La., and Rep. Bill Thomas, R-Calif., co-chairmen of the recently disbanded National Bipartisan Commission on the Future of Medicare, to increase the role of private managed care in the program. *(1999 CQ Weekly, p. 703)*

Under those proposals, known as "premium support," recipients would receive a set package of health benefits with the government's costs capped at a specific amount. Combining the two parts would be natural under that scenario.

"If we had one vote on this commission that would be unanimous, it might be" the

Quick Contents

As Congress takes up proposals to ensure the long-term viability of Medicare, there is growing consensus that any restructuring should merge Part A and Part B. And with managed care playing a greater role in the program, the distinction between the two parts becomes less and less relevant.

synthesis of the funds, Thomas said at the panel's final March 16 meeting. "It just doesn't make a lot of sense, especially in the way health care is currently delivered and will be delivered in the future, to maintain the fiction of a separate A and B fund."

Studying the Impact

Even though there is wide agreement that the program be unified, the effect on taxpayers and beneficiaries is still being analyzed. The financial impact on patients would vary, depending on whether they currently use more hospital or outpatient care.

And the financing of the program could spark a classic debate among lawmakers over who should pay for the health care of America's elderly and disabled beneficiaries, now numbering 39 million people.

Combining the trust funds would force future Congresses to find the right combination of payroll taxes, general funds mainly from income taxes and beneficiaries' premiums — a potentially difficult challenge considering the political constituencies behind each approach.

The Medicare commission disbanded after failing to agree on the best way to improve the system. Breaux's plan failed by only one vote at the commission's last meeting March 16, and he is determined to resurrect the plan. It would give beneficiaries a stipend to buy either private insurance or a government-run fee-for-service plan similar to the one that 83 percent of current beneficiaries use.

Breaux and Thomas are continuing to push for their overhaul. President Clinton is soon expected to unveil his own proposal, which is also likely to combine the parts.

'Historical Accident'

Medicare's bifurcated structure was established 34 years ago as part of a political compromise.

The Part B component, which covers doctor visits, lab work and other outpatient care, was added to President Lyndon B. Johnson's proposal for subsidized hospital insurance in 1965 at the last minute by then-House Ways and Means Chairman Wilbur Mills, D-Ark.

(1939-77). Mills made the doctors' program voluntary, with different funding than the hospital care portion. (*1965 Almanac, p. 236*)

The two divisions followed the structures set by the Blue Cross Association hospital insurance and the Blue Shield Association physicians' care programs. Those two entities had fully merged by 1982.

Critics of the current framework argue that a more united system would

Thomas, co-chairman of the Medicare commission, says the two-part system "just doesn't make a lot of sense."

CQ PHOTO / DOUGLAS GRAHAM

allow for flexibility in the program. When Medicare was created, health care was dominated by hospital stays. Since then, advancements in medicine and medical technology mean that outpatient care plays a larger role in health care. Currently, roughly 20 percent of Medicare beneficiaries require hospital care each year, while nearly two-thirds only use Part B services such as doctor visits. As medicine continues to evolve, officials would prefer to be able to adapt the program accordingly.

Under the present system, deciding whether Part A or Part B should pay for a new service is sometimes difficult. And throughout the years, the distinctions between Part A and Part B have

become less clear.

In the 1997 budget law, lawmakers "saved" money in the Part A trust fund by shifting some coverage of home health care to Part B, which then took on the additional costs.

Proponents of change point to these kinds of accounting transfers as proof that the current structure masks the difficulties facing the entire program.

"The notion of having separate funding was a historical accident," said Wilensky. "At a conceptual level, no one justifies these two pieces."

Effect on Beneficiaries

The mixing of the two funds' revenue streams and service demands will raise fundamental questions about the future direction of Medicare. Some patients would see lower costs through a combined system, while others would pay more. The impact on beneficiaries is still being studied and could change, depending on how a final plan is drafted.

The union of Part A and Part B would require creating a combined deductible. Currently the deductible for Part A is $768 for each hospital stay up to 60 days, with additional charges after that, and the deductible for Part B is $100 annually. The Breaux-Thomas plan envisioned that deductible at $400, indexed to growth in Medicare costs.

The least healthy Medicare beneficiaries — about 8 million of the 39 million — would pay a lower deductible. Those who use hospital care most would generally benefit, while others who rely more on doctors' care would likely face more out-of-pocket costs. Some of that burden could be shouldered by private supplemental Medigap insurance policies, if the patient buys it.

"The effect would be relatively small for individuals," said Bruce Vladeck, a commission member and HCFA administrator under Clinton from 1993 to 1997. "The sicker ones are better off. You have 30 million people who are worse off, but very slightly worse off, and some of those have supplemental [Medigap] insurance, anyway."

The change would also force lawmakers to come up with a fundamentally new way of looking at Medicare funding.

The merger of payroll taxes, general funds and beneficiaries' premiums would necessitate a new definition of solvency for the system as a whole.

The Breaux-Thomas idea would have required Congress to debate changes when general revenues are set to exceed 40 percent of total Medicare financing. That point would come in the next decade, according to commission staff estimates. Currently, about 37 percent of Medicare income is contributed by tax revenues.

Lawmakers working within the new construct would have to decide: Should most of the program continue to be funded by workers and employers through the 2.9 percent payroll tax, which now provides more than half the total funding? Or should beneficiaries have to pay more, either through politically unpopular premium increases or their portion of income taxes?

Critics of the payroll tax say it demands proportionately more from low-income people than from the wealthy, although that difference is less dramatic in Medicare. Opponents of higher premiums argue that seniors who have contributed to Medicare through payroll taxes in their working lives should not have to give more when they retire. And budget hawks say that general funds should not be further squeezed by entitlements. Other domestic programs will suffer, they fear, if Medicare increasingly consumes a greater share of general funds.

No Simple Explanation

Another quandary for policy-makers will be how to explain the fragile finances of the overall program to the public. The division of Medicare into two "trust funds" has given lawmakers an easy way to attract interest in the overall funding dilemma.

In Medicare financing, policy-makers have worked with two main goals in mind: preventing the exhaustion of the Part A trust fund and restraining overall program growth.

Explaining the problems with Part A are easy, since its insolvency can be viewed as analogous to bankruptcy. By 2015, the trust fund will not have enough money to cover benefits because of the number of Baby Boomers joining the program.

Less attention is focused on the

Managed Care Plans Criticized

Health care plans that participate in Medicare's managed care program have often sent "incomplete or inaccurate" information to elderly and disabled patients, according to a General Accounting Office (GAO) survey released April 13.

The GAO also criticized plans for failing to give patients enough information about certain rights — such as the ability to appeal care decisions by their plans. Because of the lack of information, the GAO said, many seniors may not realize how they can protect their interests.

The Senate Special Committee on Aging last year asked the GAO to investigate the information sent by Medicare+Choice plans, which were created in the 1997 balanced-budget act (PL 105-33) to expand Medicare's managed care options.

Of 16 managed care plans studied, all of them contained wrong or incomplete information, according to the survey. The report said nearly one-third of the surveyed health plans incorrectly told patients they must obtain a physician referral before receiving an annual mammogram screening. One plan told beneficiaries that they were entitled to a drug benefit that was lower than the benefit the plan had told the Health Care Financing Administration (HCFA) it would provide.

"The intent of Medicare+ Choice was to give older Americans more health care options," Aging Committee Chairman Charles E. Grassley, R-Iowa, said at a hearing on the issue April 13. "We wanted to make their lives easier. Instead, inadequate plan information has caused headaches. If we want Medicare beneficiaries to have more choices, we have to give them the tools to choose."

The American Association of Health Plans, a major industry lobbying group, said its members want to resolve the problems. "Our first principle is that information to beneficiaries should be accurate and understandable," said AAHP president and chief executive officer Karen Ignagni.

GAO officials also warned that the HCFA failed to adequately monitor the plans.

"HCFA has both the authority and the responsibility to ensure that Medicare [managed care plans] distribute information that helps beneficiaries," the report said. "However, its policies and practices have fallen short of that mark."

Medicare administrators say they are already working to improve oversight. By the autumn enrollment period when seniors can join managed care plans, HCFA officials expect to have more safeguards in place. Among those protections may be a pilot project to determine whether reviews by independent contractors would improve the process and a new requirement that plans summarize benefits in a way that enables seniors to make comparisons among plans.

Congress is debating whether to expand the role of private managed care in Medicare. Although most of Medicare's 39 million beneficiaries use the fee-for-service program run by the government, about 17 percent have joined managed care plans.

strain on Part B services.

Since the Part B program is funded annually through premiums and appropriations, it faces no crisis date analogous to that of Part A — but it faces fiscal pressures similar to those of its counterpart.

Despite efforts to control costs, Part B benefit outlays increased 41 percent over the past five years, according to a March 30 report released by the federal trustees who oversee the program. The program grew about 9 percent faster than the economy in that period.

"Part B deserves more attention than it gets," said Richard S. Foster, the chief HCFA actuary. "Under present law, it can't go broke . . . but it's not good to have outlays growing faster than your financing base."

Medicare's Two Parts

Medicare's bifurcated structure was set 34 years ago in a political compromise. But with the evolution of managed care, lawmakers are considering merging the two parts.

Medicare Trust Fund	How it is funded	What it covers
Part A Hospital insurance	Funded through a 2.9 percent payroll tax. Usually provided premium free to eligible recipients on the basis of past employment. Could become insolvent as early as 2015 as 77 million Baby Boomers near retirement.	Pays mainly for hospital costs, limited nursing home care and some home health services.
Part B Supplementary medical insurance	Three-quarters of its funding comes from general revenues of the federal government. One-quarter generated by monthly premium, currently $45.50. About 95 percent of eligible recipients pay these premiums.	Pays for doctors visits, lab work and other outpatient work.

Total Medicare spending as a percentage of gross domestic product is projected to grow from 2.53 percent of GDP to 5.15 percent in 2035, according to the trustees' report.

The added weight by the retirement of about 77 million Baby Boomers in about 2010 will burden the already strained system. Seniors are living longer and being supported by fewer workers. By 2030, the trustees' report predicts, there will be 2.3 workers to support every beneficiary, while in 1998 there were 3.9 workers per patient.

According to the trustees' report, the Part A trust fund had $120.4 billion in assets on Dec. 31, 1998. The Part B medical account balance was $46.2 billion on Dec. 31, 1998.

The trustees' report for each fund has been more highly publicized in recent years as lawmakers have sought to curb Medicare's growth. Politicians and administration officials have promoted the reports' yearly forecasts as warning signs that policy changes are needed.

The most recent report pushed back the insolvency date for the Part A trust fund by seven years, decreasing the pressure on politicians to act.(*1999 CQ Weekly, p. 805*)

New Trigger Needed

The near-insolvency of the Part A trust fund has been the catalyst and justification for recent discussions of Medicare funding. In 1997, when it appeared that the hospital trust fund would face bankruptcy within four years, Congress enacted a series of pay-

ment cuts in the balanced-budget law and expanded the role of private insurance to "save" the trust fund.

Under a combined system, there would no longer be the "alarm bells" and emergency status that are now associated with Part A insolvency. As a result, analysts say, some type of trigger would be needed to signal that Medicare spending was getting out of control.

The trustees would continue to report on the finances of Medicare. But some analysts fear that the 40-percent-of-general-revenues trigger would not carry the same political resonance — and urgency — as an impending "bankruptcy" of the trust fund.

And some experts would prefer a more compelling consequence for lawmakers when general revenues hit the 40 percent cap than simply the Breaux-Thomas proposal's call for "necessary and important public debate leading to potential adjustments" in financing.

"I would be much more comfortable with a provision in the law stating that to the extent that general revenues reach a certain level, that hospital rates would be cut or payroll taxes increased — anything that would force Congress to act," said former Congressional Budget Office Director Robert D. Reischauer, a senior fellow at the Brookings Institution.

If history is any guide, lawmakers would be tempted to simply dip into general revenues when Medicare spending rises.

Boosting the budget for an annual appropriation is simpler, both political-

ly and logistically, than designing a new formula for higher payroll taxes or premiums. That explains why general revenues have grown to make up three-fourths of Part B funding. The doctors' insurance program originally split the funding equally between a $3 monthly premium for patients matched by federal revenues.

Without changes in current law, the amount of total Medicare funding from general funds is projected to grow from 37 percent of program funding in fiscal 2000 to 43 percent as soon as fiscal 2005, according to commission staff estimates.

Since most analysts believe that merging the program's two parts is a long-overdue way to modernize the program's structure, lawmakers may focus on more politically appealing changes, such as adding prescription drug coverage, during Medicare debates.

Foster, the HCFA actuary, said he thinks that maintaining the two parts would be "an administrative nightmare" as managed care assumes a larger role in Medicare.

But despite the wide support for combining the trust funds, several analysts questioned whether Congress has fully digested the implications of such a move.

"It makes sense to combine the trust funds and consider them as a whole," said Marilyn Moon, one of two appointed Medicare trustees and currently an analyst at the Urban Institute, a Washington think tank. "But there are a lot of further issues that haven't been thought through yet." ◆

Clinton's plan to save Social Security stirs both controversy and hope for compromise

Opportunity Is in the Air

On its face, President Clinton's proposal to channel hundreds of billions of dollars in Social Security revenues into the stock market represented a bold stroke to harness the power of Wall Street to shore up the popular retirement program.

Underneath the plan, however, lies the cautiousness of a first-time investor.

The president's proposal would leave the basic structure of the Social Security program intact. For some people — such as poor widows — he even proposed increasing benefits. Most significantly, he veered away from what administration officials believe is a riskier proposition of replacing a portion of Social Security with private retirement accounts that individuals could invest as they saw fit.

Since he called on Congress to "save Social Security" in his 1998 State of the Union address, Clinton has been under pressure from Republicans to come up with a blueprint on how to do that. (*1998 CQ Weekly, p. 215*)

The result was a proposal that satisfied many Democrats, who had worried that the White House would embrace calls from GOP lawmakers and private industry for using the market-based accounts as a substitute, not a supplement, for basic program benefits. It angered many Republicans, who said the plan would amount to an unsustainable, big-government approach that did not address the program's long-term solvency.

Under the plan, about $2.8 trillion of the projected budget surplus would be used to bolster Social Security over the next 15 years. The government would invest a quarter of that amount in the stock market. It would use another $33 billion a year to create federally funded retirement savings accounts for low- and middle-income workers separate from Social Security.

The plan goes only about halfway toward the goal of keeping Social Security solvent for 75 years. Rather than proposing benefit cuts or tax increases

to fill the remaining gap, the White House issued a vague call for Congress to make "difficult but fully achievable choices" on a bipartisan basis.

"The president is standing on the diving board instead of jumping in the pool," said Sen. Charles E. Grassley, R-Iowa.

Democrats protested that Clinton had met GOP demands to unveil a detailed plan and said that despite the differences, it could form the basis for bipartisan negotiations.

"They [Republicans] have to stop setting the president up for failure," said Robert T. Matsui of California, the ranking Democrat on the House Ways and Means Social Security Subcommittee.

Opening the Debate

Republicans have been at the forefront of efforts to tie Social Security to the stock market, saying the government is wasting an opportunity to increase the program's financial returns. But they want individuals — not Washington — to make investment decisions.

"The president's suggestion that Social Security reform starts with government intervention in the stock market is plain wrong," said House Speaker J. Dennis Hastert, R-Ill.

Republican criticisms were seconded Jan. 20 by influential Federal Reserve Board Chairman Alan Greenspan. In testimony before the Ways and Means Committee, Greenspan reiterated his argument that it would be impossible to insulate federal investments from politics.

But he generally endorsed the administration's effort to reserve the surplus for Social Security first.

Moderates of both parties worried that instead of preparing Americans for difficult reductions in Social Security and other entitlement programs as the Baby Boom generation ages, the White House had made an impossible promise of increased retirement aid.

"His proposal established a bipartisan framework for dealing with long-term reforms," said Rep. Charles W.

Stenholm, D-Texas. "The bad part is he ducked all the heavy lifting. Depending on surplus projections that may not materialize . . . that's not going to find bipartisan support."

Complicating the debate — but possibly providing an opening for compromise — is the fact that the future of Social Security is tangled up in a larger, emerging fight over the budget surplus.

Democrats attacked House Republicans in the 1998 election campaigns for voting for an $80.1 billion tax cut that would have been funded largely through the surplus, calling it an attack on Clinton's proposal to save Social Security first. The Senate did not take up the tax cut. (*1998 CQ Weekly, p. 2656*)

This year, the House and Senate GOP are so far working in unison. They hope to tap into the surplus to fund an across-the-board tax cut of at least 10 percent.

Aside from Social Security, the administration has proposed reserving part of the surplus to shore up Medicare, which is projected to run short of funds in 2010, and pay for defense and education initiatives. (*1999 CQ Weekly, p. 176*)

"We're going to have a big argument about this, and we should," Clinton said at a rally in Buffalo, N.Y., on Jan. 20.

House Ways and Means Committee Chairman Bill Archer, R-Texas, who has criticized Clinton's plan for market investment, offered an olive branch of sorts on Jan. 21.

"We would be willing to reserve 62 percent of the surplus until Social Security has been saved," Archer said. House Minority Leader Richard A. Gephardt, D-Mo., welcomed the GOP overture, but reiterated that the White House wanted to use some of the surplus for the personal savings accounts and for ensuring the long-term solvency of Medicare.

The political positioning showed that, while the two parties are far apart on specifics, they are eager to move beyond the divisive impeachment debate to reach a deal on Social Security. (*1999 CQ Weekly, p. 183*)

PETE SOUZA / CHICAGO TRIBUNE

Greenspan, testifying Jan. 20 before the House Ways and Means Committee, said that diverting government money into the equity markets would be too risky.

Roosevelt in 1935, Social Security faces no imminent crisis; rather, there is a looming, long-term crunch as the Baby Boom generation retires, life expectancy increases and fewer workers remain in the economy to pay benefits.

Payroll taxes and trust fund balances are sufficient to cover benefits through 2032. After that point, the 12.4 percent payroll tax, half paid by workers and half by employers, will cover only about three-fourths of commitments.

Acting now would allow Congress to phase in changes over a longer period of time, allowing for more gradual policies and more equity across generations. It would also allow lawmakers to take advantage of the emerging surplus and a strong economy.

Market Intervention?

Of all the provisions in the administration's plan, the most controversial is market investment.

"Direct investment of any of the surplus by the government . . . is socialism," said Rep. E. Clay Shaw Jr., R-Fla., chairman of the House Ways and Means Social Security Subcommittee.

The idea behind direct investment is to get better earnings for the Social Security trust fund, and therefore minimize the need for benefit cuts, by realizing the higher returns of the market.

The stock market has historically averaged a 7 percent rate of return. Currently, Social Security trust funds are invested in lower-yielding, but less volatile, Treasury bonds.

While market-based proposals were unthinkable even a decade ago, booming stock prices and increasing investor sophistication have fueled the move toward private investment.

Republican opposition to the concept of direct government investment in the market is no surprise to the administration. What is troubling, White House officials say, is the degree of vitriol. They argue that their plan was designed with safeguards to prevent government abuse.

While some members of the 1994-96 Advisory Council on Social Security, for example, called for investing 40 percent of the trust fund in the stock market, the Clinton plan calls for investing about $700 billion over 15 years. That would represent about 4 percent of the total equity market and less than 15 percent of the Social Security trust fund.

Some Republicans praised Clinton for at least moving toward individual retirement accounts and said they hoped to build on the proposal. Analysts said that by channeling most of the surplus back into the Social Security trust fund, rather than spending it on tax cuts or new programs, the plan would have the important, secondary benefit of reducing the massive federal debt.

And both sides believe that after making Social Security a top priority, they cannot afford to let it die.

The fact that Congress is even debating proposals to shore up the Social Security system, which provides retirement, disability and survivors benefits to 44 million Americans, is in itself a remarkable development.

Created by President Franklin D.

The administration has yet to work out a final proposal, but officials envision an independent government board that would contract with private investment houses. To minimize market disruption, overhead costs and the potential for abuse, investments would go into broad-based investment instruments, such as mutual funds, rather than specific stocks.

Greenspan warned that it would be impossible to insulate the federal government from pressure to turn to more politically palatable, but less financially sound, investments. That would both distort the market and reduce the expected rate of return to the program.

"I am fearful that we would use those assets in a way that would create a lower rate of return for Social Security recipients and . . . create sub-optimal use of capital and a lower standard of living," Greenspan said.

In response, the White House sent Treasury Secretary Robert E. Rubin on a tour of the morning television talk shows Jan. 21 to promote the plan.

"There will be no — zero — no government involvement in the investment of the funds," Rubin said on NBC's "Today."

While the proposal to invest in the stock market has received the bulk of attention, it was not the key element in Clinton's plan for keeping the program solvent.

The administration estimates that transferring a portion of the surplus to Social Security and realizing higher market rates of return would extend the solvency of Social Security by 23 years, through 2055. The bulk of the improvement, however, would come from the transfer of the surplus, not from the stock market investment. Administration officials said the stock plan by itself accounted for about five of the additional 23 years of solvency.

Private Accounts

A second area of both division and hope for compromise is the White House's plan to create so-called Universal Savings Accounts (USAs), financed through the surplus, to supplement the basic Social Security benefit.

The plan would dedicate $33 billion a year, or about 11 percent of the projected surplus, for the next 15 years to the accounts, which would operate like 401(k) accounts. While the details are still to be worked out,

White House officials said the accounts would be intended to help low- and middle-income workers create savings pools for retirement.

In a theoretical example laid out by White House officials, a family making $40,000 a year could receive a $100 flat contribution from the federal government to set up an account. If the family contributed $600 on its own, the government could match $300 of that amount, for a total investment of $1,000. The administration has not made final decisions on how the funds would operate.

The idea already has some powerful advocates. Senate Finance Committee Chairman William V. Roth Jr., R-Del., on Jan. 20 re-introduced similar legislation. Roth's plan would use half the federal budget surplus from 2000 to 2004 to set up individual accounts. A minimum-wage earner making $12,400 a year in adjusted gross income would receive about $1,850 annually. The accounts would have to be invested in federally specified plans.

"Let's get these accounts up and running, proven and tested, while Congress considers carefully protecting and preserving Social Security for the long term," Roth said.

Harvard economist Martin Feldstein also has proposed a plan that would require individuals to invest two percent of earnings in the market. Proceeds from the accounts would be used to reduce Social Security benefits.

Many lawmakers want to go further, allowing individuals to use some or all of the Social Security payroll tax to set up individual accounts. Earnings from the accounts would be used to replace basic program benefits.

Social Security Commissioner Kenneth S. Apfel said in an interview Jan. 21 that the administration looked at such proposals but rejected them as too risky.

"We need to have more savings, but not to replace parts of the Social Security system," Apfel said. "You've got to have that benefit you can count on, whether you outlive your savings or your spouse. The creation of individual accounts as a replacement to Social Security puts individuals at risk."

Still, advocates of greater privatization hope to build on the White House proposal.

Leanne Abdnor, executive director of the Alliance for Worker Security, which represents the National Associ-

ation of Manufacturers, Business Roundtable and U.S. Chamber of Commerce, said her group would lobby hard for individual accounts to replace some program benefits, and against direct government investment.

"The members are very skeptical and cautious about an additional retirement program. I love the idea of giving workers back their money. I'm not sure it needs to be a new program," Abdnor said.

Despite Apfel's opposition, some Democrats worry that the White House's proposal is the first step toward private accounts that would replace program benefits.

And there is broad concern that, although the accounts are envisioned to last only 15 years, they would turn into a new entitlement program. Supporters said they will cross that bridge down the road.

"If you have a 10 percent across-the-board income tax rate cut . . . at the end how do you finance it? That is a much bigger problem" than extending individual accounts, said Robert Greenstein, director of the Center on Budget and Policy Priorities, a liberal think tank.

Expanding Aid

Clinton believes that the overhaul would provide an opportunity to improve the basic program. One major concern is widows, who account for nearly two-thirds of elderly women in poverty.

Under the current Social Security system, after a married individual dies, the survivor — usually a woman — receives 100 percent of the deceased spouse's benefit or her own benefit, whichever is higher. Many experts say the amount should be increased to 75 percent of the higher, joint benefits the couple received when both were alive.

While Clinton called for greater protection for women in his State of the Union address, he is not advocating funding an enhanced widow's benefit through the surplus. Rather, Congress and the White House would have to come up with billions of dollars in additional savings to pay for it. (*1998 CQ Weekly, p. 1038*)

The plan calls for eliminating the so-called Social Security earnings test. Under current law, individuals ages 65 to 70 who earn above $15,500 in 1999 will have their benefits reduced $1 for every $3 of income. ◆

For Democrats, firearms' availability is the issue; for GOP, crime and cultural decay

Beyond Guns and Violence: A Battle for House Control

In five quick days the Littleton-inspired contest over gun control turned into a crucible for effective control of the House. In the process, the gun lobby and its allies in the Republican leadership managed to shift an emotion-laden drive to expand federal regulation of firearms into a debate over responsibility for the nation's culture of violence.

Now, in the coming days and weeks, the test will be whether the GOP or President Clinton and his Democratic allies at the Capitol can use these questions to sway voters as they go to the polls in 2000.

"A lot of Democrats think they can take back the Congress on guns," said Rep. James C. Greenwood, R-Pa. "A lot of Republicans think they can hold the Congress on culture."

Senate-passed provisions that would tighten background checks of buyers at gun shows, among other steps, ran aground in a House riven by partisan politics. A watered-down package of gun curbs (HR 2122) was resoundingly defeated on June 18 — the 147-280 vote coming 59 days after the slayings at Columbine High School in Littleton, Colo., renewed momentum for gun control, which had been stalled during the four years of revived Republican control of Capitol Hill.

But the House's passage the night before of legislation (HR 1501) proposing tougher juvenile crime standards and a mix of anti-violence steps assures that there can be conference negotiations between the House and the Senate, which had passed a bill (S 254) combining juvenile justice and gun controls in May. That hands the Republican leadership — which had seemed to have a balky hold at best on the management of the debate on both sides of the Capitol — a renewed and strengthened measure of control, given their ability to name the members of the negotiating teams.

But the end product will face the scrutiny of the president and his congressional allies, who already are on the attack. Republicans are once again being labeled the lap dogs of the National Rifle Association (NRA), which lobbied intently to stanch the momentum for gun control that had seemed to be welling up on both sides of the House aisle in recent weeks.

"One more time, the Congress of the United States . . . said, 'We don't care what's necessary to protect our children. We can't possibly bear to make anyone in the NRA mad,' " Clinton said after the House votes. He spoke to reporters while at a summit in Germany, and he was scheduled to take the matter up again during his June 19 radio address.

At issue is whether to add the first new gun control law to the federal books in half a decade.

Even before the House took up its measures, Democrats threatened to add gun control amendments to fiscal 2000 appropriations bills as they come to the floor. The bill funding the Department of the Treasury and the Postal Service is expected to be their prime target, because it covers the federal agency that conducts background checks on potential gun buyers. Republican leaders say they want to move that bill through the Appropriations Committee before the July Fourth recess, set to start in two weeks.

If that plan does not work, they hope to make an election issue out of gun control. This was presaged by Patrick J. Kennedy, D-R.I., chairman of the Democratic Congressional Campaign Committee, during debate June 17 on the NRA-backed gun proposal that proved pivotal in the debate.

As the proposal edged toward a razor-thin victory, much to the dismay of most Democrats, Kennedy started a chant that sought to put a positive long-term political spin on the short-term legislative defeat.

"Six seats! Six seats!" he chanted, citing the number of House districts

that Democrats must pick up to take back control, and many of his colleagues soon chimed in.

Partisan Tensions

After the defeat on final passage June 18, Republican leaders were bitter over what they considered the politicization of the gun vote. Though 82 Republicans — or 37 percent — voted against the measure, the bulk of the opposition came from Democrats. Their 197 "no" votes account for 93 percent of the Democratic Caucus membership.

Speaker J. Dennis Hastert, R-Ill., who had promised that the GOP leadership would work to "expedite" a gun control bill, blamed the setback on Democrats "who put partisanship over progress." At a news conference, Majority Whip Tom DeLay, R-Texas, said that "the bill had four of five things they wanted [and] still was not good enough for them. So it's quite obvious to me that they're just interested in politics."

While DeLay expressed disappointment over the outcome on gun control, however, he said "I've had a great time this week," owing to the victories he won in pushing to strengthen the juvenile justice bill.

Not only was the juvenile crime bill amended to add a new collection of mandatory minimum sentences for young people who commit gun crimes, but it also was enlarged to include several provisions pushed by cultural conservatives. First among them was a provision allowing the Ten Commandments to be displayed in public settings. The bill would also bar federal judges from addressing state prison overcrowding, create nine new federal judgeships in three states, express criticism of the entertainment media for gratuitous violence and provide civil immunity to teachers who discipline students.

"None of this," said a highly skeptical John P. Murtha, D-Pa., "is going to make any difference."

The vote to pass the juvenile crime

Gun Control

In a week filled with partisan tension, lawmakers' personal experiences fueled the House gun control debate. Bob Barr, R-Ga., an NRA board member, took a telephone call in the Rayburn Room just off the House floor June 17. The day before, Carolyn McCarthy, D-N.Y., below, broke down in tears at a news conference. She was propelled into politics after her husband was slain by a gunman aboard a commuter train.

bill was a resounding 287-139, although a majority of Democrats voted against it as well. (1999 CQ Weekly, p. 1496)

Judiciary Committee Chairman Henry J. Hyde, R-Ill., pushed a provision that would have banned the sale to minors of certain violent and sexually explicit material. But his measure was rejected when civil libertarians raised First Amendment objections, retailers of videos and music complained they would not know what they could and could not legally sell — and the combined appeals won the ears of a pivotal group of Republicans. It was defeated, 146-282. (1999 CQ Weekly, p. 1490)

The Senate bill contains several modest gun control provisions, some mandatory minimums and only a few minor provisions to address the theory that cultural decline has boosted youth violence. For the Republican leaders, their ability to shape a final bill, and possibly their ability to hold their majorities in the 107th Congress, will depend on how successfully they can present their message. They argue that an effective approach to incidents such as the shooting in Littleton, Colo. — in which two teenagers killed themselves after slaying 12 schoolmates and a teacher — should deal more with the underlying cultural issues behind youth crime, and less with gun control.

Background Checks

The most controversy was generated on the gun control bill, which called for background checks of prospective buyers at gun shows but would narrow the definition of what constitutes such a show from what was passed by the Senate. The Senate measure defined a show as any event in which 50 guns were offered for sale. The House measure would have required that there be at least 10 vendors present to constitute a gun show.

Gun control supporters argued the House definition would allow a handful of gun vendors to sell huge numbers of weapons without customer checks. Opponents said it was necessary to prevent triggering the background checks for simple transactions, such as an estate sale of someone who owned at least 50 guns.

On what both sides had described as the pivotal vote, the House toned down its bill by adopting an amendment by John D. Dingell, D-Mich., that had been sanctioned by the NRA. That Dingell would promote such an amendment — and describe how he had agreed to do so after negotiating with DeLay — infuriated many Democrats and served to highlight the complicated cultural and political forces that still buffet the gun control debate. (1999 CQ Weekly, p. 1430)

Dingell's language stipulated that any background check at a gun show be completed within 24 hours. Current law allows for three business days. The issue comes into play in approximately one quarter of the background checks when a computerized database created by the 1993 Brady law (PL 103-159) is unable to provide complete information on the purchaser. In these cases federal authorities are called on to contact courthouses and state records offices by telephone.

The amendment was adopted late in the night of June 17, 218-211. (1999 CQ Weekly, p. 1496)

After that, gun control supporters offered the alternative that they had rallied behind. Sponsored by Carolyn McCarthy, D-N.Y., it would have adopted language similar to the Senate's. It was rejected 193-235. (1999 CQ Weekly, p. 1496)

The series of options was designed to keep Republicans from voting for the McCarthy amendment by allowing them choices that might fit their political needs.

For a while it looked as though DeLay and Hastert had successfully negotiated the turbulent waters of gun control, in a classic example of how victory often goes to those who frame the debate. Blocking McCarthy would have been almost impossible had they not been able to present competing options.

Only 33 Republicans — or 15 percent of those voting — voted for the McCarthy amendment, fewer than the 54 (or 31 percent) who voted for the Brady law in 1993 and fewer even than the 38 (or 22 percent) who voted for the assault weapons ban of 1994.

In contrast, Democrats cut their defectors from 69 who voted against Brady to 49 who voted against McCarthy. (1993 Almanac, p. 300, 1994 Almanac, p. 276)

One important difference was that the Democratic House of 1993 presented lawmakers with a choice of voting for the Brady legislation or nothing at all. This time, DeLay endeavored to give members in swing districts alternatives. They could vote for the underlying proposal by opposing both the Dingell and McCarthy amendments, or they could vote only for the Dingell language.

By voting for Dingell's language, they were given a rare chance to finesse the competing views of constituents. They could tell their gun control advocates that they voted for background checks, while telling gun control foes that they voted for a measure drafted by the NRA.

But in the end, all the package of amendments did was ensure that almost everyone had a gripe with the final bill. Despite support of the NRA, Dingell's plan was not enough for the staunchest gun control foes. And gun control supporters were not about to support an NRA-backed measure.

The final vote showed there will not be much cover for moderate Republicans. Christopher Shays, R-Conn., said the party has to distance itself from the NRA if it is going to portray itself as responsive to the public. "It's clear this marriage between the NRA and the Republican Party must come to an end," he said.

But Democrats' ability to score political points off the issue was dampened somewhat by the fact that DeLay handed the job of sponsoring the NRA amendment to Dingell. "The message is mixed when the senior Democrat offers the weakening amendment," said James P. Moran, D-Va.

On the other side of the equation, some Democrats may find themselves targeted by the NRA and angry gun owners for their votes for McCarthy. In the 1994 Republican sweep, a handful of Democratic losses were attributed specifically to votes to ban assault weapons.

Suburban Voters

The key to who ultimately wins on the gun control issue is how the House action plays in suburban districts. Lawmakers from suburban districts, as defined by a Congressional Quarterly study of the demographics of each of the 435 districts, have always been pivotal on gun issues. Representatives of rural areas as a rule tend to oppose gun control measures, while those from urban districts tend to support them.

The lawmakers who represent suburban districts are often the most whipsawed by gun control votes. No matter how they vote, no matter what the outcome, these issues make some of their constituents unhappy, whether they be soccer moms or weekend hunters.

The defeat of the McCarthy amendment in the House was largely the result of the fact that gun control opponents were able to hold on to most of

the suburban Republican members. In the 1994 assault weapons ban, 67 suburban Republicans voted no. (1994 Almanac, p. 48-H)

In this year's debate, 68 suburban Republicans voted against the McCarthy amendment.

Suburban and mixed district members often have to walk a fine line between the soft majority support for gun control and intense minority opposition to it. Greenwood said most of the people he actually hears from are motivated by letters they receive from the NRA.

"My district as a whole is about 75 percent in favor of common sense gun issues," said Greenwood. "Having said that, we get about 50 or 100 calls a day against these measures. They are almost without exception NRA members who receive the letters and pretty much follow the script."

Greenwood waited until the last minute to decide. He voted against Dingell's amendment and for McCarthy's.

But for all of the suburban Republicans who supported McCarthy, there were many more who voted against her measure. Emblematic of McCarthy's opposition was Rob Portman, R-Ohio. While he has traditionally voted against gun control measures, he is the type of member McCarthy would have to convince to prevail in a Republican controlled House.

Portman said his suburban Columbus voters are much more aware of the availability of guns. But he said they have heavily nuanced opinions on how to approach the issue of teen violence.

"They are much more acutely aware of the issue," he said. "But they don't believe in a silver bullet."

Even some of the most conservative members noticed an uptick of interest in gun measures. "The Columbine tragedy . . . was real heartbreak for the country," Majority Leader Dick Armey, R-Texas, said at a news conference June 15. "It was catalytic on a lot of fronts, and one of them was on guns."

Surprise Defeat for Hyde

The overwhelming defeat for the Hyde proposal to ban sales of violent material to minors came as something of a surprise. Though most Democrats were expected to vote against it, it held an appeal to many Republicans eager to take on Hollywood. In his news conference, Armey referred to it as if it were the underlying bill that would be brought to the floor, not an amendment.

But then the lobbying heated up, and it did not come just from the movie industry. Retailers, a group generally supportive of Republican policies, started calling their biggest supporters in Congress. The U.S. Chamber of Commerce actively lobbied on the issue as well.

The measure may have also suffered from a little posturing. Hyde said some of his colleagues told him that if they voted against his measure based on protecting the First Amendment, they would more easily vote against gun control by portraying themselves as defenders of the Constitution.

Indeed, a number of members of both parties invoked both the First and Second Amendments during the debate. "By the Fourth of July," said Dingell, "we will probably have successfully trampled upon the entirety of the Bill of Rights."

The Hyde measure would have provided penalties of up to five years in prison for selling or lending material to a minor that contains certain violent or sexually explicit material. In doing so it attempted to create a new standard of violence that could be constitutionally restricted. The Supreme Court has carved out a free speech exemption for obscenity, but there is no corresponding exemption for extreme violence.

The criminal sanctions would apply to violent or sexually explicit material that "the average person" would find appealing to "prurient, shameful or morbid interest," and was "patently offensive with respect to what is suitable to minors." The material would have to lack "serious literary, artistic, political or scientific value for minors," as defined by "a reasonable person." The language is similar to that in the 1973 Supreme Court case *Miller v. California* defining obscenity.

Given that the motivation for the language was ostensibly the Columbine shooting, some members found it ironic that the amendment emphasized sex over violence, giving a much broader and graphically explicit definition of sexual material than of violence.

The amendment listed acts and parts of the human anatomy that would be considered "sexually explicit" if presented. These included "actual or simulated" displays of "human male or female genitals, pubic area or buttocks with less than a full opaque covering"; "a female breast with less than a fully opaque covering of any portion thereof below the top of the nipple"; "acts of

masturbation, sodomy and or sexual intercourse"; and "covered male genitals in a discernibly turgid state."

Displays of "violent material" would have been defined as those acts that include "sadistic or masochistic flagellation by or upon a person"; "torture by or upon a person"; "acts of mutilation upon the human body"; or "rape." The specificity in both cases of sex and violence, Hyde said, was necessary to prevent vagueness, which could have a chilling effect on free speech.

McCollum's Proposal

The guts of the juvenile crime provisions were not in the bill as it came to the floor. The language the House started with merely called for a $1.5 billion authorization to states for combating teen crime.

By far the most significant amendment adopted was an omnibus juvenile crime package, sponsored by Crime Subcommittee Chairman Bill McCollum, R-Fla., that would have created a number of mandatory minimum sentences and allowed juveniles to be tried as adults in federal court. It was approved 249-181. (*1999 CQ Weekly, p. 1490*)

The amendment was, in effect, the underlying bill. Thirty-eight of the 44 amendments offered were amendments to the McCollum amendment.

McCollum's proposal spawned a classic split, with conservatives and some moderates accepting the "get-tough" approach while traditional liberals attacked it as counterproductive and inhumane.

McCollum said the juvenile justice system in American simply has not caught up with the fact that many teens are exceptionally violent and dangerous people. Democrats countered that treating teens as adult criminals will only ensure that they continue to behave violently into their adulthood.

"Lock up a 13-year-old with a murderer, a rapist and a robber, and guess what he'll want to be when he grows up?" said Melvin Watt, D-N.C.

The vote represented a complete reversal from the approach pursued earlier this year and a return to the approach used in the 105th Congress, when the House passed a tough juvenile crime bill only to see it stall in the Senate. Until the Columbine shooting, McCollum and Robert C. Scott, D-Va., had been collaborating on the bipartisan, if somewhat limited, approach espoused in HR 1501.

Indeed, the initial responses to Columbine from McCollum and Scott

were that Congress should not overreact and that the federal government's ability to combat crime is limited.

But the Columbine shooting caused an outpouring of ideas and plans to address the social decline thought to be behind it. In fact, as the debate continued, it became a forum for members' frustrations and aspirations about contemporary society and its governance.

Running through the debate were two contradictory themes: that federal government cannot possibly have much effect on the forces that would create a Littleton-like shooting, and that it should try to do just about anything it can think of.

Because gun control advocates seized immediately on the issue after the shooting, Republican members felt they needed to come up with alternatives to gun control, Greenwood said.

"The Congress would have done a lot better had it not waded into a lot of these gun and culture issues," Greenwood said. "I think things went downhill when Republicans perceived Democrats were trying to win points on guns. That's when we came up with this 'best defense is an offense' strategy."

Some amendments adopted include:

● **Ten Commandments.** By Robert B. Aderholt, R-Ala., to allow the Ten Commandments to be displayed in public places. Adopted 248-180. (*1999 CQ Weekly, p. 1492*)

● **Federal judges.** By DeLay, to limit federal judges' ability to order the release of inmates on the grounds of prison crowding. Adopted 296-133. (*1999 CQ Weekly, p. 1490*)

● **Prison funding.** By Matt Salmon, R-Ariz., to penalize states whose convicts commit crimes in other states after release. The cost of incarcerating the criminal in the second state would be docked from the first state's federal crime assistance fund and transferred to the second. Adopted 412-15. *1999 CQ Weekly, p. 1490*)

● **Hollywood.** By Jo Ann Emerson, R-Mo., criticizing the entertainment industry for the use of pointless acts of brutality in movies, television, music and video games. Adopted by voice vote.

● **Disabled children.** By Charlie Norwood, R-Ga., to allow schools to discipline children with mental or physical disabilities the same way that other children are disciplined if they come to school with a weapon or illegal drugs. Adopted 300-128. (*1999 CQ Weekly, p. 1494*) ◆

Appendix

The Legislative Process in Brief

Note: Parliamentary terms used below are defined in the glossary.

Introduction of Bills

A House member (including the resident commissioner of Puerto Rico and non-voting delegates of the District of Columbia, Guam, the Virgin Islands and American Samoa) may introduce any one of several types of bills and resolutions by handing it to the clerk of the House or placing it in a box called the hopper. A senator first gains recognition of the presiding officer to announce the introduction of a bill. If objection is offered by any senator, the introduction of the bill is postponed until the following day.

As the next step in either the House or Senate, the bill is numbered, referred to the appropriate committee, labeled with the sponsor's name and sent to the Government Printing Office so that copies can be made for subsequent study and action. Senate bills may be jointly sponsored and carry several senators' names. Until 1978, the House limited the number of members who could cosponsor any one bill; the ceiling was eliminated at the beginning of the 96th Congress. A bill written in the executive branch and proposed as an administration measure usually is introduced by the chairman of the congressional committee that has jurisdiction.

Bills — Prefixed with HR in the House, S in the Senate, followed by a number. Used as the form for most legislation, whether general or special, public or private.

Joint Resolutions — Designated H J Res or S J Res. Subject to the same procedure as bills, with the exception of a joint resolution proposing an amendment to the Constitution. The latter must be approved by two-thirds of both houses and is thereupon sent directly to the administrator of general services for submission to the states for ratification instead of being presented to the president for his approval.

Concurrent Resolutions — Designated H Con Res or S Con Res. Used for matters affecting the operations of both houses. These resolutions do not become law.

Resolutions — Designated H Res or S Res. Used for a matter concerning the operation of either house alone and adopted only by the chamber in which it originates.

Committee Action

With few exceptions, bills are referred to the appropriate standing committees. The job of referral formally is the responsibility of the Speaker of the House and the presiding officer of the Senate, but this task usually is carried out on their behalf by the parliamentarians of the House and Senate. Precedent, statute and the jurisdictional mandates of the committees as set forth in the rules of the House and Senate determine which committees receive what kinds of bills. An exception is the referral of private bills, which are sent to whatever committee is designated by their sponsors. Bills are technically considered "read for the first time" when referred to House committees.

When a bill reaches a committee it is placed on the committee's calendar. At that time the bill comes under the sharpest congressional focus. Its chances for passage are quickly determined — and the great majority of bills falls by the legislative roadside. Failure of a committee to act on a bill is equivalent to killing it; the measure can be withdrawn from the committee's purview only by a discharge petition signed by a majority of the House membership on House bills, or by adoption of a special resolution in the Senate. Discharge attempts rarely succeed.

The first committee action taken on a bill usually is a request for comment on it by interested agencies of the government. The committee chairman may assign the bill to a subcommittee for study and hearings, or it may be considered by the full committee. Hearings may be public, closed (executive session) or both. A subcommittee, after considering a bill, reports to the full committee its recommendations for action and any proposed amendments.

The full committee then votes on its recommendation to the House or Senate. This procedure is called "ordering a bill reported." Occasionally a committee may order a bill reported unfavorably; most of the time a report, submitted by the chairman of the committee to the House or Senate, calls for favorable action on the measure since the committee can effectively "kill" a bill by simply failing to take any action.

After the bill is reported, the committee chairman instructs the staff to prepare a written report. The report describes the purposes and scope of the bill, explains the committee revisions, notes proposed changes in existing law and, usually, includes the views of the executive branch agencies consulted. Often committee members opposing a measure issue dissenting minority statements that are included in the report.

Usually, the committee "marks up" or proposes amendments to the bill. If they are substantial and the measure is complicated, the committee may order a "clean bill" introduced, which will embody the proposed amendments. The original bill then is put aside and the clean bill, with a new number, is reported to the floor.

The chamber must approve, alter or reject the committee amendments before the bill itself can be put to a vote.

Floor Action

After a bill is reported back to the house where it originated, it is placed on the calendar.

There are five legislative calendars in the House, issued in one cumulative calendar titled *Calendars of the United States House of Representatives and History of Legislation.* The House

How a Bill Becomes Law

This graphic shows the most typical way in which proposed legislation is enacted into law. There are more complicated, as well as simpler, routes, and most bills never become law. The process is illustrated with two hypothetical bills, House bill No. 1 (HR 1) and Senate bill No. 2 (S 2). Bills must be passed by both houses in identical form before they can be sent to the president. The path of HR 1 is traced by a black line, that of S 2 by a gray line. In practice, most bills begin as similar proposals in both houses.

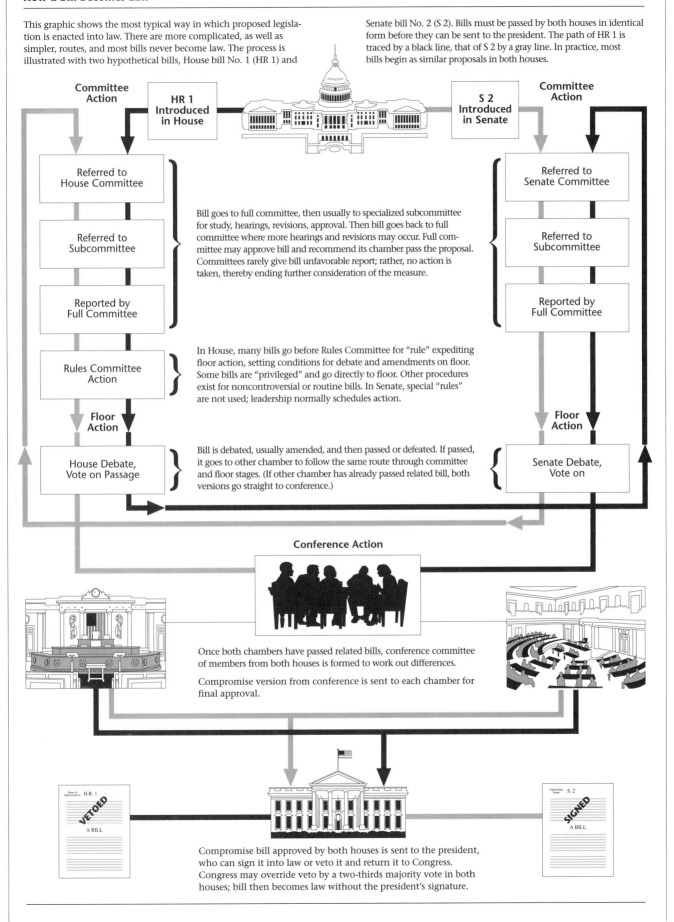

Committee Action

HR 1 Introduced in House

S 2 Introduced in Senate

Committee Action

Referred to House Committee

Referred to Subcommittee

Reported by Full Committee

Bill goes to full committee, then usually to specialized subcommittee for study, hearings, revisions, approval. Then bill goes back to full committee where more hearings and revisions may occur. Full committee may approve bill and recommend its chamber pass the proposal. Committees rarely give bill unfavorable report; rather, no action is taken, thereby ending further consideration of the measure.

Referred to Senate Committee

Referred to Subcommittee

Reported by Full Committee

Rules Committee Action

In House, many bills go before Rules Committee for "rule" expediting floor action, setting conditions for debate and amendments on floor. Some bills are "privileged" and go directly to floor. Other procedures exist for noncontroversial or routine bills. In Senate, special "rules" are not used; leadership normally schedules action.

Floor Action

House Debate, Vote on Passage

Bill is debated, usually amended, and then passed or defeated. If passed, it goes to other chamber to follow the same route through committee and floor stages. (If other chamber has already passed related bill, both versions go straight to conference.)

Floor Action

Senate Debate, Vote on

Conference Action

Once both chambers have passed related bills, conference committee of members from both houses is formed to work out differences.

Compromise version from conference is sent to each chamber for final approval.

H.R. 1
VETOED
A BILL

S. 2
SIGNED
A BILL

Compromise bill approved by both houses is sent to the president, who can sign it into law or veto it and return it to Congress. Congress may override veto by a two-thirds majority vote in both houses; bill then becomes law without the president's signature.

calendars are:

The Union Calendar to which are referred bills raising revenues, general appropriations bills and any measures directly or indirectly appropriating money or property. It is the Calendar of the Committee of the Whole House on the State of the Union.

The House Calendar to which are referred bills of public character not raising revenue or appropriating money.

The Corrections Calendar to which are referred bills to repeal rules and regulations deemed excessive or unnecessary when the Corrections Calendar is called the second and fourth Tuesday of each month. (Instituted in the 104th Congress to replace the seldom-used Consent Calendar.) A three-fifths majority is required for passage.

The Private Calendar to which are referred bills for relief in the nature of claims against the United States or private immigration bills that are passed without debate when the Private Calendar is called the first and third Tuesdays of each month.

The Discharge Calendar to which are referred motions to discharge committees when the necessary signatures are signed to a discharge petition.

There is only one legislative calendar in the Senate and one "executive calendar" for treaties and nominations submitted to the Senate. When the Senate Calendar is called, each senator is limited to five minutes' debate on each bill.

Debate. A bill is brought to debate by varying procedures. If a routine measure, it may await the call of the calendar. If it is urgent or important, it can be taken up in the Senate either by unanimous consent or by a majority vote. The majority leader, in consultation with the minority leader and others, schedules the bills that will be taken up for debate.

In the House, precedence is granted if a special rule is obtained from the Rules Committee. A request for a special rule usually is made by the chairman of the committee that favorably reported the bill, supported by the bill's sponsor and other committee members. The request, considered by the Rules Committee in the same fashion that other committees consider legislative measures, is in the form of a resolution providing for immediate consideration of the bill. The Rules Committee reports the resolution to the House where it is debated and voted on in the same fashion as regular bills. If the Rules Committee fails to report a rule requested by a committee, there are several ways to bring the bill to the House floor — under suspension of the rules, on Calendar Wednesday or by a discharge motion.

The resolutions providing special rules are important because they specify how long the bill may be debated and whether it may be amended from the floor. If floor amendments are banned, the bill is considered under a "closed rule," which permits only members of the committee that first reported the measure to the House to alter its language, subject to chamber acceptance.

When a bill is debated under an "open rule," amendments may be offered from the floor. Committee amendments always are taken up first but may be changed, as may all amendments up to the second degree; that is, an amendment to an amendment to an amendment is not in order.

Duration of debate in the House depends on whether the bill is under discussion by the House proper or before the House when it is sitting as the Committee of the Whole House on the State of the Union. In the former, the amount of time for debate either is determined by special rule or is allocated with an hour for each member if the measure is under consideration without a rule. In the Committee of the Whole the amount of time agreed on for general debate is equally divided between proponents and opponents. At the end of general discussion, the bill is read section by section for amendment. Debate on an amendment is limited to five minutes for each side; this is called the "five-minute rule." In practice, amendments regularly are debated more than ten minutes, with members gaining the floor by offering pro forma amendments or obtaining unanimous consent to speak longer than five minutes.

Senate debate usually is unlimited. It can be halted only by unanimous consent by "cloture," which requires a three-fifths majority of the entire Senate except for proposed changes in the Senate rules. The latter requires a two-thirds vote.

The House considers almost all important bills within a parliamentary framework known as the Committee of the Whole. It is not a committee as the word usually is understood; it is the full House meeting under another name for the purpose of speeding action on legislation. Technically, the House sits as the Committee of the Whole when it considers any tax measure or bill dealing with public appropriations. It also can resolve itself into the Committee of the Whole if a member moves to do so and the motion is carried. The Speaker appoints a member to serve as the chairman. The rules of the House permit the Committee of the Whole to meet when a quorum of 100 members is present on the floor and to amend and act on bills, within certain time limitations. When the Committee of the Whole has acted, it "rises," the Speaker returns as the presiding officer of the House and the member appointed chairman of the Committee of the Whole reports the action of the committee and its recommendations. The Committee of the Whole cannot pass a bill; instead it reports the measure to the full House with whatever changes it has approved. The full House then may pass or reject the bill — or, on occasion, recommit the bill to committee. Amendments adopted in the Committee of the Whole may be put to a second vote in the full House.

Votes. Voting on bills may occur repeatedly before they are finally approved or rejected. The House votes on the rule for the bill and on various amendments to the bill. Voting on amendments often is a more illuminating test of a bill's support than is the final tally. Sometimes members approve final passage of bills after vigorously supporting amendments that, if adopted, would have scuttled the legislation.

The Senate has three different methods of voting: an untabulated voice vote, a standing vote (called a division) and a recorded roll call to which members answer "yea" or "nay" when their names are called. The House also employs voice and standing votes, but since January 1973 yeas and nays have been recorded by an electronic voting device, eliminating the need for time-consuming roll calls.

Another method of voting, used in the House only, is the teller vote. Traditionally, members filed up the center aisle past counters; only vote totals were announced. Since 1971, one-fifth of a quorum can demand that the votes of individual members be recorded, thereby forcing them to take a public position on amendments to key bills. Electronic voting now is commonly used for this purpose.

After amendments to a bill have been voted upon, a vote may be taken on a motion to recommit the bill to committee. If carried, this vote removes the bill from the chamber's calendar and is usually a death blow to the bill. If the motion is unsuccessful, the bill then is "read for the third time." An actual reading usually is dispensed with. Until 1965, an opponent of a bill could delay this move by objecting and asking for a full reading of an engrossed (certified in final form) copy of the bill. After the "third reading," the vote on final passage is taken.

Examples of Legislative Documents

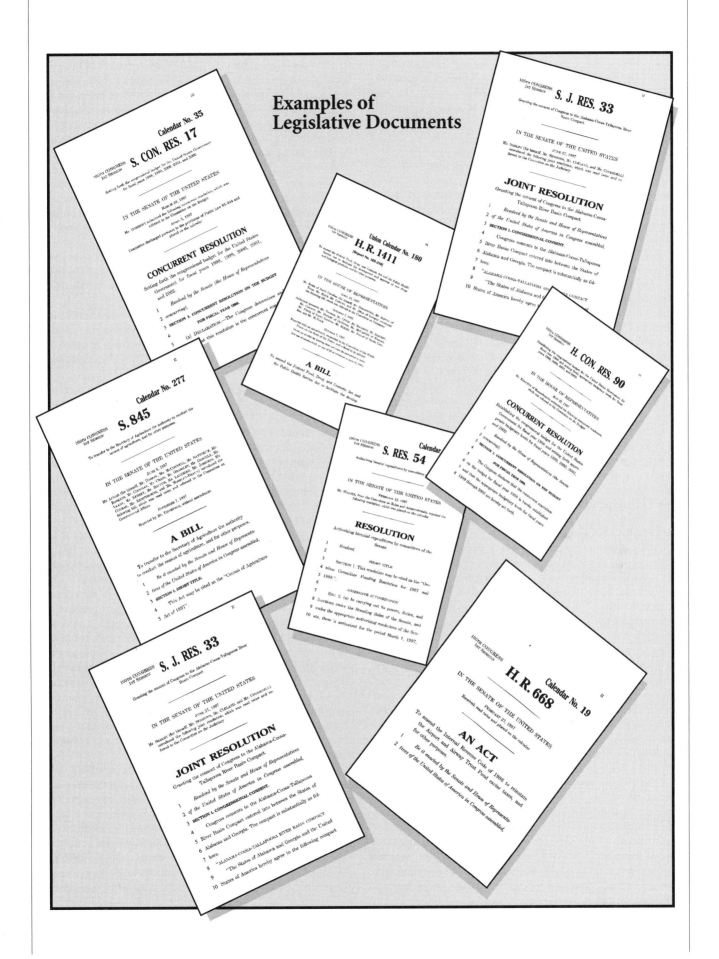

The final vote may be followed by a motion to reconsider, and this motion may be followed by a move to lay the motion on the table. Usually, those voting for the bill's passage vote for the tabling motion, thus safeguarding the final passage action. With that, the bill has been formally passed by the chamber. While a motion to reconsider a Senate vote is pending on a bill, the measure cannot be sent to the House.

Action in Second House

After a bill is passed it is sent to the other chamber. This body may then take one of several steps. It may pass the bill as is — accepting the other chamber's language. It may send the bill to committee for scrutiny or alteration, or reject the entire bill, advising the other house of its actions. Or it simply may ignore the bill submitted while it continues work on its own version of the proposed legislation. Frequently, one chamber may approve a version of a bill that is greatly at variance with the version already passed by the other house, and then substitute its contents for the language of the other, retaining only the latter's bill number.

A provision of the Legislative Reorganization Act of 1970 permits a separate House vote on any non-germane amendment added by the Senate to a House-passed bill and requires a majority vote to retain the amendment. Previously the House was forced to act on the bill as a whole; the only way to defeat the non-germane amendment was to reject the entire bill.

Often the second chamber makes only minor changes. If these are readily agreed to by the other house, the bill then is routed to the president. However, if the opposite chamber significantly alters the bill submitted to it, the measure usually is "sent to conference." The chamber that has possession of the "papers" (engrossed bill, engrossed amendments, messages of transmittal) requests a conference and the other chamber must agree to it. If the second house does not agree, the bill dies.

Conference, Final Action

Conference. A conference works out conflicting House and Senate versions of a legislative bill. The conferees usually are senior members appointed by the presiding officers of the two houses, from the committees that managed the bills. Under this arrangement the conferees of one house have the duty of trying to maintain their chamber's position in the face of amending actions by the conferees (also referred to as "managers") of the other house.

The number of conferees from each chamber may vary, the range usually being from three to nine members in each group, depending upon the length or complexity of the bill involved. There may be five representatives and three senators on the conference committee, or the reverse. But a majority vote controls the action of each group so that a large representation does not give one chamber a voting advantage over the other chamber's conferees.

Theoretically, conferees are not allowed to write new legislation in reconciling the two versions before them, but this curb sometimes is bypassed. Many bills have been put into acceptable compromise form only after new language was provided by the conferees. The 1970 Reorganization Act attempted to tighten restrictions on conferees by forbidding them to introduce any language on a topic that neither chamber sent to conference or to modify any topic beyond the scope of the different House and Senate versions.

Frequently the ironing out of difficulties takes days or even weeks. Conferences on involved appropriations bills sometimes are particularly drawn out.

As a conference proceeds, conferees reconcile differences between the versions, but generally they grant concessions only insofar as they remain sure that the chamber they represent will accept the compromises. Occasionally, uncertainty over how either house will react, or the positive refusal of a chamber to back down on a disputed amendment, results in an impasse, and the bills die in conference even though each was approved by its sponsoring chamber.

Conferees sometimes go back to their respective chambers for further instructions, when they report certain portions in disagreement. Then the chamber concerned can either "recede and concur" in the amendment of the other house or "insist on its amendment."

When the conferees have reached agreement, they prepare a conference report embodying their recommendations (compromises). The report, in document form, must be submitted to each house.

The conference report must be approved by each house. Consequently, approval of the report is approval of the compromise bill. In the order of voting on conference reports, the chamber which asked for a conference yields to the other chamber the opportunity to vote first.

Final Steps. After a bill has been passed by both the House and Senate in identical form, all of the original papers are sent to the enrolling clerk of the chamber in which the bill originated. He then prepares an enrolled bill, which is printed on parchment paper. When this bill has been certified as correct by the secretary of the Senate or the clerk of the House, depending on which chamber originated the bill, it is signed first (no matter whether it originated in the Senate or House) by the Speaker of the House and then by the president of the Senate. It is next sent to the White House to await action.

If the president approves the bill, he signs it, dates it and usually writes the word "approved" on the document. If he does not sign it within 10 days (Sundays excepted) and Congress is in session, the bill becomes law without his signature.

However, should Congress adjourn before the 10 days expire, and the president has failed to sign the measure, it does not become law. This procedure is called the pocket veto.

A president vetoes a bill by refusing to sign it and, before the 10-day period expires, returning it to Congress with a message stating his reasons. The message is sent to the chamber that originated the bill. If no action is taken on the message, the bill dies. Congress, however, can attempt to override the president's veto and enact the bill, "the objections of the president to the contrary notwithstanding." Overriding a veto requires a two-thirds vote of those present, who must number a quorum and vote by roll call.

Debate can precede this vote, with motions permitted to lay the message on the table, postpone action on it or refer it to committee. If the president's veto is overridden by a two-thirds vote in both houses, the bill becomes law. Otherwise it is dead.

When bills are passed finally and signed, or passed over a veto, they are given law numbers in numerical order as they become law. There are two series of numbers, one for public and one for private laws, starting at the number "1" for each two-year term of Congress. They are then identified by law number and by Congress — for example, Private Law 21, 97th Congress; Public Law 250, 97th Congress (or PL 97–250).

The Budget Process in Brief

Through the budget process, the president and Congress decide how much to spend and tax during the upcoming fiscal year. More specifically, they decide how much to spend on each activity, ensure that the government spends no more and spends it only for that activity, and report on that spending at the end of each budget cycle.

The President's Budget

The law requires that, by the first Monday in February, the president submit to Congress his proposed federal budget for the next fiscal year, which begins on October 1. In order to accomplish this, the president establishes general budget and fiscal policy guidelines. Based on these guidelines, executive branch agencies make requests for funds and submit them to the White House's Office of Management and Budget (OMB) nearly a year prior to the start of a new fiscal year. The OMB, receiving direction from the president and administration official, reviews the agencies' requests and develops a detailed budget by December. From December to January the OMB prepares the budget documents, so that the president can deliver it to Congress in February.

The president's budget is the executive branch's plan for the next year — but it is just a proposal. After receiving it, Congress has its own budget process to follow from February to October. Only after Congress passes the required spending bills — and the president signs them — has the government created its actual budget.

Action in Congress

Congress first must pass a "budget resolution" — a framework within which the members of Congress will make their decisions about spending and taxes. It includes targets for total spending, total revenues, and the deficit, and allocations within the spending target for the two types of spending — discretionary and mandatory.

Discretionary spending, which currently accounts for about 33 percent of all federal spending, is what the president and Congress must decide to spend for the next year through the thirteen annual appropriations bills. It includes money for such activities as the FBI and the Coast Guard, for housing and education, for NASA and highway and bridge construction, and for defense and foreign aid.

Mandatory spending, which currently accounts for 67 percent of all spending, is authorized by laws that have already been passed. It includes entitlement spending — such as for Social Security, Medicare, veterans' benefits, and food stamps — through which individuals receive benefits because they are eligible based on their age, income, or other criteria. It also includes interest on the national debt, which the government pays to individuals and institutions that hold Treasury bonds and other government securities. The only way the president and Congress can change the spending on entitlement and other mandatory programs is if they change the laws that authorized the programs.

Currently, the law imposes a limit or "cap" through 1998 on total annual discretionary spending. Within the cap, however, the president and Congress can, and often do, change the spending levels from year to year for the thousands of individual federal programs.

In addition, the law requires that legislation that would raise mandatory spending or lower revenues — compared to existing law — be offset by spending cuts or revenue increases. This requirement, called "pay-as-you-go" is designed to prevent new legislation from increasing the deficit.

Once Congress passes the budget resolution, it turns its attention to passing the thirteen annual appropriations bills and, if it chooses, "authorizing" bills to change the laws governing mandatory spending and revenues.

Congress begins by examining the president's budget in detail. Scores of committees and subcommittees hold hearings on proposals under their jurisdiction. The House and Senate Armed Services Authorizing Committees, and the Defense and Military Construction Subcommittees of the Appropriations Committees, for instance, hold hearings on the president's defense budget. The White House budget director, cabinet officers, and other administration officials work with Congress as it accepts some of the president's proposals, rejects others, and changes still others. Congress can change funding levels, eliminate programs, or add programs not requested by the president. It can add or eliminate taxes and other sources of revenue, or make other changes that affect the amount of revenue collected. Congressional rules require that these committees and subcommittees take actions that reflect the congressional budget resolution.

The president's budget, the budget resolution, and the appropriations or authorizing bills measure spending in two ways — "budget authority" and "outlays." Budget authority is what the law authorizes the federal government to spend for certain programs, projects, or activities. What the government actually spends in a particular year, however, is an outlay. For example, when the government decides to build a space exploration system, the president and Congress may agree to appropriate $1 billion in budget authority. But the space system may take ten years to build. Thus, the government may spend $100 million in outlays in the first year to begin construction and the remaining $900 million during the next nine years as the construction continues.

Congress must provide budget authority before the federal agencies can obligate the government to make outlays. When Congress fails to complete action on one or more of the regular annual appropriations bills before the fiscal year begins on October 1, budget authority may be made on a temporary basis through continuing resolutions. Continuing resolutions make budget authority available for limited periods of time, generally at rates related through some formula to the rate provided in the previous year's appropriation.

Monitoring the Budget

Once Congress passes and the president signs the federal appropriations bills or authorizing laws for the fiscal year, the government monitors the budget through (1) agency program managers and budget officials, including the Inspectors General, who report only to the agency head; (2) the Office of Management and Budget; (3) congressional committees; and (4) the General Accounting Office, an auditing arm of Congress.

This oversight is designed to (1) ensure that agencies comply with legal limits on spending, and that they use budget authority only for the purposes intended; (2) see that programs are operating consistently with legal requirements and existing policy; and (3) ensure that programs are well managed and achieving the intended results.

The president may withhold appropriated amounts from obligation only under certain limited circumstances — to provide for contingencies, to achieve savings made possible through changes in requirements or greater efficiency of operations, or as otherwise provided by law. The Impoundment Control Act of 1974 specifies the procedures that must be followed if funds are withheld. Congress can also cancel previous authorized budget authority by passing a rescissions bill — but it also must be signed by the president.

Glossary of Congressional Terms

Absolute Majority—A vote requiring approval by a majority of all members of a house rather than a majority of members present and voting. Also referred to as constitutional majority.

Act—(1) A bill passed in identical form by both houses of Congress and signed into law by the president or enacted over his veto. A bill also becomes an act without the president's signature if he does not return it to Congress within 10 days (Sundays excepted) and if Congress has not adjourned within that period. (2) Also, the technical term for a bill passed by at least one house and engrossed.

Adjourn for More Than Three Days—Under Article I, Section 5 of the Constitution, neither house may adjourn for more than three days without the approval of the other. The necessary approval is given in a concurrent resolution and agreed to by both houses, which may permit one or both to take such an adjournment.

Adjournment Sine Die—Final adjournment of an annual or two-year session of Congress; literally, adjournment without a day. The two houses must agree to a privileged concurrent resolution for such an adjournment. A sine die adjournment precludes Congress from meeting again until the next constitutionally fixed date of a session (January 3 of the following year) unless Congress determines otherwise by law or the president calls it into special session. Article II, Section 3 of the Constitution authorizes the president to adjourn both houses until such time as he thinks proper when the two houses cannot agree to a time of adjournment, but no president has ever exercised this authority.

Adjournment to a Day (and Time) Certain—An adjournment that fixes the next date and time of meeting for one or both houses. It does not end an annual session of Congress.

Advice and Consent—The Senate's constitutional role in consenting to or rejecting the president's nominations to executive branch and judicial offices and the treaties he submits. Confirmation of nominees requires a simple majority vote of the full Senate. Treaties must be approved by a two-thirds majority of senators present and voting.

Amendment—A formal proposal to alter the text of a bill, resolution, amendment, motion, treaty, or some other text. Technically, it is a motion. An amendment may strike out (eliminate) part of a text, insert new text, or strike out and insert—that is, replace all or part of the text with new text. The texts of amendments considered on the floor are printed in full in the *Congressional Record*.

Amendment in the Nature of a Substitute—Usually, an amendment to replace the entire text of a measure. It strikes out everything after the enacting clause and inserts a version that may be somewhat, substantially, or entirely different. When a committee adopts extensive amendments to a measure, it often incorporates them into such an amendment. Occasionally, the term is applied to an amendment that replaces a major portion of a measure's text.

Annual Authorization—Legislation that authorizes appropriations for a single fiscal year and usually for a specific amount. Under the rules of the authorization-appropriation process, an annually authorized agency or program must be reauthorized each year if it is to receive appropriations for that year. Sometimes Congress fails to enact the reauthorization but nevertheless provides appropriations to continue the program, circumventing the rules by one means or another.

Appeal—A member's formal challenge of a ruling or decision by the presiding officer. On appeal, a house or a committee may overturn the ruling by majority vote. The right of appeal ensures the body against arbitrary control by the chair. Appeals are rarely made in the House and are even more rarely successful. Rulings are more frequently appealed in the Senate and occasionally overturned, in part because its presiding officer is not the majority party's leader, as in the House.

Apportionment—The action, after each decennial census, of allocating the number of members in the House of Representatives to each state. By law, the total number of House members (not counting delegates and a resident commissioner) is fixed at 435. The number allotted to each state is based approximately on its proportion of the nation's total population. Since the Constitution guarantees each state one representative no matter how small its population, exact proportional distribution is virtually impossible. The mathematical formula currently used to determine the apportionment is called the Method of Equal Proportions. (*See Method of Equal Proportions.*)

Appropriation—(1) Legislative language that permits a federal agency to incur obligations and make payments from the Treasury for specified purposes, usually during a specified period of time. (2) The specific amount of money made available by such language. The Constitution prohibits payments from the Treasury except "in Consequence of Appropriations made by Law." With some exceptions, the rules of both houses forbid consideration of appropriations for purposes that are unauthorized in law or of appropriation amounts larger than those authorized in law. The House of Representatives claims the exclusive right to originate appropriation bills—a claim the Senate denies in theory but accepts in practice.

Authorization—(1) A statutory provision that establishes or continues a federal agency, activity or program for a fixed or indefinite period of time. It may also establish policies and restrictions and deal with organizational and administrative matters. (2) A statutory provision that authorizes appropriations for an agency, activity, or program. The appropriations may be authorized for one year, several years, or an indefinite period of time, and the authorization may be for a specific amount of money or an indefinite amount ("such sums as may be necessary"). Authorizations of specific amounts are construed as ceilings on the amounts that subsequently may be appropriated in an appropriation bill, but not as minimums; either house may appropriate lesser amounts or nothing at all.

Backdoor Spending Authority—Authority to incur obligations that evades the normal congressional appropriations process because it is provided in legislation other than appropriation acts. The most common forms are borrowing authority, contract authority, and entitlement authority.

Baseline—A projection of the levels of federal spending, revenues, and the resulting budgetary surpluses or deficits for the upcoming and subsequent fiscal years, taking into account laws enacted to date and assuming no new policy decisions. It provides a benchmark for measuring the budgetary effects of proposed changes in federal revenues or spending, assuming certain economic conditions.

Bill—The term for the chief vehicle Congress uses for enacting laws. Bills that originate in the House of Representatives are designated as H.R., those in the Senate as S., followed by a number assigned in the order in which they are introduced during a two-year Congress. A bill becomes a law if passed in identical language by both houses and signed by the president, or passed over his veto, or if the president fails to sign it within 10 days after he has received it while Congress is in session.

Bills and Resolutions Introduced—Members formally present measures to their respective houses by delivering them to a clerk in the chamber when their house is in session. Both houses permit any number of members to join in introducing a bill or resolution. The first member listed on the measure is the sponsor; the other members listed are its cosponsors.

Bills and Resolutions Referred—After a bill or resolution is introduced, it is normally sent to one or more committees that have jurisdiction over its subject, as defined by House and Senate rules and precedents. A Senate measure is usually referred to the committee with jurisdiction over the predominant subject of its text, but it may be sent to two or more committees by unanimous consent or on a motion offered jointly by the majority and minority leaders. In the House, a rule requires the Speaker to refer a measure to the committee that has primary jurisdiction. The Speaker is also authorized to refer measures sequentially to additional committees.

Borrowing Authority—Statutory authority permitting a federal agency, such as the Export-Import Bank, to borrow money from the public or the Treasury to finance its operations. It is a form of backdoor spending. To bring such spending under the control of the congressional appropriation process, the Congressional Budget Act requires that new borrowing authori-

ty shall be effective only to the extent and in such amounts as are provided in appropriations acts.

Budget—A detailed statement of actual or anticipated revenues and expenditures during an accounting period. For the national government, the period is the federal fiscal year (October 1–September 30). The budget usually refers to the president's budget submission to Congress early each calendar year. The president's budget estimates federal government income and spending for the upcoming fiscal year and contains detailed recommendations for appropriation, revenue, and other legislation. Congress is not required to accept or even vote directly on the president's proposals, and it often revises the president's budget extensively. (*See Fiscal Year.*)

Budget Act—Common name for the Congressional Budget and Impoundment Control Act of 1974, which established the basic procedures of the current congressional budget process; created the House and Senate budget committees; and enacted procedures for reconciliation, deferrals, and rescissions. (*See Budget Process, Deferral, Impoundment, Reconciliation, Rescission. See also Gramm-Rudman-Hollings Act of 1985.*)

Budget and Accounting Act of 1921—The law that, for the first time, authorized the president to submit to Congress an annual budget for the entire federal government. Prior to the act, most federal agencies sent their budget requests to the appropriate congressional committees without review by the president.

Budget Authority—Generally, the amount of money that may be spent or obligated by a government agency or for a government program or activity. Technically, it is statutory authority to enter into obligations that normally result in outlays. The main forms of budget authority are appropriations, borrowing authority, and contract authority. It also includes authority to obligate and expend the proceeds of offsetting receipts and collections. Congress may make budget authority available for only one year, several years, or an indefinite period, and it may specify definite or indefinite amounts.

Budget Process—(1) In Congress, the procedural system it uses (a) to approve an annual concurrent resolution on the budget that sets goals for aggregate and functional categories of federal expenditures, revenues, and the surplus or deficit for an upcoming fiscal year; and (b) to implement those goals in spending, revenue, and, if necessary, reconciliation and debt-limit legislation. (2) In the executive branch, the process of formulating the president's annual budget, submitting it to Congress, defending it before congressional committees, implementing subsequent budget-related legislation, impounding or sequestering expenditures as permitted by law, auditing and evaluating programs, and compiling final budget data. The Budget and Accounting Act of 1921 and the Congressional Budget and Impoundment Control Act of 1974 established the basic elements of the current budget process. Major revisions were enacted in the Gramm-Rudman-Hollings Act of 1985 and the Budget Enforcement Act of 1990.

Budget Resolution—A concurrent resolution in which Congress establishes or revises its version of the federal budget's broad financial features for the upcoming fiscal year and several additional fiscal years. Like other concurrent resolutions, it does not have the force of law, but it provides the framework within which Congress subsequently considers revenue, spending, and other budget-implementing legislation. The framework consists of two basic elements: (1) aggregate budget amounts (total revenues, new budget authority, outlays, loan obligations and loan guarantee commitments, deficit or surplus, and debt limit); and (2) subdivisions of the relevant aggregate amounts among the functional categories of the budget. Although it does not allocate funds to specific programs or accounts, the budget committees' reports accompanying the resolution often discuss the major program assumptions underlying its functional amounts. Unlike those amounts, however, the assumptions are not binding on Congress.

By Request—A designation indicating that a member has introduced a measure on behalf of the president, an executive agency, or a private individual or organization. Members often introduce such measures as a courtesy because neither the president nor any person other than a member of Congress can do so. The term, which appears next to the sponsor's name, implies that the member who introduced the measure does not necessarily endorse it. A House rule dealing with by-request introductions dates from 1888, but the practice goes back to the earliest history of Congress.

Calendar—A list of measures or other matters (most of them favorably reported by committees) that are eligible for floor consideration. The House has five calendars; the Senate has two. A place on a calendar does not guarantee consideration. Each house decides which measures and matters it will take up, when, and in what order, in accordance with its rules and practices.

Calendar Wednesday—A House procedure that on Wednesdays permits its committees to bring up for floor consideration nonprivileged measures they have reported The procedure is so cumbersome and susceptible to dilatory tactics, however, that committees rarely use it.

Call of the Calendar—Senate bills that are not brought up for debate by a motion, unanimous consent, or a unanimous consent agreement are brought before the Senate for action when the calendar listing them is "called." Bills must be called in the order listed. Measures considered by this method usually are noncontroversial, and debate on the bill and any proposed amendments is limited to a total of five minutes for each senator.

Caucus—(1) A common term for the official organization of each party in each house. (2) The official title of the organization of House Democrats. House and Senate Republicans and Senate Democrats call their organizations "conferences." (3) A term for an informal group of members who share legislative interests, such as the Black Caucus, Hispanic Caucus, and Children's Caucus.

Censure—The strongest formal condemnation of a member for misconduct short of expulsion. A house usually adopts a resolution of censure to express its condemnation, after which the presiding officer reads its rebuke aloud to the member in the presence of his colleagues.

Chamber—The Capitol room in which a house of Congress normally holds its sessions. The chamber of the House of Representatives, officially called the Hall of the House, is considerably larger than that of the Senate because it must accommodate 435 representatives, four delegates, and one resident commissioner. Unlike the Senate chamber, members have no desks or assigned seats. In both chambers, the floor slopes downward to the well in front of the presiding officer's raised desk. A chamber is often referred to as "the floor," as when members are said to be on or going to the floor. Those expressions usually imply that the member's house is in session.

Christmas Tree Bill—Jargon for a bill adorned with amendments, many of them unrelated to the bill's subject, that provide benefits for interest groups, specific states, congressional districts, companies, and individuals.

Classes of Senators—A class consists of the 33 or 34 senators elected to a six-year term in the same general election. Since the terms of approximately one-third of the senators expire every two years, there are three classes.

Clean Bill—After a House committee extensively amends a bill, it often assembles its amendments and what is left of the bill into a new measure that one or more of its members introduces as a "clean bill." The revised measure is assigned a new number.

Clerk of the House—An officer of the House of Representatives responsible principally for administrative support of the legislative process in the House. The clerk is invariably the candidate of the majority party.

Cloture—A Senate procedure that limits further consideration of a pending proposal to 30 hours in order to end a filibuster. Sixteen senators must first sign and submit a cloture motion to the presiding officer. One hour after the Senate meets on the second calendar day thereafter, the chair puts the motion to a yea-and-nay vote following a live quorum call. If three-fifths of all senators (60 if there are no vacancies) vote for the motion, the Senate must take final action on the cloture proposal by the end of the 30 hours of consideration and may consider no other business until it takes that action. Cloture on a proposal to amend the Senate's standing rules requires approval by two-thirds of the senators present and voting.

Code of Official Conduct—A House rule that bans certain actions by House members, officers, and employees; requires them to conduct themselves in ways that "reflect creditably" on the House; and orders them to adhere to the spirit and the letter of House rules and those of its committees. The code's provisions govern the receipt of outside compensation, gifts, and honoraria, and the use of campaign funds; prohibit members from using their clerk-hire allowance to pay anyone who does not perform duties commensurate with that pay; forbids discrimination in members' hiring or treatment of employees on the grounds of race, color, religion, sex, handicap, age, or national origin; orders members convicted of a crime who might be punished by imprisonment of two or more years not to participate in committee business or vote on the floor until exonerated or reelected; and restricts employees' contact with federal agencies on matters in which they have a significant financial interest. The Senate's rules contain some similar prohibitions.

College of Cardinals—A popular term for the subcommittee chairmen of the appropriations committees, reflecting their influence over appropriation measures. The chairmen of the full appropriations committees are sometimes referred to as popes.

Committee—A panel of members elected or appointed to perform some service or function for its parent body. Congress has four types of committees: standing, special or select, joint, and, in the House, a Committee of the Whole.

Committees conduct investigations, make studies, issue reports and recommendations, and, in the case of standing committees, review and prepare measures on their assigned subjects for action by their respective houses. Most committees divide their work among several subcommittees. With rare exceptions, the majority party in a house holds a majority of the seats on its committees, and their chairmen are also from that party.

Committee of the Whole—Common name of the Committee of the Whole House on the State of the Union, a committee consisting of all members of the House of Representatives. Measures from the union calendar must be considered in the Committee of the Whole before the House officially completes action on them; the committee often considers other major bills as well. A quorum of the committee is 100, and it meets in the House chamber under a chairman appointed by the Speaker. Procedures in the Committee of the Whole expedite consideration of legislation because of its smaller quorum requirement, its ban on certain motions, and its five-minute rule for debate on amendments. Those procedures usually permit more members to offer amendments and participate in the debate on a measure than is normally possible. The Senate no longer uses a Committee of the Whole.

Committee Veto—A procedure that requires an executive department or agency to submit certain proposed policies, programs, or action to designated committees for review before implementing them. Before 1983, when the Supreme Court declared that a legislative veto is unconstitutional, these provisions permitted committees to veto the proposals. They no longer do so, and the term is now something of a misnomer. Nevertheless, agencies usually take the pragmatic approach of trying to reach a consensus with the committees before carrying out their proposals, especially when an appropriations committee is involved.

Concurrent Resolution—A resolution that requires approval by both houses but is not sent to the president for his signature and therefore cannot have the force of law. Concurrent resolutions deal with the prerogatives or internal affairs of Congress as a whole. Designated H. Con. Res. in the House and S. Con. Res. in the Senate, they are numbered consecutively in each house in their order of introduction during a two-year Congress.

Conference—(1) A formal meeting or series of meetings between members representing each house to reconcile House and Senate differences on a measure (occasionally several measures). Since one house cannot require the other to agree to its proposals, the conference usually reaches agreement by compromise. When a conference completes action on a measure, or as much action as appears possible, it sends its recommendations to both houses in the form of a conference report, accompanied by an explanatory statement. (2) The official title of the organization of all Democrats or Republicans in the Senate and of all Republicans in the House of Representatives. (*See Party Caucus.*)

Confirmations—(*See Nomination.*)

Congress—(1) The national legislature of the United States, consisting of the House of Representatives and the Senate. (2) The national legislature in office during a two-year period. Congresses are numbered sequentially; thus, the 1st Congress of 1789–1791 and the 102d Congress of 1991–1993. Before 1935, the two-year period began on the first Monday in December of odd-numbered years. Since then it has extended from January of an odd-numbered year through noon on January 3 of the next odd-numbered year. A Congress usually holds two annual sessions, but some have had three sessions and the 67th Congress had four. When a Congress expires, measures die if they have not yet been enacted.

Congressional Record—The daily, printed, and substantially verbatim account of proceedings in both the House and Senate chambers. Extraneous materials submitted by members appear in a section titled "Extensions of Remarks." A "Daily Digest" appendix contains highlights of the day's floor and committee action plus a list of committee meetings and floor agendas for the next day's session.

Although the official reporters of each house take down every word spoken during the proceedings, members are permitted to edit and "revise and extend" their remarks before they are printed. In the Senate section, all speeches, articles, and other material submitted by senators but not actually spoken or read on the floor are set off by large black dots, called bullets. However, bullets do not appear when a senator reads part of a speech and inserts the rest. In the House section, undelivered speeches and materials are printed in a distinctive typeface. The term "permanent *Record*" refers to the bound volumes of the daily *Records* of an entire session of Congress.

Congressional Terms of Office—A term normally begins on January 3 of the year following a general election and runs two years for representatives and six years for senators. A representative chosen in a special election to fill a vacancy is sworn in for the remainder of his predecessor's term. An individual appointed to fill a Senate vacancy usually serves until the next general election or until the end of the predecessor's term, whichever comes first. Some states, however, require their governors to call a special election to fill a Senate vacancy shortly after an appointment has been made.

Continuing Resolution (CR)—A joint resolution that provides funds to continue the operation of federal agencies and programs at the beginning of a new fiscal year if their annual appropriation bills have not yet been enacted; also called continuing appropriations.

Contract Authority—Statutory authority permitting an agency to enter into contracts or incur other obligations even though it has not received an appropriation to pay for them. Congress must eventually fund them because the government is legally liable for such payments. The Congressional Budget Act of 1974 requires that new contract authority may not be used unless provided for in advance by an appropriation act, but it permits a few exceptions.

Controllable Expenditures—Federal spending that is permitted but not mandated by existing authorization law and therefore may be adjusted by congressional action in appropriation bills. (*See Appropriation.*)

Correcting Recorded Votes—The rules of both houses prohibit members from changing their votes after a vote result has been announced. Nevertheless, the Senate permits its members to withdraw or change their votes, by unanimous consent, immediately after the announcement. In rare instances, senators have been granted unanimous consent to change their votes several days or weeks after the announcement.

Votes tallied by the electronic voting system in the House may not be changed. But when a vote actually given is not recorded during an oral call of the roll, a member may demand a correction as a matter of right. On all other alleged errors in a recorded vote, the Speaker determines whether the circumstances justify a change. Occasionally, members merely announce that they were incorrectly recorded; announcements can occur hours, days, or even months after the vote and appear in the *Congressional Record*.

Corrections Calendar—Members of the House may place on this calendar bills reported favorably from committee that repeal rules and regulations considered excessive or unnecessary. Bills on the Corrections Calendar normally are called on the second and fourth Tuesday of each month at the discretion of the Speaker in consultation with the minority leader. A bill must be on the calendar for at least three legislative days before it can be brought up for floor consideration. Once on the floor, a bill is subject to one hour of debate equally divided between the chairman and ranking member of the committee of jurisdiction. A vote may be called on whether to recommit the bill to committee with or without instructions. To pass, a three-fifths majority, or 261 votes if all House members vote, is required.

Cosponsor—A member who has joined one or more other members to sponsor a measure. (*See Bills and Resolutions Introduced.*)

Current Services Estimates—Executive branch estimates of the anticipated costs of federal programs and operations for the next and future fiscal years at existing levels of service and assuming no new initiatives or changes in existing law. The president submits these estimates to Congress with his annual budget and includes an explanation of the underlying economic and policy assumptions on which they are based, such as anticipated rates of inflation, real economic growth, and unemployment, plus program caseloads and pay increases.

Custody of the Papers—Possession of an engrossed measure and certain related basic documents that the two houses produce as they try to resolve their differences over the measure.

Dance of the Swans and the Ducks—A whimsical description of the gestures some members use in connection with a request for a recorded vote, especially in the House. When a member wants his colleagues to stand in support of the request, he moves his hands and arms in a gentle upward motion resembling the beginning flight of a graceful swan. When he wants his colleagues to remain seated in order to avoid such a vote, he moves his hands and arms in a vigorous downward motion resembling a diving duck.

Dean—Within a state's delegation in the House of Representatives, the member with the longest continuous service.

Debt Limit—The maximum amount of outstanding federal public debt permitted by law. The limit (or ceiling) covers virtually all debt incurred by the government except agency debt. Each congressional budget resolution sets forth the new debt limit that may be required under its provisions.

Deferral—An impoundment of funds for a specific period of time that may not extend beyond the fiscal year in which it is proposed. Under the Impoundment Control Act of 1974, the president must notify Congress that he is deferring the spending or obligation of funds provided by law for a project or activity. Congress can disapprove the deferral by legislation.

Deficit—The amount by which the government's outlays exceed its budget receipts for a given fiscal year. Both the president's budget and the annual congressional budget resolution provide estimates of the deficit or surplus for the upcoming and several future fiscal years.

Degrees of Amendment—Designations that indicate the relationships of amendments to the text of a measure and to each other. In general, an amendment offered directly to the text of a measure is an amendment in the first degree, and an amendment to that amendment is an amendment in the second degree. Both houses normally prohibit amendments in the third degree—that is, an amendment to an amendment to an amendment.

Dilatory Tactics—Procedural actions intended to delay or prevent action by a house or a committee. They include, among others, offering numerous motions, demanding quorum calls and recorded votes at every opportunity, making numerous points of order and parliamentary inquiries, and speaking as long as the applicable rules permit. The Senates rules permit a battery of dilatory tactics, especially lengthy speeches, except under cloture. In the House, possible dilatory tactics are more limited. Speeches are always subject to time limits and debate-ending motions. Moreover, a House rule instructs the Speaker not to entertain dilatory motions and lets the Speaker decide whether a motion is dilatory. However, the Speaker may not override the constitutional right of a member to demand the yeas and nays, and in practice usually waits for a point of order before exercising that authority. (*See Cloture.*)

Discharge a Committee—Remove a measure from a committee to which it has been referred in order to make it available for floor consideration. Noncontroversial measures are often discharged by unanimous consent. However, because congressional committees have no obligation to report measures referred to them, each house has procedures to extract controversial measures from recalcitrant committees. Six discharge procedures are available in the House of Representatives. The Senate uses a motion to discharge, which is usually converted into a discharge resolution.

Discharge Calendar—The House calendar to which motions to discharge committees are referred when they have the required number of signatures (218) and are awaiting floor action.

Discharge Petition—(*See Discharge a Committee.*)

Discharge Resolution—In the Senate, a special motion that any senator may introduce to relieve a committee from consideration of a bill before it. The resolution can be called up for Senate approval or disapproval in the same manner as any other Senate business. (*House procedure, see Discharge a Committee.*)

Division Vote—A vote in which the chair first counts those in favor of a proposition and then those opposed to it, with no record made of how each member votes. In the Senate, the chair may count raised hands or ask senators to stand, whereas the House requires members to stand; hence, often called a standing vote. Committees in both houses ordinarily use a show of hands. A division usually occurs after a voice vote and may be demanded by any member or ordered by the chair if there is any doubt about the outcome of the voice vote. The demand for a division can also come before a voice vote. In the Senate, the demand must come before the result of a voice vote is announced. It may be made after a voice vote announcement in the House, but only if no intervening business has transpired and only if the member was standing and seeking recognition at the time of the announcement. A demand for the yeas and nays or, in the house, for a recorded vote, takes precedence over a division vote.

Enacting Clause—The opening language of each bill, beginning "Be it enacted by the Senate and House of Representatives of the United States of America in Congress assembled..." This language gives legal force to measures approved by Congress and signed by the president or enacted over his veto. A successful motion to strike it from a bill kills the entire measure.

Engrossed Bill—The official copy of a bill or joint resolution as passed by one chamber, including the text as amended by floor action, and certified by the clerk of the House or the secretary of the Senate (as appropriate). Amendments by one house to a measure or amendments of the other also are engrossed. House engrossed documents are printed on blue paper; the Senate's are printed on white paper.

Enrolled Bill—The final official copy of a bill or joint resolution passed in identical form by both houses. An enrolled bill is printed on parchment. After it is certified by the chief officer of the house in which it originated and signed by the House Speaker and the Senate president pro tempore, the measure is sent to the president for his signature.

Entitlement Program—A federal program under which individuals, businesses, or units of government that meet the requirements or qualifications established by law are entitled to receive certain payments if they seek such payments. Major examples include Social Security, Medicare, Medicaid, unemployment insurance, and military and federal civilian pensions. Congress cannot control their expenditures by refusing to appropriate the sums necessary to fund them because the government is legally obligated to pay eligible recipients the amounts to which the law entitles them.

Executive Calendar—The Senate's calendar for committee reports on its executive business, namely treaties and nominations. The calendar numbers indicate the order in which items were referred to the calendar but have no bearing on when or if the Senate will consider them. The Senate, by motion or unanimous consent, resolves itself into executive session to consider them

Executive Document—A document, usually a treaty, sent by the president to the Senate for approval. It is referred to a committee in the same manner as other measures. Executive documents are designated as Executive A, 102d Congress, 1st Session; Executive B; and so on.

Executive Order—A unilateral proclamation by the president that has a policy-making or legislative impact. Members of Congress have challenged some executive orders on the grounds that they usurped the authority of the legislative branch. Although the Supreme Court has ruled that a particular order exceeded the president's authority, it has upheld others as falling within the president's general constitutional powers.

Executive Privilege—The assertion that presidents have the right to withhold certain information from Congress. Presidents have based their claim on: (1) the constitutional separation of powers; (2) the need for secrecy in military and diplomatic affairs; (3) the need to protect individuals from unfavorable publicity; (4) the need to safeguard the confidential exchange of ideas in the executive branch; and (5) the need to protect individuals who provide confidential advice to the president.

Executive Session—A meeting of a Senate or House committee (or occasionally of either chamber) that only its members may attend. Witnesses regularly appear at committee meetings in executive session — for example, Defense Department officials during presentations of classified defense information. Other members of Congress may be invited, but the public and press are not to attend.

Expenditures—The actual spending of money as distinguished from the appropriation of funds. Expenditures are made by the disbursing officers of the administration; appropriations are made only by Congress. The two are rarely identical in any fiscal year. In addition to some current budget authority, expenditures may represent budget authority made available one, two, or more years earlier.

Expulsion—A member's removal from office by a two-thirds vote of his house; the super majority is required by the Constitution. It is the most severe and most rarely used sanction a house can invoke against a member. Although the Constitution provides no explicit grounds for expulsion, the courts have ruled that it may be applied only for misconduct during a member's term of office, not for conduct before the member's election. Generally, neither house will consider expulsion of a member convicted of a crime until the judicial processes have been exhausted. At that stage, members sometimes resign rather than face expulsion. In 1977 the House adopted a rule urging members convicted of certain crimes to voluntarily abstain from voting or participating in other legislative business.

Federal Debt—The total amount of monies borrowed and not yet repaid by the federal government. Federal debt consists of public debt and agency debt. Public debt is the portion of the federal debt borrowed by the Treasury or the Federal Financing Bank directly from the public or from another federal fund or account. For example, the Treasury regularly borrows money from the Social Security trust fund. Public debt accounts for about 99 percent of the federal debt. Agency debt refers to the debt incurred by federal agencies like the Export-Import Bank, but excluding the Treasury and the Federal Financing Bank, which are authorized by law to borrow funds from the public or from another government fund or account.

Filibuster—The use of obstructive and time-consuming parliamentary tactics by one member or a minority of members to delay, modify, or defeat proposed legislation or rules changes. Filibusters are also sometimes used to delay urgently needed measures in order to force the body to accept other legislation. The Senate's rules permitting unlimited debate and the extraordinary majority it requires to impose cloture make filibustering particularly effective in that chamber. Under the stricter rules of the House, filibusters in that body are short-lived and therefore ineffective and rarely attempted

Fiscal Year—The federal government's annual accounting period. It begins October 1 and ends on the following September 30. A fiscal year is designated by the calendar year in which it ends and is often referred to as FY. Thus, fiscal year 1992 began October 1, 1991, ended September 30, 1992, and is called FY92. In theory, Congress is supposed to complete action on all budgetary measures applying to a fiscal year before that year begins. It rarely does so.

Five-Minute Rule—In its most common usage, a House rule that limits debate on an amendment offered in Committee of the Whole to five minutes for its sponsor and five minutes for an opponent. In practice, the committee routinely permits longer debate by two devices: the offering of pro forma amendments, each debatable for five minutes, and unanimous consent for a member to speak longer than five minutes. Also a House rule that limits a committee member to five minutes when questioning a witness at a hearing until each member has had an opportunity to question that witness.

Floor Manager—A majority party member responsible for guiding a measure through its floor consideration in a house and for devising the political and procedural strategies that might be required to get the measure passed. The presiding officer gives the floor manager priority recognition to debate, offer amendments, oppose amendments, and make crucial procedural motions.

Frank—Informally, a member's legal right to send official mail postage free under his or her signature; often called the franking privilege. Technically, it is the autographic or facsimile signature used on envelopes instead of stamps that permits members and certain congressional officers to send their official mail free of charge. The franking privilege has been authorized by law since the first Congress, except for a few months in 1873. Congress reimburses the U.S. Postal Service for the franked mail it handles.

Function or Functional Category—A broad category of national need and spending of budgetary significance. A category provides an accounting method for allocating and keeping track of budgetary resources and expenditures for that function because it includes all budget accounts related to the functions subject or purpose such as agriculture, administration of justice, commerce and housing and energy. Functions do not necessari-

ly correspond with appropriations acts or with the budgets of individual agencies.

Germane—Basically, on the same subject as the matter under consideration. A House rule requires that all amendments be germane. In the Senate, only amendments proposed to general appropriation bills and budget resolutions or under cloture must be germane. Germaneness rules can be evaded by suspension of the rules in both houses, by unanimous consent agreements in the Senate, and by special rules from the Rules Committee in the House.

Gerrymandering—The manipulation of legislative district boundaries to benefit a particular party, politician, or minority group. The term originated in 1812 when the Massachusetts legislature redrew the lines of state legislative districts to favor the party of Gov. Elbridge Gerry, and some critics said one district looked like a salamander.

Gramm-Rudman-Hollings Act of 1985—Common name for the Balanced Budget and Emergency Deficit Control Act of 1985, which established new budget procedures intended to balance the federal budget by fiscal year 1991—a goal subsequently extended to 1993. The act's chief sponsors were senators Phil Gramm (R-Texas), Warren Rudman (R-N.H.), and Ernest Hollings (D-S.C.).

Grandfather Clause—A provision in a measure, law, or rule that exempts an individual, entity, or a defined category of individuals or entities from complying with a new policy or restriction. For example, a bill that would raise taxes on persons who reach the age of 65 after a certain date inherently grandfathers out those who are 65 before that date. Similarly, a Senate rule limiting senators to two major committee assignments also grandfathers some senators who were sitting on a third major committee prior to a specified date.

Grants-in-Aid—Payments by the federal government to state and local governments to help provide for assistance programs or public services.

Hearing—(1) Committee or subcommittee meetings to receive testimony from witnesses on proposed legislation during investigations or for oversight purposes. Relatively few bills are important enough to justify formal hearings. Witnesses often include experts, government officials, spokespersons for interested groups, officials of the General Accounting Office, and members of Congress. Also, the printed transcripts of hearings.

Hold—A senator's request that his or her party leaders delay floor consideration of certain legislation or presidential nominations. The majority leader usually honors a hold for a reasonable period of time, especially if its purpose is to assure the senator that the matter will not be called up during his or her absence or to give the senator time to gather necessary information.

Hold-Harmless Clause—In legislation providing a new formula for allocating federal funds, a clause to ensure that recipients of those funds do not receive less in a future year than they did in the current year if the new formula would result in a reduction for them. Similar to a grandfather clause, it has been used most frequently to soften the impact of sudden reductions in federal grants. (*See Grandfather Clause.*)

Hopper—A box on the clerk's desk in the House chamber into which members deposit bills and resolutions to introduce them. In House jargon, to drop a bill in the hopper is to introduce it.

Hour Rule—(1) A House rule that permits members, when recognized, to hold the floor in debate for no more than one hour each. The majority party member customarily yields one-half the time to a minority member. Although the hour rule applies to general debate in Committee of the Whole as well as in the House, special rules routinely vary the length of time for such debate and its control to fit the circumstances of particular measures.

House—The House of Representatives, as distinct from the Senate, although each body is a "house" of Congress.

House as in Committee of the Whole—A hybrid combination of procedures from the general rules of the House and from the rules of the Committee of the Whole, sometimes used to expedite consideration of a measure on the floor.

House Calendar—The calendar reserved for all public bills and resolutions that do not raise revenue or directly or indirectly appropriate money or property when they are favorably reported by House committees.

House Manual—A commonly used title for the handbook of the rules of the House of Representatives, published in each Congress. Its official title is *Constitution, Jefferson's Manual, and Rules of the House of Representatives*.

House of Representatives—The house of Congress in which states are represented roughly in proportion to their populations, but every state is guaranteed at least one representative. By law, the number of voting representatives is fixed at 435. Four delegates and one resident commissioner also serve in the House; they may vote in their committees and in Committee of the Whole but not in the House sitting as the House. Although the House and Senate have equal legislative power, the Constitution gives the House sole authority to originate revenue measures. The House also claims the right to originate appropriation measures, a claim the Senate disputes in theory but concedes in practice. The House has the sole power to impeach, and it elects the president when no candidate has received a majority of the electoral votes. It is sometimes referred to as the lower body.

Immunity—(1) Members' constitutional protection from lawsuits and arrest in connection with their legislative duties. They may not be tried for libel or slander for anything they say on the floor of a house or in committee. Nor may they be arrested while attending sessions of their houses or when traveling to or from sessions of Congress, except when charged with treason, a felony, or a breach of the peace. (2) In the case of a witness before a committee, a grant of protection from prosecution based on that person's testimony to the committee. It is used to compel witnesses to testify who would otherwise refuse to do so on the constitutional ground of possible self-incrimination. Under such a grant, none of a witness testimony may be used against

him or her in a court proceeding except in a prosecution for perjury or for giving a false statement to Congress.

Impeachment—The first step to remove the president, vice president, or other federal civil officers from office and to disqualify them from any future federal office "of honor, Trust or Profit." An impeachment is a formal charge of treason, bribery, or "other high Crimes and Misdemeanors." The House has the sole power of impeachment and the Senate the sole power of trying the charges and convicting. The House impeaches by a simple majority vote; conviction requires a two-thirds vote of all senators present.

Impoundment—An executive branch action or inaction that delays or withholds the expenditure or obligation of budget authority provided by law. The Impoundment Control Act of 1974 classifies impoundments as either deferrals or rescissions, requires the president to notify Congress about all such actions, and gives Congress authority to approve or reject them. The Constitution is unclear on whether a president may refuse to spend appropriated money, but Congress usually expects the president to spend at least enough to achieve the purposes for which the money was provided whether or not he agrees with those purposes.

Item Veto—A procedure (sometimes called a line-item veto), available in 1997 for the first time, permitting a president to cancel amounts of new discretionary appropriations (budget authority), as well as new items of direct spending (entitlements) and certain limited tax benefits, unless Congress disapproves by law within a limited period of time. After the president signs a bill, he may act within five calendar days to propose the cancellation of one or more such items; a cancellation becomes permanent unless, within 30 days, Congress passes a joint resolution to disapprove it. The president may veto such a joint resolution; in that case, it requires a two-thirds vote in both houses to override the president's veto of the joint resolution disapproving his action. The authority to cancel amounts of new discretionary appropriations applies only to amounts specifically identified in the law or one of the accompanying standing or conference committee reports. The authority for this procedure expires at the end of 2004 unless Congress extends it by law.

Joint Committee—A committee composed of members selected from each house. The functions of most joint committees involve investigation, research, or oversight of agencies closely related to Congress. Permanent joint committees, created by statute, are sometimes called standing joint committees. Once quite numerous, only four joint committees remained as of 1997: Joint Economic, Joint Taxation, Joint Library, and Joint Printing. No joint committee has authority to report legislation.

Joint Resolution—A legislative measure that Congress uses for purposes other than general legislation. Like a bill, it has the force of law when passed by both houses and either approved by the president or passed over the president's veto. Unlike a bill, a joint resolution enacted into law is not called an act; it retains its original title.

Most often, joint resolutions deal with such relatively limited matters as the correction of errors in existing law, continuing appropriations, a single appropriation, or the establishment of permanent joint committees. Unlike bills, however, joint resolutions also are used to propose constitutional amendments; these do not require the president's signature and become effective only when ratified by three-fourths of the states. The House designates joint resolutions as H.J. Res., the Senate as S.J. Res. Each house numbers its joint resolutions consecutively in the order of introduction during a two-year Congress.

Journal—The official record of House or Senate actions, including every motion offered, every vote cast, amendments agreed to, quorum calls, and so forth. Unlike the *Congressional Record,* it does not provide reports of speeches, debates, statements, and the like. The Constitution requires each house to maintain a *Journal* and to publish it periodically.

King of the Mountain (or Hill Rule)—*(See Queen of the Hill Rule.)*

Lame Duck—Jargon for a member who has not been reelected, or did not seek reelection, and is serving the balance of his or her term.

Lame Duck Session—A session of a Congress held after the election for the succeeding Congress, so-called after the lame duck members still serving.

Law—An act of Congress that has been signed by the president, passed over the president's veto, or allowed to become law without the president's signature.

Legislative Day—The day that begins when a house meets after an adjournment and ends when it next adjourns. Because the House of Representatives normally adjourns at the end of a daily session, its legislative and calendar days usually coincide. The Senate, however, frequently recesses at the end of a daily session, and its legislative day may extend over several calendar days, weeks, or months. Among other uses, this technicality permits the Senate to save time by circumventing its morning hour, a procedure required at the beginning of every legislative day

Legislative Veto—A procedure, declared unconstitutional in 1983, that allowed Congress or one of its houses to nullify certain actions of the president, executive branch agencies, or independent agencies. Sometimes called congressional vetoes or congressional disapprovals. Following the Supreme Court's 1983 decision, Congress amended several legislative veto statutes to require enactment of joint resolutions, which are subject to presidential veto, for nullifying executive branch actions.

Live Pair—A voluntary and informal agreement between two members on opposite sides of an issue under which the member who is present for a recorded vote withholds or withdraws his or her vote because the other member is absent.

Loan Guarantee—A statutory commitment by the federal government to pay part or all of a loans principal and interest to a lender or the holder of a security in case the borrower defaults.

Lobby—To try to persuade members of Congress to propose, pass, modify, or defeat proposed legislation or to change or repeal existing laws. A lobbyist attempts to promote his or her own preferences or those of a group, organization, or industry. Originally the term referred to persons frequenting the lobbies or corridors of legislative chambers in order to speak to lawmakers. In a general sense, lobbying includes not only direct contact with members but also indirect attempts to influence them, such as writing to them or persuading others to write or visit them, attempting to mold public opinion toward a desired legislative goal by various means, and contributing or arranging for contributions to members election campaigns. The right to lobby stems from the First Amendment to the Constitution, which bans laws that abridge the right of the people to petition the government for a redress of grievances.

Logrolling—Jargon for a legislative tactic or bargaining strategy in which members try to build support for their legislation by promising to support legislation desired by other members or by accepting amendments they hope will induce their colleagues to vote for their bill.

Mace—The symbol of the office of the House sergeant at arms. Under the direction of the Speaker, the sergeant at arms is responsible for preserving order on the House floor by holding up the mace in front of an unruly member, or by carrying the mace up and down the aisles to quell boisterous behavior. When the House is in session, the mace sits on a pedestal at the Speaker's right; when the House is in Committee of the Whole, it is moved to a lower pedestal. The mace is 46 inches high and consists of 13 ebony rods bound in silver and topped by a silver globe with a silver eagle, wings outstretched, perched on it.

Majority Leader—The majority party's chief floor spokesman, elected by that party's caucus—sometimes called floor leader. In the Senate, the majority leader also develops the party's political and procedural strategy, usually in collaboration with other party officials and committee chairmen. He negotiates the Senates agenda and committee ratios with the minority leader and usually calls up measures for floor action. The chamber traditionally concedes to the majority leader the right to determine the days on which it will meet and the hours at which it will convene and adjourn. In the House, the majority leader is the Speaker's deputy and heir apparent. He helps plan the floor agenda and the party's legislative strategy and often speaks for the party leadership in debate.

Majority Whip—In effect, the assistant majority leader, in either the House or Senate. His job is to help marshal majority forces in support of party strategy and legislation.

Manual—The official handbook in each house prescribing in detail its organization, procedures, and operations.

Marking Up a Bill—Going through the contents of a piece of legislation in committee or subcommittee to, for example, consider its provisions in large and small portions, act on amendments to provisions and proposed revisions to the language, and insert new sections and phraseology. If the bill is extensively amended, the committee's version may be introduced as a separate bill, with a new number, before being considered by the full House or Senate. *(See Clean Bill.)*

Method of Equal Proportions—The mathematical formula used since 1950 to determine how the 435 seats in the House of Representatives should be distributed among the 50 states in the apportionment following each decennial census. It minimizes as much as possible the proportional difference between the average district population in any two states. Because the Constitution guarantees each state at least one representative, 50 seats are automatically apportioned. The formula calculates priority numbers for each state, assigns the first of the 385 remaining seats to the state with the highest priority number, the second to the state with the next highest number, and so on until all seats are distributed. *(See Apportionment.)*

Midterm Election—The general election for members of Congress that occurs in November of the second year in a presidential term.

Minority Leader—The minority party's leader and chief floor spokesman, elected by the party caucus; sometimes called minority floor leader. With the assistance of other party officials and the ranking minority members of committees, the minority leader devises the party's political and procedural strategy.

Minority Whip—Performs duties of whip for the minority party. *(See also Majority Whip.)*

Minority Staff—Employees who assist the minority party members of a committee. Most committees hire separate majority and minority party staffs, but they also may hire nonpartisan staff.

Motion—A formal proposal for a procedural action, such as to consider, to amend, to lay on the table, to reconsider, to recess, or to adjourn. It has been estimated that at least 85 motions are possible under various circumstances in the House of Representatives, somewhat fewer in the Senate. Not all motions are created equal; some are privileged or preferential and enjoy priority over others. And some motions are debatable, amendable or divisible, while others are not.

Nomination—A proposed presidential appointment to a federal office submitted to the Senate for confirmation. Approval is by majority vote. The Constitution explicitly requires confirmation for ambassadors, consuls, public Ministers (department heads), and Supreme Court justices. By law, other federal judges, all military promotions of officers, and many high-level civilian officials must be confirmed.

Oath of Office—Upon taking office, members of Congress must swear or affirm that they will "support and defend the Constitution . . . against all enemies, foreign and domestic," that they will "bear true faith and allegiance" to the Constitution, that they take the obligation "freely, without any mental reservation or purpose of evasion," and that they will "well and faithfully discharge the duties" of their office. The oath is required by the Constitution; the wording is prescribed by a statute. All House members must take the oath at the beginning of each new Congress.

Obligations—Orders placed, contracts awarded, services received, and similar transactions during a given period that will require payments during the same or future period. Such amounts include outlays for which obligations had not been previously recorded and reflect adjustments for differences between obligations previously recorded and actual outlays to liquidate those obligations.

Omnibus Bill—A measure that combines the provisions of several disparate subjects into a single and often lengthy bill.

One-Minute Speeches—Addresses by House members at the beginning of a legislative day. The speeches may cover any subject but are limited to one minute's duration.

Order of Business (House)—The sequence of events during the meeting of the House on a new legislative day prescribed by a House rule; also called the general order of business. The sequence consists of (1) the chaplain's prayer; (2) approval of the *Journal*; (3) pledge of allegiance (4) correction of the reference of public bills; (5) disposal of business on the Speaker's table; (6) unfinished business; (7) the morning hour call of committees and consideration of their bills (largely obsolete); (8) motions to go into Committee of the Whole; and (9) orders of the day (also obsolete). In practice, on days specified in the rules, the items of business that follow approval of the *Journal* are supplanted in part by the special order of business (for example, the corrections, discharge, or private calendars or motions to suspend the rules) and on any day by other privileged business (for example, general appropriation bills and special rules) or measures made in order by special rules. By this combination of an order of business with privileged interruptions, the House gives precedence to certain categories of important legislation, brings to the floor other major legislation from its calendars in any order it chooses, and provides expeditious processing for minor and noncontroversial measures.

Order of Business (Senate)—The sequence of events at the beginning of a new legislative day prescribed by Senate rules. The sequence consists of (1) the chaplain's prayer; (2) *Journal* reading and correction; (3) morning business in the morning hour; (4) call of the calendar during the morning hour; and (5) unfinished business.

Outlays—Amounts of government spending. They consist of payments, usually by check or in cash, to liquidate obligations incurred in prior fiscal years as well as in the current year, including the net lending of funds under budget authority. In federal budget accounting, net outlays are calculated by subtracting the amounts of refunds and various kinds of reimbursements to the government from actual spending.

Override a Veto—Congressional enactment of a measure over the president's veto. A veto override requires a recorded two-thirds vote of those voting in each house, a quorum being present. Because the president must return the vetoed measure to its house of origin, that house votes first, but neither house is required to attempt an override, whether immediately or at all. If an override attempt fails in the house of origin, the veto stands and the measure dies.

Oversight—Congressional review of the way in which federal agencies implement laws to ensure that they are carrying out the intent of Congress and to inquire into the efficiency of the implementation and the effectiveness of the law. The Legislative Reorganization Act of 1946 defined oversight as the function of exercising continuous watchfulness over the execution of the laws by the executive branch.

Pairing—A procedure that permits two or three members to enter into voluntary arrangements that offset their votes so that one or more of the members can be absent without changing the result. The names of paired members and their positions on the vote (except on general pairs) appear in the *Congressional Record*. Members can be paired on one vote or on a series of votes.

Parliamentarian—The official advisor to the presiding officer in each house on questions of procedure. The parliamentarian and his assistants also answer procedural questions from members and congressional staff, refer measures to committees on behalf of the presiding officer, and maintain compilations of the precedents. The House parliamentarian revises the House Manual at the beginning of every Congress and usually reviews special rules before the Rules Committee reports them to the House. Either a parliamentarian or an assistant is always present and near the podium during sessions of each house.

Party Caucus—Generic term for each party's official organization in each house. Only House Democrats officially call their organization a caucus. House and Senate Republicans and Senate Democrats call their organizations conferences. The party caucuses elect their leaders, approve committee assignments and chairmanships (or ranking minority members, if the party is in the minority), establish party committees and study groups, and discuss party and legislative policies. On rare occasions, they have stripped members of committee seniority or expelled them from the caucus for party disloyalty.

Petition—A request or plea sent to one or both chambers from an organization or private citizens' group asking support of particular legislation or favorable consideration of a matter not yet receiving congressional attention. Petitions are referred to appropriate committees.

Pocket Veto—The indirect veto of a bill as a result of the president withholding approval of it until after Congress has adjourned sine die. A bill the president does not sign, but does not formally veto while Congress is in session, automatically becomes a law 10 days (excluding Sundays) after it is received. But if Congress adjourns its annual session during that 10-day period, the measure dies even if the president does not formally veto it.

Point of Order—A parliamentary term used in committee and on the floor to object to an alleged violation of a rule and to demand that the chair enforce the rule. The point of order immediately halts the proceedings until the chair decides whether the contention is valid.

Pork or Pork Barrel Legislation—Pejorative terms for federal appropriations, bills, or policies that provide funds to benefit a legislator's district or state, with the implication that the legislator presses for enactment of such benefits to ingratiate himself or herself with constituents rather than on the basis of an impartial, objective assessment of need or merit.

The terms are often applied to such benefits as new parks, post offices, dams, canals, bridges, roads, water projects, sewage treatment plants, and public works of any kind, as well as demonstration projects, research grants, and relocation of government facilities. Funds released by the president for various kinds of benefits or government contracts approved by him allegedly for political purposes are also sometimes referred to as pork.

Postcloture Filibuster—A filibuster conducted after the Senate invokes cloture. It employs an array of procedural tactics rather than lengthy speeches to delay final action. The Senate curtailed the postcloture filibusters effectiveness by closing a variety of loopholes in the cloture rule in 1979 and 1986.

President of the Senate—The vice president of the United States in his constitutional role as presiding officer of the Senate. The Constitution permits the vice president to cast a vote in the Senate only to break a tie, but he is not required to do so.

President Pro Tempore—Under the Constitution, an officer elected by the Senate to preside over it during the absence of the vice president of the United States. Often referred to as the "pro tem," he is usually the majority party senator with the longest continuous service in the chamber and also, by virtue of his seniority, a committee chairman. When attending to committee and other duties, the president pro tempore appoints other senators to preside.

Previous Question—A nondebatable motion which, when agreed to by majority vote, usually cuts off further debate, prevents the offering of additional amendments, and brings the pending matter to an immediate vote. It is a major debate-limiting device in the House; it is not permitted in Committee of the Whole or in the Senate.

Printed Amendment—A House rule guarantees five minutes of floor debate in support and five minutes in opposition, and no other debate time, on amendments printed in the Congressional Record at least one day prior to the amendment's consideration in the Committee of the Whole. In the Senate, although amendments may be submitted for printing, they have no parliamentary standing or status. An amendment submitted for printing in the Senate, however, may be called up by any senator.

Private Bill—A bill that applies to one or more specified persons, corporations, institutions, or other entities, usually to grant relief when no other legal remedy is available to them. Many private bills deal with claims against the federal government, immigration and naturalization cases, and land titles.

Private Calendar—Commonly used title for a calendar in the House reserved for private bills and resolutions favorably reported by committees. The private calendar is officially called the Calendar of the Committee of the Whole House.

Privilege—An attribute of a motion, measure, report, question, or proposition that gives it priority status for consideration. Privileged motions and motions to bring up privileged questions are not debatable.

Privileged Questions—The order in which bills, motions, and other legislative measures are considered by Congress is governed by strict priorities. A motion to table, for instance, is more privileged than a motion to recommit. Thus, a motion to recommit can be superseded by a motion to table, and a vote would be forced on the latter motion only. A motion to adjourn, however, takes precedence over a tabling motion and thus is considered of the "highest privilege." (*See also Questions of Privilege*.)

Pro Forma Amendment—In the House, an amendment that ostensibly proposes to change a measure or another amendment by moving "to strike the last word" or "to strike the requisite number of words." A member offers it not to make any actual change in the measure or amendment but only to obtain time for debate.

Proxy Voting—The practice of permitting a member to cast the vote of an absent colleague in addition to his own vote. Proxy voting is prohibited on the floors of the House and Senate, but the Senate permits their committees to authorize proxy voting, and most do. In 1995, House rules were changed to prohibit proxy voting in committee.

Public Law—A public bill or joint resolution enacted into law. It is cited by the letters P.L. followed by a hyphenated number. The digits before the hyphen indicate the number of the Congress in which it was enacted; the digits after the hyphen indicate its position in the numerical sequence of public measures that became law during that Congress. For example, the Budget Enforcement Act of 1990 became P.L. 101-508 because it was the 508th measure in that sequence for the 101st Congress. (*See also Private Bill.*)

Queen of the Hill Rule—A special rule from the House Rules Committee that permits votes on a series of amendments, especially complete substitutes for a measure, in a specified order, but directs that the amendment receiving the greatest number of votes shall be the winning one. This kind of rule permits the House to vote directly on a variety of alternatives to a measure. In doing so, it sets aside the precedent that once an amendment has been adopted, no further amendments may be offered to the text it has amended. Under an earlier practice, the Rules Committee reported "king of the hill" rules under which there also could be votes on a series of amendments, again in a specified order. If more than one of the amendments was adopted under this kind of rule, it was the last amendment to receive a majority vote that was considered as having been finally adopted, whether or not it had received the greatest number of votes.

Questions of Privilege—These are matters affecting members of Congress individually or collectively. Matters affecting the rights, safety, dignity, and integrity of proceedings of the House or Senate as a whole are questions of privilege in both chambers.

Questions involving individual members are called questions of "personal privilege." A member rising to ask a question of personal privilege is given precedence over almost all other proceedings. An annotation in the House rules points out that the privilege rests primarily on the Constitution, which gives a member a conditional immunity from arrest and an unconditional freedom to speak in the House. (*See also Privileged Questions.*)

Quorum—The minimum number of members required to be present for the transaction of business. Under the Constitution, a quorum in each house is a majority of its members: 218 in the House and 51 in the Senate when there are no vacancies. By House rule, a quorum in Committee of the Whole is 100. In practice, both houses usually assume a quorum is present even if it is not, unless a member makes a point of no quorum in the House or suggests the absence of a quorum in the Senate. Con-

sequently, each house transacts much of its business, and even passes bills, when only a few members are present.

For House and Senate committees, chamber rules allow a minimum quorum of one-third of a committee's members to conduct most types of business.

Ramseyer Rule—A House rule that requires a committee's report on a bill or joint resolution to show the changes the measure, and any committee amendments to it, would make in existing law.

Readings of Bills—Traditional parliamentary procedure required bills to be read three times before they were passed. This custom is of little modern significance. Normally a bill is considered to have its first reading when it is introduced and printed, by title, in the *Congressional Record*. In the House, its second reading comes when floor consideration begins. (This is the most likely point at which there is an actual reading of the bill, if there is any.) The second reading in the Senate is supposed to occur on the legislative day after the measure is introduced, but before it is referred to committee. The third reading (again, usually by title) takes place when floor action has been completed on amendments.

Reapportionment—(*See Apportionment.*)

Recess—(1) A temporary interruption or suspension of a meeting of a chamber or committee. Unlike an adjournment, a recess does not end a legislative day. Because the Senate often recesses from one calendar day to another, its legislative day may extend over several calendar days, weeks, or even months. (2) A period of adjournment for more than three days to a day certain, especially over a holiday or in August during odd-numbered years.

Recognition—The power of recognition of a member is lodged in the Speaker of the House and the presiding officer of the Senate. The presiding officer names the member who will speak first when two or more members simultaneously request recognition.

Recommit—To send a measure back to the committee that reported it; sometimes called a straight motion to recommit to distinguish it from a motion to recommit with instructions. A successful motion to recommit kills the measure unless it is accompanied by instructions.

Reconciliation—A procedure for changing existing revenue and spending laws to bring total federal revenues and spending within the limits established in a budget resolution. Congress has applied reconciliation chiefly to revenues and mandatory spending programs, especially entitlements. Discretionary spending is controlled through annual appropriation bills.

Reconsider a Vote—A motion to reconsider the vote by which an action was taken has, until it is disposed of, the effect of putting the action in abeyance. In the Senate, the motion can be made only by a member who voted on the prevailing side of the original question or by a member who did not vote at all. In the House, it can be made only by a member on the prevailing side.

A common practice in the Senate after close votes on an issue is a motion to reconsider, followed by a motion to table the motion to reconsider. On this motion to table, senators vote as they voted on the original question, which allows the motion to table to prevail, assuming there are no switches. The matter then is finally closed and further motions to reconsider are not entertained. In the House, as a routine precaution, a motion to reconsider usually is made every time a measure is passed. Such a motion almost always is tabled immediately, thus shutting off the possibility of future reconsideration, except by unanimous consent.

Motions to reconsider must be entered in the Senate within the next two days of actual session after the original vote has been taken. In the House they must be entered either on the same day or on the next succeeding day the House is in session.

Recorded Vote—(1) Generally, any vote in which members are recorded by name for or against a measure; also called a record vote or roll-call vote. The only recorded vote in the Senate is a vote by the yeas and nays and is commonly called a roll-call vote. (2) Technically, a recorded vote is one demanded in the House of Representatives and supported by at least one-fifth of a quorum (44 members) in the House sitting as the House or at least 25 members in Committee of the Whole.

Report—(1) As a verb, a committee is said to report when it submits a measure or other document to its parent chamber. (2) A clerk is said to report when he or she reads a measure's title, text, or the text of an amendment to the body at the direction of the chair. (3) As a noun, a committee document that accompanies a reported measure. It describes the measure, the committee's views on it, its costs, and the changes it proposes to make in existing law; it also includes certain impact statements. (4) A committee document submitted to its parent chamber that describes the results of an investigation or other study or provides information the committee is required to provide by rule or law.

Reprimand—A formal condemnation of a member for misbehavior, considered a milder reproof than censure. The House of Representatives first used it in 1976. The Senate has not used the term. (*See also Censure, Code of Official Conduct, Expulsion.*)

Rescission—A provision of law that repeals previously enacted budget authority in whole or in part. Under the Impoundment Control Act of 1974, the president can impound such funds by sending a message to Congress requesting one or more rescissions and the reasons for doing so. If Congress does not pass a rescission bill for the programs requested by the president within 45 days of continuous session after receiving the message, the president must make the funds available for obligation and expenditure. If the president does not, the comptroller general of the United States is authorized to bring suit to compel the release of those funds. A rescission bill may rescind all, part, or none of an amount proposed by the president, and may rescind funds the president has not impounded.

Resolution—(1) A simple resolution; that is, a nonlegislative measure effective only in the house in which it is proposed and not requiring concurrence by the other chamber or approval by the president. Simple resolutions are designated H. Res. in the House and S. Res. in the Senate. Simple resolutions express nonbinding opinions on policies or issues or deal with the internal affairs or prerogatives of a house. (2) Any type of resolution: simple, concurrent, or joint. (*See Concurrent Resolution, Joint Resolution.*)

Revise and Extend One's Remarks—A unanimous consent request to publish in the *Congressional Record* a statement a member did not deliver on the floor, a longer statement than the one made on the floor, or miscellaneous extraneous material.

Rider—Congressional slang for an amendment unrelated or extraneous to the subject matter of the measure to which it is attached. Riders often contain proposals that are less likely to become law on their own merits as separate bills, either because of opposition in the committee of jurisdiction, resistance in the other house, or the probability of a presidential veto. Riders are more common in the Senate.

Rule—(1) A permanent regulation that a house adopts to govern its conduct of business, its procedures, its internal organization, behavior of its members, regulation of its facilities, duties of an officer, or some other subject it chooses to govern in that form. (2) In the House, a privileged simple resolution reported by the Rules Committee that provides methods and conditions for floor consideration of a measure or, rarely, several measures.

Secretary of the Senate—The chief administrative and budgetary officer of the Senate. The secretary manages a wide range of functions that support the operation of the Senate as an organization as well as those functions necessary to its legislative process, including recordkeeping, document management, certifications, housekeeping services, administration of oaths, and lobbyist registrations.

Select or Special Committee—A committee established by a resolution in either house for a special purpose and, usually, for a limited time. Most select and special committees are assigned specific investigations or studies, but are not authorized to report measures to their chambers.

Senate—The house of Congress in which each state is represented by two senators; each senator has one vote. Article V of the Constitution declares that "No State, without its Consent, shall be deprived of its equal Suffrage in the Senate." The Constitution also gives the Senate equal legislative power with the House of Representatives. Although the Senate is prohibited from originating revenue measures, and as a matter of practice it does not originate appropriation measures, it can amend both. Only the Senate can give or withhold consent to treaties and nominations from the president. It also acts as a court to try impeachments by the House and elects the vice president when no candidate receives a majority of the electoral votes. It is often referred to as "the upper body," but not by members of the House.

Senate Manual—The handbook of the Senate's standing rules and orders and the laws and other regulations that apply to the Senate, usually published once each Congress.

Senatorial Courtesy—The Senate's practice of declining to confirm a presidential nominee for an office in the state of a senator of the president's party unless that senator approves.

Sequestration—A procedure for canceling budgetary resources that is, money available for obligation or spending to enforce budget limitations established in law. Sequestered funds are no longer available for obligation or expenditure.

Sine Die—*(See Adjournment Sine Die.)*

Slip Law—The first official publication of a measure that has become law. It is published separately in unbound, single-sheet form or pamphlet form. A slip law usually is available two or three days after the date of the law's enactment.

Speaker—The presiding officer of the House of Representatives and the leader of its majority party. The Speaker is selected by the majority party and formally elected by the House at the beginning of each Congress. Although the Constitution does not require the Speaker to be a member of the House, in fact, all Speakers have been members.

Special Session—A session of Congress convened by the president, under his constitutional authority, after Congress has adjourned sine die at the end of a regular session. *(See Adjournment Sine Die.)*

Spending Authority—The technical term for backdoor spending. The Congressional Budget Act of 1974 defines it as borrowing authority, contract authority, and entitlement authority for which appropriation acts do not provide budget authority in advance. Under the Budget Act, legislation that provides new spending authority may not be considered unless it provides that the authority shall be effective only to the extent or in such amounts as provided in an appropriation act.

Sponsor—The principal proponent and introducer of a measure or an amendment.

Standing Committee—A permanent committee established by a House or Senate standing rule or standing order. The rule also describes the subject areas on which the committee may report bills and resolutions and conduct oversight. Most introduced measures must be referred to one or more standing committees according to their jurisdictions.

Standing Vote—An alternative and informal term for a division vote, during which members in favor of a proposal and then members opposed stand and are counted by the chair. *(See Division Vote.)*

Star Print—A reprint of a bill, resolution, amendment, or committee report correcting technical or substantive errors in a previous printing; so called because of the small black star that appears on the front page or cover.

Statutes at Large—A chronological arrangement of the laws enacted in each session of Congress. Though indexed, the laws are not arranged by subject matter nor is there an indication of how they affect or change previously enacted laws. The volumes are numbered by Congress, and the laws are cited by their volume and page number. The Gramm-Rudman-Hollings Act, for example, appears as 99 Stat. 1037.

Strike from the *Record*—Expunge objectionable remarks from the *Congressional Record*, after a member's words have been taken down on a point of order.

Strike Out the Last Word—A motion whereby a House member is entitled to speak for five minutes on an amendment then being debated by the chamber. A member gains recognition from the chair by moving to "strike out the last word" of the amendment or section of the bill under consideration. The motion is proforma, requires no vote, and does not change the amendment being debated.

Substitute—A motion, amendment, or entire bill introduced in place of the pending legislative business. Passage of a substitute measure kills the original measure by supplanting it. The substitute also may be amended. *(See also Amendment in the Nature of a Substitute.)*

Sunshine Rules—Rules requiring open committee hearings and business meetings, including markup sessions, in both houses, and also open conference committee meetings. However, all may be closed under certain circumstances and using certain procedures required by the rules.

Super Majority—A term sometimes used for a vote on a matter that requires approval by more than a simple majority of those members present and voting; also referred to as extraordinary majority.

Supplemental Appropriation Bill—A measure providing appropriations for use in the current fiscal year, in addition to those already provided in annual general appropriation bills. Supplemental appropriations are often for unforeseen emergencies.

Suspension of the Rules (House)—An expeditious procedure for passing relatively noncontroversial or emergency measures by a two-thirds vote of those members voting, a quorum being present.

Suspension of the Rules (Senate)—A procedure to set aside one or more of the Senate's rules; it is used infrequently, and then most often to suspend the rule banning legislative amendments to appropriation bills.

Table a Bill—Motions to table, or to "lay on the table," are used to block or kill amendments or other parliamentary questions. When approved, a tabling motion is considered the final disposition of that issue. One of the most widely used parliamentary procedures, the motion to table is not debatable, and adoption requires a simple majority vote.

In the Senate, however, different language sometimes is used. The motion may be worded to let a bill "lie on the table," perhaps for subsequent "picking up." This motion is more flexible, keeping the bill pending for later action, if desired. Tabling motions on amendments are effective debate-ending devices in the Senate.

Teller Vote—A voting procedure, formerly used in the House, in which members cast their votes by passing through the center aisle to be counted, but not recorded by name, by a member from each party appointed by the chair. The House deleted the procedure from its rules in 1993, but during floor discussion of the deletion a leading member stated that a teller vote would still be available in the event of a breakdown of the electronic voting system.

Treaty—A formal document containing an agreement between two or more sovereign nations. The Constitution authorizes the president to make treaties, but he must submit them to the Senate for its approval by a two-thirds vote of the senators present. Under the Senate's rules, that vote actually occurs on a resolution of ratification. Although the Constitution does not give the House a direct role in approving treaties, that body has sometimes insisted that a revenue treaty is an invasion of its prerogatives. In any case, the House may significantly affect the application of a treaty by its equal role in enacting legislation to implement the treaty.

Trust Funds—Special accounts in the Treasury that receive earmarked taxes or other kinds of revenue collections, such as user fees, and from which payments are made for special purposes or to recipients who meet the requirements of the trust funds as established by law. Of the more than 150 federal government trust funds, several finance major entitlement programs, such as Social Security, Medicare, and retired federal employees' pensions. Others fund infrastructure construction and improvements, such as highways and airports.

Unanimous Consent—Without an objection by any member. A unanimous consent request asks permission, explicitly or implicitly, to set aside one or more rules. Both houses and their committees frequently use such requests to expedite their proceedings.

Unanimous Consent Agreement—A device used in the Senate to expedite legislation. Much of the Senate's legislative business, dealing with both minor and controversial issues, is conducted through unanimous consent or unanimous consent agreements. On major legislation, such agreements usually are printed and transmitted to all senators in advance of floor debate. Once agreed to, they are binding on all members unless the Senate, by unanimous consent, agrees to modify them. An agreement may list the order in which various bills are to be considered, specify the length of time bills and contested amendments are to be debated and when they are to be voted upon, and, frequently, require that all amendments introduced be germane to the bill under consideration. In this regard, unanimous consent agreements are similar to the "rules" issued by the House Rules Committee for bills pending in the House.

Unfunded Mandate—Generally, any provision in federal law or regulation that imposes a duty or obligation on a state or local government or private sector entity without providing the necessary funds to comply. The Unfunded Mandates Reform Act of 1995 amended the Congressional Budget Act of 1974 to provide a mechanism for the control of new unfunded mandates.

Union Calendar—A calendar of the House of Representatives for bills and resolutions favorably reported by committees that raise revenue or directly or indirectly appropriate money or property. In addition to appropriation bills, measures that authorize expenditures are also placed on this calendar. The calendar's full title is the Calendar of the Committee of the Whole House on the State of the Union.

U.S. Code—Popular title for the *United States Code: Containing the General and Permanent Laws of the United States in Force on. . . .* It is a consolidation and partial codification of the general and permanent laws of the United States arranged by subject under 50 titles. The first six titles deal with general or political subjects, the other 44 with subjects ranging from agriculture to war, alphabetically arranged. A supplement is published after each session of Congress, and the entire Code is revised every six years.

Veto—The president's disapproval of a legislative measure passed by Congress. He returns the measure to the house in which it originated without his signature but with a veto message stating his objections to it. When Congress is in session, the president must veto a bill within 10 days, excluding Sundays, after he has received it; otherwise it becomes law without his signature. The 10-day clock begins to run at midnight following his receipt of the bill. (*See also Committee Veto, Item Veto, Override a Veto, Pocket Veto.*)

Voice Vote—A method of voting in which members who favor a question answer aye in chorus, after which those opposed answer no in chorus, and the chair decides which position prevails.

War Powers Act of 1973—An act that requires the president "in every possible instance" to consult Congress before he commits U.S. forces to ongoing or imminent hostilities. If he commits them to a combat situation without congressional consultation, he must notify Congress within 48 hours. Unless Congress declares war or otherwise authorizes the operation to continue, the forces must be withdrawn within 60 or 90 days, depending on certain conditions.

Whip—The majority or minority party member in each house who acts as assistant leader, helps plan and marshal support for party strategies, encourages party discipline, and advises his leader on how his colleagues intend to vote on the floor. In the Senate, the Republican whip's official title is assistant leader.

Without Objection—Used in lieu of a vote on noncontroversial motions, amendments, or bills that may be passed in either the House or Senate if no member voices an objection.

Yeas and Nays—A vote in which members usually respond "aye" or "no" (despite the official title of the vote) on a question when their names are called in alphabetical order. The Constitution requires the yeas and nays when a demand for it is supported by one-fifth of the members present, and it also requires an automatic yea-and-nay vote on overriding a veto. Senate precedents require the support of at least one-fifth of a quorum, a minimum of 11 members with the present membership of 100.

Yielding—When a member has been recognized to speak, no other member may speak unless he or she obtains permission from the member recognized. This permission is called yielding and usually is requested in the form, "Will the gentleman yield to me?" While this activity occasionally is seen in the Senate, the Senate has no rule or practice to parcel out time.

Zone Whip—A member responsible for whip duties concerning his or her party colleagues from specific geographical areas.

Constitution of the United States

We the People of the United States, in Order to form a more perfect Union, establish Justice, insure domestic Tranquility, provide for the common defence, promote the general Welfare, and secure the Blessings of Liberty to ourselves and our Posterity, do ordain and establish this Constitution for the United States of America.

ARTICLE I

Section 1. All legislative Powers herein granted shall be vested in a Congress of the United States, which shall consist of a Senate and House of Representatives.

Section 2. The House of Representatives shall be composed of Members chosen every second Year by the People of the several States, and the Electors in each State shall have the Qualifications requisite for Electors of the most numerous Branch of the State Legislature.

No Person shall be a Representative who shall not have attained to the age of twenty five Years, and been seven Years a Citizen of the United States, and who shall not, when elected, be an Inhabitant of that State in which he shall be chosen.

[Representatives and direct Taxes shall be apportioned among the several States which may be included within this Union, according to their respective Numbers, which shall be determined by adding to the whole Number of free Persons, including those bound to Service for a Term of Years, and excluding Indians not taxed, three fifths of all other Persons.][1] The actual Enumeration shall be made within three Years after the first Meeting of the Congress of the United States, and within every subsequent Term of ten Years, in such Manner as they shall by Law direct. The Number of Representatives shall not exceed one for every thirty Thousand, but each State shall have at Least one Representative; and until such enumeration shall be made, the State of New Hampshire shall be entitled to chuse three, Massachusetts eight, Rhode-Island and Providence Plantations one, Connecticut five, New-York six, New Jersey four, Pennsylvania eight, Delaware one, Maryland six, Virginia ten, North Carolina five, South Carolina five, and Georgia three.

When vacancies happen in the Representation from any State, the Executive Authority thereof shall issue Writs of Election to fill such Vacancies.

The House of Representatives shall chuse their Speaker and other Officers; and shall have the sole Power of Impeachment.

Section 3. The Senate of the United States shall be composed of two Senators from each State, [chosen by the Legislature thereof,][2] for six Years; and each Senator shall have one Vote.

Immediately after they shall be assembled in Consequence of the first Election, they shall be divided as equally as may be into three Classes. The Seats of the Senators of the first Class shall be vacated at the Expiration of the second Year, of the second Class at the Expiration of the fourth Year, and of the third Class at the Expiration of the sixth Year, so that one third may be chosen every second Year; [and if Vacancies happen by Resignation, or otherwise, during the Recess of the Legislature of any State, the Executive thereof may make temporary Appointments until the next Meeting of the Legislature, which shall then fill such Vacancies.][3]

No Person shall be a Senator who shall not have attained to the Age of thirty Years, and been nine Years a Citizen of the United States, and who shall not, when elected, be an Inhabitant of that State for which he shall be chosen.

The Vice President of the United States shall be President of the Senate, but shall have no Vote, unless they be equally divided.

The Senate shall chuse their other Officers, and also a President pro tempore, in the Absence of the Vice President, or when he shall exercise the Office of President of the United States.

The Senate shall have the sole Power to try all Impeachments. When sitting for that Purpose, they shall be on Oath or Affirmation. When the President of the United States is tried, the Chief Justice shall preside: And no Person shall be convicted without the Concurrence of two thirds of the Members present.

Judgment in Cases of Impeachment shall not extend further than to removal from Office, and disqualification to hold and enjoy any Office of honor, Trust or Profit under the United States: but the Party convicted shall nevertheless be liable and subject to Indictment, Trial, Judgment and Punishment, according to Law.

Section 4. The Times, Places and Manner of holding Elections for Senators and Representatives, shall be prescribed in each State by the Legislature thereof; but the Congress may at any time by Law make or alter such Regulations, except as to the Places of chusing Senators.

The Congress shall assemble at least once in every Year, and such Meeting shall [be on the first Monday in December],[4] unless they shall by Law appoint a different Day.

Section 5. Each House shall be the Judge of the Elections, Returns and Qualifications of its own Members, and a Majority of each shall constitute a Quorum to do Business; but a smaller Number may adjourn from day to day, and may be authorized to compel the Attendance of absent Members, in such Manner, and under such Penalties as each House may provide.

Each House may determine the Rules of its Proceedings, punish its Members for disorderly Behaviour, and, with the Concurrence of two thirds, expel a Member.

Each House shall keep a Journal of its Proceedings, and from time to time publish the same, excepting such Parts as may in their Judgment require Secrecy; and the Yeas and Nays of the Members of either House on any question shall, at the Desire of one fifth of those Present, be entered on the Journal.

Neither House, during the Session of Congress, shall, without the Consent of the other, adjourn for more than three days, nor to any other Place than that in which the two Houses shall be sitting.

Section 6. The Senators and Representatives shall receive a Compensation for their Services, to be ascertained by Law, and paid out of the Treasury of the United States. They shall in all Cases, except Treason, Felony and Breach of the Peace, be privileged from Arrest during their Attendance at the Session of their respective Houses, and in going to and returning from the same; and for any Speech or Debate in either House, they shall not be questioned in any other Place.

No Senator or Representative shall, during the Time for which he was elected, be appointed to any civil Office under the Authority of the United States, which shall have been created, or the Emoluments whereof shall have been encreased during such time; and no Person holding any Office under the United States, shall be a Member of either House during his Continuance in Office.

Section 7. All Bills for raising Revenue shall originate in the House of Representatives; but the Senate may propose or concur with Amendments as on other Bills.

Every Bill which shall have passed the House of Representatives and the Senate, shall, before it become a Law, be presented to the President of the United States; If he approve he shall sign it, but if not he shall return it, with his Objections to that House in which it shall have originated, who shall enter the Objections at large on their Journal, and proceed to reconsider it. If after such Reconsideration two thirds of that House shall agree to pass the Bill, it shall be sent, together with the Objections, to the other House, by which it shall likewise be reconsidered, and if approved by two thirds of that House, it shall become a Law. But in all such Cases the Votes of both Houses shall be determined by yeas and Nays, and the Names of the Persons voting for and against the Bill shall be entered on the Journal of each House respectively. If any Bill shall not be returned by the President within ten Days (Sundays excepted) after it shall have been presented to him, the Same shall be a Law, in like Manner as if he had signed it, unless the Congress by their Adjournment prevent its Return, in which Case it shall not be a Law.

Every Order, Resolution, or Vote to which the Concurrence of the Senate and House of Representatives may be necessary (except on a question of Adjournment) shall be presented to the President of the United States; and before the Same shall take Effect, shall be approved by him, or being disapproved by him, shall be repassed by two thirds of the Senate and House of Representatives, according to the Rules and Limitations prescribed in the Case of a Bill.

Section 8. The Congress shall have Power To lay and collect Taxes, Duties, Imposts and Excises, to pay the Debts and provide for the common Defence and general Welfare of the United States; but all Duties, Imposts and Excises shall be uniform throughout the United States;

To borrow Money on the credit of the United States;

To regulate Commerce with foreign Nations, and among the several States, and with the Indian Tribes;

To establish an uniform Rule of Naturalization, and uniform Laws on the subject of Bankruptcies throughout the United States;

To coin Money, regulate the Value thereof, and of foreign Coin, and fix the Standard of Weights and Measures;

To provide for the Punishment of counterfeiting the Securities and current Coin of the United States;

To establish Post Offices and post Roads;

To promote the Progress of Science and useful Arts, by securing for limited Times to Authors and Inventors the exclusive Right to their respective Writings and Discoveries;

To constitute Tribunals inferior to the supreme Court;

To define and punish Piracies and Felonies committed on the high Seas, and Offences against the Law of Nations;

To declare War, grant Letters of Marque and Reprisal, and make Rules concerning Captures on Land and Water;

To raise and support Armies, but no Appropriation of Money to that Use shall be for a longer Term than two Years;

To provide and maintain a Navy;

To make Rules for the Government and Regulation of the land and naval Forces;

To provide for calling forth the Militia to execute the Laws of the Union, suppress Insurrections and repel Invasions;

To provide for organizing, arming, and disciplining, the Militia, and for governing such Part of them as may be employed in the Service of the United States, reserving to the States respectively, the Appointment of the Officers, and the Authority of training the Militia according to the discipline prescribed by Congress;

To exercise exclusive Legislation in all Cases whatsoever, over such District (not exceeding ten Miles square) as may, by Cession of particular States, and the Acceptance of Congress, become the Seat of the Government of the United States, and to exercise like Authority over all Places purchased by the Consent of the Legislature of the State in which the Same shall be, for the Erection of Forts, Magazines, Arsenals, dock-Yards, and other needful Buildings; — And

To make all Laws which shall be necessary and proper for carrying into Execution the foregoing Powers, and all other Powers vested by this Constitution in the Government of the United States, or in any Department or Officer thereof.

Section 9. The Migration or Importation of such Persons as any of the States now existing shall think proper to admit, shall not be prohibited by the Congress prior to the Year one thousand eight hundred and eight, but a Tax or duty may be imposed on such Importation, not exceeding ten dollars for each Person.

The Privilege of the Writ of Habeas Corpus shall not be suspended, unless when in Cases of Rebellion or Invasion the public Safety may require it.

No Bill of Attainder or ex post facto Law shall be passed.

No Capitation, or other direct, Tax shall be laid, unless in Proportion to the Census or Enumeration herein before directed to be taken.[5]

No Tax or Duty shall be laid on Articles exported from any State.

No Preference shall be given by any Regulation of Commerce or Revenue to the Ports of one State over those of another; nor shall Vessels bound to, or from, one State, be obliged to enter, clear, or pay Duties in another.

No Money shall be drawn from the Treasury, but in Consequence of Appropriations made by Law; and a regular Statement and Account of the Receipts and Expenditures of all public Money shall be published from time to time.

No Title of Nobility shall be granted by the United States: And no Person holding any Office of Profit or Trust under them, shall, without the Consent of the Congress, accept of any present, Emolument, Office, or Title, of any kind whatever, from any King, Prince, or foreign State.

Section 10. No State shall enter into any Treaty, Alliance, or Confederation; grant Letters of Marque and Reprisal; coin Money; emit Bills of Credit; make any Thing but gold and silver Coin a Tender in Payment of Debts; pass any Bill of Attainder, ex post facto Law, or Law impairing the Obligation of Contracts, or grant any Title of Nobility.

No State shall, without the Consent of the Congress, **lay** any Imposts or Duties on Imports or Exports, except what may be absolutely necessary for executing it's inspection Laws: and the net Produce of all Duties and Imposts, laid by any State on Imports or Exports, shall be for the Use of the Treasury of the United States; and all such Laws shall be subject to the Revision and Controul of the Congress.

No State shall, without the Consent of Congress, lay any Duty of Tonnage, keep Troops, or Ships of War in time of Peace, enter into any Agreement or Compact with another State, or with a foreign Power, or engage in War, unless actually invaded, or in such imminent Danger as will not admit of delay.

ARTICLE II

Section 1. The executive Power shall be vested in a President of the United States of America. He shall hold his Office during the Term of four Years, and, together with the Vice President, chosen for the same Term, be elected, as follows

Each State shall appoint, in such Manner as the Legislature thereof may direct, a Number of Electors, equal to the whole Number of Senators and Representatives to which the State may be entitled in the Congress: but no Senator or Representative, or Person holding an Office of Trust or Profit under the United States, shall be appointed an Elector.

[The Electors shall meet in their respective States, and vote by Ballot for two Persons, of whom one at least shall not be an Inhabitant of the same State with themselves. And they shall make a List of all the Persons voted for, and of the Number of Votes for each; which List they shall sign and certify, and transmit sealed to the Seat of the Government of the United States, directed to the President of the Senate. The President of the Senate shall, in the Presence of the Senate and House of Representatives, open all the Certificates, and the Votes shall then be counted. The Person having the greatest Number of Votes shall be the President, if such Number be a Majority of the whole Number of Electors appointed; and if there be more than one who have such Majority, and have an equal Number of Votes, then the House of Representatives shall immediately chuse by Ballot one of them for President; and if no Person have a Majority, then from the five highest on the list the said House shall in like Manner chuse the President. But in chusing the President, the Votes shall be taken by States, the Representation from each State having one Vote; A quorum for this Purpose shall consist of a Member or Members from two thirds of the States, and a Majority of all the States shall be necessary to a Choice. In every Case, after the Choice of the President, the Person having the greatest Number of Votes of the Electors shall be the Vice President. But if there should remain two or more who have equal Votes, the Senate shall chuse from them by Ballot the Vice President.][6]

The Congress may determine the Time of chusing the Electors, and the Day on which they shall give their Votes; which Day shall be the same throughout the United States.

No Person except a natural born Citizen, or a Citizen of the United States, at the time of the Adoption of this Constitution, shall be eligible to the Office of President; neither shall any Person be eligible to that Office who shall not have attained to the Age of thirty five Years, and been fourteen Years a Resident within the United States.

In Case of the Removal of the President from Office, or of his Death, Resignation, or Inability to discharge the Powers and Duties of the said Office,[7] the Same shall devolve on the Vice President, and the Congress may by Law provide for the Case of Removal, Death, Resignation or Inability, both of the President and Vice President, declaring what Officer shall then act as President, and such Officer shall act accordingly, until the Disability be removed, or a President shall be elected.

The President shall, at stated Times, receive for his Services, a Compensation, which shall neither be encreased nor diminished during the Period for which he shall have been elected, and he shall not receive within that Period any other Emolument from the United States, or any of them.

Before he enter on the Execution of his Office, he shall take the following Oath or Affirmation: — "I do solemnly swear (or affirm) that I will faithfully execute the Office of President of the United States, and will to the best of my Ability, preserve, protect and defend the Constitution of the United States."

Section 2. The President shall be Commander in Chief of the Army and Navy of the United States, and of the Militia of the several States, when called into the actual Service of the United States; he may require the Opinion, in writing, of the principal Officer in each of the executive Departments, upon any Subject relating to the Duties of their respective Offices, and he shall have Power to grant Reprieves and Pardons for Offences against the United States, except in Cases of Impeachment.

He shall have Power, by and with the Advice and Consent of the Senate, to make Treaties, provided two thirds of the Senators present concur; and he shall nominate, and by and with the Advice and Consent of the Senate, shall appoint Ambassadors, other public Ministers and Consuls, Judges of the supreme Court, and all other Officers of the United States, whose Appointments are not herein otherwise provided for, and which shall be established by Law: but the Congress may by Law vest the Appointment of such inferior Officers, as they think proper, in the President alone, in the Courts of Law, or in the Heads of Departments.

The President shall have Power to fill up all Vacancies that may happen during the Recess of the Senate, by granting Commissions which shall expire at the End of their next Session.

Section 3. He shall from time to time give to the Congress Information of the State of the Union, and recommend to their Consideration such Measures as he shall judge necessary and expedient; he may, on extraordinary Occasions, convene both Houses, or either of them, and in Case of Disagreement between them, with Respect to the Time of Adjournment, he may adjourn them to such Time as he shall think proper; he shall receive Ambassadors and other public Ministers; he shall take Care that the Laws be faithfully executed, and shall Commission all the Officers of the United States.

Section 4. The President, Vice President and all civil Officers of the United States, shall be removed from Office on Impeachment for, and Conviction of, Treason, Bribery, or other high Crimes and Misdemeanors.

ARTICLE III

Section 1. The judicial Power of the United States, shall be vested in one supreme Court, and in such inferior Courts as the Congress may from time to time ordain and establish. The Judges, both of the supreme and inferior Courts, shall hold their

Offices during good Behaviour, and shall, at stated Times, receive for their Services, a Compensation, which shall not be diminished during their Continuance in Office.

Section 2. The judicial Power shall extend to all Cases, in Law and Equity, arising under this Constitution, the Laws of the United States, and Treaties made, or which shall be made, under their Authority; — to all Cases affecting Ambassadors, other public Ministers and Consuls; — to all Cases of admiralty and maritime Jurisdiction; — to Controversies to which the United States shall be a Party; — to Controversies between two or more States; — between a State and Citizens of another State;[8] — between Citizens of different States; — between Citizens of the same State claiming Lands under Grants of different States, and between a State, or the Citizens thereof, and foreign States, Citizens or Subjects.

In all Cases affecting Ambassadors, other public Ministers and Consuls, and those in which a State shall be Party, the supreme Court shall have original Jurisdiction. In all the other Cases before mentioned, the supreme Court shall have appellate Jurisdiction, both as to Law and Fact, with such Exceptions, and under such Regulations as the Congress shall make.

The Trial of all Crimes, except in Cases of Impeachment, shall be by Jury; and such Trial shall be held in the State where the said Crimes shall have been committed; but when not committed within any State, the Trial shall be at such Place or Places as the Congress may by Law have directed.

Section 3. Treason against the United States, shall consist only in levying War against them, or in adhering to their Enemies, giving them Aid and Comfort. No Person shall be convicted of Treason unless on the Testimony of two Witnesses to the same overt Act, or on Confession in open Court.

The Congress shall have Power to declare the Punishment of Treason, but no Attainder of Treason shall work Corruption of Blood, or Forfeiture except during the Life of the Person attainted.

ARTICLE IV

Section 1. Full Faith and Credit shall be given in each State to the public Acts, Records, and judicial Proceedings of every other State. And the Congress may by general Laws prescribe the Manner in which such Acts, Records and Proceedings shall be proved, and the Effect thereof.

Section 2. The Citizens of each State shall be entitled to all Privileges and Immunities of Citizens in the several States.

A Person charged in any State with Treason, Felony, or other Crime, who shall flee from Justice, and be found in another State, shall on Demand of the executive Authority of the State from which he fled, be delivered up, to be removed to the State having Jurisdiction of the Crime.

[No Person held to Service or Labour in one State, under the Laws thereof, escaping into another, shall, in Consequence of any Law or Regulation therein, be discharged from such Service or Labour, but shall be delivered up on Claim of the Party to whom such Service or Labour may be due.][9]

Section 3. New States may be admitted by the Congress into this Union; but no new State shall be formed or erected within the Jurisdiction of any other State; nor any State be formed by the Junction of two or more States, or Parts of States, without the Consent of the Legislatures of the States concerned as well as of the Congress.

The Congress shall have Power to dispose of and make all needful Rules and Regulations respecting the Territory or other Property belonging to the United States; and nothing in this Constitution shall be so construed as to Prejudice any Claims of the United States, or of any particular State.

Section 4. The United States shall guarantee to every State in this Union a Republican Form of Government, and shall protect each of them against Invasion; and on Application of the Legislature, or of the Executive (when the Legislature cannot be convened) against domestic Violence.

ARTICLE V

The Congress, whenever two thirds of both Houses shall deem it necessary, shall propose Amendments to this Constitution, or, on the Application of the Legislatures of two thirds of the several States, shall call a Convention for proposing Amendments, which, in either Case, shall be valid to all Intents and Purposes, as Part of this Constitution, when ratified by the Legislatures of three fourths of the several States, or by Conventions in three fourths thereof, as the one or the other Mode of Ratification may be proposed by the Congress; Provided [that no Amendment which may be made prior to the Year One thousand eight hundred and eight shall in any Manner affect the first and fourth Clauses in the Ninth Section of the first Article; and][10] that no State, without its Consent, shall be deprived of its equal Suffrage in the Senate.

ARTICLE VI

All Debts contracted and Engagements entered into, before the Adoption of this Constitution, shall be as valid against the United States under this Constitution, as under the Confederation.

This Constitution, and the Laws of the United States which shall be made in Pursuance thereof; and all Treaties made, or which shall be made, under the Authority of the United States, shall be the supreme Law of the Land; and the Judges in every State shall be bound thereby, any Thing in the Constitution or Laws of any State to the Contrary notwithstanding.

The Senators and Representatives before mentioned, and the Members of the several State Legislatures, and all executive and judicial Officers, both of the United States and of the several States, shall be bound by Oath or Affirmation, to support this Constitution; but no religious Test shall ever be required as a Qualification to any Office or public Trust under the United States.

ARTICLE VII

The Ratification of the Conventions of nine States, shall be sufficient for the Establishment of this Constitution between the States so ratifying the Same.

Done in Convention by the Unanimous Consent of the States present the Seventeenth Day of September in the Year of our Lord one thousand seven hundred and Eighty seven and of the Independence of the United States of America the Twelfth. IN WITNESS whereof We have hereunto subscribed our Names,

George Washington,
President and
deputy from Virginia.

New Hampshire:	John Langdon
	Nicholas Gilman.
Massachusetts:	Nathaniel Gorham,
	Rufus King.
Connecticut:	William Samuel Johnson,
	Roger Sherman.

New York:	Alexander Hamilton.
New Jersey:	William Livingston, David Brearley, William Paterson, Jonathan Dayton.
Pennsylvania:	Benjamin Franklin, Thomas Mifflin, Robert Morris, George Clymer, Thomas FitzSimons, Jared Ingersoll, James Wilson, Gouverneur Morris.
Delaware:	George Read, Gunning Bedford Jr., John Dickinson, Richard Bassett, Jacob Broom.
Maryland:	James McHenry, Daniel of St. Thomas Jenifer, Daniel Carroll.
Virginia:	John Blair, James Madison Jr.
North Carolina:	William Blount, Richard Dobbs Spaight, Hugh Williamson.
South Carolina:	John Rutledge, Charles Cotesworth Pinckney, Charles Pinckney, Pierce Butler.
Georgia:	William Few, Abraham Baldwin.

[The language of the original Constitution, not including the Amendments, was adopted by a convention of the states on September 17, 1787, and was subsequently ratified by the states on the following dates: Delaware, December 7, 1787; Pennsylvania, December 12, 1787; New Jersey, December 18, 1787; Georgia, January 2, 1788; Connecticut, January 9, 1788; Massachusetts, February 6, 1788; Maryland, April 28, 1788; South Carolina, May 23, 1788; New Hampshire, June 21, 1788.

Ratification was completed on June 21, 1788.

The Constitution subsequently was ratified by Virginia, June 25, 1788; New York, July 26, 1788; North Carolina, November 21, 1789; Rhode Island, May 29, 1790; and Vermont, January 10, 1791.]

Amendments

Amendment I

(First ten amendments ratified December 15, 1791.)

Congress shall make no law respecting an establishment of religion, or prohibiting the free exercise thereof; or abridging the freedom of speech, or of the press; or the right of the people peaceably to assemble, and to petition the Government for a redress of grievances.

Amendment II

A well regulated Militia, being necessary to the security of a free State, the right of the people to keep and bear Arms, shall not be infringed.

Amendment III

No Soldier shall, in time of peace be quartered in any house, without the consent of the Owner, nor in time of war, but in a manner to be prescribed by law.

Amendment IV

The right of the people to be secure in their persons, houses, papers, and effects, against unreasonable searches and seizures, shall not be violated, and no Warrants shall issue, but upon probable cause, supported by Oath or affirmation, and particularly describing the place to be searched, and the persons or things to be seized.

Amendment V

No person shall be held to answer for a capital, or otherwise infamous crime, unless on a presentment or indictment of a Grand Jury, except in cases arising in the land or naval forces, or in the Militia, when in actual service in time of War or public danger; nor shall any person be subject for the same offence to be twice put in jeopardy of life or limb; nor shall be compelled in any criminal case to be a witness against himself, nor be deprived of life, liberty, or property, without due process of law; nor shall private property be taken for public use, without just compensation.

Amendment VI

In all criminal prosecutions, the accused shall enjoy the right to a speedy and public trial, by an impartial jury of the State and district wherein the crime shall have been committed, which district shall have been previously ascertained by law, and to be informed of the nature and cause of the accusation; to be confronted with the witnesses against him; to have compulsory process for obtaining witnesses in his favor, and to have the Assistance of Counsel for his defence.

Amendment VII

In Suits at common law, where the value in controversy shall exceed twenty dollars, the right of trial by jury shall be preserved, and no fact tried by a jury, shall be otherwise re-examined in any Court of the United States, than according to the rules of the common law.

Amendment VIII

Excessive bail shall not be required, nor excessive fines imposed, nor cruel and unusual punishments inflicted.

Amendment IX

The enumeration in the Constitution, of certain rights, shall not be construed to deny or disparage others retained by the people.

Amendment X

The powers not delegated to the United States by the Constitution, nor prohibited by it to the States, are reserved to the States respectively, or to the people.

Amendment XI (Ratified February 7, 1795)

The Judicial power of the United States shall not be construed to extend to any suit in law or equity, commenced or prosecuted against one of the United States by Citizens of another State, or by Citizens or Subjects of any Foreign State.

Amendment XII (Ratified June 15, 1804)

The Electors shall meet in their respective states and vote by ballot for President and Vice-President, one of whom, at least, shall not be an inhabitant of the same state with themselves; they shall name in their ballots the person voted for as President, and in distinct ballots the person voted for as Vice-President, and they shall make distinct lists of all persons voted for as President, and of all persons voted for as Vice-President, and of the number of votes for each, which lists they shall sign and certify, and transmit sealed to the seat of the government of the United States, directed to the President of the Senate; — The President of the Senate shall, in the presence of the Senate and House of Representatives, open all the certificates and the votes shall then be counted; — The person having the greatest number of votes for President, shall be the President, if such number be a majority of the whole number of Electors appointed; and if no person have such majority, then from the persons having the highest numbers not exceeding three on the list of those voted for as President, the House of Representatives shall choose immediately, by ballot, the President. But in choosing the President, the votes shall be taken by states, the representation from each state having one vote; a quorum for this purpose shall consist of a member or members from two-thirds of the states, and a majority of all the states shall be necessary to a choice. [And if the House of Representatives shall not choose a President whenever the right of choice shall devolve upon them, before the fourth day of March next following, then the Vice-President shall act as President, as in the case of the death or other constitutional disability of the President. —][11] The person having the greatest number of votes as Vice-President, shall be the Vice-President, if such number be a majority of the whole number of Electors appointed, and if no person have a majority, then from the two highest numbers on the list, the Senate shall choose the Vice-President; a quorum for the purpose shall consist of two-thirds of the whole number of Senators, and a majority of the whole number shall be necessary to a choice. But no person constitutionally ineligible to the office of President shall be eligible to that of Vice-President of the United States.

Amendment XIII (Ratified December 6, 1865)

Section 1. Neither slavery nor involuntary servitude, except as a punishment for crime whereof the party shall have been duly convicted, shall exist within the United States, or any place subject to their jurisdiction.

Section 2. Congress shall have power to enforce this article by appropriate legislation.

Amendment XIV (Ratified July 9, 1868)

Section 1. All persons born or naturalized in the United States, and subject to the jurisdiction thereof, are citizens of the United States and of the State wherein they reside. No State shall make or enforce any law which shall abridge the privileges or immunities of citizens of the United States; nor shall any State deprive any person of life, liberty, or property, without due process of law; nor deny to any person within its jurisdiction the equal protection of the laws.

Section 2. Representatives shall be apportioned among the several States according to their respective numbers, counting the whole number of persons in each State, excluding Indians not taxed. But when the right to vote at any election for the choice of electors for President and Vice President of the United States, Representatives in Congress, the Executive and Judicial officers of a State, or the members of the Legislature thereof, is denied to any of the male inhabitants of such State, being twenty-one years of age,[12] and citizens of the United States, or in any way abridged, except for participation in rebellion, or other crime, the basis of representation therein shall be reduced in the proportion which the number of such male citizens shall bear to the whole number of male citizens twenty-one years of age in such State.

Section 3. No person shall be a Senator or Representative in Congress, or elector of President and Vice President, or hold any office, civil or military, under the United States, or under any State, who, having previously taken an oath, as a member of Congress, or as an officer of the United States, or as a member of any State legislature, or as an executive or judicial officer of any State, to support the Constitution of the United States, shall have engaged in insurrection or rebellion against the same, or given aid or comfort to the enemies thereof. But Congress may by a vote of two-thirds of each House, remove such disability.

Section 4. The validity of the public debt of the United States, authorized by law, including debts incurred for payment of pensions and bounties for services in suppressing insurrection or rebellion, shall not be questioned. But neither the United States nor any State shall assume or pay any debt or obligation incurred in aid of insurrection or rebellion against the United States, or any claim for the loss or emancipation of any slave; but all such debts, obligations and claims shall be held illegal and void.

Section 5. The Congress shall have power to enforce, by appropriate legislation, the provisions of this article.

Amendment XV (Ratified February 3, 1870)

Section 1. The right of citizens of the United States to vote shall not be denied or abridged by the United States or by any State on account of race, color, or previous condition of servitude.

Section 2. The Congress shall have power to enforce this article by appropriate legislation.

Amendment XVI (Ratified February 3, 1913)

The Congress shall have power to lay and collect taxes on incomes, from whatever source derived, without apportionment among the several States, and without regard to any census or enumeration.

Amendment XVII (Ratified April 8, 1913)

The Senate of the United States shall be composed of two Senators from each State, elected by the people thereof, for six years; and each Senator shall have one vote. The electors in each State shall have the qualifications requisite for electors of the most numerous branch of the State legislatures.

When vacancies happen in the representation of any State in the Senate, the executive authority of such State shall issue writs of election to fill such vacancies: *Provided,* That the legislature of any State may empower the executive thereof to make temporary appointments until the people fill the vacancies by election as the legislature may direct.

This amendment shall not be so construed as to affect the election or term of any Senator chosen before it becomes valid as part of the Constitution.

Amendment XVIII (Ratified January 16, 1919)[13]

Section 1. After one year from the ratification of this article the manufacture, sale, or transportation of intoxicating liquors within, the importation thereof into, or the exportation thereof from the United States and all territory subject to the jurisdiction thereof for beverage purposes is hereby prohibited.

Section 2. The Congress and the several States shall have concurrent power to enforce this article by appropriate legislation.

Section 3. This article shall be inoperative unless it shall have been ratified as an amendment to the Constitution by the legislatures of the several States, as provided in the Constitution, within seven years from the date of the submission hereof to the States by the Congress.

Amendment XIX (Ratified August 18, 1920)

The right of citizens of the United States to vote shall not be denied or abridged by the United States or by any State on account of sex.

Congress shall have power to enforce this article by appropriate legislation.

Amendment XX (Ratified January 23, 1933)

Section 1. The terms of the President and Vice President shall end at noon on the 20th day of January, and the terms of Senators and Representatives at noon on the 3d day of January, of the years in which such terms would have ended if this article had not been ratified; and the terms of their successors shall then begin.

Section 2. The Congress shall assemble at least once in every year, and such meeting shall begin at noon on the 3d day of January, unless they shall by law appoint a different day.

Section 3.[14] If, at the time fixed for the beginning of the term of the President, the President elect shall have died, the Vice President elect shall become President. If a President shall not have been chosen before the time fixed for the beginning of his term, or if the President elect shall have failed to qualify, then the Vice President elect shall act as President until a President shall have qualified; and the Congress may by law provide for the case wherein neither a President elect nor a Vice President elect shall have qualified, declaring who shall then act as President, or the manner in which one who is to act shall be selected, and such person shall act accordingly until a President or Vice President shall have qualified.

Section 4. The Congress may by law provide for the case of the death of any of the persons from whom the House of Representatives may choose a President whenever the right of choice shall have devolved upon them, and for the case of the death of any of the persons from whom the Senate may choose a Vice President whenever the right of choice shall have devolved upon them.

Section 5. Sections 1 and 2 shall take effect on the 15th day of October following the ratification of this article.

Section 6. This article shall be inoperative unless it shall have been ratified as an amendment to the Constitution by the legislatures of three-fourths of the several States within seven years from the date of its submission.

Amendment XXI (Ratified December 5, 1933)

Section 1. The eighteenth article of amendment to the Constitution of the United States is hereby repealed.

Section 2. The transportation or importation into any State, Territory, or possession of the United States for delivery or use therein of intoxicating liquors, in violation of the laws thereof, is hereby prohibited.

Section 3. This article shall be inoperative unless it shall have been ratified as an amendment to the Constitution by conventions in the several States, as provided in the Constitution, within seven years from the date of the submission hereof to the States by the Congress.

Amendment XXII (Ratified February 27, 1951)

Section 1. No person shall be elected to the office of the President more than twice, and no person who has held the office of President, or acted as President, for more than two years of a term to which some other person was elected President shall be elected to the office of the President more than once. But this Article shall not apply to any person holding the office of President when this Article was proposed by the Congress, and shall not prevent any person who may be holding the office of President, or acting as President, during the term within which this Article become operative from holding the office of President or acting as President during the remainder of such term.

Section 2. This article shall be inoperative unless it shall have been ratified as an amendment to the Constitution by the legislatures of three-fourths of the several States within seven years from the date of its submission to the States by the Congress.

Amendment XXIII (Ratified March 29, 1961)

Section 1. The District constituting the seat of Government of the United States shall appoint in such manner as the Congress may direct:

A number of electors of President and Vice President equal to the whole number of Senators and Representatives in Congress to which the District would be entitled if it were a State, but in no event more than the least populous State; they shall be in addition to those appointed by the States, but they shall be considered, for the purposes of the election of President and Vice President, to be electors appointed by a State; and they shall meet in the District and perform such duties as provided by the twelfth article of amendment.

Section 2. The Congress shall have power to enforce this article by appropriate legislation.

Amendment XXIV (Ratified January 23, 1964)

Section 1. The right of citizens of the United States to vote in any primary or other election for President or Vice President, for electors for President or Vice President, or for Senator or Representative in Congress, shall not be denied or abridged by the United States or any State by reason of failure to pay any poll tax or other tax.

Section 2. The Congress shall have power to enforce this article by appropriate legislation.

Amendment XXV (Ratified February 10, 1967)

Section 1. In case of the removal of the President from office or of his death or resignation, the Vice President shall become President.

Section 2. Whenever there is a vacancy in the office of the Vice President, the President shall nominate a Vice President who shall take office upon confirmation by a majority vote of both Houses of Congress.

Section 3. Whenever the President transmits to the President pro tempore of the Senate and the Speaker of the House of Representatives his written declaration that he is unable to discharge the powers and duties of his office, and until he transmits to them a written declaration to the contrary, such powers and duties shall be discharged by the Vice President as Acting President.

Section 4. Whenever the Vice President and a majority of either the principal officers of the executive departments or of such other body as Congress may by law provide, transmit to the President pro tempore of the Senate and the Speaker of the House of Representatives their written declaration that the President is unable to discharge the powers and duties of his office, the Vice President shall immediately assume the powers and duties of the office as Acting President.

Thereafter, when the President transmits to the President pro tempore of the Senate and the Speaker of the House of Representatives his written declaration that no inability exists, he shall resume the powers and duties of his office unless the Vice President and a majority of either the principal officers of the executive department or of such other body as Congress may by law provide, transmit within four days to the President pro tempore of the Senate and the Speaker of the House of Representatives their written declaration that the President is unable to discharge the powers and duties of his office. Thereupon Congress shall decide the issue, assembling within forty-eight hours for that purpose if not in session. If the Congress, within twenty-one days after receipt of the latter written declaration, or, if Congress is not in session, within twenty-one days after Congress is required to assemble, determines by two-thirds vote of both Houses that the President is unable to discharge the powers and duties of his office, the Vice President shall continue to discharge the same as Acting President; otherwise, the President shall resume the powers and duties of his office.

Amendment XXVI (Ratified July 1, 1971)

Section 1. The right of citizens of the United States, who are eighteen years of age or older, to vote shall not be denied or abridged by the United States or by any State on account of age.

Section 2. The Congress shall have power to enforce this article by appropriate legislation.

Amendment XXVII (Ratified May 7, 1992)

No law varying the compensation for the services of the Senators and Representatives shall take effect, until an election of Representatives shall have intervened.

Notes

1. The part in brackets was changed by section 2 of the Fourteenth Amendment.
2. The part in brackets was changed by the first paragraph of the Seventeenth Amendment.
3. The part in brackets was changed by the second paragraph of the Seventeenth Amendment.
4. The part in brackets was changed by section 2 of the Twentieth Amendment.
5. The Sixteenth Amendment gave Congress the power to tax incomes.
6. The material in brackets has been superseded by the Twelfth Amendment.
7. This provision has been affected by the Twenty-fifth Amendment.
8. These clauses were affected by the Eleventh Amendment.
9. This paragraph has been superseded by the Thirteenth Amendment.
10. Obsolete.
11. The part in brackets has been superseded by section 3 of the Twentieth Amendment.
12. See the Nineteenth and Twenty-sixth Amendments.
13. This Amendment was repealed by section 1 of the Twenty-first Amendment.
14. See the Twenty-fifth Amendment.

SOURCE: U.S. Congress, House, Committee on the Judiciary, *The Constitution of the United States of America, as Amended*, 100th Cong., 1st sess., 1987, H Doc 100-94.

Congressional Information on the Internet

A huge array of congressional information is available for free at Internet sites operated by the federal government, colleges and universities, and commercial firms. The sites offer the full text of bills introduced in the House and Senate, voting records, campaign finance information, transcripts of selected congressional hearings, investigative reports, and much more.

THOMAS

The most important site for congressional information is THOMAS (*http://thomas.loc.gov*), which is named for Thomas Jefferson and operated by the Library of Congress. THOMAS's highlight is its databases containing the full text of all bills introduced in Congress since 1989, the full text of the *Congressional Record* since 1989, and the status and summary information for all bills introduced since 1973.

THOMAS also offers special links to bills that have received or are expected to receive floor action during the current week and newsworthy bills that are pending or that have recently been approved. Finally, THOMAS has selected committee reports, answers to frequently asked questions about accessing congressional information, publications titled *How Our Laws Are Made* and *Enactment of a Law*, and links to lots of other congressional Web sites.

House of Representatives

The U.S. House of Representatives site (*http://www.house. gov*) offers the schedule of bills, resolutions, and other legislative issues the House will consider in the current week. It also has updates about current proceedings on the House floor and a list of the next day's meeting of House committees. Other highlights include a database that helps users identify their representative, a directory of House members and committees, the House ethics manual, links to Web pages maintained by House members and committees, a calendar of congressional primary dates and candidate-filing deadlines for ballot access, the full text of all amendments to the Constitution that have been ratified and those that have been proposed but not ratified, and lots of information about Washington, D.C., for visitors.

Another key House site is The Office of the Clerk On-line Information Center (*http://clerkweb.house.gov*), which has records of all roll-call votes taken since 1990. The votes are recorded by bill, so it is a lengthy process to compile a particular representative's voting record. The site also has lists of committee assignments, a telephone directory for members and committees, mailing label templates for members and committees, rules of the current Congress, election statistics from 1920 to the present, biographies of Speakers of the House, biographies of women who have served since 1917, and a virtual tour of the House Chamber.

One of the more interesting House sites is operated by the Subcommittee on Rules and Organization of the House

Committee on Rules (*http://www.house.gov/rules/crs_reports. htm*). Its highlight is dozens of Congressional Research Service reports about the legislative process. Some of the available titles include *Legislative Research in Congressional Offices: A Primer, How to Follow Current Federal Legislation and Regulations, Investigative Oversight: An Introduction to the Law, Practice, and Procedure of Congressional Inquiry,* and *Presidential Vetoes 1789–1996: A Summary Overview.*

A final House site is the Internet Law Library (*http://law. house.gov*). This site has a searchable version of the U.S. Code, which contains the text of public laws enacted by Congress, and a tutorial for searching the Code. There also is a huge collection of links to other Internet sites that provide state and territorial laws, laws of other nations, and treaties and international laws.

Senate

At least in the Internet world, the Senate is not as active as the House. Its main Web site (*http://www.senate.gov*) has records of all roll-call votes taken since 1989 (arranged by bill), brief descriptions of all bills and joint resolutions introduced in the Senate during the past week, and a calendar of upcoming committee hearings. The site also provides the standing rules of the Senate, a directory of senators and their committee assignments, lists of nominations that the president has submitted to the Senate for approval, links to Web pages operated by senators and committees, and a virtual tour of the Senate.

Information about the membership, jurisdiction, and rules of each congressional committee is available at the U.S. Government Printing Office site (*http://www.access.gpo.gov/congress/ index.html*). It also has transcripts of selected congressional hearings, the full text of selected House and Senate reports, and the House and Senate rules manuals.

General Reference

An excellent place to explore voting records of individual members of Congress is Congressional Quarterly's VoteWatch (*http://cnn.com/ALLPOLITICS/cq/resources/votewatch*), a project of CNN and Congressional Quarterly. The site provides key voting records for the previous 18 months and can be searched by the name of the representative or senator, state, district, Zip Code, popular bill name, or subject. Accompanying news stories explain each vote. Another feature, Rate Your Rep, allows users to compare their positions on key issues with those of their representative and senators (*http://www-cgi.cnn.com/cgi-bin/election/ raterep/raterep.sh*).

To find key CQ news stories explaining current events in Congress, visit the AllPolitics site (*http://cnn.com/ALLPOLITICS*). To learn more about CQ's other news and legislative tracking web sites, visit *http://www.cq.com.*

The U.S. General Accounting Office, the investigative arm of Congress, operates a site (*http://www.gao.gov*) that provides the full text of its reports from 1996 to the present. The reports cover a wide range of topics: aviation safety, combating terrorism, counternarcotics efforts in Mexico, defense contracting, electronic warfare, food assistance programs, Gulf War illness, health insurance, illegal aliens, information technology, long-term care, mass transit, Medicare, military readiness, money laundering, national parks, nuclear waste, organ donation, student loan defaults, and the Year 2000 computing crisis, among others.

The GAO Daybook is an excellent current awareness tool. This electronic mailing list distributes a daily list of reports and testimony released by the GAO. Subscriptions are available by sending an E-mail message to *majordomo@www.gao.gov*, and in the message area typing "subscribe daybook" (without the quotation marks).

Current budget and economic projections are provided at the Congressional Budget Office Web site *(http://www.cbo.gov)*. The site also has reports about the economic and budget outlook for the next decade, the president's budget proposals, federal civilian employment, Social Security privatization, tax reform, water use conflicts in the West, marriage and the federal income tax, and the role of foreign aid in development, among other topics. Other highlights include monthly budget updates, historical budget data, cost estimates for bills reported by congressional committees, and transcripts of congressional testimony by CBO officials.

Campaign Finance

Several Internet sites provide detailed campaign finance data for congressional elections. The official site is operated by the Federal Election Commission *(http://www.fec.gov)*, which regulates political spending. The site's highlight is its database of campaign reports filed from May 1996 to the present by House and presidential candidates, political action committees, and political party committees. Senate reports are not included because they are filed with the Secretary of the Senate. The reports in the FEC's database are scanned images of paper reports filed with the commission.

The FEC site also has summary financial data for House and Senate candidates in the current election cycle, abstracts of court decisions pertaining to federal election law from 1976 to 1997, a graph showing the number of political action committees in existence each year from 1974 to the present, and a directory of national and state agencies that are responsible for releasing information about campaign financing, candidates on

the ballot, election results, lobbying, and other issues. Another useful feature is a collection of brochures about federal election law, public funding of presidential elections, the ban on contributions by foreign nationals, independent expenditures supporting or opposing a candidate for federal office, contribution limits, filing a complaint, researching public records at the FEC, and other topics. Finally, the site provides the FEC's legislative recommendations, its annual report, a report about its first twenty years in existence, the FEC's monthly newsletter, several reports about voter registration, election results for the most recent presidential and congressional elections, and campaign guides for corporations and labor organizations, congressional candidates and committees, political party committees, and nonconnected committees.

The best online source for campaign finance data is FECInfo *(http://www.tray.com/fecinfo)*, which is operated by former Federal Election Commission employee Tony Raymond. FECInfo's searchable databases provide extensive itemized information about receipts and expenditures by federal candidates and political action committees from 1980 to the present. The data, which are obtained from the FEC, are quite detailed. For example, for candidates contributions can be searched by Zip Code. The site also has data on soft money contributions, lists of the top political action committees in various categories, lists of the top contributors from each state, and much more.

Another interesting site is Campaign Finance Data on the Internet *(http://www.soc.american.edu/campfin)*, which is operated by the American University School of Communication. It provides electronic files from the FEC that have been reformatted in .dbf format so they can be used in database programs such as Paradox, Access, and FoxPro. The files contain data on PAC, committee, and individual contributions to individual congressional candidates.

More campaign finance data is available from the Center for Responsive Politics *(http://www.opensecrets.org)*, a public interest organization. The center provides a list of all "soft money" donations to political parties of $100,000 or more in the current election cycle and data about "leadership" political action committees associated with individual politicians. Other databases at the site provide information about travel expenses that House members received from private sources for attending meetings and other events, activities of registered federal lobbyists, and activities of foreign agents who are registered in the United States.

Index

Index

Index